Accountability in State Legislatures

Chicago Studies in American Politics

A SERIES EDITED BY SUSAN HERBST, LAWRENCE R. JACOBS, ADAM J. BERINSKY, AND FRANCES LEE;

BENJAMIN I. PAGE, EDITOR EMERITUS

Also in the series:

Additional series titles follow the index.

Accountability in State Legislatures

STEVEN ROGERS

THE UNIVERSITY OF CHICAGO PRESS   CHICAGO AND LONDON

The University of Chicago Press, Chicago 60637
The University of Chicago Press, Ltd., London
© 2023 by The University of Chicago
Published 2023
Printed in the United States of America

32 31 30 29 28 27 26 25 24 23   1 2 3 4 5

ISBN-13: 978-0-226-82722-3 (cloth)
ISBN-13: 978-0-226-82724-7 (paper)
ISBN-13: 978-0-226-82723-0 (e-book)
DOI: https://doi.org/10.7208/chicago/9780226827230.001.0001

Library of Congress Cataloging-in-Publication Data

Names: Rogers, Steven (Political scientist), author.
Title: Accountability in state legislatures / Steven Rogers.
Other titles: Chicago studies in American politics.
Description: Chicago : The University of Chicago Press, 2023. | Series: Chicago studies in American politics | Includes bibliographical references and index.
Identifiers: LCCN 2022053773 | ISBN 9780226827223 (cloth) | ISBN 9780226827247 (paperback) | ISBN 9780226827230 (ebook)
Subjects: LCSH: Government accountability—United States. | State governments—United States. | Legislators—United States.
Classification: LCC JK2495 .R64 2023 | DDC 328.3/456—dc23/eng/20221205
LC record available at https://lccn.loc.gov/2022053773

TO PETER AND SUSAN ROGERS

Contents

Preface

The seeds of this project were planted when a Kirkwood High School history teacher, Stephen Platte, convinced a new freshman to join a mock state government program.[1] Following in my sister's footsteps, I joined as a lobbyist, not a legislator. My peers later elected this lobbyist to be their governor, and I represented Missouri's Youth in Government program at a conference in Washington, DC. There, I learned of my future alma mater, the George Washington University, and later interned for US Representative Russ Carnahan. Near the end of that job, I asked Carnahan's chief of staff where I should work next. He responded that Carnahan had had good experiences with the Democratic Legislative Campaign Committee (DLCC)—the national organization to elect Democratic state legislators—during Carnahan's days in the Missouri state legislature. Like most Americans, I knew little about state politics (chapters 4 and 5). But I loved elections. I applied to work for the DLCC, beginning a career immersed in state legislative elections.

As my career shifted to academia, my new colleagues did much more than provide feedback on the following pages. I am particularly grateful to Larry Bartels and Sarah Binder. Larry's generosity led to many happy hours and shaped how I think about political science more than anyone.[2] I likely would not be a political scientist without Sarah's continued guidance, especially in unbreakable email threads. I also owe a debt of gratitude to Nolan McCarty and Josh Clinton. Nolan's feedback and perspective made me and my work stronger, but I am even more appreciative of how he stood up for me and made sacrifices to put what was best for me first. Josh taught me some of my most useful academic and "above my pay grade" lessons, but I truly won't forget how he stuck with me and helped me during some of my lowest of lows.

FIGURE O.I. An early conversation between Josh Clinton and Steven Rogers. The fuller explanation ended up needing more than figure 1.1.

The following chapters use stories of state legislators to make points about accountability, and here I will use a story of political scientists to make a point about the state politics research community. At my first State Politics and Policy Conference (SPPC), I presented a dissertation chapter that would become the start of this book. Jerry Wright and Tom Carsey engaged with my presentation. Even though it was clear early on that Rogers's view differed from those of Erikson, Wright, and McIver, Jerry invited me to his table at dinner with his *Statehouse Democracy* co-authors and students that evening.[3] A senior scholar making such a gesture to a graduate student he had never met is impressively commonplace within the welcoming state politics community, whose research and helpful advice leave fingerprints throughout this manuscript. I am particularly grateful for all that Jason Windett, Justin Kirkland, Nate Birkhead, and Michael Nelson have done to make this book stronger and aid my career.

This manuscript benefited from the feedback of many. Larry Bartels, Seth Benson, Andrew Hall, Emily Heman, Jim Heman, Michael Sances, John Sides, Michael Nelson's graduate state politics class, and two very constructive anonymous reviewers generously provided comments on the full manuscript. I additionally appreciated helpful discussions with Douglas Arnold, Deborah Beim, Adam Bonica, Dan Butler, Brandice Canes-Wrone, Ellen Carnaghan, Nicholas Carnes, Adam Dynes, Bob Erikson, John Geer, Alan Greenblatt, Morgan Hazelton, Marc Hetherington, Robert Hogan, Dan Hopkins, Molly Jackman, Saul Jackman, Vlad Kogan, Chryl Laird, Eric Lawrence, David Lewis, Scott Limbocker, Seth Masket, Marc Meredith, William McCormick, Matthew Nanes, Bruce Oppenheimer, Efren Perez, Steve Puro, Andrew Reeves, Mark Richardson, Jeff Tessin, Chris Warshaw, Alan Wiseman, Jennifer Wolak, and John Zaller, along with seminar participants at Princeton University, George Washington University, Stanford University, Washington University, and Vanderbilt University. I am also grateful for feedback from many constructive audiences and discussants at the American Political Science Association (APSA), Midwest Political Science Association (MPSA), and Southern Political Science Association (SPSA) annual meetings.

In addition to stories about obscure state legislators, this book brings together data to better understand the American electoral system. It can be easy to look at a scatterplot but fail to appreciate what it took to create each dot. The data points in this book that piece together a story about accountability are the result of the tremendous efforts by Peter Koppstein, Michelle Anderson, Carl Klarner, Michael Davies, the Cooperative Election Study, the National Institute on Money in State Politics, the National Committee for an Effective Congress, the Center for American Women and Politics, and the Pew Research Center. Todd Maske, Ben Melusky, Gary Jacobson, Pev Squire, Jordan Butcher, Boris Shor, Jonathon Winburn, and the Center for Effective Lawmaking also generously shared data sets for the following analyses. My plots, figures, and analyses are also the result of Billiken research assistants' hard work. Adam Kneepkens, Abby Faust, Emily Johansson, Patrick Monahan, Sequoyah Lopez, Dan Carter, Kaitlin Klasen, Tegan Hoover, Jeffery Seib, and Lucie Wood completed tasks ranging from looking up the results of thousands of primary elections to completing the grimmer job of identifying whether state legislators had left the chamber feet first. My research also benefited from the assistance and support of the Center for the Study of Democratic Politics, the Center for Democratic Institutions, and the Saint Louis University

Research Institute. I am additionally thankful for the University of Chicago Press's support, along with Sara Doskow, Chuck Meyers, and Frances
Lee's guidance in the publishing process.

Even with the tremendous professional support I have received, neither this project nor my career would have been possible without family,
and in particular, my parents, Peter and Susan Rogers, to whom this book
is dedicated. Few others try to do what is right more than Peter, and to
steal the words of a good friend, "you cannot out-nice Sue Rogers." While
the following pages reflect more of the glass-half-empty perspective, Peter
and Sue have made the glasses of the lives they touched a little fuller.

CHAPTER ONE

Introduction

State lawmakers decide who can bear arms, join arms in matrimony, and even participate in our democracy. Formally, the US Constitution says: "The powers not delegated to the United States by the Constitution, nor prohibited by it to the States, are reserved to the States respectively, or to the people" (Amendment X). As gridlock has increased in Washington, DC, legislators in state capitals have exercised their constitutionally authorized powers and become more active in lawmaking (Binder 2015; Grumbach 2018). On average, each state legislature now passes over twice as many bills as Congress (Justice 2015). As either national and state lawmakers make policies devoted to the economy, education, health care, religious freedom, the environment, racial and gender equality, infrastructure, abortion, and criminal justice—to name a few—both the Founding Fathers and political scientists largely agree that "a dependence on the people is, no doubt, the primary control on the government" (Madison or Hamilton 1788).

In theory, elections in the United States create such a dependence. Once elected, little directly constrains officeholders' behavior, but if these representatives govern irresponsibly, they can be replaced. By providing voters opportunities to hold those in power accountable, elections establish a fundamental connection between citizens and elites that can motivate elected officials to act in the interests of those they represent. Electoral connections help explain national lawmaking (e.g., Mayhew 1974), but despite state governments' considerable power, it is more often assumed than shown that most state lawmakers are similarly "dependent on the people." Nor do we well understand to what degree any such "electoral connections" operate across the American states. In this book, I investigate whether there is support for such assumptions and address a core question about American democracy: do elections hold state legislators accountable for their own performance?

To answer this question, I draw upon what political scientists think they know about American politics to understand better what is unknown about state legislative elections. My study examines the major stages of the electoral process, looking at both elites' decisions to run for state office and voters' decisions at the ballot box. I utilize state legislators', reporters', activists', and voters' accounts about state legislative elections along with statistical analyses that employ one of the most comprehensive collections of measures of representation and public opinion across the American states. But even simple statistics cause worry for the electoral foundation of statehouse democracy. Over 80 percent of voters do not know who their state legislator is, 40 percent of voters do not know which political party controls their legislature, and over a third of incumbent legislators regularly do not face a challenger in either the primary or general election. Together, these conditions would seemingly make it difficult to hold state legislators accountable. How does someone reward or punish those in power if they rarely know who is in charge? And how do you throw someone out of office if they run for reelection unopposed?

National trends in legislative elections further indicate that state legislators' electoral fates have little to do with what legislators do themselves. Instead, evidence suggests that state electoral outcomes are largely an unintended consequence of a complicated, federalist system of government. Figure 1.1 plots the nationwide seat change for the Democratic Party in state (solid black line) and US House elections (grey dashed line) over the past century. The similarity between congressional and state election outcomes is striking. In years when Democrats or Republicans made substantial gains in congressional elections, these parties were also successful in state legislative elections across the country.

But why should that be the case? State legislatures often have different priorities than Congress, and legislatures in different states enact different policies with varying success. State governments spend at least five times more on education (National Center for Education Statistics 2019) and prisons (Kearney et al. 2014) than the federal government. Throughout American history, state legislatures have differently affected millions of Americans' personal lives simply because of where Americans lived.[1] A woman can legally get an abortion in Illinois, but state law prohibits this procedure across the Mississippi River in Missouri (Kitchener et al. 2022). A man could marry another man in New York but not Ohio until *Obergefell v. Hodges* struck down an Ohio state law (Barlow 2015). Men and

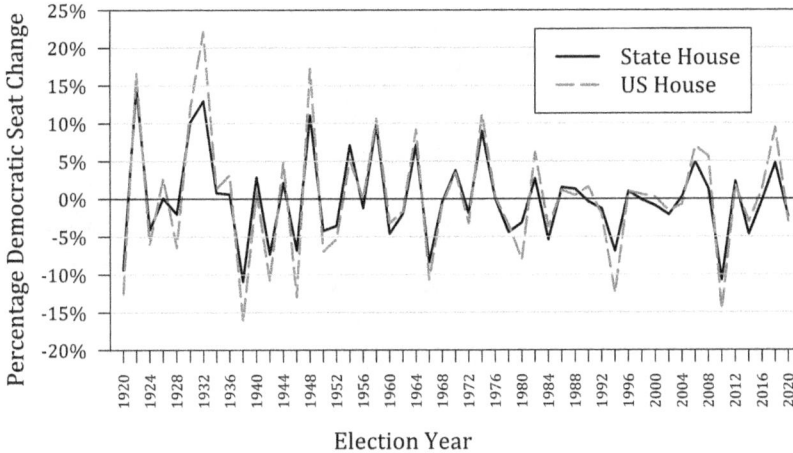

FIGURE I.I. Nationwide percentage of seats won or lost by the Democratic Party in state house or US House elections from 1920 to 2020.

women can smoke marijuana in Colorado but not in neighboring Kansas due to differing laws across these states (National Conference of State Legislatures 2022). Lawmakers from one state may also do their jobs much better than lawmakers in another state. When rating policy outcomes across all the states, the *US News and World Report* rated New Jersey as the best state in education but forty-first in infrastructure. Meanwhile, Nevada ranked best in infrastructure but fortieth in education (*US News and World Report* 2021).

Despite these and other considerable differences across the states, the national partisan tides that produce significant turnover in Congress almost invariably also produce significant turnover in state legislatures. Democrats, for example, lost seats in all but three legislatures in 1994, and in 1974, Republicans lost seats in all but five. Health care reforms or Watergate may explain federal elections' outcomes in these years, but state legislators had little to do with these federal events. The near-perfect correlation between seat change in federal and state elections (0.96) shown in figure I.I by no means proves meaningful electoral connections fail to exist in states, but it casts a cloud of doubt.

This book's findings help confirm these doubts by systematically exposing cracks in the foundations of statehouse democracy. Is electoral accountability utterly absent from American state legislatures? Certainly not. But most of the behavior of state legislators has relatively little impact on the outcomes of their own elections. The following chapters reveal meager evidence of accountability in state legislatures: legislators are not severely punished at the ballot box for poor state-level policy outcomes, legislative records, or overall performance. These results imply that state legislators have little electoral incentive to behave responsibly, and what state legislators need to do to be reelected, such as support popular policies, *differs* from what their federal counterparts need to do. States offer political scientists attractive variation to study American politics, but my findings indicate that theories of legislative behavior developed and tested at the national level do not always cleanly translate to the "laboratories of democracy."

My analyses of state legislative elections have important implications for how scholars study American politics, but their central message concerns electoral accountability in state legislatures. To begin conveying this message, this chapter outlines some of the purposes and expectations of elections in the American system. First, I revisit and detail problems posed by representative government and outline solutions to this problem offered by seminal theories of elections and representation focused on accountability and selection. After establishing that elections are not purely selection mechanisms and that there are unrepresentative legislators to hold accountable, I offer readers conceptual and empirical benchmarks for accountability in state legislatures. I then conclude with a plan of how I will assess the extent to which state legislative elections meet expectations for accountability in American state legislatures.

A Problem with Representative Government

After the failure of the Articles of Confederation, the Founding Fathers wrestled with how to allocate federal and state power, ultimately coming to a resolution where "the federal Constitution forms a happy combination . . . the great and aggregated interests being referred to the national, the local and particular to the State legislatures" (Madison 1787). These national and subnational governments' power has varied over time, along with the issues these institutions address. However, a common theme throughout American history is that the federal and state levels of government derive their legitimacy from the consent of the governed.

Voters provide this consent by electing political candidates to represent them in these governments. This consent is one of many agreements Americans make with other individuals to provide a service. Whether hiring a local teenager to mow the lawn or a stockbroker to manage a retirement portfolio, Americans often delegate responsibilities to other individuals. Contemporary society would be difficult to conceptualize without such deals, or in economic terms, such *principal-agent relationships*. Some agreements, however, can lead to undesirable behaviors where the agent does not act in the principal's best interest. For example, a stockbroker may make riskier investments with a client's money than they would with the broker's own savings, perhaps in hopes of receiving higher commission fees. Such problems are known as moral hazards. More formally, a moral hazard problem arises when Parties A and B enter an agreement, and Party B engages in certain behaviors because Party B knows Party A will bear the negative consequences for that behavior. In the previous example, the client (Party A) bears the greater risk of negative consequences for the stockbroker's (Party B) investment decisions. Alternatively, consider an agreement between a driver and a car-insurance company where the insurance company will pay for any damages that result from a car accident caused by the driver. With car insurance, the insurance company (Party A) foots the bill for an accident by a risky driver (Party B) who cuts someone off on the highway.

Examples of moral hazards involving insurance companies and stockbrokers are commonly heard in business or economics classes, but moral hazards also concern those who study politics and representation. Instead of a stockbroker and client, consider a legislator and his constituents. In a representative government, legislators and constituents form agreements where constituents permit legislators to act on their behalf in government. There is nothing, however, that commands a legislator to act in his constituents' best interest. For instance, constituents can allow legislators to levy taxes so the government can spend this money. At the legislator's discretion, tax revenues could then pay for schools; however, they might instead be used to finance a new stadium for a sports league that—coincidentally—has generously donated to a legislator's reelection campaign. A situation can arise where most citizens may prefer to build needed schools, but a legislator wants a sports stadium. The two parties then have conflicting interests, but under the agreement established under a republican form of government, legislators decide how to spend tax revenues, even if such spending is not in the people's interest.[2]

Herein lies a fundamental problem posed by representative government. Those in power are "hired" by voters to represent constituents' interests, but once elected, little constrains officeholders' behavior. Citizens may want or need new schools, but nothing forces representatives to build them. This lack of control over those in power has long been recognized. The Founding Fathers, for example, acknowledged that:

> If angels were to govern men, neither external nor internal controls on government would be necessary. In framing a government which is to be administered by men over men, the great difficulty lies in this: you must first enable the government to control the governed; and in the next place oblige it to control itself.

The Founding Fathers also offered a potential solution to this moral hazard problem and immediately continued:

> A dependence on the people is, no doubt, the primary control on the government. (Madison or Hamilton 1788)

A primary purpose of elections is to create such a dependence. If voters have the opportunity to electorally punish those in power for doing a bad job, elected officials' job security depends on the people. As long as those in power want to keep their jobs, elected officials theoretically have an incentive to represent or act in their constituents' interests. When legislators' own behavior determines their election outcomes, elections help create a system of accountability intended to discourage undesirable behavior by legislators and solve the moral hazard problem posed by representative government.

Holding Representatives Electorally Accountable

Political scientists most often attribute electoral accountability to be the result of "retrospective voting." V. O. Key, for example, considers elections in a reward-punishment framework and portrays "the electorate in its great, and principal, role as an appraiser of past events, part performance, and past actions. It judges retrospectively" (Key 1966, 61). Given many voters' disinterest in politics (e.g., Delli Carpini and Keeter 1997), an appealing trait of retrospective voting theories is that they require relatively little of the electorate. As compared to "prospective voting"—where voters acquire knowledge of future policy plans to forecast what will happen—it is almost always easier to make decisions in an election based on assessing what has already happened (Downs 1957, 40).[3] Anticipating voters' decisions at the ballot box, legislators who want to keep their jobs take a judging retrospective electorate into account in their own decisions of how to behave in the legislature.

Voters can evaluate legislators' performance and employ retrospective accountability in at least two ways: individually and collectively. First, voters can reward or punish legislators for their individual actions. An example of this individual accountability view is when election outcomes follow predictions of the *median voter theorem*. Chapter 6 more formally explains this theorem, but the theorem's underlying logic is that if a legislator supports a bill that the median (or pivotal) voter opposes, this voter can, in turn, cast a ballot against that legislator in the next election, forcing the legislator from office.[4] The anticipation of such election monitoring encourages the legislator to support policies that align with the voter's interest. Voters can also hold legislators individually accountable for other actions, such as failing to write good bills or provide constituency services. Again, in these cases, theories of retrospective voting predict that a legislator fears being held individually accountable and changes their behavior to avoid electoral punishment.

Holding legislators accountable for their individual behavior, however, may be a tall ask of voters, particularly at the state level. Few voters know who their state legislator is, let alone what they do from day to day (chapters 4 and 5). To simplify the accountability process, voters can instead rely on "heuristics," such as party labels, to hold those in power collectively accountable for their collective performance (Schattschneider 1942). The most common form of collective accountability resembles the idea of responsible party government, where voters only need to know which party is in power and reward or punish that party for doing a good or bad job. Again, the underlying assumption is that those in power (i.e., political parties) want to stay in power. Party members then anticipate election monitoring, which motivates legislators to produce good policies. Otherwise, party members will be held collectively accountable and lose their jobs. Systems of individual or collective accountability each connect how legislators perform in office to how they perform in elections, thereby helping solve the moral hazard problem posed by representative government.

Policymaking and Accountability in States

Of central concern to this book is uncovering the extent to which systems of individual or collective accountability exist in state legislative elections and thereby promote desirable state-level policymaking. The founders

8

CHAPTER ONE

envisioned state governments to be central to American lives. Madison argued, "The powers reserved to the several States will extend to all the objects which, in the ordinary course of affairs, concern the lives, liberties, and properties of the people, and the internal order, improvement, and prosperity of the State" (Madison 1788, *Federalist* no. 45).

Since the founding, the federal government's power has undeniably grown, but more recently, states have become increasingly important to Americans' everyday lives. For example, since the 1970s, state governments have increased their fiscal activity and size relative to the federal government. For every dollar in federal tax revenues, state governments raised $0.25 in 1970 but $0.32 in 2020. These increases contributed to state government tax revenues exceeding $1 trillion for the first time in 2018. During this time, state government expenditures as a percentage of US GDP rose from approximately 7 to 12 percent, which contributed to the growing relative number of individuals employed by state governments. In 1970, there were 1.3 state employees for every federal government employee, but in 2020 the ratio grew to 2.3.[5] State governments additionally have considerable influence over federal dollars (Nathan and Gais 2001). For example, letting states decide whether to expand Medicaid under the Affordable Care Act sent billions of dollars to state governments and exemplifies states' increasing power over Americans' lives.

In the last half-century, states have also increasingly dictated the rights and services afforded to their citizens. In an appropriately titled article, "From Backwaters to Major Policymakers," Jacob Grumbach (Grumbach 2018; see also Grossmann 2019) studies sixteen different policy areas, such as abortion, guns, and health care, and shows that many states had similar policies in the 1970s, but since the turn of the century policies across states have become increasingly varied. Grumbach (2022, 51–52) later highlights how states' policies have changed in greater detail. For example, for abortion and gun control policies:

Abortion: In 1973, states only differed in Medicaid coverage for abortions and other minor regulations. By 2014 the most restrictive states mandated waiting periods, parental notification, counseling, licensed physicians, a twenty week gestation limit, and restricted insurance coverage for abortion.

Gun Control: In 1970, the least strict states allowed open carry and the strictest states required dealer licenses and purchase background checks. By 2014, the least strict states had added Stand Your Ground Laws, while the strictest states banned assault weapons and mandated registration and waiting periods for purchases.

States have substantial policymaking power, and some political science research suggests that state governments generally produce representative policies. For example, Robert Erikson, Gerald Wright, and John McIver provide one of the most impressive studies of state-level representation in the last half-century: *Statehouse Democracy*. These authors argue that "state political structures do a good job delivering more liberal policies to more liberal states and more conservative policies to more conservative states" (Erikson, Wright, and McIver 1993, 95). More recently, Caughey and Warshaw (2022, 4, 14) examine 186 state-level policies from 1935 to 2020 and assert that state policymaking "is probably more responsive than it was when *Statehouse Democracy* was written." To explain these findings, these political scientists point to electoral accountability:

> Ultimately, our message about representation in the states is a simple one. At the ballot box, state electorates hold a strong control over the ideological direction of policies in their states. In anticipation of election monitoring, state legislatures and other policymakers take public opinion into account when enacting state policy. (Erikson, Wright, and McIver 1993, 247)

> By enabling voters to hold incumbents accountable, [elections] incentivize officials to react preemptively to public opinion. (Caughey and Warshaw 2022, 5)

Statehouse Democracy and *Dynamic Democracy* paint relatively rosy pictures of politics in the American states. The bloom on this rose is rooted in elections helping "control" state-level policymaking. Political scientists provide evidence that such accountability exists across many of the different levels of government in the United States. At the federal level, national elections appear to hold both political parties (e.g., Tufte 1975) and members of Congress (e.g., Canes-Wrone, Brady, and Cogan 2002) accountable for how they govern. At the state level, voters hold governors responsible for their management of the economy (e.g., Niemi, Stanley, and Vogel 1995) and taxes (e.g., Besley and Case 1995). And at the local level, voters electorally punish mayors for potholes (Burnett and Kogan 2017) and school board officials for low test scores (Payson 2017). Voter behavior certainly does not always meet democratic ideals in American elections (see Warshaw 2019 for a review). Still, some evidence of electoral accountability exists—both above and below state legislators in our federal system.

With state legislatures being "closer to the people," we may think that state legislators are more likely to be held accountable than their federal counterparts (Madison 1788, *Federalist* no. 46). However, despite the evidence of electoral connections for members of Congress, the evidence that state legislators have similar reasons to worry about punishment at the ballot box is limited. This is surprising given some assertions made about the health of democracy in the American states. Erikson, Wright, and McIver, for example, claim that "parties are rewarded and punished based on how well they represent state opinion" (Erikson, Wright, and McIver 1993, 124), but their most direct test of this assumption only shows that states with higher levels of Democratic partisan identifiers are more likely to elect Democratic legislators, averaged over a six-year period.[6] That Democratic voters are electing more Democratic legislators serves as evidence that a type of state-level electoral connection exists, but does a match between policymakers' party membership and their constituents' party identification constitute meaningful electoral accountability?

Research on the relationship between state legislators' performance and election outcomes has grown in recent years but often remains narrow in scope. Prior studies focused on individual accountability find that more "extreme" state legislators fare worse in state legislative elections. However, these studies typically examine a single election year (e.g., Birkhead 2015), less than a third of states (e.g., Hogan 2008), or do little to explain why we find more or less evidence of accountability in certain states (e.g., Caughey and Warshaw 2022). These works undoubtedly enhance our understanding of accountability in state legislatures but leave many important questions unanswered.

More attention is given to the role of parties and collective accountability in state legislatures. Research shows that approval of the state legislature's performance is associated with a state's policy liberalism, the ideological extremity of state legislative parties, and the unemployment rate (J. E. Cohen 2020; Langehennig, Zamadics, and Wolak 2019; Richardson Jr., Konisky, and Milyo 2012; Richardson and Milyo 2016). These studies, however, do not assess whether voters' approval of the legislature is meaningful for their decisions in state legislative elections. Research more directly focused on state legislative election outcomes most often studies the role of the economy, but outside of a single study that controls for divided government (Lowry, Alt, and Ferree 1998), I know of no published work outside my own that accounts for which party controls the state house, leaving

it unclear whether the party in control of the state legislature has an electoral incentive to produce strong economic policy.[7] Instead, more work finds
that national economic conditions strongly relate to state legislative election outcomes rather than local economic conditions (e.g., Chubb 1988).

Voters' responses to the national economy in state legislative elections
are likely partly responsible for the nationwide trends illustrated in figure 1.1. Nationalized voter behavior is becoming increasingly important
to explain outcomes in federal and state elections. Gary Jacobson (2021,
503, fig. 4; 2015), for example, documents the "extremely close connection
between presidential and congressional voting," where the bivariate correlation between district-level congressional and presidential vote grew
from 0.80 in the 2000 election to 0.95 in the 2016 election. Dan Hopkins
(2018) provides arguably the most thorough treatment of nationalization
at the state level in the appropriately titled *The Increasingly United States*.
Hopkins shows that state party platforms are becoming more and more
similar across states, which—combined with more nationalized media—
leads voters to perceive America's two major parties to offer "the same
choices across the country" (2018, 3) and vote similarly in mayoral, gubernatorial, and presidential elections.

Jacobson and Hopkins better our understanding of nationalized politics' implications for elections for members of Congress, governors, and
mayors. Each of these public officials performs different duties but frequently shares the common party labels of Republican or Democrat. State
legislators also share these labels, but voters are typically less aware of what
goes on in their legislature (chapter 5), giving these labels increased importance. It is not, however, well understood if elites and voters in a nationalized political context meaningfully use party labels and cues to hold
state legislators collectively accountable. If legislators and their parties do
not face meaningful sanctions for *their own* bad policies or poor performance, it spells trouble for elections solving the moral hazard posed by representative government.

An Alternative Solution: Selecting the Right Representatives

In the following chapters, I investigate the extent to which elections create
incentives for state lawmakers to represent their constituents' interests. I
show that evidence of accountability exists but is scarce. Accountability
as a solution to a moral hazard problem is the most common conceptualization of how elections produce a representative government, but it is not

the only one. An alternative explanation is that elections instead solve an adverse-selection problem (see Ashworth 2012 for a review). As described below, this perspective views the purpose of elections to be to select the best representative and not necessarily to motivate or change an individual representative's behavior. The adverse-selection perspective of elections is important to consider—especially before reading a book devoted to accountability—because if voters selected perfect representatives, it would be impossible to find evidence of voters punishing poor performance or holding legislators accountable, as there would be no bad eggs in the state capitol.

An adverse-selection problem can arise when two parties enter an agreement but one party has greater information (e.g., regarding the good or service exchanged) before making the agreement. Reconsider the above example of the driver and car-insurance company. Before purchasing insurance, the driver knows his accident history, but the insurance company does not. If the insurance company knew a driver had previously been issued three speeding tickets and caused two car accidents, the company might not want to enter an agreement with this reckless driver as compared to another driver who had a spotless record. Adverse selection occurs when the driver does not disclose this information, and the insurance company enters an agreement it would not have if fully informed.

Voters face a similar problem to the insurance company. Voters do not always know whether a candidate for office is a "good" or "bad" driver of policymaking before entering a representation agreement. Repeated elections, however, provide voters multiple opportunities to select a "good" representative versus a "bad" one. James Fearon nicely explains this idea in his chapter "Electoral Accountability and the Control of Politicians: Selecting Good Types versus Sanctioning Poor Performance":

> It might be entirely reasonable to imagine the best possible solution is to try to elect good types of candidates, and to view repeated elections as repeated opportunities to *sort among types* rather than as mechanisms for controlling problems of moral hazard for elected officials. In this view, one votes against an incumbent if economic or other circumstances are bad not in order to give the new officeholder an incentive to work harder or more responsibly, but rather just to try a new random "draw" from the pool of types. (Fearon 1999, 69)

A critical distinction between the adverse-selection and moral hazard perspectives is that under an adverse-selection perspective the voter is

All State House Members in 2003

State House Members who served 2003 - 2010

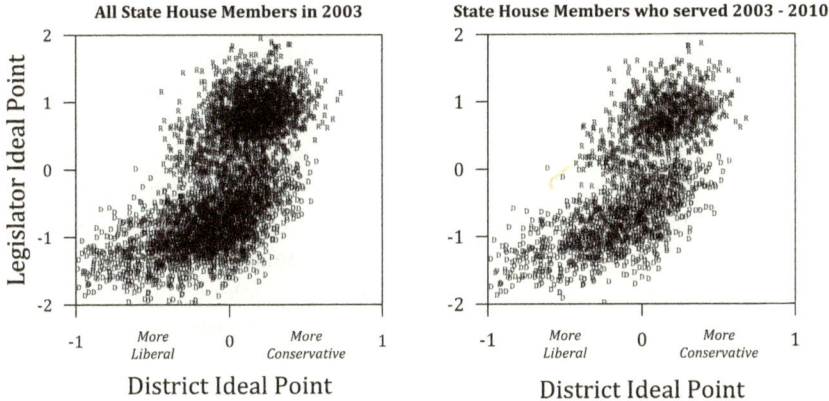

FIGURE 1.2. State house members' ideal points plotted against district ideal points. The left panel includes all state legislators who served in 2003, and the right panel includes only those legislators who served from 2003 to 2010.

faced with the problem of selecting the correct type rather than trying to create incentives for a representative's behavior.[8] Applying the idea of adverse selection to the example of car insurance, a driver has a true type, either good or bad, and this type will become evident by his driving record. The insurance company will then learn more about the driver's true type after a few years; better identify him as a good or bad driver or type; and decide to keep the driver as a client, charge a higher premium, or cease offering him insurance. Similarly, a voter does not know much about a candidate's type in the candidate's first election, but after observing the candidate perform in office, the voter can either select to keep the candidate to serve again or select a different candidate.[9]

The selection interpretation of elections is important to consider, especially when my claim is that the evidence of electoral accountability in state legislatures is meager at best. If voters selected perfectly representative legislators through repeated elections, it would be difficult to find empirical evidence of accountability. Voters cannot punish unrepresentative legislators if all legislators are "good types" and there are no unrepresentative legislators to punish. But a look at legislators' representation suggests some "bad types" likely serve in legislatures.[10] Figure 1.2 plots measures of legislators' ideology derived by Boris Shor and Nolan McCarty (2011) against measures of voters' ideology in their district derived by Chris Tausanovitch and Chris Warshaw (2013).[11] The left and right panels of figure 1.2 illustrate the relationship between these ideological measures for all state house members who served in 2003 (left panel) and those who voters repeatedly selected to serve from 2003 to 2010 (right panel).

If voters only selected representative legislators, more-liberal legislators should represent more-liberal districts, and more-conservative legislators should represent more-conservative districts. Going from the left to right of either panel in figure 1.2, we generally see this trend. However, when we look at the panels from top to bottom, we see that many state legislators with different ideological positions (y-axis) represent ideologically similar constituencies (x-axis). For example, consider two state legislators who served in the Michigan legislature at the same time in 2003: Democrat William DeWeese and Republican Scott Boyd. According to Shor and McCarty's estimates of legislator ideology, DeWeese's ideal point is -0.7, reflecting liberal representation, and Boyd's ideal point is 0.7, reflecting conservative representation. Meanwhile, according to Tausanovitch and Warshaw's district ideology estimates, DeWeese and Boyd's districts' ideal points are approximately 0. DeWeese and Scott then provide vastly different representation for ideologically similar districts. Given the different scales of the legislator and district ideal point measures, it is unknown where ideal representation falls, and I do not claim that all state legislators poorly represent their districts. Either DeWeese or Boyd may have done excellent jobs. However, if two legislators' ideology (y-axis) falls on a single type of district ideology (x-axis), at least one legislator is likely out of step with their district.

The left panel of figure 1.2 suggests that the example of DeWeese and Boyd is not unique.[12] Many ideologically similar districts often select ideologically different representatives. The interpretation of elections as a solution to an adverse-selection problem, however, argues that voters will select good-type legislators as voters learn the legislator's type over the course of repeated elections. To investigate whether this is the case, the right panel of figure 1.2 is similar to the left panel but only includes legislators who were repeatedly selected to serve from 2003 to 2010. In other words, these representatives served in 2010 after voters had at least eight years to learn a representative's type. Again, many ideologically similar constituencies still continue to select ideologically dissimilar state legislators, including DeWeese and Boyd, who provided very different representation to their similar districts throughout the decade. Again, it is unknown whether DeWeese or Boyd was more out of step with their district, but overall, the right panel of figure 1.2 suggests there are plenty of "bad-type" or out-of-step legislators to hold accountable.

The patterns in figure 1.2 cast doubt that all voters use elections to solve

an adverse-selection problem, but some voters likely use elections to select policymakers who will work toward voters' policy goals. For example,
studies provide evidence that American legislative election outcomes are
partly explained by the theory of "balancing" (e.g., Alesina and Rosenthal
1989). The premise of the balancing argument is that some voters want moderate policies, and these policies are more likely to be produced when different parties control different branches of government. The voter will then
cast ballots with the motivation to create a divided government to ideologically balance the executive and legislative branches of government, with
hopes that divided government will produce more-moderate policies.

Political scientists often use balancing to account for why the president's
party regularly loses congressional seats in midterm elections, which is more
commonly explained by theories of voter turnout (e.g., A. Campbell 1960)
or referendum voting (e.g., Tufte 1975).[13] Studies of state elections also produce evidence consistent with the balancing argument (Bailey and Fullmer
2011; Folke and Snyder 2012; Caughey and Warshaw 2022). For example,
focusing on what I hereafter refer to as "state-level balancing," Caughey
and Warshaw show that when a Republican wins the governorship, the Democratic legislative party is more successful in the next election. Similarly,
legislative Republicans experience more success when there is a Democrat in the governor's mansion. From these findings, Caughey and Warshaw
(2022, 96) argue that "state electors seem to hold state parties accountable
for their policymaking, shifting support to the opposition party in an effort to counterbalance excessive policy changes."[14]

State-level balancing can explain state election outcomes, but again, an
important aspect of state elections is that they are embedded in a federal
system. Voters who seek moderate policies then may try to balance the federal and state levels of government. Robert Erikson, Olle Folke, and James
Snyder (2015, 493) offer such an extension of the balancing argument in
their study of presidential elections:

> In a presidential election year, voters believe that the previous gubernatorial
> election generated policies downstream that tilt generally in the direction of
> the Governor's party ... One mechanism for pushing the overall policy bundle
> back toward the center is to elect the opposite party in the presidential election.

Erikson and his coauthors find that a presidential candidate loses 3 to
4 percent of the vote if a governor of the same party won the previous election. This finding is consistent with the argument that voters' balancing leads
to state election outcomes (i.e., gubernatorial election results) impacting

federal elections (i.e., presidential elections). The logic of balancing, however, can also be applied to federal election outcomes affecting state elections. Suppose the federal government produces an extreme conservative policy. In that case, voters can use state elections to put more-liberal policymakers in state office to create a more moderate overall policy bundle. If voters engage in such a behavior, it can be considered "federal-state balancing."

Both "state-level balancing" and "federal-state balancing" can explain state legislative election outcomes, which is of central importance to this book. The following chapters then investigate balancing in state legislative elections by studying how the governor's and president's legislative co-partisans fare electorally during state and federal midterm elections. To simplify presentation, I use the term "balancing" to refer to the governor's or president's party doing worse in state legislative elections during the midterm. Readers should carefully consider what these results mean empirically and normatively. As discussed in chapter 5, many empirical results consistent with the balancing explanation are also consistent with other explanations of election outcomes, such as those centered on voter turnout. However, empirical evidence consistent with a theory does not necessarily prove a particular theory.

Normatively, it is less clear the extent to which balancing is a meaningful form of accountability. Recall that the assumed solution to the moral hazard problem posed by representative government is that voters' responses to legislators' behavior incentivize policymakers to act in voters' interests. However, if voters cast ballots for or against legislators simply based on what party controls the governor's mansion or the White House, what incentive does a legislator have to perform well? As acknowledged by Caughey and Warshaw (2022, 95), "most voters' balancing decisions may therefore be 'crude' in the sense that they punish the majority party mechanically, without regard to how it has governed in the preceding term." If legislators' party affiliations with the executive branches of government mechanically determine legislators' electoral fates, a legislator's personal actions do less to impact whether they are reelected. If such balancing occurs, it diminishes elections' strength as an accountability mechanism, at least in my judgment.

Standards for Electoral Accountability

The picture of accountability in state legislatures presented in this book is not reassuring and dashes many hopes that elections effectively solve the moral hazard problem posed by representative government. While it is too strong to say that relationships between legislators' behavior and election outcomes fail to exist in state legislatures, the weakness of electoral connections does not constitute a healthy democratic process, again, in my judgment. But as it is a voter's decision regarding how to cast their ballot, it is up to the reader to digest my findings to determine whether state legislative elections meet their standards for electoral accountability. There undoubtedly is disagreement on what this standard should be, but making this determination at some level requires we ask: what are the requirements for elections to serve as accountability mechanisms?

The many facets of elections make it challenging to boil electoral accountability down to simple boxes to check. As a starting point, I offer readers conditions for accountability laid out by G. Bingham Powell in his book *Elections as Instruments for Democracy*:

> What must we expect from the electoral and policymaking setting if citizens are to use this powerful instrument of democracy appropriately and effectively? A first condition is that citizens must know who is responsible for making policy. A second condition is that they must have a fair opportunity to cast a meaningful vote for or against the policymakers. Given these two conditions, they could use their votes to retain the good policymakers and send the bad ones packing. (Powell 2000, 51)

Powell's conditions align with most democratic theory concerning elections, and the logic mirrors that of both the Founding Fathers and V. O. Key. It would be difficult for a "dependence upon the people" to be the "primary control of government" if these people did not "know who is responsible for making policy." Predictions of retrospective voting would similarly be difficult to fulfill if voters did not have "a fair opportunity" to vote against the policymakers and such votes were not "meaningful." I then use the above conditions for accountability to help guide normative interpretations of this book's findings.

Powell's requirements establish conceptual criteria for what is necessary for elections to provide accountability, but it is not always clear what empirically constitutes a "meaningful vote" or "healthy" amount of accountability. Unlike a physician who can measure whether a patient's temperature is 98.6°F (37°C), a political scientist cannot necessarily tell if the statistical relationship between an election result and representation indicates the presence of a healthy amount of accountability. Most can agree that some relationship between representation or performance and elections is better than no relationship, but what the relationship "should" be is again debatable.

Given this uncertainty, it is useful to compare findings regarding something we know less about—state legislatures—to an American legislature we think we know much more about: Congress. To offer such comparisons throughout this book, I evaluate the levels of accountability both in this national legislature and in state legislatures. State governments have considerable authority over American lives and offer attractive institutional variation to test theories developed in the congressional setting. If both members of Congress and state legislators are responsible for laws that impact Americans' daily lives, there is little reason in my judgment to hold state legislators to a lower electoral standard.

The Search for Accountability

The following chapters examine elites' and voters' behavior to assess whether state legislative elections meet the above standards for accountability. My search for accountability begins where electoral competition typically starts: with candidates' decisions to run for the legislature. A voter will not have a "fair opportunity" to hold their legislator electorally accountable if the legislator is not on the ballot or if there is no one else to vote for. However, 20 percent of incumbents regularly do not seek reelection, and a third of incumbents who do seek reelection do not face either a primary or general election challenger. Chapter 2 shows that increased time demands, such as longer legislative sessions, family obligations, and lower pay lead to fewer legislators seeking reelection and fewer "fair opportunities" for voters to hold their legislators accountable. There is also often hope that poorly performing legislators will be scared to run for reelection. However, I find limited evidence that legislators retire more frequently during a weak economy and no substantial evidence that legislators retire after providing poor representation in recent elections. Such reelection strategies by incumbents leave worse-performing legislators in office.

Voters also do not have the "fair opportunity" to hold their legislators electorally accountable if there is no one else to vote for. Chapter 3 shows that major-party challengers, like incumbents, less often run when the time demands of serving in the legislature are high or pay is low. However, challengers also take more-strategic advantage of political conditions. I find district partisanship is an increasingly important predictor of challenger decision-making, and—promisingly for accountability—challengers run more often when incumbents oversee weak economies or provide poor representation. However, challengers also more frequently challenge incumbents who are members of the president's party, particularly during unpopular presidencies. With these national influences, whether legislators face electoral competition is then often dictated by political conditions outside of state legislators' own control.

Analyses in chapter 4 turn to Powell's other condition for accountability and investigate the extent to which voters "know who is responsible for making policy." Over 20 percent fewer voters know which party controls the state house than the US House, and far fewer voters know who their state legislator is. Voters are more knowledgeable about their state legislature in states with unified government and where the news media devotes more resources to covering state government, providing a potential avenue to close the knowledge gap. However, increasing media coverage alone may not be a feasible solution to inform voters to more desirable levels. Making voters as knowledgeable about their state legislature as they are of Congress would likely require tripling the amount of news coverage of state governments. Such increases in the media corps covering state government are unlikely to happen anytime soon, as the number of reporters devoted to covering state government has declined by a third since the turn of the century.

Few voters may know who their legislators are, and fewer challengers may run. Nevertheless, some challengers run, and some voters know who is responsible for making policy, leading to the possibility of accountability. Chapter 5 begins to more directly address the question of whether voters themselves hold state legislators accountable for what they do. Specifically, I ask voters to explain in their own words: "Was there anything in particular you [liked/disliked] about the [Democratic/Republican] candidate in the election for the [name of lower state legislative chamber]?" Forty-two percent of respondents gave a "no" response when indicating their likes of a candidate, 39 percent gave a "no" response when indicating their dislikes of a candidate, and 30 percent gave a "no" response to *both* questions. When asked if they could remember anything their representative had done for their district, 60 percent of voters explicitly answered "no," and 18 percent responded with some version of "don't know." Voters not having opinions of their state legislative candidates, not knowing anything their state legislator has done, or not being able to recall who their state legislator is contributes to a shaky foundation for accountability in state legislatures.

Chapters 6 and 7 investigate the extent to which voters hold their legislators individually and collectively accountable. In chapter 6, I discover
that legislators do not face meaningful electoral consequences for their ideological representation. Voters, furthermore, do not appear to hold legislators individually accountable for their roll-call positions on controver-
sial issues such as collective bargaining or immigration. I also find that
voters in an overwhelming majority of states do not reward legislators for
their effectiveness, such as their ability to get legislation passed. Together,
these findings are consistent with the takeaways from chapters 4 and 5 that
voters know little about their legislators and do not provide substantial evidence that what individual legislators do themselves resonates much with
most voters.

Given the low levels of voter knowledge, few may be surprised that voters do not hold legislators accountable for their individual behavior. As
discussed above, party labels can simplify the accountability process, and
in chapter 7, I examine surveys and election results since the 1970s to evaluate the degree to which state-level party retrospective voting is present in
state legislative elections. State-level economic conditions, policy performance, and voters' assessments of the legislature appear to relate little—if
at all—to the electoral success of the party in control of the legislature. Voters who are more knowledgeable about the legislature are more likely to
hold the parties in power accountable, but I discover that even when the
legislature performs well, misinformed voters at times mistakenly reward
members of the minority party. Across both informed and uninformed voters, evaluations of the president are better predictors of state legislative
vote choice than voters' assessments of the legislature. State legislators'
electoral fates then are more closely tied to the performance of the White
House than the state house, casting doubt on prior explanations of state-
level representation and the notion that "all politics are local."

Neither elites nor voters then appear to meaningfully threaten a state
legislative incumbent's job security, at least via the general election. The
general election, however, is not the only way for a legislator to leave office.
If legislators want to keep their jobs, they also must survive the primary
election. The state legislative primary can provide a form of "accountability," at least to primary voters. However, chapter 8 reaffirms one American
politics textbook's characterization that a state legislative primary is "not
unlike the common cold. It is a nuisance, but seldom fatal" (Bibby 2003,
172).[15] Fewer than 15 percent of incumbents face an in-party primary challenger, and over 98 percent of incumbents win their primary races. Con-

cerning for polarization in state legislatures, legislators who provide more ideologically extreme representation or vote more frequently with the majority of their party face fewer primary challengers, and Democratic legislators who provide more-liberal representation of their districts experience more electoral success. Rewards for party loyalty or ideological extremity offer a type of accountability. However, this form of accountability motivates legislators to represent extreme voters or their partisan base rather than their whole district, perhaps creating undesirable incentives for representation, at least of the median voter.

My search for accountability concludes with a review of my findings and their implications that will disappoint many but likely truly surprise few: elections do little to hold most state legislators accountable. This sad state of statehouse democracy's electoral foundation is the culmination of decisions made by both political elites and voters. Neither elites nor voters are fools, but both are trapped in a complicated, federal system of government. In such a system, state lawmakers have few incentives to change their behavior to match most voters' preferences. It is ultimately up to the reader to determine whether state legislative elections meet their standards for electoral accountability. If the evidence I offer satisfies the reader's own standards, my findings provide reassurance that statehouse democracy rests on a solid foundation. But if they do not, it casts doubt on the founders' proposition that elections provide a meaningful "dependence on the people" to control the "angels" in American legislatures (Madison or Hamilton 1788).

Legislators Not Seeking Reelection

You Can't Fire Me If I Quit

In 1987, Emile "Peppi" Bruneau sought reelection to represent the 94th Louisiana state house district and handily defeated Barbara Arnold with 10,615 votes to 2,649. After serving a four-year term, Bruneau ran for reelection again in 1991. No one challenged the sitting state representative, and he successfully reclaimed his seat. Bruneau ran again in 1995 and 1999, and once more in 2003, but each time faced no opposition. The 2,649 votes for Arnold in 1987 would be the last ballots cast against a Bruneau for decades. Peppi Bruneau retired from the legislature in 2007, and in the special election to fill his seat, voters chose Nick Lorusso over Peppi's son, Jeb Bruneau, by a margin of 60 percent to 40 percent. Later, in the general election, Lorusso defeated Peppi's other son Adrian 49 percent to 21 percent.

Some Bruneau family members were clearly unpopular with 94th District voters, but voters' dissatisfaction with Peppi's performance could not be expressed at the ballot box due to a lack of opposition candidates followed by Peppi's retirement. Peppi's electoral "success" seems remarkable but reflects a fairly common obstacle for accountability in state legislatures. Millions of voters do not have "a fair opportunity to cast a meaningful vote for or against the policymakers" (Powell 2000, 51) because their state legislator does not seek reelection, or opposition candidates do not run against the incumbent.

Figure 2.1 highlights the severity of this problem for accountability by breaking down legislators' potential paths to leaving office or reelection. Specifically, it shows the percentages of state legislators in single-member districts who retired, ran for reelection, faced primary and general election challengers, and won primary or general elections from 2001 to 2020.

All Incumbents

5% 81% 14%

Involuntarily Retire | Seek Reelection | Voluntarily Retire

17% 83%

Contested Primary | Uncontested Primary

15% 41% 43% 43% 56%

Lost Primary Election | Contested General | Uncontested General | Uncontested General | Contested General

7% 93% 100% 100% 91% 9%

Lost General Election | Won General Election | Lost General Election

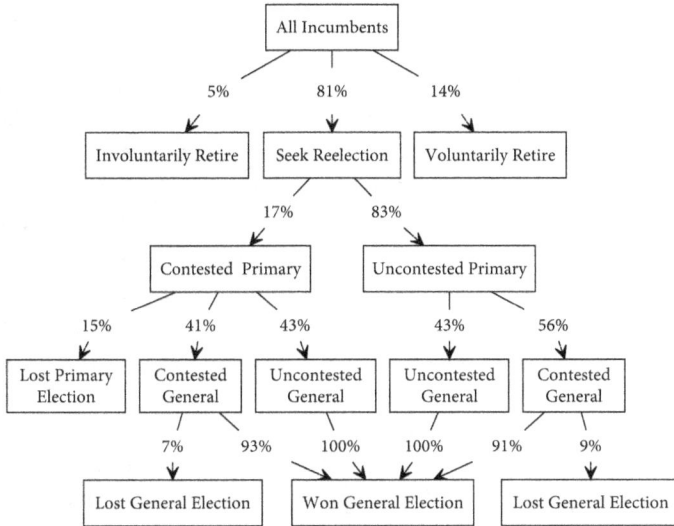

FIGURE 2.1. Legislators' paths to retirement or reelection. Percentages in this figure represent the percentage of legislators from the previous stage who appeared in the following stage. For example, 81 percent of all incumbents sought reelection. Of these incumbents, 17 percent then had a contested primary. Of these incumbents, 15 percent lost their primary elections. Together, 2 percent of all incumbents lost in a contested primary election (81 percent x 17 percent x 15 percent).

Percentages in this figure represent the percentage of legislators from the previous stage who appeared in the following stage. For example, approximately 14 percent of state legislators voluntarily left the legislature (e.g., resigned or chose not to run for reelection), and 5 percent involuntarily left office (e.g., faced term limits or died). By comparison, less than 10 percent of members of Congress voluntarily retired during this time (Brookings Institute 2021).

State legislators who sought reelection often faced little competition. Eighty-three percent did not face opposition in their primary election, 45 percent did not face opposition in the general election, and 38 percent did not face *either* a primary or general election challenger. Combined with those legislators who retire, voters in over half of state legislative districts do not have the "fair opportunity" to hold their state legislators accountable.

The fact that so many voters cannot cast ballots against their state legislators presents a considerable obstacle to accountability in state legislatures. Recall, the underlying assumption behind the idea that elections solve the moral hazard problem posed by representative government is that legislators do not want to lose their jobs. There are two main ways a legislator can lose their job. First, the incumbent does not seek reelection. And second, the incumbent loses to a primary or general election challenger. Whether the first event happens nearly always depends on one political elite's—the incumbent's—decision, with the main exception being term limits. The second event can only occur if another political elite—the challenger—decides to run against the incumbent. Elites then largely decide whether voters have a fair opportunity to hold their legislators accountable well before Election Day. Knowing why political elites run for the state legislature is therefore critical to understanding accountability in state legislatures.

In this chapter, I lay out and test theories that potentially explain why incumbents decide to retire from the legislature or run for reelection. The following chapter builds on these explanations to better understand when and why challengers run against incumbents. Incumbents' and challengers' decisions are rooted in the potential costs and benefits of serving in the legislature. Both appear to consider the personal sacrifices they must make to serve in the legislature. Incumbents less often seek reelection when they have a family, and challengers are less likely to run when serving in the legislature requires a long drive to the state capital. Incumbents and challengers also strategically decide when to run for office. They run more often in favorable districts to their party, and challengers more frequently run against unrepresentative incumbents, which provides voters with more fair opportunities to hold poorly performing legislators accountable. However, I find less evidence that incumbents who provide worse representation of their districts retire at higher rates in more-recent elections, suggesting that instead of running scared, few legislators are scared to run—even if they provided poor representation.

The Decision to Run

When deciding to run for the state legislature, a candidate asks themselves many of the same questions most Americans ask before pursuing a new job. "What sacrifices will I make for this job?" or "Do I have any chance of getting the job?" More formally, the decision to run for office can be broken down into whether the probability of obtaining the seat (p) times the benefit of holding the seat (B) exceeds the costs of running for office and serving in the legislature (C). A candidate should run when $pB > C$ (e.g., G. Black 1972). This three-term expression is, however, deceptively simple. To figure out B and C, incumbents need to weigh the tradeoffs between personal obligations, public service, and other—sometimes more prestigious and lucrative—opportunities. Calculating p requires incumbents to consider challengers' and voters' responses to political conditions ranging from representation to the economy.

Some of these factors more directly relate to policymaking than others, but each is crucial for understanding elections' ability to create incentives for representation. If an incumbent knows he is not running for reelection—either for personal reasons or because he thinks he cannot win—he has less incentive to consider voters' interests when making laws. A retiring legislator can cast roll calls and create a policy that suits his own interests without much repercussion, as voters have little means to punish the incumbent if he does not appear on the ballot in the next election. Understanding accountability in state legislatures then requires understanding the reasons behind state legislators' decisions to run for reelection, both personal and political.

The Personal Decision: Family, Time, and Money

(Most) everyone has a life outside their job, and political elites similarly have responsibilities beyond their political duties. For instance, it is almost cliché for a retiring politician to say they want to spend more time with their family. However, this oft-given reason is frequently accepted because Americans can relate. Many mothers and fathers, including those in the legislature, find it somewhat or very difficult "to balance the responsibilities of their job and family" (Pew Research Center 2013).[1] For instance, when resigning from the California state senate, Senator Michael Rubio said, "my family comes first," citing his special-needs fourteen-month-old daughter and the 300-mile drive to Sacramento from his district (McGreevy 2013).

To better understand how many candidates share Senator Rubio's family concerns, David Broockman, Nicholas Carnes, Melody Crowder-Meyer, and Christopher Skovron conducted the National Candidate Study, which surveyed the 10,131 people running for state legislature in 2012. 1,907 state legislative candidates and incumbents answered questions about their backgrounds and impressions of state legislative politics. I thank Nicholas Carnes and his coauthors for generously sharing these survey results to use in this book.[2] Like Senator Rubio, 53 percent of state legislators and 55 percent

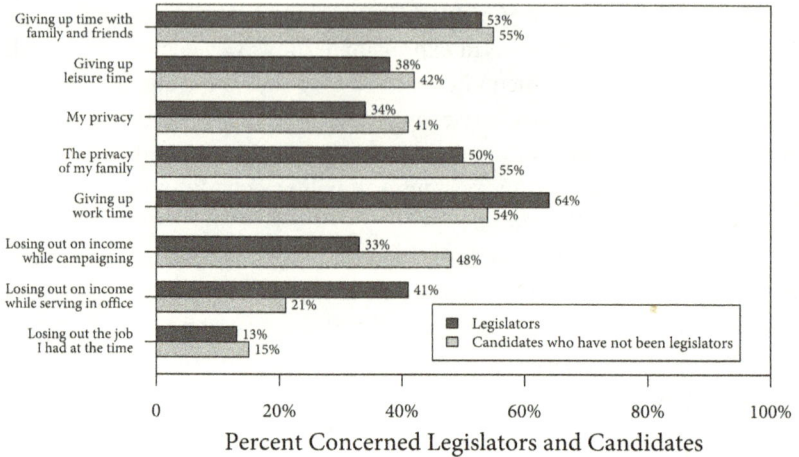

Percent Concerned Legislators and Candidates

FIGURE 2.2. State legislators and candidates' responses to: "Many people who think about running for office choose not to because of the many personal challenges entailed in seeking public service. When you first ran for elected political office, did you feel seriously concerned about any of the following? (check all that apply)" in the 2012 National Candidate Study.

of other state legislative candidates nationwide told the National Candidate Study they were concerned with "giving up time with family and friends" when first deciding to seek public office (figure 2.2).

Not all legislators feel the same family obligations when considering running for office. Such pressures often fall more heavily on women. For example, when describing her decision to run for the legislature, one state representative told Susan Carroll and Kira Sanbonmatsu:

> I do think it is harder for women to make that decision to spend a lot of time away from their kids . . . I decided to do this when my kids were about three and six, but I put it off until they graduated high school. That is because I represent a rural district, and their whole school life I would have been in [the state capital], and it wasn't a cost I wanted to pay . . . And for men . . . if they are married, they have someone at home who can tend to the home fires. (Carroll and Sanbonmatsu 2013, 46)

Men have increasingly become more responsible for tending to the home fires in recent years, but women still report spending twice as much time on childcare than men (Pew Research Center 2013). Competing work-life demands affect women's career trajectories in law or business (for reviews, see Kay and Gorman 2008 and Phillips and Imhoff 1997), and women are descriptively underrepresented in public office. Carroll and Sanbonmatsu (2013, 45) posit that few women run for office partly because of women's greater consideration of "how candidacy and office-holding would affect the lives of others with whom the potential candidate has close relationships" compared to men.[3] Similarly, more women than men incumbents told the National Candidate Study that they were concerned about how running for office would mean giving up time with family and friends. If this is the case, it potentially explains why women legislators are less likely to be married or have children (Carroll and Sanbonmatsu 2013, tables 2.5 and 2.8; Lawless and Fox 2010, table 4.3) and why Rachel Silbermann finds that living an "hour further from the state capital decreases a district's likelihood of having a woman candidate by a full 6.8 percentage points" (Silbermann 2015, 134; see also Freeman and Lyons 1992 and Smith et al. 2015).

Party leaders consider family and time obligations when recruiting candidates. When discouraging a thirty-year-old mother of two from running, Ohio senate majority leader Tom Patton stated, "I don't know if anybody explained to her we've got to spend three nights a week in Columbus. So, how does that work out for you? I waited until I was 48 and my kids were raised, and at least adults, before we took the opportunity to try" (Pelzer 2016). Nationally, when asked, "What do you look for in a candidate?," 1,118 county-level Republican and Democratic party chairs rated a candidate having "a flexible work schedule" as more important than previously holding elected office, serving in a community leadership position, or being independently wealthy (Broockman et al. 2014).

Legislative leaders are also partly concerned about work schedules because the current generation of state legislators spends more time in the capital than their predecessors. Peverill Squire has impressively documented institutional changes in state legislatures since the country's founding, focusing on a concept known as "legislative professionalism." Political scientists consider a legislature more professional as its institutions (i.e., salaries, legislative session length, and staff) resemble Congress. Focusing on the time demands placed upon legislators, Squire found that most state legislatures met biennially in the 1960s, but in 2014, forty-six legislatures met every year (Squire 2012, table 7.1; 2017). Further increasing demands placed upon state legislators, most legislatures met for twenty-eight days or fewer in 1909, but by 2014, most met for at least fifty days (Jewell 1982, Squire 2017).

Legislators themselves determine how long they will meet, and they evaluate the costs and benefits of longer legislative sessions. The Rhode Island legislature, for example, considered moving from being "part-time" to "full-time" in 2006. Some legislators, such as State Representative Raymond Gallison, felt that "if we went to a full-time legislature, we wouldn't have the rush at the end of the session that we always do, where things seem to break down and some of the most important bills get lost" (Gregg, Mayerowitz, and Gudrais 2006). However, not all representatives shared Gallison's enthusiasm for longer sessions. As Representative Stephen Ucci expressed, "I think we do enough damage being in here part-time. The last thing people need is to have us here full-time" (Gregg, Mayerowitz, and Gudrais 2006).[4] Ucci is likely not alone in his concern. A survey of over two thousand state legislators from the 1980s found that majority-party legislators who served in legislatures in longer sessions were less satisfied with the bills they passed (Francis 1985).

A state legislator may find himself struggling to produce quality bills and, in turn, put in long hours at the office if he is relatively inexperienced at the job. Forty-nine percent of state legislative candidates told the National Candidate Study that they had never previously held elected office, and 17 percent indicated they were concerned about the difficulties of holding offices. Once elected, many of these candidates can rely on the over thirty thousand state legislative staff members across the country to help them transition to their new job (National Conference of State Legislatures 2021a). Studies of state legislatures find that, as in Congress, newer legislators (e.g., freshman members) depend more on staff than more senior members do (Weissert and Weissert 2000; K. Hoffman 2006), and staff help newly elected legislators learn the "capitol way" (Weissert and Weissert 2000, 1138). While much is required of newly elected state legislators, staff can address constituency concerns and research legislation, making the job easier and less time-consuming.

Rhode Island ultimately decided to remain part-time, but the time commitment necessary to serve in this legislature is now more than in most states. Using data collected by Squire, figure 2.3 illustrates the average number of days legislators spent in session per year from 2013 to 2014. State legislatures meet for approximately fifty days a year, on average, and Rhode Island legislators, on average, meet for almost seventy days per year. Time commitments are smaller in some legislatures. New Hampshire legislators only meet for twenty-one days per year. Meanwhile, the Massachusetts, California, and Ohio legislatures meet for over one hundred days each year. Incumbents in California and Ohio then face a work-life balance dilemma and must decide if they want to spend considerable time in Sacramento or Columbus instead of being at home with their loved ones.

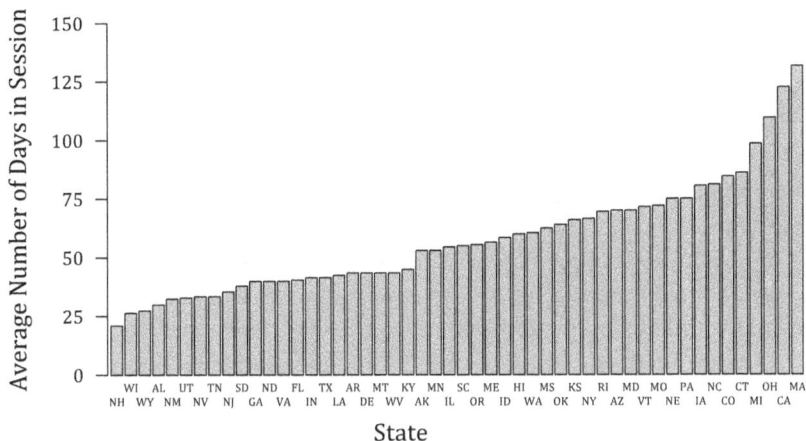

FIGURE 2.3. The average number of days state legislatures met per year from 2013 to 2014.

When contemplating what longer legislative sessions would be for those who served in the Rhode Island legislature, another issue that arose in the debate regarding whether to become a full-time legislature was: could legislators meet the demands of both their legislative and outside careers? Steve Nardelli, a lobbyist for charter schools, characterized the Rhode Island legislature as one "where you've got lawyers, teachers, real-estate agents . . . people that can afford to be there, where John Q. Public really can't" (Gregg, Mayerowitz, and Gudrais 2006). Senate Majority Leader M. Teresa Paiva expressed similar concerns that she was "not sure what full-time means . . . Does it mean that [Rep.] Paul Crowley can't own his restaurant because he's a legislator?" State legislators across the country share similar financial worries. When asked by the National Candidate Study about their concerns before running for public office, 13 percent of incumbents expressed concern about "losing the job I had at the time," 41 percent worried about "losing their income from their job" by serving in the legislature, and 64 percent were "worried about giving up work time" (figure 2.2).

Before serving in the state capitol, many legislators often had well-paying careers. Todd Maske (2019) remarkably documented the occupations of state legislators. Maske found that approximately 17 percent of legislators who served from 1991 to 2011 were once lawyers, and over 20 percent were business owners, executives, or managers.[5] Many legislators intend to return to these often better-paying careers and sometimes continue them while serving in the legislature. In 2002, John Carey and coauthors (2008) asked approximately three thousand legislators: "After service in the present chamber, what are you likely to do?" Approximately 28 percent of legislators said they would return to their nonpolitical careers after serving in elected office.[6] Jerome Maddox (2004, table 4) similarly found that reducing a legislator's salary from $50,000 to $20,000 increases the probability a legislator has a career outside the legislature by .096.

These findings reflect Connecticut State Senator Norm Needleman's motivations when introducing a bill to raise Connecticut legislators' pay in 2020. Needleman told the *Connecticut Mirror*, "I personally know of legislators who've had to leave because of the money. They couldn't support their family, living in basement apartments." These Connecticut legislators who had to carefully manage their personal budgets to serve in the legislature were also responsible for overseeing $30 billion in state spending in 2020 (Urban Institute 2022). When addressing the implications of low legislative salaries for policymaking, Needleman continued, "I hate to be as crass as to say 'You get what you pay for,' but we're paying people $30,000—they get a little bit of money to chair a committee, they get a little bit of money for mileage—and believe it or not, there are many people in that legislature who have to live on that" (Phaneuf 2020).

Low salaries have long frustrated legislators. Over a decade earlier, one anonymous legislator told Grant Reeher: "I just wish that I could do [legislative service] and send my kid to college" (Reeher 2006, 131). Many parents can attest to the skyrocketing college-tuition costs in the 2000s, but perhaps less known is how little state legislative salaries have increased. When adjusted for inflation, the average state-legislator salary in 1970 was $43,521 but $38,370 in 2021, and legislators in ten states saw no pay increases from 2001 to 2021 (National Conference of State Legislatures 2021b). Louisiana legislators received a salary increase in 2009, but this was their first raise since 1980. When speaking about Louisiana's salary situation, Representative Joe Harrison stated that he had "colleagues in the Legislature who are leaving simply because they can no longer afford to serve" (Cullen 2011).

Legislators report that time and financial sacrifices weigh upon their decisions to stay in the legislature, but are these simply noncontroversial answers or real reasons for why legislators do not seek reelection, denying voters the "fair opportunity" to hold them accountable? There are many explanations for variation in legislative turnover, such as types of districts (e.g., Niemi and Winsky 1987), levels of professionalism (e.g., Rosenthal

1974), and term limits (e.g., Moncrief et al. 2004). But outside of recent work by Benjamin Melusky (2018) and Jordan Butcher (2022), nearly all studies of turnover that consider more than a handful of states focus on overall turnover, which includes exits from the legislature both voluntarily by legislator choice and involuntarily by election. As discussed below, a legislator may "voluntarily" retire because he thinks he will lose the next election — such as for his representation — but there may be other reasons why a legislator voluntarily retires — such as if a legislator has a family — that would be less likely explanations for why a legislator would lose an election.

To clarify the reasons why state legislators voluntarily leave the office and, in turn, deny voters the ability to have a fair opportunity to hold their legislators accountable, I estimate a series of statistical models that evaluate how personal considerations and political conditions relate to the likelihood an individual state legislator retires from the legislature. The dependent variable of interest is whether an incumbent state legislator voluntarily did not seek reelection. These analyses exclude legislators who involuntarily left the legislature (i.e., due to term limits or death). In this and the following chapters (chapters 3, 6, and 8), I focus on elections to state legislative chambers where only one candidate could win an election. For example, analyses include New Hampshire state senate elections, which exclusively had single-member elections, but excludes the New Hampshire state house, which had both multi-member and single-member elections. I also exclude Louisiana elections due to its runoff system and Nebraska due to its nonpartisan elections.

My analyses first consider how time and finances relate to legislators' retirement decisions. I assess the importance of time demands in at least three ways. First, I account for the length of a legislature's session (Bowen and Greene 2014). Second, I consider a legislative district's distance from the capital, assuming that legislators who live farther from the state capital will spend more time away from their everyday lives.[7] Third, for elections from 2001 to 2010, I account for whether a legislator was married or had children. To assess the importance of finances, I consider legislators' salaries, campaign costs, and potential other job opportunities. To capture campaign costs, I account for the average amount a candidate raised in a legislative chamber in that election year and whether a state had a public campaign-finance option. For occupations, I account for whether a legislator's previous profession was as a lawyer, doctor, or business professional and, as explained in greater detail below, whether a state has restrictions on a legislator becoming a lobbyist following their service in the legislature.

The analyses in the current and following chapters also study the extent to which legislators' gender and race relate to state legislative election outcomes. As discussed above, societal expectations for men and women often differ, and political scientists show that voters at times perceive women candidates as more liberal than otherwise comparable men candidates (e.g., McDermott 1997; see also Hayes and Lawless 2016). Theoretically, such political perceptions or stereotypes can have important implications for both elite and voter-level decision-making. For example, if a woman incumbent is perceived to be more liberal due to her gender, we may expect her to receive fewer votes from more-conservative voters.

Empirically, investigations of the electoral implications of such stereotypes have produced differing conclusions (Bos, Schneider, and Utz, 2018). However, when focusing on elites' behavior, Jennifer Lawless and Kathryn Pearson (2008) show that Republican women incumbents, perceived as more liberal, face more competition in primaries than their Democratic counterparts. Studying voters' behavior, Jeffrey Koch (2000) finds that gender ideological stereotypes increase the perceived ideological distance between Democratic women candidates and voters, thereby decreasing their electoral prospects. Sarah Anzia and Rachel Bedford (2022) find gender stereotypes and cues particularly relevant in local elections, where voters have less information, as often is the case in state legislative elections. Focusing on race, Matthew Jacobsmeier (2015) similarly shows that voters perceive African American members of Congress to be more liberal.

If such stereotypes exist in state legislative elections, they may not be all that inaccurate. Using the ideological measures of representation or legislators' ideal points (e.g., those presented in figure 1.2), where lower ideal points reflect more-liberal representation, the average woman legislator's ideal point is -0.36. Meanwhile, the average man legislator's ideal point is 0.08. Within the Democratic party, the average woman and man legislator ideal points are -1.00 and -0.81; in the Republican party, these figures are 0.75 and 0.80.[8] Given that voters have limited information about their state legislators (chapters 4 and 5), voters may rely on stereotypes of legislators' representation when deciding whom to support in state legislative elections.

To account for elites' and voters' differing responses to and perceptions of minority legislators, I identify women and nonwhite legislators using data from the Center for American Women in Politics (2022) and Carl Klarner (2021). Given prior evidence that the impact of gender and race can differ by party, I additionally account for whether such legislators are members of the Democratic or Republican parties. In the current chapter, I use these variables to evaluate whether minority legislators are more likely to retire, and in the following chapters, I study how these variables relate to other elites' and voters' behavior.

My study of legislators' retirement also considers legislators' other personal characteristics, such as their age and marital status, and whether they have children. Benjamin Melusky (2018) generously shared these data on most legislators who served from 2001 to 2010. While these data are incomplete, I want to emphasize that gathering personal data on state legislators is difficult, and Melusky's work is an outstanding contribution. Research assistants and I independently attempted to fill in the blanks but could not do so for all legislators who served in this time period. I present findings that include these personal variables for analyses of the 2001 to 2010 elections. I additionally present separate studies that exclude personal variables for 2001 to 2010, 2011 to 2020, and the 2001 to 2020 elections.

My models also account for political characteristics unique to the incumbent (representation, time served in the legislature, party affiliation, past electoral success), legislative district (district-level presidential vote, district population), state (term limits, amount of staff per legislator), and temporal political conditions (the state economy, approval of the president, whether the election took place in the midterm).[9] I address many of these variables' substantive importance at greater length below, and table A.2.1 provides summary statistics of variables used in this and the following chapters' analyses.

For my statistical tests, I use probit regressions to estimate the relationship between the above independent variables and legislators' retirement in districts where elections only elected one state legislator. Estimations include random effects for states (table A.2.2). Table A.2.3 provides results of similar statistical models with fewer control variables. To give substantive meaning to relationships, I convert probit estimates to predicted probabilities or differences in probabilities for a given change in an independent variable (table 2.1). For example, using the analyses in the final column of table A.2.2, the first row of table 2.1 shows that increasing the length of a legislative session by one hundred days increases the probability that a legislator retires by 0.014 when studying the 2001 to 2020 elections.[10]

Time, Family, and Finances

My statistical analyses help affirm that "wanting to spend more time with family" is not just a cliché. Legislators do not seem to want to spend long

TABLE 2.1 **Personal variables' relationship with retirement**

Variable	Change in variable value	2001–2010 Model with personal variables	2011–2020 Model without personal variables	2001–2020 Model without personal variables
Length of legislative session	Increase of 100 days	+0.000 (0.006)	+0.013* (0.005)	+0.014* (0.004)
District distance from capital	Increase of 100 kilometers	−0.000 (0.002)	+0.001 (0.002)	−0.000 (0.002)
Married	Single to married	+0.026* (0.006)		
Children	No children to children	−0.029* (0.006)		
Age	Increase 10 years	+0.008* (0.002)		
Incumbent gender	Man to woman	+0.002 (0.006)	+0.000 (0.006)	−0.004 (0.004)
Nonwhite legislator	White to nonwhite	−0.020* (0.010)	−0.021* (0.010)	−0.021* (0.007)

This table reports the differences in the average predicted probabilities of an incumbent retirement associated with changing the variable value listed in the second column. Standard errors are in parentheses; *$p < 0.05$.

hours at the state capitol. Again, when focusing on the 2001 to 2020 elections, increasing the session length by one hundred days increases the predicted probability of a legislator retiring. However, I do not find that legislators who represent districts farther from the state capital are more likely to retire (table 2.1, second row). Focusing on family, I find that the probability of a married legislator retiring is 0.026 higher than the comparable probability for unmarried legislators. But perhaps surprisingly, parents are less likely to retire, all else equal.

When assessing the relationship between parenthood and legislator retirement, there are important differences between younger and older legislators to consider. For example, older state legislators who are parents likely have more free time on their hands since their kids have moved out of the house, which seems to drive this overall result. For legislators who are sixty years old, not having kids compared to having kids decreases the probability of retirement by 0.033 (t-statistic of difference 4.76). The difference for legislators who are thirty years old is a 0.005 increase in the probability of retirement (t-statistic of difference 0.294). Otherwise stated, when a legislator's nest is empty, they appear to keep themselves busy at the state capital.

Despite the many work and life expectations held of women, I find little evidence that women legislators are more likely to retire than men legislators (table 2.1, sixth row). Wives and mothers are no more likely to retire than husbands or fathers, a result that holds even when the focus is restricted to legislators younger than sixty years old (see online appendix). Unlike studies of US House elections (Fox and Lawless 2005), I do not find that women state legislators are more likely to retire if they have served longer in the legislature or represent more-competitive districts. Nor do I find that women legislators are more likely to retire if their session lengths are longer or their districts are farther from the state capital.[11] Meanwhile, nonwhite legislators are approximately 0.02 less likely to retire than white legislators.

It may be surprising that variables such as gender or a legislator's district's distance from the capital do not systematically relate to retirement, but in a methodological aside, it is important to bring attention to limitations the present study faces. One limitation is that who serves in legislatures is not random. To better understand this limitation, reconsider the above findings concerning a district's distance to the capital. It may be tempting to infer from the lack of correlation between distance from capital and retirement that state legislators are not bothered by long drives to work. But suppose those who dislike long drives never run for the state legislature in the first place. For instance, recall Silbermann offers evidence that increased time away from home deters women from seeking state legislative office.[12] If people who dislike long drives do not run for the legislature, there is a selection effect that shapes who is in the legislature and, in turn, examined in my study. This selection effect can bias our results and make finding a statistical relationship between the two variables more difficult. Otherwise stated, even though there is not a statistically significant relationship between an independent and dependent variable, we cannot be fully confident there is no relationship.

When interpreting this chapter's findings, like those where legislators retire to "spend more time with their family," it is also important to keep in mind another commonly used phrase: correlation does not imply causation. In this book, I repeatedly show how a change in one independent variable relates to a change in the dependent variable of interest, such as a legislator's retirement or reelection vote share. Such theoretically motivated and tested associations are often informative but do not necessarily imply that the independent variable causes the dependent variable. Another variable or explanation could be responsible for the change in the dependent variable. My analyses attempt to account for these alternative explanations by "controlling" for other variables, generally following an all-else-equal assumption, as is done in most work that studies elections. However, as with any statistical assumption, it limits interpretations. Here, reconsider the above findings concerning parenthood. My initial statistical test did not consider that parenting responsibilities vary for thirty-year-olds versus sixty-year-olds and found that legislators who are parents are less likely to retire, all else equal. Once I accounted for a more complete theoretical prediction where the time costs of parenthood will not impact all moms and dads equally but will instead vary by age, statistical analyses revealed a different finding. In the following pages, I make an honest effort to provide theoretically sound statistical tests and to highlight other methodological limitations of my analyses. And I encourage readers to keep such limitations and assumptions in mind when reading this or any other social science research.[13]

Returning to legislators' costs-and-benefits calculus when deciding to retire, table 2.2 presents relationships between some of legislators' financial considerations and retirement. Over 50 percent of legislators told the National Candidate Study that they were concerned with the "need to raise money" before their first time running for public office. Consistent with these survey responses, legislators who serve in chambers where it takes more money on average to win elections are more likely to retire, at least in more-recent elections (table 2.2, first row). Meanwhile, in states that offer a public-finance option, which presumably should reduce campaign costs for legislators, the probability of a legislator retiring is 0.048 higher when considering elections from 2001 to 2020 (table 2.2, third row). A potential reason for this latter finding is that legislators are more likely to face major-party challengers in public-finance states (chapter 3; see also Mancinelli 2022), which incumbents may foresee and thereby be deterred from seeking reelection.

Legislators also claim they leave public office "simply because they can no longer afford to serve," and higher salaries appear to be one way to keep legislators in the state capital. Similar to prior work that finds legislators who are paid better serve longer careers or are less likely to retire (Squire 1988; Melusky 2018), I find that increasing a legislator's salary by $10,000 decreases the probability of retirement by 0.007 (table 2.2, third row).[14] Legislators also appear to be able to afford to serve in the legislature if they previously had a well-paying career. Legislators whose most recent occupation was either in business or law were at least 0.045 less likely to retire. Findings concerning doctors are similar but do not meet conventional levels of statistical significance. If individuals from more white-collar professions are more likely to stay in legislatures, there may be a reason to be concerned that occupational and class biases shape lawmaking as found in Congress (e.g., Carnes 2013).[15]

TABLE 2.2 **Financial variables' relationship with retirement**

Variable	Change in variable value	2001–2010 Model with personal variables	2011–2020 Model without personal variables	2001–2020 Model without personal variables
Average cost of campaign	Increase of $50,000	+0.001 (0.004)	+0.013* (0.006)	0.020* (0.003)
Public-finance option	All states without option to all states with option	0.018 (0.016)	+0.020* (0.029)	0.048* (0.018)
Legislative salary	Increase of $10,000	−0.001 (0.001)	−0.007* (0.002)	−0.007* (0.001)
Occupation: lawyer	Not lawyer to lawyer	−0.073* (0.007)	−0.028* (0.007)	−0.045* (0.005)
Occupation: business	Not business to business	−0.081* (0.006)	−0.022* (0.006)	−0.046* (0.005)
Occupation: doctor	Not doctor to doctor	−0.031 (0.025)	−0.016 (0.021)	−0.023 (0.015)

This table reports the differences in the average predicted probabilities of an incumbent retirement associated with changing the variable value listed in the second column. Standard errors are in parentheses; *$p < 0.05$.

Value of Legislative Office

Not all lawyers stay in the legislature. Former Florida senate president Joe Negron, for instance, resigned two years into a four-year term to return to the Akerman law firm. Negron told the *Orlando Sentinel*: "I'm a lawyer first, a legislator second . . . This was one part of my life that I greatly value . . . but my primary professional identity is as a lawyer. I'm back in the office. I enjoy what I do." Negron's decision to return to his law firm was likely not only motivated by a passion for the law. When Negron left the legislature, he was no longer eligible to run for reelection due to term limits.

By limiting the length of legislative careers, term limits wipe away some potential benefits legislators accrue while serving, such as legislative experience or prestige in the chamber. Such experience appears to factor into legislators' calculus when deciding to seek reelection. For example, chamber leaders wield more power than other legislators in most legislatures, and leaders appear less willing to step away from these positions. The first row of table 2.3 indicates that the predicted probability of a chamber leader retiring is 0.102 less than the typical legislator. Similarly, freshman legislators who just worked hard in their first campaign for their current seat are at least 0.067 less likely to retire from the legislature than other members (table 2.3, second row). The value of the office itself—beyond direct dollars and cents—then likely shapes whether voters have the fair opportunity to hold their state legislator accountable.

TABLE 2.3 **State legislative chamber variables' relationship with retirement**

Variable	Change in variable value	2001–2010 Model with personal variables	2011–2020 Model without personal variables	2001–2020 Model without personal variables
Chamber leader	Non-leader to leader	−0.115* (0.006)	−0.060* (0.011)	−0.102* (0.007)
Freshman member	Non-freshman to freshman	−0.067* (0.005)	−0.077* (0.006)	−0.076* (0.005)
Terms served	Increase from 3 to 5 terms	+0.016* (0.002)	+0.016* (0.002)	+0.016* (0.001)
Term limits	All states have term limits	+0.058* (0.012)	+0.056* (0.018)	+0.045* (0.015)
Minority-party seat share	Increase of 10 percent	0.004 (0.004)	+0.005 (0.005)	−0.008* (0.003)
Majority-party member	Minority- to majority-party member	−0.012* (0.005)	+0.010 (0.006)	−0.003 (0.004)
Revolving-door policy	All states without policy to all states with policy	−0.014 (0.010)	−0.007 (0.015)	+0.016* (0.007)

This table shows differences in the average predicted probabilities of an incumbent retirement associated with changing the variable value listed in the second column. Standard errors are in parentheses; *$p < 0.05$.

If legislators cannot hold onto their seats due to term limits, it reduces the value of these seats. Studying term limits and state legislative elections from 2000 to 2001 in twenty states, Jeffrey Lazarus (2006) found that legislators in term-limit states were less likely to seek reelection. My analyses reaffirm Lazarus's findings. Legislators who serve in states with term limits are at least 0.045 more likely to retire than legislators who serve in a state without term limits (table 2.3, fourth row). Recall that the present analyses remove legislators who could not seek reelection due to term limits (i.e., those serving in their final term), so this estimate does not capture legislators who were forced to retire. Term limits then, directly and indirectly, reduce the number of "fair opportunities" voters have to hold their legislators accountable. Term limits directly prevent legislators from running and facing voters, and by preventing legislators from indefinitely running for reelection, term limits indirectly encourage legislators to leave the legislature early.

The Revolving Door

Term limits prevent many legislators from continuing to utilize their experience in the state capital, at least as state legislators. Legislators can still take advantage of their legislative skills in their next jobs.[16] They are often uniquely familiar with a state's lawmaking process and have relationships with other state legislators, which can be valuable for organizations wanting to shape policy, such as interest groups. As characterized by the majority leader of the Minnesota Senate, "[former members] make very good lobbyists for a client to pick up because they understand the place" (Stassen-Berger 2015). Becoming a lobbyist can also help alleviate some state legislators' financial worries. When describing his decision to become a lobbyist, former Indiana Democratic legislator Louis Mahern stated:

> I can stay in the state Senate, which I've been in for 16 years, attend meetings at night and weekends, and stand for reelection at $25,000 a year with per diem, or I can go out in the hall and not have to go to meetings at night, only follow the legislation that my clients care about, and make $200,000 a year . . . You can only resist that for so long. I have to start thinking about my financial future or my children's education. (Tolchin and Tolchin 2010, 70)

The transition of government officials to becoming lobbyists is often characterized as going through the "revolving door." The First Amendment to the US Constitution ensures the right "to petition the Government," but if a state representative goes through the revolving door to a well-paying lobbyist job, it can lead to voters not having the fair opportunity to hold their legislator accountable for unpopular policy.

One example of a legislator becoming a lobbyist was State Representative Kevin McCarthy in Illinois. Shortly prior to leaving the legislature, McCarthy introduced legislation in the Illinois General Assembly that gave utility companies "the ability to raise . . . rates with less regulatory oversight" (Erickson 2012). Specifically, in exchange for $2.6 billion in consumer rate hikes over ten years, Commonwealth Edison (Illinois's largest utility company) pledged to digitize Illinois's electrical grid (Guerrero and Wernau 2013). After McCarthy introduced his bill, Commonwealth Edison's president lauded the legislation, stating that "the Illinois General Assembly has taken on the critically important task of determining the proper policy path to make a 21st-century electric grid a reality" (*Energy Times*, 2011). McCarthy's controversial bill meanwhile faced opposition from the Citizens Utility Board, the Illinois Environmental and Policy Center, and the American Association of Retired People. The legislation only became law after the General Assembly overrode a gubernatorial veto, after which the president of Commonwealth Edison released a statement thanking "our supporters in the General Assembly for their leadership"

(Wernau 2011). After these incidents, it must have only been a coincidence that Representative McCarthy retired two months following the bill's adoption, registered as a lobbyist, and took Commonwealth Edison on as a client (McQueary 2012).

McCarthy joined thirty-nine other former Illinois state legislators who at the time were already lobbyists (Erickson 2012) and is not the only former legislator who sought to exit from the legislative chamber to the lobby of the state capital. In John Carey and coauthors' survey of approximately three thousand legislators, more than 15 percent of state legislators stated they intended to become a lobbyist or consultant after their legislative career (2008). Of the 46,994 lobbyists registered with the state government in 2011, approximately 2.2 percent were once state legislators (Strickland 2020), and many legislators make quick exits through the revolving door like McCarthy. In 2016, of the forty-four Michigan lobbyists who were once state legislators, 63 percent had registered as lobbyists within a year of leaving office (Mauger and Roelofs 2017). Similarly, as of 2015, sixteen of the thirty-nine former state legislators who had become lobbyists in Minnesota did so less than a year after leaving the legislature (Stassen-Berger 2015).

To slow the rate at which the revolving door spins, state governments have imposed restrictions on how long a state legislator must wait after leaving office before becoming a lobbyist. In 2005, twenty-five states had at least a one-year "cooling off" period before a former state legislator could register as a lobbyist (Holman 2005). By 2011, thirty-two states had revolving-door policies; in 2019, thirty-eight states had such policies (Holman and Reddy 2011; Holman and Esser 2019).[17] When studying the number of lobbyists in 1989 and 2011 who were once state legislators, James Strickland finds that "each additional 12 months of waiting time [to become a lobbyist] results in about three fewer revolvers" (Strickland 2020, 76).

Strickland shows that revolving-door policies mean fewer legislators become lobbyists after leaving the legislature. But do revolving-door policies deter legislators from leaving the legislature itself? When I focus on a legislator's decision to leave the legislature instead of whether a former legislator becomes a lobbyist, statistical evidence of relationships between revolving-door policies and legislative retirement is mixed. When separately studying the 2001 to 2010 and 2011 to 2020 elections, the statistical relationship between legislative retirement and revolving-door policies does not meet conventional levels of statistical significance. However, when studying the full 2001 to 2020 time period, a state having a revolving-door policy is associated with an 0.016 increase in the likelihood that a legislator retires, suggesting that a legislator who knows they have to wait to become a lobbyist leaves the legislature a little earlier than they otherwise would. However, the certainty of this relationship is sensitive to whether analyses account for if a legislator's district had been recently redistricted (table A.2.4).

Again, it is important to consider that a lack of statistical certainty or a null result does not imply there is no relationship. For instance, a legislator may want to spend more time with their family, and once they decide to leave the legislature, they then choose to become a lobbyist. Family may be why they left, and becoming a lobbyist a later decision. The above accounts from state legislators also suggest some legislators consider becoming lobbyists, and there are stark examples of revolving-door policies impacting legislators' decision to leave the legislature. For instance, six days before Missouri's cooling-off period was to extend from six to twenty-four months, former state senator Jake Hummel stated he resigned to be able to work for the AFL-CIO sooner (Lieb 2018), a decision that is consistent with Strickland's findings.[18]

The Strategic Decision to Run

Time and financial sacrifices are captured by the B and C terms in the reelection-decision calculus of $pB > C$. When deciding whether it is worth seeking another term, a legislator must also consider the p term: the probability of being reelected. Like many other retiring legislators, McCarthy, for example, stated that the decision to leave the legislature was right for his family (Associated Press 2011). Personal considerations probably played some role in McCarthy's decision, but a fuller account of McCarthy's decision likely should include his electoral prospects in 2012, which were not great. McCarthy won reelection in 2006 and 2008 unopposed but only received 52 percent of the vote against a relatively unknown Republican candidate in 2010 (Hanania 2011). Redistricting additionally set McCarthy up to run against another incumbent in 2012. All of this was before McCarthy passed the utility-regulation bill that the governor, lieutenant governor, attorney general, and voters opposed. In a statewide survey of Illinois, most respondents indicated "they wouldn't vote for a legislator who allows electric utilities to raise their rates annually," which is just what McCarthy spearheaded (USNewswire 2011).

McCarthy then faced the decision of whether to pursue a potentially tough reelection campaign, where the probability of reelection was lower, or to not run at all. McCarthy ultimately chose not to run, which many political scientists would likely call a "strategic retirement."[19] Like any retirement, McCarthy's decision denied voters the fair opportunity to hold their state legislator accountable, but McCarthy's behavior may not be completely bad for representation in state legislatures. If McCarthy retired because he thought his representation would be unpopular with voters, elections may indirectly produce better representation by scaring unrepresentative legislators from seeking reelection with the threat of accountability. A mere threat can be meaningful. For instance, Alexander Fouirnaies and Andrew Hall (2022) find that legislators who can seek reelection—as opposed to those who cannot due to term limits—sponsor more bills and miss fewer floor votes. Similarly, legislators who decide to seek reelection more often cast roll-call votes that align with their district's preferences (Giger, Kluver, and Witko, 2019). The threat of election alone then appears to shape representation in state legislatures.

The District

When legislators calculate their p term or decide whether to strategically retire, they likely ask themselves questions many other political candidates ask, such as "Who are the voters in the district?", "How have I represented the district?", or "Is this an opportune time to run?" Focusing on the first question, political scientists have well documented that voters' party identification strongly predicts how successful a party's candidate will be in an election (e.g., A. Campbell et al. 1960). While some work finds some voters have different levels of partisanship at the state and national levels (e.g., Jennings and Niemi 1966), more recently, political scientists demonstrate that voters' partisanship at the federal and state levels has become increasingly aligned. For instance, Caughey and Warshaw (2018, 73, fig. 3.8; see also Hopkins 2018) use survey data since the 1930s to show that there has been an ideological nationalization of partisanship. These authors claim that the labels of "Democrat" and "Republican" "have the same ideological meaning everywhere in the country" and "[t]he typical Democratic identifier is much more similar to Democrats in other states than they once were."

Chapter 6 shows how partisanship has become increasingly important for voters in state legislative elections. In turn, an incumbent concerned

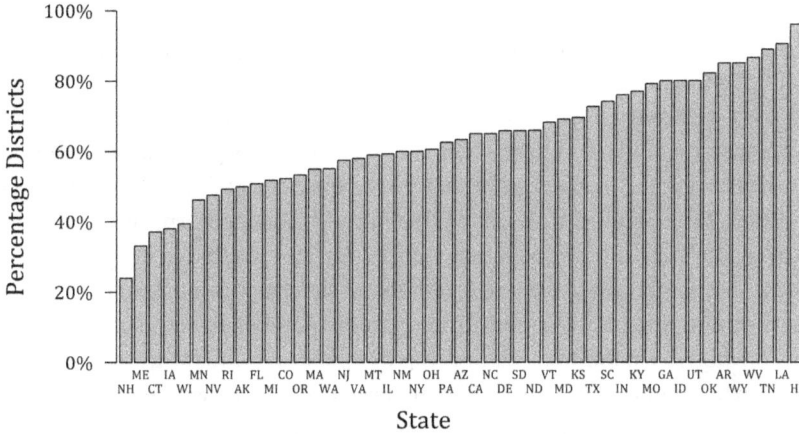

FIGURE 2.4. Percentages of state house seats where average Democratic vote share in the 2012 and 2016 presidential elections was less than 40 percent or greater than 60 percent.

about winning must consider how much the district already favors his party before running for reelection, particularly after district lines have been redrawn. Many complain that redistricting and gerrymandering create too many "safe" congressional districts—or those where it is difficult for one party to lose (e.g., Hulse 2016). However, even mapmakers who want to create more balanced districts face obstacles. Voters with similar political views increasingly live closer to one another or "geographically sort," creating homogenous political communities (Brown and Enos 2021; Levendusky 2009; Oppenheimer 2005). State legislative districts are often geographically smaller than congressional districts, making it especially difficult to create constituencies with diverse populations.

Safe districts are becoming increasingly prevalent at the state level. When defining a district as "safe" when one party received at least 60 percent of the presidential vote, 50 percent of state legislative districts were safe in 2000. In 2008, this percentage rose to 57 percent. And in 2016, this percentage reached 65 percent. Meanwhile, "only" 61 percent of US House districts were safe in 2016. Using averaged results from the 2012 and 2016 elections, figure 2.4 presents the percentage of such safe state house districts within each state. Over 60 percent of states have more safe house districts than the US House. In Hawaii and Louisiana, over 90 percent of state house seats are safe, and the number of safe seats within a state often disproportionally favors a single party. In fifteen states, most state house districts are safe Republican districts, and in six states, most state house districts are safe Democratic districts. In some states, nearly every district favors one party. Only one West Virginia state house district supported Obama in 2012 with more than 53 percent of the vote, and in Hawaii and Vermont, Obama won at least 52 percent of the vote in *every* state house district.

Returning to Illinois's 37th state house district, McCarthy's district was not safe for a Democrat. Barack Obama received 54 percent of the vote in McCarthy's district in 2008, but after redistricting, Obama only received 40 percent of the vote in 2012. In addition to reducing the number of friendly partisans in a legislator's constituency, redistricting can lead to fewer voters having an established relationship or "personal vote" with their incumbent, which political scientists show reduces US House members' vote share (Ansolabehere, Snyder, and Stewart 2000). McCarthy's foresight of the partisan makeup of his district likely shaped his decision to retire, as it likely does for legislators across the country. When considering all elections from 2001 to 2020, incumbents are at least 0.045 more likely to retire immediately after a district is redistricted.

Incumbents also appear to increasingly consider how safe their district is before deciding to run for reelection. From 2001 to 2010, a standard-deviation or 13 percent increase in district partisanship was associated with an 0.014 decrease in the probability of legislator retirement. In elections from 2011 to 2020, the comparable decrease in probability was 0.025. This strengthening relationship, combined with the increased number of safe seats, suggests that legislators being comfortable with their probability of victory in more-partisan districts leads to voters having more "fair opportunities" to hold their incumbent accountable. However, these opportunities will disproportionately present themselves in safe seats, where the incumbent is unlikely to lose even if they perform poorly (Rogers 2017; see also chapters 6 and 8).

Anticipated Individual Accountability for Legislators' Representation

When McCarthy had to decide whether run for reelection, he had just spearheaded the passage of unpopular legislation. Chapter 6 offers evidence that state legislators are more likely to lose, albeit slightly, if they provide worse representation. If this is the case, an unrepresentative legislator's anticipated probability of victory should be lower, thereby increasing their likelihood of retirement following $pB < C$. Studies of Congress provide evidence that poor representation can lead to more legislative retirements.

Moore and Hibbing (1998) show that US House members who are "ideo-logical misfits" with their party—as measured by their Conservative Coali-tion roll-call score—are more likely to retire (p. 1104). Studying the 1992 election, Sean Theriault (1998) shows that a standard-deviation change in "district compatibility"—created using interest-group scores—leads to a .097 increase in the likelihood that an incumbent voluntarily leaves the US House (table 2). Such findings suggest that members of Congress an-ticipate being held individually accountable by voters. Despite congres-sional findings, I am unaware of research that investigates how state leg-islators' representation relates to state legislative incumbents' retirement decisions.

To assess whether a relationship between state legislators' representa-tion and retirement exists, I employ two measures of legislators' represen-tation. The first measure aims to test underlying predictions of the median voter theorem and capture the ideological distance between a legislator and his district. The median voter theorem generally predicts that legisla-tors should experience more electoral success when their representation better reflects their district ideology (see chapter 6 for a fuller explanation of this theorem). To create a measure of legislators' "ideological distance from their district," I calculate the distance between a state legislator's and his district's "ideal points." Political scientists frequently use ideal point estimates to quantify ideology on a numerical scale (e.g., from -1 to 1, with lower numbers reflecting liberal ideology; see Poole and Rosenthal 2000). For state legislators, I employ ideal points derived from legislators' re-sponses to surveys and roll-call records (Shor and McCarty 2011). For leg-islative districts, I use ideal points based on the demographic characteris-tics of a district and voters' responses to political surveys (Tausanovitch and Warshaw 2013). These legislator and district ideal points are the same as those presented in figure 1.2.

After putting legislator and district ideal points on a common scale us-ing ordinary least-square regressions (see Rogers 2017 for more detail), I measure the *ideological distance* between a legislator and their district. For an example of this measure, reconsider McCarthy's Illinois's 37th state house district.[20] McCarthy's legislative ideal point was -0.48. The estimated dis-trict ideal point for Illinois's 37th District was 0.19. McCarthy's ideologi-cal distance from his district was then 0.67 (absolute value of [-0.48–0.19]), which is roughly equivalent to the mean (0.72) and median (0.70) values of this ideological-distance measure whose standard deviation is 0.37. Smaller values of the ideological-distance metric suggest that an incumbent better represents their district in the legislature, and larger values indicate an incumbent provides worse representation.

The second measure of representation employed is a legislator's "party loyalty," or how often a legislator votes with their party. Research on US House elections finds that voters reward and punish legislators for their ideological representation along with voting with their party more in Congress (Carson et al. 2010). As put by Jamie Carson and his coauthors, the reasoning behind this relationship is that

> voters may be much more comfortable identifying themselves as Democrats and Republicans than they are liberals or conservatives . . . If so, they would have a much stronger reaction to political actions taken by a legislator in terms of the legislator's partisan opposition than his or her ideological opposition. (Carson et al. 2010, 601)

To assess whether voters exhibit such behavior to punish state legislators for such "party loyalty," my statistical models include a measure of the percentage of votes in which a legislator voted with a majority of their party in the most recent legislative session. I derive this measure from roll-call votes collected by Shor and McCarty (2011).[21]

If unrepresentative legislators fear being held individually accountable, legislators who are more distant from their district should be more likely to leave the legislature voluntarily, but the evidence to support this assumption is becoming increasingly discouraging. When studying elections from 2001 to 2010, a standard-deviation increase in the ideological-distance measure—which captures a legislator providing worse representation—was associated with a 0.004 increase in the likelihood of a legislator's retirement, but this difference does not meet conventional levels of statistical significance. However, when studying elections from the following decade, the same change in representation was associated with a 0.005 decrease in the likelihood of retirement. Unrepresentative legislators were then perhaps more likely to retire in the 2001 to 2010 elections, removing them from office, but less likely to retire in the 2011 to 2020 elections.

Legislators who voted with their party 13 percent more often than average—reflecting a standard deviation in a legislator's party-loyalty score—were 0.066 less likely to retire, but again the relationship between representation and retirement changed over time. From 2001 to 2010, such a change in party loyalty is associated with a 0.040 decrease in the probability of retirement. But the comparable decrease in probability when studying the 2011 to 2020 elections was 0.080. By increasingly running for reelection, unrepresentative and party-loyal legislators do allow voters the fair opportunity to hold them accountable. However, these findings are also potentially discouraging for representation in state legislatures. Given most legislators cruise to reelection (figure 2.1, chapter 6), these results suggest that more undesirable legislators ultimately will return to the state capitol.[22]

Anticipated Collective Accountability for State and National Political Conditions

When calculating their probability of victory, legislators are also likely to consider the larger political climate and whether voters will hold them collectively accountable. If times are good, incumbents may anticipate coasting to reelection, but if times are bad, they may retire to avoid being swept up in political tides. Legislators do not always admit they retire for such reasons, but many likely do. As Gary Jacobson and Sam Kernell (1983, 50), in their reflection on the number of Republican retirements in Congress during the Watergate era, curiously note: "Something about the 1974 election made family men out of a disproportionate number of Republican congressmen." There is mixed evidence that federal legislators retire in fear of being held collectively accountable. Jennifer Wolak (2007) finds higher levels of US House retirements when voters disapprove of Congress. However, neither Wolak nor Moore and Hibbing (1998) find that presidential approval or the economy relate to congressional retirements (see also Swain, Borrelli, and Reed, 1999). Again, I am unaware of research investigating whether state legislators are more likely to retire due to political conditions that change over time, such as the economy.

I evaluate how larger political conditions relate to legislators' retirement decisions in three ways. First, I return to the theory of balancing described in this book's introduction. Following the logic that if incumbents anticipate that voters will balance the executive and legislative branches of government, the governor's legislative co-partisans should anticipate such balancing and less electoral success in state midterm elections and be more likely to retire. Second, given the rise in the nationalization of state politics, I expect legislative co-partisans of an unpopular president to be more likely to retire. Third, and more directly tied to state-level accountability, incumbents presumably should be less confident in their reelection prospects during weak economies and be more likely to retire. For these latter

TABLE 2.4 **Political variables' relationship with retirement**

Variable	Change in variable value	2001–2010 Model with personal variables	2011–2020 Model without personal variables	2001–2020 Model without personal variables
District partisanship	Increase of	−0.014*	−0.025*	−0.019*
	1 standard deviation	(0.002)	(0.003)	(0.002)
	(approx. 13 percent)			
Redistricting	District redistricted	+0.032*	+0.031*	+0.045*
	before election	(0.009)	(0.007)	(0.005)
Ideological distance	Increase of	+0.004	−0.005*	−0.001
	1 standard deviation	(0.003)	(0.003)	(0.002)
Party loyalty	Increase of	−0.040*	−0.080*	−0.066*
	13 percent	(0.002)	(0.004)	(0.003)
State economy	Increase of	−0.005*	−0.004*	0.001
	1 standard deviation	(0.002)	(0.002)	(0.002)
	(approx. 2 percent)			

This table shows differences in the average predicted probabilities of an incumbent retirement associated with changing the variable value listed in the second column. Standard errors are in parentheses; *$p < 0.05$.

analyses, I use the president's average approval rating in the Gallup poll the three months prior to the primary election and the annual change in logged, real state personal income as measured in the second quarter. My focus on these time periods follows studies of federal elections and aims to capture economic and political conditions for the approximate time when many incumbents need to finalize their decision to run for reelection.

State legislators appear to anticipate being held accountable for the state economy more than they anticipate voters will engage in balancing behavior in state legislative elections. For instance, 2 percent economic growth in the state economy—reflecting approximately a standard-deviation change in this measure—decreases the predicted probability of a state legislator retiring by at least 0.004 in elections from either 2001 to 2010 or 2011 to 2020 (table 2.4, bottom row).[23] Statistical analyses, meanwhile, provide less evidence that state legislators anticipate voters will balance the executive and legislative branches of state government by voting against members of the governor's party in state midterm elections. Nor do analyses suggest that members of the president's party are more likely to retire in federal midterm elections or when the president is unpopular.[24]

Legislators' responses to state economic conditions provide some good news for representation in state legislatures, but state legislators may want to consider more than just state politics. Legislators more often retire when the economy is weak, which is consistent with the argument that legislators strategically retire to avoid anticipated electoral punishment. Such behavior may decrease voters' fair opportunities to hold their state legislators accountable but results in fewer legislators returning to the state capitol who poorly managed the economy. Meanwhile, the above analyses provide little evidence that state legislators consider national politics before running for reelection, which may deserve reconsideration. As documented in the following chapters—state legislators of the president's party are more likely to face challengers, receive fewer votes, and fail to be reelected than other state legislators. The president's state legislative copartisans then face an uphill battle to return to the state house, and they may want to think about "spending more time with the family" when the national political climate is bad for their party.

Recap

Political elites largely determine whether voters will have a "fair opportunity" to hold their state legislators accountable, and approximately 14 percent of state legislators voluntarily decide to leave office each election year. When sitting legislators make this decision, they weigh the costs and benefits of serving and forecast their probability of reelection. Legislators retire more often when time demands are high and pay is low. Reflecting the diminished value of legislative office, voters additionally have fewer opportunities to hold their legislators accountable in term-limit states, even when legislators can run for reelection. Perhaps promising for representation in state legislatures, legislators slightly less often seek reelection during a weaker economy, reflecting their fear of being held accountable for their poor performance. However, more legislators appear to retire in response to recently redrawn districts or to the partisan makeup of their district, factors that have little to do with legislators' own performance.

It is hard to criticize legislators for spending more time with their families or taking a better job or avoiding an unfavorable electorate, but 14 percent of legislators choosing not to seek reelection is not a small number, especially in the context of other percentages presented in figure 2.1. Over twice as many legislators voluntarily retire rather than lose reelection, and in the 2020 election, voluntary retirements denied at least 59 million Americans the fair opportunity to hold their state legislators accountable. Such foreseen retirement—even rooted in reasons such as family—diminishes legislators' electoral incentive to represent their districts before leaving office. Kevin McCarthy may have cared little that most Illinoisans opposed his utility bill, especially if he knew there was a payday as a lobbyist at the end of the line. McCarthy no longer needed voters' electoral support for his career, so why care about his constituents in his newly redistricted and less-partisan-friendly district? State legislative elections then do less to solve the moral hazard problem posed by representative government, at least for those legislators who decide not to pursue reelection.

No one can serve in a job forever, and approximately 81 percent of legislators regularly seek reelection, potentially giving voters a fair opportunity to reward or punish their legislators for good or bad performance. The potential for accountability, however, will only be fulfilled if voters have an alternative candidate to support, which is not always the case. Remember, Emile "Peppi" Bruneau ran for reelection over two decades. But no one ran against him. To stay in the state legislature, Bruneau did not have to be an effective policymaker, provide services to constituents, or even kiss a baby. Louisiana voters could not cast a ballot against Bruneau because they had no other choice. Regrettably, relatively few voters have choices in state legislative elections, and we will better see why this is the case in the next chapter.

Appendix

TABLE A.2.1 **Summary statistics**

Variable	Min.	Max	Median	Mean	SD
Incumbent voluntarily retires	0.00	1.00	0.00	0.15	0.35
Incumbent contested in primary election	0.00	1.00	0.00	0.18	0.38
Incumbent wins primary election	0.00	1.00	1.00	0.97	0.16
Incumbent contested in general election	0.00	1.00	1.00	0.78	0.41
Incumbent wins general election	0.00	1.00	1.00	0.95	0.22
Inc. gen. election two-party vote share	0.00	100.00	71.59	76.85	21.07
Ideological distance from district	0.00	3.18	0.70	0.72	0.37
Party loyalty	6.16	100.00	91.20	87.40	12.96
Change in annual log of Q2 state personal income	−0.08	0.14	0.02	0.03	0.03
Change in annual log of Q4 state personal income	−0.06	0.22	0.03	0.03	0.03
Married	0.00	1.00	1.00	0.85	0.36
Children	0.00	1.00	1.00	0.79	0.41
Age	19.00	99.00	56.00	55.69	11.77
Terms served	1.00	26.00	3.00	3.66	3.17
Business profession	0.00	1.00	0.00	0.11	0.32
Lawyer	0.00	1.00	0.00	0.09	0.28
Doctor	0.00	1.00	0.00	0.01	0.09

Variable	Min.	Max	Median	Mean	SD
Legislator salary (in thousands of 2010 dollars)	0.00	285.76	54.43	74.28	59.64
Legislative staff per member	0.35	19.66	3.61	4.98	3.86
Session length	39.00	521.30	143.55	172.24	104.08
Public-finance campaign option	0.00	1.00	0.00	0.11	0.31
Logged average amount to win race (state-year)	8.45	14.59	11.36	11.30	1.11
Term limits enacted	0.00	1.00	0.00	0.37	0.48
Revolving-door restriction	0.00	1.00	1.00	0.65	0.48
Incumbent-party pres. vote	9.41	98.76	61.16	61.61	13.34
Prev. incumbent-party vote share	0.00	100.00	71.45	76.90	21.39
Seat previously contested	0.00	1.00	1.00	0.59	0.49
Minority-party seat share	0.00	0.50	0.38	0.37	0.10
Logged full-time reporters	0.00	4.19	2.57	2.49	0.66
District size (logged)	9.01	13.74	10.95	10.94	0.90
Freshman incumbent	0.00	1.00	0.00	0.27	0.44
Midterm appointee	0.00	1.00	0.00	0.04	0.18
Chamber leader	0.00	1.00	0.00	0.04	0.19
Woman legislator	0.00	1.00	0.00	0.23	0.42
Nonwhite legislator	0.00	1.00	0.00	0.16	0.36
Member of the Democratic Party	0.00	1.00	0.00	0.49	0.50
Member of chamber-majority Party	0.00	1.00	1.00	0.63	0.48
Member of governor's party	0.00	1.00	1.00	0.54	0.50
Member of president's party	0.00	1.00	0.00	0.50	0.50
Midterm election (federal)	0.00	1.00	0.00	0.48	0.50
Midterm election (state)	0.00	1.00	1.00	0.50	0.50
Off-year election	0.00	1.00	0.00	0.04	0.21
Redistricted district	0.00	1.00	0.00	0.25	0.43
State senator	0.00	1.00	0.00	0.23	0.42

Summary statistics of variables used in the main analyses in chapters 2, 3, 6, and 8. The online appendix provides more detail about these measures.

TABLE A.2.2 **Legislator retirement**

	Include personal variables 2001–2010	Exclude personal variables 2001–2010	Exclude personal variables 2011–2020	Exclude personal variables 2001–2020
Ideological distance from district	0.254[*]	0.255[*]	0.138	0.218[*]
	(0.122)	(0.113)	(0.089)	(0.067)
Ideological distance squared	−0.105	−0.112	−0.117[*]	−0.125[*]
	(0.078)	(0.072)	(0.046)	(0.037)
Party loyalty	−0.020[*]	−0.026[*]	−0.034[*]	−0.029[*]
	(0.001)	(0.001)	(0.001)	(0.001)
Change in annual log of Q2 state personal income	−1.348[*]	−1.281[*]	−1.005[*]	−0.365
	(0.566)	(0.532)	(0.383)	(0.264)
Pre-primary presidential approval	−0.006[*]	−0.006[*]	−0.020[*]	−0.003[*]
	(0.002)	(0.002)	(0.008)	(0.001)

continues

	Include personal variables 2001–2010	Exclude personal variables 2001–2010	Exclude personal variables 2011–2020	Exclude personal variables 2001–2020
Pres. approval x pres. party member	0.002 (0.002)	0.001 (0.002)	0.026* (0.012)	0.002 (0.001)
Married	0.155* (0.039)			
Children	0.222 (0.132)			
Age	−0.069* (0.008)			
Age x age	0.001* (0.000)			
Age x children	−0.007* (0.002)			
Age x terms served	−0.001* (0.000)			
Business profession	−0.595* (0.058)	−0.635* (0.054)	−0.108* (0.033)	−0.251* (0.027)
Lawyer	−0.518* (0.064)	−0.519* (0.059)	−0.146* (0.039)	−0.250* (0.031)
Doctor	−0.189 (0.172)	−0.233 (0.159)	−0.083 (0.107)	−0.126 (0.088)
Legislator salary (in thousands of 2010 dollars)	−0.000 (0.001)	−0.000 (0.001)	−0.004* (0.001)	−0.004* (0.001)
Legislative staff per member	0.015 (0.011)	0.011 (0.011)	0.020 (0.014)	−0.005 (0.012)
Session length	−0.000 (0.000)	−0.000 (0.000)	0.001* (0.000)	0.001* (0.000)
Distance to capital (logged)	−0.002 (0.012)	0.000 (0.012)	0.003 (0.012)	−0.001 (0.008)
Public-finance campaign option	0.095 (0.083)	0.095 (0.084)	0.094 (0.129)	0.223* (0.076)
Logged average amount to win race (state-year average)	0.013 (0.046)	0.010 (0.045)	0.113* (0.051)	0.183* (0.032)
Revolving-door restriction	−0.066 (0.050)	−0.031 (0.048)	−0.035 (0.072)	0.082* (0.036)
Term limits enacted	0.296* (0.057)	0.277* (0.058)	0.264* (0.082)	0.223* (0.070)
Redistricted district	0.169* (0.048)	0.160* (0.044)	0.144* (0.031)	0.211* (0.023)
Incumbent-party pres. vote	−0.006* (0.001)	−0.006* (0.001)	−0.010* (0.001)	−0.007* (0.001)
Previous incumbent-party vote share	0.005* (0.001)	0.005* (0.001)	0.008* (0.001)	0.006* (0.001)
Seat previously contested	0.202* (0.060)	0.193* (0.056)	0.326* (0.058)	0.248* (0.040)
Minority-party seat share	0.253 (0.239)	0.313 (0.233)	0.234 (0.247)	−0.399* (0.150)
District size (logged)	−0.052 (0.062)	−0.038 (0.061)	−0.057 (0.068)	−0.012 (0.051)
Terms served	0.108* (0.025)	0.034* (0.004)	0.038* (0.004)	0.039* (0.003)

	Include personal variables 2001–2010	Exclude personal variables 2001–2010	Exclude personal variables 2011–2020	Exclude personal variables 2001–2020
Freshman incumbent	−0.420*	−0.434*	−0.413*	−0.423*
	(0.038)	(0.034)	(0.033)	(0.024)
Chamber leader	−1.192*	−1.234*	−0.339*	−0.707*
	(0.105)	(0.105)	(0.069)	(0.053)
Midterm appointee	−1.573*	−1.530*	−1.146*	−1.214*
	(0.225)	(0.149)	(0.101)	(0.079)
Woman legislator	0.007	−0.054	0.009	−0.024
	(0.047)	(0.043)	(0.039)	(0.029)
Woman legislator x Democratic	0.005	0.011	−0.018	0.003
Party member	(0.062)	(0.057)	(0.053)	(0.039)
Nonwhite legislator	−0.113	−0.135	−0.086	−0.102
	(0.103)	(0.101)	(0.085)	(0.065)
Nonwhite legislator x Democratic	−0.007	0.027	−0.047	−0.019
Party member	(0.113)	(0.110)	(0.095)	(0.071)
Member of the Democratic Party	−0.145*	−0.138*	−0.076*	−0.105*
	(0.039)	(0.036)	(0.038)	(0.021)
Member of chamber-majority party	−0.064*	−0.053*	0.046	−0.015
	(0.026)	(0.024)	(0.028)	(0.018)
Member of governor's party	−0.046	−0.032	0.025	−0.003
	(0.032)	(0.030)	(0.036)	(0.023)
Member of president's party	−0.048	−0.032	−1.198*	−0.072
	(0.082)	(0.077)	(0.544)	(0.067)
Midterm election (federal)	0.134*	0.101*	−0.126*	−0.001
	(0.049)	(0.045)	(0.058)	(0.026)
Midterm election (state)	−0.061	−0.083*	−0.015	−0.058*
	(0.041)	(0.038)	(0.039)	(0.027)
Member of governor's party x	0.022	0.032	−0.047	−0.000
midterm election (state)	(0.050)	(0.047)	(0.046)	(0.032)
Member of president's party x	0.008	0.052	0.116	0.021
midterm election (federal)	(0.059)	(0.055)	(0.071)	(0.032)
Off-year election	0.243	0.264*	−0.647*	−0.203
	(0.131)	(0.133)	(0.191)	(0.173)
State senator	0.275*	0.247*	0.122*	0.046
	(0.052)	(0.050)	(0.054)	(0.042)
Constant	2.305*	1.346*	1.844*	−0.376
	(0.529)	(0.479)	(0.651)	(0.426)
N	21,537	24,093	22,329	46,422
Log-likelihood	−6,902.4	−7,944.0	−8,165.6	−16,291.0

This table reports the results of probit regressions in which the outcome of interest is whether an incumbent state legislator voluntarily left the legislature. Standard errors are in parentheses; *$p < 0.05$.

TABLE A.2.3 **Legislator retirement—reduced models**

	Include personal variables 2001–2010	Exclude personal variables 2001–2010	Exclude personal variables 2011–2020	Exclude personal variables 2001–2020
Ideological distance from district	0.068	0.035	−0.091*	−0.015
	(0.039)	(0.036)	(0.032)	(0.024)
Change in annual log of Q2 state personal income	−0.672	−0.715	−0.812*	−0.445
	(0.454)	(0.424)	(0.324)	(0.246)
Party loyalty	−0.017*	−0.022*	−0.027*	−0.024*
	(0.001)	(0.001)	(0.001)	(0.001)
Incumbent-party pres. vote	−0.007*	−0.007*	−0.009*	−0.007*
	(0.001)	(0.001)	(0.001)	(0.001)
Previous incumbent-party vote share	0.004*	0.004*	0.008*	0.005*
	(0.001)	(0.001)	(0.001)	(0.001)
Seat previously contested	0.197*	0.188*	0.338*	0.241*
	(0.057)	(0.053)	(0.056)	(0.038)
Member of president's party	0.038	0.030	−0.005	0.009
	(0.048)	(0.045)	(0.030)	(0.022)
Member of the Democratic Party	−0.141*	−0.123*	−0.058*	−0.103*
	(0.033)	(0.030)	(0.024)	(0.016)
Freshman incumbent	−0.556*	−0.598*	−0.600*	−0.593*
	(0.033)	(0.030)	(0.030)	(0.021)
Midterm election (federal)	0.123*	0.104*	−0.058	−0.017
	(0.037)	(0.034)	(0.032)	(0.022)
Member of president's party x midterm election (federal)	0.007	0.036	0.022	0.039
	(0.051)	(0.048)	(0.046)	(0.031)
Married	0.142*			
	(0.037)			
Children	−0.203*			
	(0.031)			
Age	0.006*			
	(0.001)			
Constant	0.040	0.887*	1.279*	1.034*
	(0.177)	(0.149)	(0.156)	(0.107)
N	21,621	24,250	22,825	47,075
Log-likelihood	−7,308.5	−8,463.9	−8,578.3	−17,127.1

This table reports the results of probit regressions in which the outcome of interest is whether an incumbent state legislator voluntarily left the legislature. Standard errors are in parentheses; *$p < 0.05$.

TABLE A.2.4 **Legislator retirement—exclude redistricted districts**

	Include personal variables 2001–2010	Exclude personal variables 2001–2010	Exclude personal variables 2011–2020	Exclude personal variables 2001–2020
Ideological distance from district	0.070	0.059	−0.120*	−0.037
	(0.049)	(0.045)	(0.039)	(0.029)
Party loyalty	−0.023*	−0.029*	−0.036*	−0.032*
	(0.001)	(0.001)	(0.001)	(0.001)

	Include personal variables 2001–2010	Exclude personal variables 2001–2010	Exclude personal variables 2011–2020	Exclude personal variables 2001–2020
Change in annual log of Q2 state personal income	−1.737* (0.637)	−1.753* (0.600)	−1.232* (0.442)	−0.429 (0.274)
Pre-primary presidential approval	−0.007* (0.003)	−0.006* (0.002)	−0.028* (0.009)	−0.000 (0.002)
Pres. approval x pres. party member	0.003 (0.003)	0.001 (0.003)	0.035* (0.014)	0.001 (0.003)
Married	0.190* (0.046)			
Children	0.338* (0.157)			
Age	−0.085* (0.010)			
Age x age	0.001* (0.000)			
Age x children	−0.008* (0.003)			
Age x terms served	−0.001* (0.000)			
Business profession	−0.577* (0.063)	−0.611* (0.059)	0.083* (0.038)	−0.142* (0.030)
Lawyer	−0.551* (0.072)	−0.540* (0.067)	0.065 (0.045)	−0.141* (0.035)
Doctor	−0.170 (0.183)	−0.193 (0.169)	0.101 (0.125)	−0.015 (0.099)
Legislator salary (in thousands of 2010 dollars)	−0.000 (0.001)	−0.000 (0.001)	−0.002* (0.001)	−0.003* (0.001)
Legislative staff per member	0.016 (0.011)	0.013 (0.012)	0.015 (0.015)	−0.002 (0.012)
Session length	0.000 (0.000)	0.000 (0.000)	0.000 (0.000)	0.001* (0.000)
Distance to capital (logged)	0.006 (0.014)	0.010 (0.014)	0.006 (0.014)	0.005 (0.010)
Public-finance campaign option	0.048 (0.085)	0.056 (0.087)	0.116 (0.139)	0.200* (0.087)
Logged average amount to win race (state-year average)	0.006 (0.051)	−0.000 (0.051)	0.179* (0.060)	0.232* (0.038)
Revolving-door restriction	−0.041 (0.053)	0.002 (0.052)	−0.028 (0.082)	0.059 (0.043)
Term limits enacted	0.353* (0.059)	0.339* (0.062)	0.303* (0.088)	0.292* (0.080)
Incumbent-party pres. vote	−0.001 (0.001)	−0.001 (0.001)	−0.002 (0.001)	−0.001 (0.001)
Previous incumbent-party vote share	−0.004 (0.002)	−0.004 (0.002)	−0.002 (0.002)	−0.004* (0.001)
Seat previously contested	−0.099 (0.088)	−0.100 (0.082)	−0.004 (0.079)	−0.067 (0.056)
Minority-party seat share	0.431 (0.259)	0.410 (0.258)	0.347 (0.281)	−0.131 (0.167)

continues

	Include personal variables 2001–2010	Exclude personal variables 2001–2010	Exclude personal variables 2011–2020	Exclude personal variables 2001–2020
District size (logged)	−0.059	−0.053	−0.142	−0.114
	(0.066)	(0.067)	(0.080)	(0.059)
Terms served	0.128*	0.036*	0.034*	0.039*
	(0.029)	(0.005)	(0.004)	(0.003)
Freshman incumbent	−0.420*	−0.432*	−0.462*	−0.458*
	(0.046)	(0.040)	(0.041)	(0.028)
Chamber leader	−1.073*	−1.119*	−0.181*	−0.574*
	(0.115)	(0.114)	(0.076)	(0.058)
Midterm appointee	−1.748*	−1.757*	−1.268*	−1.411*
	(0.267)	(0.182)	(0.127)	(0.098)
Woman legislator	0.044	−0.023	0.033	0.001
	(0.055)	(0.050)	(0.046)	(0.033)
Woman legislator x Democratic Party member	−0.023	−0.014	−0.046	−0.023
	(0.072)	(0.066)	(0.062)	(0.045)
Nonwhite legislator	−0.129	−0.160	0.019	−0.051
	(0.119)	(0.117)	(0.095)	(0.073)
Nonwhite legislator x Democratic Party member	0.009	0.045	−0.158	−0.080
	(0.132)	(0.128)	(0.107)	(0.081)
Member of the Democratic Party	−0.117*	−0.114*	−0.070	−0.074*
	(0.047)	(0.043)	(0.046)	(0.027)
Member of chamber-majority party	−0.069*	−0.059*	0.044	−0.016
	(0.031)	(0.028)	(0.033)	(0.021)
Member of governor's party	−0.028	−0.015	0.016	0.009
	(0.039)	(0.036)	(0.041)	(0.026)
Member of president's party	−0.101	−0.025	−1.669*	−0.069
	(0.161)	(0.144)	(0.650)	(0.130)
Midterm election (federal)	0.123*	0.103*	−0.170*	0.018
	(0.055)	(0.051)	(0.073)	(0.031)
Midterm election (state)	−0.066	−0.098*	−0.002	−0.053
	(0.047)	(0.044)	(0.046)	(0.031)
Member of governor's party x midterm election (state)	0.004	0.018	0.011	0.017
	(0.057)	(0.053)	(0.053)	(0.037)
Member of president's party x midterm election (federal)	0.036	0.068	0.241*	0.062
	(0.066)	(0.062)	(0.090)	(0.038)
Off-year election	0.329*	0.371*	−0.578*	−0.133
	(0.134)	(0.139)	(0.204)	(0.176)
State senator	0.329*	0.295*	0.157*	0.133*
	(0.056)	(0.055)	(0.063)	(0.048)
Constant	3.533*	2.331*	3.040*	0.711
	(0.586)	(0.526)	(0.752)	(0.481)
N	16,396	18,455	16,897	35,352
Log-likelihood	−4,986.8	−5,783.8	−6,004.7	−11,954.6

This table reports the results of probit regressions in which the outcome of interest is whether an incumbent state legislator voluntarily left the legislature, excluding districts that were redistricted since the most recent election. Standard errors are in parentheses; *p < 0.05.

Challengers in State Legislative Elections

A Lack of Choice

S tate legislators' retirements deny millions of voters a "fair opportunity" to hold their state representative accountable. Perhaps a more disturbing aspect of state legislative elections is that even when legislators do seek reelection, a greater number of voters do not have a fair opportunity to hold these legislators accountable in either the primary or general election. Over a third of reelection-seeking state legislators do not face either a primary or general election challenger and win reelection just by signing up (figure 2.1). These state legislators may have done such an excellent job that no one felt it necessary to run against them. Our core understanding of democracy, however, operates with the assumption that elections will offer voters a choice. An absence of state legislative challengers deprives voters of this choice and ultimately of the ability to hold their state legislators electorally accountable.

To highlight the lack of choice in recent state legislative elections, figure 3.1 presents competition levels in US and single-member district state legislative races from 1970 to 2020 (Boatright 2018; Klarner 2021). From 1991 to 2020, 83 percent of state legislators did not face opposition in their primary election (figure 3.1, dashed black line), and 47 percent did not face opposition in the general election (figure 3.1, solid black line), a rate over 25 percent lower than in US House elections (figure 3.1, solid grey line). Together, 35 percent of state legislators did not face *either* a primary or general election challenger.

Competition has not always been so meager in state legislatures. In 1970, approximately 84 percent of state legislative incumbents who sought

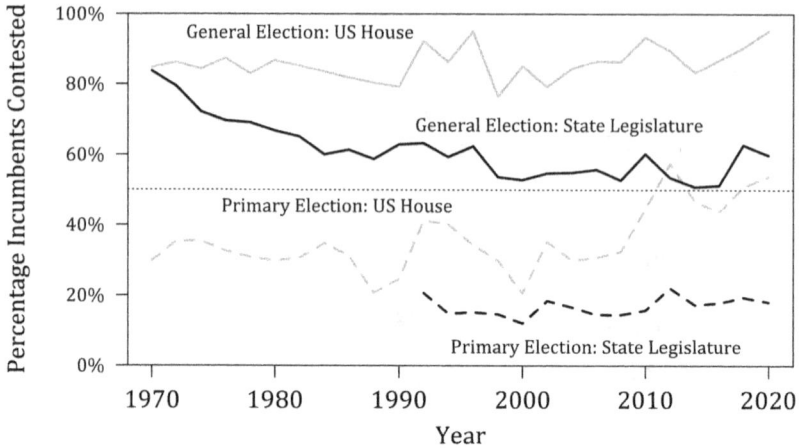

FIGURE 3.1. Percentages of US House and state legislative incumbents who faced a major-party or primary challenger.

reelection faced a major-party challenger, just shy of the 85 percent of US House incumbents who faced similar competition the same year. The 1960s and 1970s were likely a high point for state legislative competition, but even competition in the first half of the twentieth century was probably higher than in more-recent elections. State legislative election returns for all states before the 1970s are not readily available, but Barry Burden and Rochelle Snyder (2020) identified levels of contestation in ten state legislatures since 1920. Burden and Snyder defined contestation as a race featuring more than one candidate on the ballot, thereby including races with and without incumbents. From 1920 to 1970, at least 70 percent of state legislative races were contested each election year, and only in 1928 and 1930 were fewer than 75 percent of races contested. When comparing competition at the federal and state levels, Burden and Snyder (2020, 250) show that "before the 1960s, the 10-state sample suggests that Congress and state legislatures were following similar patterns without much of a trend" but later diverge. There was only one election after 1970 where at least 75 percent of races were contested in these ten states.

State legislative competition may be historically low, but contemporary voters have relatively more fair opportunities to hold state legislators accountable in some states. Figure 3.2 shows the percentage of state house incumbents who faced challengers in general and primary elections from 2001 to 2020 by state. Over 90 percent of incumbents regularly face general election challengers in Michigan and Minnesota, but such high levels of competition appear to be more of the exception rather than the rule. Fewer than half of incumbents regularly face a general election challenger in approximately one-third of states. For instance, less than a fourth of Arkansas state house incumbents faced either a primary or general election challenger. Many state legislators serving in Little Rock then reclaimed their jobs just by signing up.

Ideally, incumbents would have to do more than sign up to serve in the legislature. A "fair opportunity to cast a meaningful vote for or against the policymakers" only exists when an alternative candidate to the incumbent is on the ballot. Challengers also promote representation and hold legislators responsible for their actions in other ways. They spur debate between those in and out of power, forcing representatives to consider a broader set of interests (Key 1949, 303–10). This increased attention to issues can benefit voters who do not pay active attention to state legislative politics (subjects addressed in chapters 4 and 5). They also help voters identify the bad eggs in the legislature. As characterized by Douglas Arnold in his study of Congress, "few challengers fail to sift through incumbents' records in search of the smoking gun. They then employ their newly discovered evidence to persuade citizens how poorly their current representatives have served their interest" (Arnold 1992, 49). Perhaps reflecting state legislators' recognition

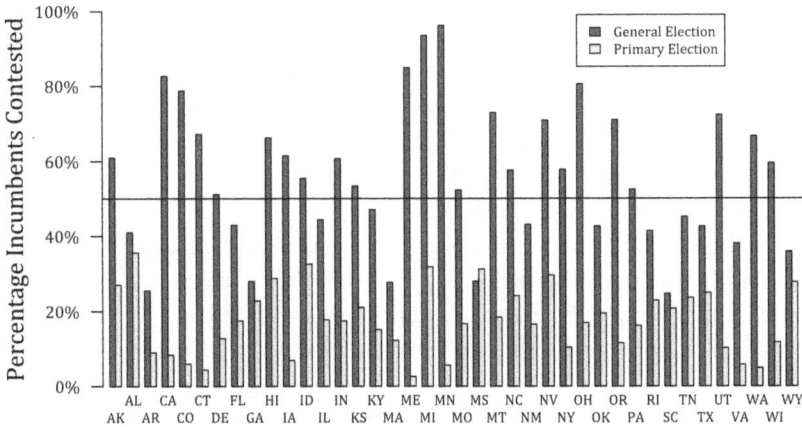

FIGURE 3.2. Percentages of state house incumbents challenged in general and primary elections from 2002 to 2020 in single-member districts.

that relatively few challengers are available to sift through state legislative incumbents' records, state legislators elected in unopposed elections more often miss roll-call votes (Konisky and Ueda 2011).

Challengers are important for representation and accountability in state legislatures but are too often absent in state legislative elections.[1] In this chapter, I build on the previous chapter and my earlier work (Rogers 2015) and address how candidates' personal and strategic decision-making is partly responsible for the lack of challengers in state legislative elections. Challengers do not run for the legislature for some of the same reasons incumbents do not seek reelection, such as time commitments and less favorable partisan districts. However, the state economy and incumbents' representation appear to be more-prominent factors in challengers' decision-making. Challengers more often run against incumbents who provide worse representation and oversee weak state economies, particularly when the incumbent is a member of the party in power. Such elite-level behavior gives more voters "fair opportunities" to hold unrepresentative incumbents individually accountable and state parties collectively accountable.

More troubling for accountability, a remedy to make state legislative elections as competitive as US House elections is not immediately apparent. Statistical analyses suggest that even under extreme institutional arrangements and political conditions, such as higher state legislative salaries and weak economies, which presumably should promote challenger entry in state legislatures, competition levels fail to match those typically found in US House elections. Of further concern, state legislative challengers also strategically respond to politics outside of state legislative incumbents' control. They run more often against the president's legislative co-partisans, especially when the president is unpopular. Despite actions at the White House having little to do with what happens in the state house, national politics influence state-level politicians' decision-making. Such strategic behavior by challengers reduces elections' ability to solve the moral hazard problem posed by representative government.

In this chapter, I focus on major-party challengers in general elections, but incumbents can also face challengers in primary elections (figure 3.1). I delay more in-depth discussion of primary elections until chapter 8 for clarity in presentation, as theoretical expectations for primary and general elections challengers' decision-making differ in important ways. For instance, in the primary election, an in-party challenger may anticipate more success in a partisan district. Meanwhile, in the general election, a major-party challenger may anticipate more success in a moderate district. Chapters 3 through 7 are not critical reading for my analyses of primary competition, and readers interested in more sequentially following the electoral process can skip to chapter 8 before returning to the following studies.

A Challenger's Decision to Run

Understanding when and why voters have "fair opportunities" to hold their state legislators accountable in the general election again requires examining political elites' decisions. A good starting point to build this understanding is revisiting what we learned in the previous chapter, as a candidate's decision to challenge an incumbent is similar to an incumbent's decision to run for reelection. Returning to the deceptively simple equation of $pB > C$, a candidate must weigh the costs of running for and serving in the legislature against the benefits of winning and the likelihood they will win. Costs again include the personal sacrifices a candidate makes, such as spending time at the state capitol instead of at home. Benefits can include salary or a legislator's policymaking power. Finally, the probability that a candidate will win theoretically depends on political conditions surrounding the election, such as the partisan makeup of a district and the incumbent's performance.

Figure 3.3 begins to highlight how the costs and benefits of running for office broadly relate to challenger entry and presents the percentages of incumbents who faced major-party challengers from 2001 to 2020 under different political contexts. For example, the previous chapter showed that women legislators were no more likely to retire from the legislature, but the first two sets of bars in figure 3.3. indicate that women legislators more often face challengers.[2] On average, incumbents additionally face more competition if they serve in state legislatures with higher salaries or represent more-marginal districts, where the incumbent's party received less than 60 percent of the presidential vote (figure 3.3, second and third set of bars), which is also consistent with findings concerning legislators' retirement.[3] Voters in these states and districts then appear to have more fair opportunities to hold their incumbents accountable, which is good. However, to solve the moral hazard problem presented by representative government, it is important that legislators' elections are tied to factors they can control. And unless they want to move out of their district or state, an individual legislator has relatively little power over the partisan makeup of their district or over their individual salary.

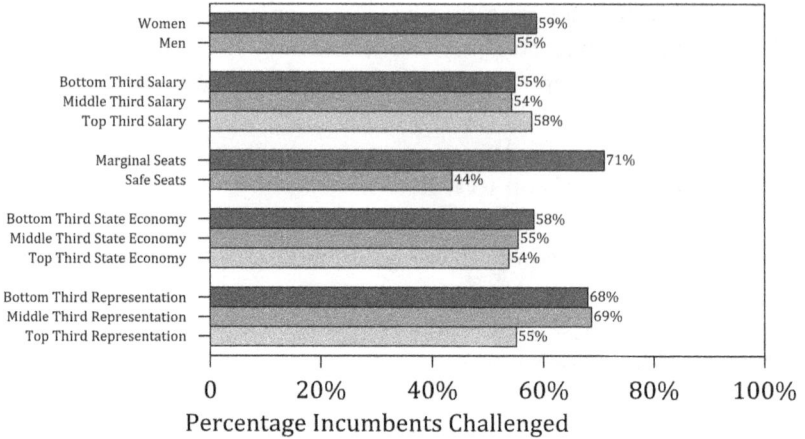

FIGURE 3.3. Percentages of state house incumbents who have major party challengers, broken down by incumbents' differing gender, state legislative salaries, or political conditions.

The bottom two sets of bars in figure 3.3 focus on variables more directly connected to a legislator's actions or performance: the state economy and representation. I divide electoral contests into bottom-third, middle-third, and top-third percentiles based on the state economy or an incumbent's representation, where the top thirds reflect the better economies and representation. To measure the state economy, I again use a state's income growth in the second quarter of the election year, approximately the time a challenger would need to decide to run for office. For representation, I use the ideological-distance measure described in the previous chapter. When the economy is weak (figure 3.3, fourth set of bars) and incumbents provide relatively worse representation (figure 3.3, fifth set of bars), incumbents face more challengers. Such findings are promising for accountability, as they suggest that when legislators perform poorly, voters have more opportunities to hold them accountable.[4]

For reasons similar to those detailed in the previous chapter, the above factors potentially shape a challenger's $pB > C$ calculus. To more systematically investigate the relative importance of personal and political considerations for voters' opportunities to hold their state legislators accountable, I estimate statistical models that predict whether a legislator faced a challenger when seeking reelection. Statistical models are similar to those in the previous chapter, but the dependent variable is whether a major-party challenger ran when an incumbent sought reelection.[5] For my statistical tests, I use probit regressions to estimate the relationship between the above independent variables and state legislative challenger entry. To evaluate how variables' importance has changed over time, I additionally assess the relationship separately for the 2001 to 2010 and 2011 to 2020 elections. Each estimation includes random effects for states. To give substantive meaning to relationships, I convert probit estimates (table 3.1) to predicted probabilities or differences in probabilities (e.g., table 3.2). For example, using results from the final column of table 3.1, the first row of table 3.2 indicates that the probability that a woman legislator faces a challenger is at least 0.014 higher than the comparable probability for a man legislator.

Time and Money

Legislative service can require considerable time for not much pay, and these factors weigh upon even very ambitious politicians' decisions to run for the state legislature. In his memoirs, Barack Obama wrote about his decision to seek public office for the first time and run for the Illinois legislature. These reflections included listing the "pros and cons" of being a state senator. One "pro" for Obama was that "the Illinois state legislature was in session only a few weeks out of the year, which meant [Obama] could continue teaching and working at the law firm" (Obama 2020, 24). However, Obama also reflected on the "con" of the I-55 traffic as he left Chicago, followed by "miles and miles of corn" with limited radio options during the three-and-a-half-hour drive to Springfield (Obama 2020, 31).

Other state legislative candidates also seem to contemplate how long it will take them to get to the state capital. For every 100 kilometers an incumbent's district is farther away from the state capital, an incumbent is .015 less likely to face a challenger in the general election (table 3.2, second row). Unlike findings concerning legislators' retirement, there is less robust evidence that a legislature's session length systematically relates to challenger entry (table 3.2, third row). When considering elections from 2001 to 2010, the length of state legislative sessions has a negative relationship with challenger entry. However, from 2011 to 2020, this relationship is positive but does not meet conventional levels of statistical significance (t-statistic of difference 1.48). Estimates from the 2001 to 2020 elections suggest that increasing the length of a legislative session by one hundred days decreases the likelihood of a challenger by 0.006, but this estimate also fails to meet conventional levels of statistical significance (t-statistic of difference 1.22).

TABLE 3.1 **Challenger entry**

	2001–2010	2001–2010	2011–2020	2011–2020	2001–2020	2001–2020
Ideological distance	0.390* (0.033)	0.597* (0.098)	0.326* (0.031)	0.420* (0.083)	0.395* (0.022)	0.562* (0.060)
Ideological distance squared		−0.166* (0.063)		−0.084* (0.043)		−0.134* (0.033)
Party loyalty	−0.002 (0.001)	−0.002 (0.001)	−0.001 (0.001)	−0.002 (0.001)	−0.002* (0.001)	−0.003* (0.001)
Change in annual log of Q2 state personal income	−0.284 (0.383)	−1.019* (0.428)	0.036 (0.309)	−0.991* (0.330)	−0.402 (0.227)	−1.033* (0.239)
Legislator salary (in thousands of 2010 dollars)		0.002 (0.001)		0.001 (0.001)		0.002* (0.001)
Legislative staff per member		−0.049* (0.021)		−0.045* (0.021)		−0.014 (0.014)
Session length		−0.001* (0.000)		0.000 (0.000)		−0.000 (0.000)
Public-finance campaign option		0.138 (0.096)		0.597* (0.253)		0.262* (0.072)
Logged average amount to win race (state-year average)		0.258* (0.046)		0.320* (0.053)		0.269* (0.029)
Term limits enacted		0.083 (0.102)		−0.000 (0.162)		0.112 (0.092)
Redistricted district		−0.024 (0.031)		−0.127* (0.028)		−0.069* (0.019)
Distance to capital (logged)		−0.048* (0.010)		−0.065* (0.011)		−0.054* (0.008)
Incumbent-party presidential vote	−0.024* (0.001)	−0.024* (0.001)	−0.030* (0.001)	−0.032* (0.001)	−0.026* (0.001)	−0.027* (0.001)
Previous incumbent-party vote share	−0.010* (0.001)	−0.010* (0.001)	−0.007* (0.001)	−0.008* (0.001)	−0.008* (0.001)	−0.009* (0.001)

	(1)	(2)	(3)	(4)	(5)	(6)
Seat previously contested	0.222* (0.045)	0.177* (0.046)	0.282* (0.047)	0.224* (0.049)	0.279* (0.032)	0.220* (0.033)
Minority-party seat share		-0.254 (0.266)		0.712* (0.261)		0.214 (0.136)
District size (logged)		0.008 (0.070)		-0.119 (0.078)		-0.017 (0.051)
Terms served		-0.011* (0.004)		-0.007 (0.004)		-0.010* (0.003)
Freshman incumbent	-0.015 (0.023)	-0.088* (0.027)	0.057* (0.025)	0.023 (0.028)	0.016 (0.017)	-0.043* (0.019)
Chamber leader		-0.158* (0.043)		-0.023 (0.057)		-0.113* (0.034)
Midterm appointee		0.192* (0.079)		0.123 (0.086)		0.111 (0.057)
Woman legislator		0.063 (0.039)		0.008 (0.037)		0.035 (0.027)
Woman legislator x Democratic Party member		0.005 (0.050)		0.081 (0.050)		0.025 (0.035)
Nonwhite legislator		-0.053 (0.086)		0.075 (0.082)		0.028 (0.058)
Nonwhite legislator x Democratic Party member o		-0.088 (0.093)		-0.050 (0.090)		-0.104 (0.064)
Member of the Democratic Party	0.193* (0.028)	0.211* (0.032)	-0.270* (0.023)	-0.245* (0.031)	-0.095* (0.015)	-0.059* (0.019)
Member of chamber-majority party		0.158* (0.021)		0.221* (0.027)		0.208* (0.016)
Member of governor's party		-0.005 (0.028)		0.106* (0.034)		0.012 (0.021)
Member of governor's party x state midterm		-0.069 (0.040)		-0.069 (0.043)		-0.031 (0.028)
Member of president's party	0.343* (0.039)	0.332* (0.040)	0.168* (0.028)	0.173* (0.029)	0.060* (0.020)	0.076* (0.020)

continues

TABLE 3.1 (*continued*)

	2001–2010	2001–2010	2011–2020	2011–2020	2001–2020	2001–2020
Member of president's party x midterm (federal)	0.011	0.003	0.299*	0.302*	0.265*	0.241*
	(0.042)	(0.044)	(0.043)	(0.044)	(0.028)	(0.029)
Midterm election (federal)	0.008	0.015	-0.097*	-0.087	-0.104*	-0.066*
	(0.029)	(0.034)	(0.030)	(0.035)	(0.020)	(0.023)
Midterm election (state)		-0.020		0.135*		0.026
		(0.033)		(0.037)		(0.024)
Off-ear election		-0.119		-0.112		-0.056
		(0.338)		(0.331)		(0.317)
State senator		-0.099		-0.116		-0.116*
		(0.064)		(0.064)		(0.044)
Constant	1.932*	-0.450	2.378*	0.271	2.171*	-0.367
	(0.156)	(0.654)	(0.165)	(0.673)	(0.121)	(0.482)
N	21,201	21,096	19,523	19,340	40,724	40,436
Log-likelihood	-11,546.8	-11,378.0	-10,323.5	-10,106.0	-22,048.1	-21,663.0

This table reports the results of probit regressions in which the outcome of interest is whether a major party challenger ran against an incumbent state legislator from 2001 to 2020. Standard errors are in parentheses; $*p < 0.05$.

TABLE 3.2 **Predicted changes in probability of a challenger**

Variable	Change in variable value	Change in probability		
		2001–2010	2011–2020	2001–2020
Incumbent gender	Man to woman	+0.020*	+0.015*	+0.014*
		(0.007)	(0.007)	(0.005)
District distance from capital	Increase of 100 kilometers	−0.014*	−0.018*	−0.015*
		(0.003)	(0.003)	(0.002)
Length of legislative session	Increase of 100 days	−0.021*	+0.009	−0.006
		(0.009)	(0.006)	(0.005)
Publicly financed campaign	All states without public-finance option to all states with public-finance option	+0.041*	+0.162*	+0.077*
		(0.029)	(0.065)	(0.021)
Average cost of campaign	Increase of $10,000	+0.010*	0.010*	+0.010*
		(0.002)	(0.002)	(0.001)
Legislator salary	Increase of $10,000	+0.006	+0.003	+0.006*
		(0.004)	(0.004)	(0.002)
District partisanship	Increase of 13 percent	−0.010*	−0.133*	−0.114*
		(0.005)	(0.005)	(0.004)

This table reports the differences in average predicted probabilities of an incumbent facing a challenger associated with changing variable value listed in the second column. Standard errors are in parentheses; *$p < 0.05$.

Challengers also have financial worries about running for and serving in the state capitol. Fifty-nine percent of candidates told the National Candidate Study that they were seriously concerned about "the need to raise lots of money" when deciding to run for the state legislature. These survey responses are consistent with research that finds "more restrictive campaign finance laws increase the likelihood of challenger emergence" (Hamm and Hogan 2008, 464; Malhotra 2008; Mayer and Wood 1995; Werner and Mayer 2007). Despite survey findings, my analyses provide mixed evidence that finances weigh heavily in challengers' decisions. I find that the probability of a challenger is at least .041 greater in states where candidates have the option to receive public money to fund their campaigns (table 3.2, fourth row), where campaign financial demands are presumably lower. However, more expensive campaigns positively correlate with challenger entry. Specifically, a $10,000 increase in the average cost of a state legislative campaign is associated with an increase in the probability of a state legislative challenger of 0.010 (table 3.2, fifth row). Such findings may reflect that those states with more expensive campaigns also have a more established party apparatus to recruit challengers.

State legislative candidates also worry about their potential lost salary. When asked by the National Candidate Study, 13 percent of candidates expressed concern about "losing the job I had at the time" before running for public office, and 31 percent worried about "losing their income from their job" by serving in the legislature (figure 2.2). Such survey responses echo the sentiment of a Colorado state legislative candidate who spoke to Moncrief, Squire, and Jewell for their book *Who Runs for Legislature*. From 1998 to 1999, the salary of Colorado state legislators increased from $17,500 to $30,000, and when describing his decision to run for office after this change, this Colorado candidate said, "I couldn't run before because the $17,500 was too low" (quoted in Moncrief, Squire, and Jewell 2001, 22). When studying the 2001 to 2020 elections, statistical analyses suggest increasing legislators' salaries by $10,000 associates with a predicted 0.006 increase in the probability of a major-party challenger (table 3, sixth row). Together with the findings in chapter 2, higher salaries appear to be one avenue to have legislators seek reelection and face challengers, providing voters more fair opportunities to hold their legislators accountable.

The Strategic Decision to Run

Time and pay are a few of the considerations that a potential candidate has before running for the state legislature. Some candidates may run as sacrificial lambs or to gain experience (Canon 1993), but most challengers want to win. At least among those who run for office, state legislative candidates generally express confidence about their election prospects. Only 22 percent of state legislative candidates told the National Candidate Study in 2012 that they were concerned about losing the election. As with incumbents deciding to seek reelection, we should theoretically expect most challengers to strategically choose when to enter races when their probability of victory is higher (Canon and Sousa 1992; Jacobson and Kernell 1983; Maestas et al. 2006).

One such strategic candidate was Jeanne Kirkton. Kirkton was a Democratic city council member in Webster Groves, Missouri. As the 2006 election season began, it was well-known that Kirkton wanted to serve in the state legislature. In Kirkton's state house district, Democratic presidential candidate John Kerry received 49 percent of the vote in 2004, and Barack Obama carried the district by a more considerable margin four years later, suggesting the district was winnable for a Democrat. Kirkton's district at the time was represented by Kathlyn Fares. Fares was a pro-choice Republican and small business owner, thereby making her a more-moderate Republican representing a moderate district. Kirkton stated she "considered running against Kathlyn Fares . . . but [Kirkton] didn't believe she was beatable" (email message to author, 2014). Fares then went on to defeat a less experienced Democratic challenger after Kirkton opted not to run in 2006. Kirkton's determination that Fares was not "beatable" was the likely culmination of asking herself questions many strategic candidates ask themselves before running for public office: Who are the voters in the district? How has the incumbent represented the district? Is this an opportune time to run? Again, these questions are not only crucial for candidates' strategy but also for accountability in state legislatures, as they determine whether a voter will have a fair opportunity to hold their representative accountable.

The District

Focusing on the first question, a challenger concerned about winning must consider who potential voters are. For example, how much does the district already favor the incumbent's party? We know from the previous chapter that the incumbent's party receives at least 60 percent of the presidential vote in most state legislative districts, and even casual observers of politics recognize it would be foolish for a Democrat to expect to win in a district where voters are overwhelmingly Republican. The last row of table 3.2 indicates that challengers are not fools. A standard-deviation or 13 percent increase in the average presidential vote share for the incumbent's party in a district reduces the predicted probability of a major-party opponent to an incumbent by 0.114. The abundance of partisan state legislative districts is then partly responsible for the low levels of competition in state legislatures.

Similar to findings concerning incumbents seeking reelection, district partisanship appears to be increasingly consequential to explain whether an incumbent will face a major-party challenger. To illustrate this growing importance, I reconduct the analyses in table 3.1 but only examine two-year periods of elections at a time (e.g., 2001 and 2002 or 2003 and 2004). I then calculate the change in the probability of a challenger associated with a 13 percent increase in district partisanship. The black dots in figure 3.4 reflect these estimates, and the black loess curve helps show trends over time. For instance, in the 2001 and 2002 elections, a standard-deviation change in partisanship *reduced* the probability of a major-party challenger by approximately 0.09. In the 2019 and 2020 elections, a similar change in partisanship reduced the probability of a challenger by approximately 0.17.

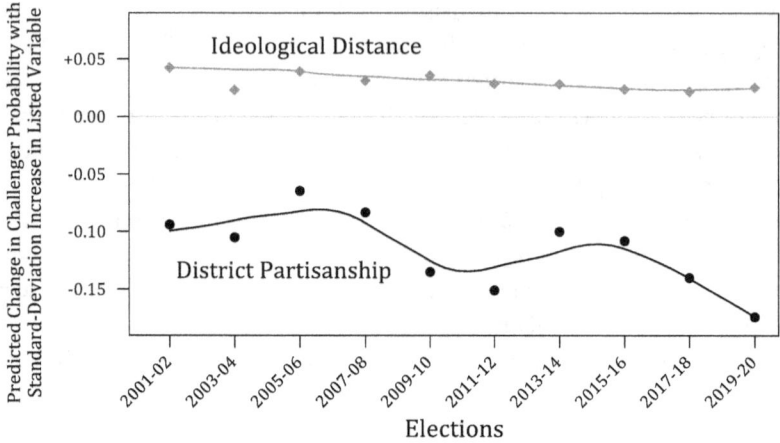

FIGURE 3.4. Predicted differences in probability of challenger entry associated with a standard-deviation change in the ideological-distance or district-partisanship measures.

Legislators are then increasingly less likely to face major-party challengers in partisan districts. In light of the growing number of partisan districts in state legislatures, such findings raise concerns about voters' opportunities to hold their legislators accountable.

Challenger entry is relatively low in state legislative elections, but can changes to state legislative institutions, such as campaign-finance laws and legislative districts, be potential remedies? Unfortunately, even dramatic changes to institutions will likely not be enough to increase levels of challenger entry in state legislatures to those found at the federal level. Under the hypothetical scenario where every state legislator received a salary equal to the highest in the country (i.e., California); served the fewest average days in session (i.e., New Hampshire); had the most staff (i.e., California), and had the option to publicly finance their campaign (i.e., Arizona or Maine), the predicted probability of a state legislative challenger (0.72) is still less than that found in a typical US House election (0.85). To make challenger entry in congressional and state legislative elections comparable, one would also need to change the district partisanship for the incumbents' party to 42 percent in every district.

These hypotheticals extrapolate statistical analyses to uncertain extremes, but they help illustrate an important point.[6] Changes to state legislative institutions can improve the conditions for accountability, but there is likely no immediately feasible remedy to the low number of state legislative challengers. All state legislatures could have salaries like California and Michigan legislators, but legislators infrequently give themselves raises. It is also doubtful that every state will considerably reduce session lengths, especially as state legislators handle more and more policymaking (Grumbach 2018). Even if every legislature did so, it is likely impossible for legislatures to redraw districts to have the needed partisan balance. If we redrew a Democratic incumbent's district to be 42 instead of 62 percent Democratic to achieve desired competition, this Democrat would likely lose their seat to a Republican. However, the new Republican incumbent now holds a 58 percent Republican seat, a district that Democratic challengers will now likely avoid. This scenario additionally does not even consider that drawing moderate districts is increasingly difficult due to geographic sorting. Together, there does not seem to be a quick and feasible institutional fix to this accountability problem.

Representation

When Jeanne Kirkton considered taking on Kathlyn Fares in 2006, the 91st Missouri state house district was a trending Democratic district where Democratic presidential candidate John Kerry had received 49 percent of the vote two years prior. Given district partisanship's importance for election outcomes, it may seem surprising that Kirkton—a Democrat—did not run for the state legislature. However, when explaining her decision not to run against Fares, Kirkton expressed that it would be difficult to beat a "popular moderate Republican legislator" (Kirkton 2014, personal communication). Fares's roll-call voting record was more liberal than those of most Missouri state house members (Shor and McCarty 2011), making her a moderate Republican representing a moderate district.

If Kirkton was worried about maximizing her probability of victory, spatial theories of elections suggest that representative legislators will receive larger vote shares (e.g., Downs 1957), a proposition that is supported by empirical studies of congressional elections (e.g., Canes-Wrone, Brady, and Cogan 2002). If these theories of electoral competition apply to voters' behavior in state legislative elections, Kirkton's reasoning that it would be difficult to defeat Fares made staying out of the race a sound decision. More importantly for accountability, if legislators who provide good representation are less likely to face a challenger, incumbents like Fares have an electoral incentive to represent their districts.

Promising for accountability, less representative incumbents across the country more often face challengers. The predicted probability of an incumbent facing a challenger is 0.602. When increasing the ideological distance by a standard deviation for all legislators, the predicted probability of a challenger rises to 0.637, and a three-standard-deviation change increases this probability to 0.673. To underscore the magnitude of this difference, this 0.071 increase is the most substantial relationship state legislators' ideological representation has with elites' or voters' behavior in state legislative elections within this entire book's analyses. Elites, such as challengers, then appear to play a very important role in creating incentives for legislators to represent their districts. If legislators fail to do so, they will more likely have a contested race in the general election.

The relationship between legislators' ideological representation and challenger entry appears to have been relatively stable from 2001 to 2020. The grey diamonds in figure 3.4 illustrate the difference in the predicted probability of a major-party challenger associated with the same standard-deviation increase in ideological distance. From 2001 to 2010, a standard-deviation change in ideological distance was associated with a 0.033 increase in the probability of a major-party challenger. In the 2011 to 2020 elections, this difference in probability falls slightly to 0.029, but the difference between these differences in probabilities does not meet conventional levels of statistical significance.

The Right Time to Run

A legislator's district and representation then partly determine whether state legislators face challengers. However, strategic candidates must also consider when to seek public office. Conditions surrounding state legislative contests change from one election to the next and can impact a challenger's probability of election and strategy. Gary Jacobson and Samuel Kernell notably lay out the logic and potential benefits of such strategies in their book *Strategy and Choice in Congressional Elections*:

> National events and conditions shape the expectations of potential candidates and their supporters about their party's electoral prospects. Their expectations affect their strategies and thus their behavior. And this, in turn, structures the choices voters are offered in districts across the nation. The election outcome becomes in part the aggregate consequence of many political making strategic decisions about their political careers. (1983, 24)

Jacobson and Kernell specifically argue that congressional candidates strategically take advantage of a president's popularity and begin their book with the example of how the 1974 election was a "disaster" for congressional Republicans following Watergate. At this time, President Nixon's average approval rating was in the mid-twenties. Consistent with the idea that congressional Democratic candidates took advantage of unfavorable political conditions for Republicans, Democrats challenged all but one of the 165 Republican US House members who sought reelection. This common strategy by Democrats gave voters many opportunities to hold the federal Republican party collectively accountable.

Jacobson and Kernell's theory of strategic challengers most straightforwardly translates to the state level when thought of in the context of the governor and the state legislature. Candidates at the state legislative level may anticipate the governor's coattails influencing their own electoral success (Hogan 2005). If this is the case, the opposition party's members should be more likely to run when the governor is unpopular. If voters act on and challengers respond to anti-gubernatorial sentiment, challengers' strategies not only increase their probability of victory but also connect the performance of the governor's party to its members' electoral security, promoting collective accountability for members of the state parties.

A complication for applying Jacobson and Kernell's underlying theory of strategic challengers to state legislative elections is that state legislatures are embedded within a larger federal system. In the American federal system, national and state candidates often share party labels, and as discussed in greater detail in chapter 7, national politics can influence state-level electoral outcomes (e.g., Carsey and Wright 1998; Chubb 1988; Hopkins 2018). Just as they may ride gubernatorial coattails within a state, a potential state legislative candidate may anticipate taking advantage of an anti-presidential wave. Returning to the example of the 1974 election—where all but one US House Republican faced a Democratic challenger—Democrats similarly challenged every Republican state legislator in over fifty state legislative chambers, well over twice the comparable figure for Democrats (Tidmarch, Lonergan, and Sciortino 1986). State legislative Republicans then faced increased opposition during the Watergate era, even when these legislators had little to do with federal politics.

Patterns of state legislative candidate entry are similar in more-recent elections. Following September 11th, President Bush enjoyed approval ratings exceeding 70 percent until the summer of 2002, and in the November election that year, approximately 51 percent of Democrats and Republicans in state legislatures faced major-party competition. However, as Bush became unpopular, there were consequences for his state legislative co-partisans. In both the 2006 and 2008 elections, almost 60 percent of Republican state legislators faced a Democratic opponent. Meanwhile, most Democratic incumbents went unopposed in these two elections. However, in the 2010 election, which followed the passage of an unpopular federal health care reform bill, during the Obama administration, over 66 percent of Democratic state legislative incumbents were challenged, but most Republicans faced no opponent.

State legislators subsequently recognized that the president's unpopularity could work in their favor. After the 2012 candidate-filing deadline in Tennessee, only 40 percent of Tennesseans approved of Barack Obama's performance as president, and Republican state house representative Glen Casada claimed, "That is the biggest thing working for us: President Obama and the anti-president attitude" (Cass 2012). Chapter 7 will show that Casada was likely right in terms of voter decision-making. Regarding challengers' decision-making in Tennessee, Casada was also likely right. Democrats chose not to challenge Republicans in over a third of Tennessee state house districts, implying that Republicans only had to win thirteen of forty-five contested elections to retain their majority in the Tennessee state house.

Challengers' strategies that account for larger political conditions are one consequence of how federalism can produce mixed implications for accountability in state legislatures. Suppose a candidate runs against a member of a state party who oversaw an economic downturn. In that case, voters have some opportunity to hold the party in power collectively responsible for their management of the economy. However, if a state-level challenger considers national conditions before deciding to run against an incumbent, the implications for accountability are less clear. A congressional challenger who responds to national political conditions promotes collective partisan accountability, as members of Congress directly influence the national government (Jacobson 1989). State legislators, meanwhile, are responsible for state policymaking, so if challengers systematically respond to national conditions, this does less to create incentives for state-level representation. Concerns arise if state legislative incumbents foresee the ability to ride favorable national political conditions to unopposed reelection and pursue state policy goals with less fear of being held electorally accountable.

To better understand the extent to which larger political contexts factor into challengers' decision-making, I evaluate the impact of larger political conditions and levels of collective accountability in three ways. First, I follow the logic that if challengers anticipate that voters will "balance" the executive and legislative branches of government, the governor's legislative co-partisans should face more challengers in state midterm elections. Second, I assess whether incumbents face fewer challengers during strong state economies. Third, I investigate the implications of the American federal system and study whether the president's popularity relates to challenger entry in state legislative elections.

For the latter two analyses, if state legislative candidates' strategies resemble those of their federal counterparts and foster collective accountability, political conditions' impact on candidates' entry decisions should differ by which parties controlled political institutions. Democratic candidates, for example, should be more likely to challenge Republican incumbents when a Republican legislature or governor oversaw weak economies. Similarly, if challengers respond to national politics, Democrats should be more likely to run during unpopular Republican presidencies. To determine whether state legislative challengers respond to economic conditions or presidential approval, I conduct analyses similar to those in table 3.1 but separate incumbents by whether they were members of the legislative majority, governor's, or president's party (tables A.3.1 and A.3.2).

Strategic Responses to State-Level Conditions

State legislative challengers appear to respond strategically to some state political conditions, often giving voters more opportunities to hold those in power accountable. For instance, across both gubernatorial and state midterm elections, the probability of a legislative majority-party state legislator facing a challenger is 0.062 higher than the same probability for a minority-party legislator. However, minority-party legislators are more likely to face challengers when the minority party has a greater share of seats. When a minority party holds 49 instead of 39 percent of the seats in a chamber, the probability of a minority-party legislator facing a challenger increases by 0.032 (table A.3.1, column 2). Such findings suggest that legislative majority parties recognize that their chamber control is in danger and recruit more candidates to protect this chamber.

Challengers also give voters more opportunities to hold state legislators who oversaw weak economies collectively accountable. Figure 3.5 presents the relationship between economic growth on the average predicted probability of a challenger for all incumbents (top circle) and members of different parties (other circles as indicated by the y-axis). When there

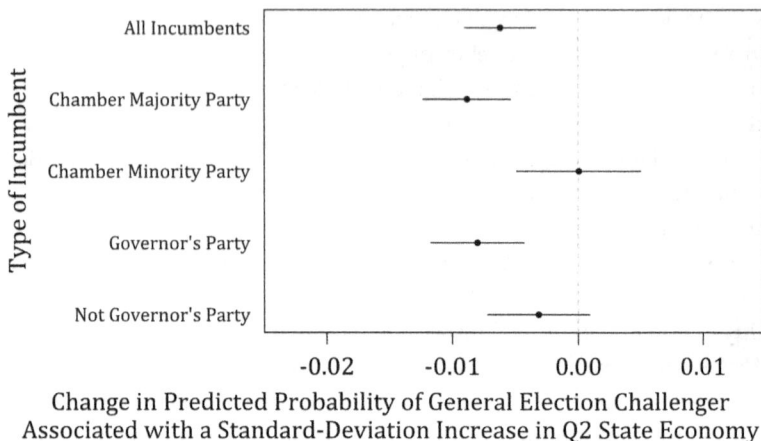

Change in Predicted Probability of General Election Challenger
Associated with a Standard-Deviation Increase in Q2 State Economy

FIGURE 3.5. Predicted differences in the probability of a major-party challenger associated with 2 percent economic growth in the state economy.

is 2 percent economic growth in the state economy, the probability that a state legislative incumbent faces a challenger falls by approximately 0.006. Challengers also more often run against the governing state parties during weak economies. For example, 2 percent economic growth decreases the probability of a challenger to a majority-party incumbent by 0.009 (figure 3.5, second circle). Meanwhile, statistical analyses predict that such growth increases the likelihood that a minority-party legislator faces a challenger by less than 0.000 (figure 3.5, third circle, t-statistic of difference 0.02).

Challengers additionally seem to follow entry strategies comparable to their federal counterparts where they challenge the party in control of the executive branch during weak economies. In state legislatures from 2001 to 2020, I find that 2 percent state economic growth is associated with a 0.008 decrease in the probability that a governor's-party legislator faces a challenger (figure 3.5, fourth circle). This gubernatorial-state legislative challenger relationship parallels the presidential-congressional challenger relationship and indicates that members of the governor's party then have an incentive to create strong state economies. Otherwise, they will be more likely to face competition in their next general election. In 2006 Missouri's economy grew by almost 3.5 percent, and Fares was a member of the governor's party, which may have contributed to Kirkton's thinking that Fares was "not beatable." The above findings again provide evidence that state legislative challengers consider how state lawmakers perform in office, providing voters more opportunities to hold their legislators accountable.

Members of the governor's party are more likely to be challenged during weak economies, which is consistent with the notion that challengers anticipate voters will punish the governor's party for a weak economy. There is, however, less evidence that challengers run more often in state midterm elections in anticipation of voters balancing the executive and legislative branches of government. From 2001 to 2010, members of the governor's party were no more likely to be challenged than other legislators in state midterms, and from 2011 to 2020, members of the governor's party were 0.022 less likely to face a challenger. Meanwhile, members of the state house majority party are at least 0.047 more likely to be challenged than minority-party members across both gubernatorial and state midterm elections.

Strategic Responses to National-Level Conditions

State-level conditions, such as the economy and which parties control state governments, appear to factor into challengers' strategies. Still, when calculating their probability of victory, challengers must also consider that state governments are embedded in a national political system. For example, reconsider the federal-state balancing theory discussed in the introduction. If centrist voters want to "balance" the policies made by the president, they can vote against the president's party members in state elections. Chapter 6 provides evidence that voters engage in such behavior in state legislative elections, but of interest to this study of elite behavior is understanding: do challengers respond to national political conditions?

The answer is: Yes, they do. The president's state legislative co-partisans are more likely to face challengers than legislators unaffiliated with the president's party to a considerable degree. The predicted probability that a president's party state legislator faces a challenger is 0.625 when considering all elections, 0.651 in federal midterm elections, and 0.626 in state midterm elections. Meanwhile, the comparable probabilities for non–president's party legislators are 0.568, 0.557, and 0.569. The 0.094 difference in probability that members of the president's party face a challenger in federal midterm elections is larger than the 0.062 difference in probabilities of a challenger across state house majority-party versus minority-party incumbents across any type of election. National politics then appears to loom large in state legislative challengers' decisions.

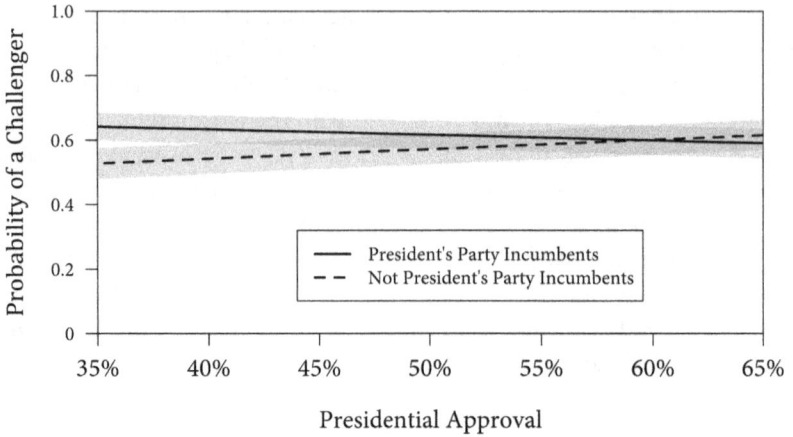

FIGURE 3.6. Predicted probability of a challenger under different levels of presidential approval.

The president's legislative co-partisans additionally more often face opposition candidates when the president is unpopular. Figure 3.6 illustrates
incumbents' probabilities of facing a challenger under different levels of
presidential approval (see table A.3.2 for estimates). A 10 percent increase
in presidential approval decreases the predicted probability of a member
of the president's party facing an opponent by approximately 0.017 (figure 3.6, solid black line). For legislators unaffiliated with the president's
party, a 10 percent increase in presidential approval increases the probability of a challenger by approximately 0.029. The relationships between
presidential approval and challenger entry are more substantial than those
between the state economy and challenger entry for either the legislative
majority or the governor's party, and they appear to be growing in strength.
I find that during the 2001 to 2010 elections, a 10 percent change in presidential approval was associated with a 0.018 change in the probability a
president's legislative co-partisan faces a challenger. Meanwhile, the comparable difference in probability in the 2011 to 2020 elections more than
doubles to 0.049. A substantial amount of presidential politics appears to
be going into the p term when challengers calculate $pB > C$.

    Such presidential findings raise concern for accountability in state leg-
islatures. To solve the moral hazard problem posed by representative government, legislators' actions need to be connected to their own performance. A state legislator chooses their party affiliation, but they have little
control over which party controls the White House and how the president

performs. Meanwhile, it seems that the party affiliation of the president and presidential approval matter a great deal for whether a state legislator faces a challenger. Recall that all else equal, members of the president's party are already more likely to face challengers. Only when the president's approval rating exceeds 61 percent are the president's legislative co-partisans as likely to face a challenger as state legislators unaffiliated with the president's party.[7] To provide context for whether these levels of popularity are achievable, Barack Obama and Donald Trump's average approval ratings were 48 and 41 percent, and Trump's approval rating never exceeded 49 percent. In most elections, the president's state legislative co-partisans are then more likely to face a challenger, even though they have little control over federal politics.

Recap

This chapter continued our investigation of how elites' decisions shape voters' "fair opportunities" to hold state legislators accountable. An important — if not the most important — takeaway from this chapter is a simple statistic: over one-third of incumbents do not face a challenger in either the primary or general election. Before there is a meaningful discussion concerning voters holding state legislators accountable, it is essential to recognize that elites' decisions prevent millions of voters from even having the opportunity to hold their American legislators accountable. A staggering number of legislators win reelection by just signing up for another term.

Most state legislators, however, face opponents when they seek reelection, and political institutions and conditions help explain where competition is most likely to happen. Work environments with fewer demands upon an individual's time or finances, such as those with shorter drives to the capital or publicly financed campaigns, reduce the costs of serving in the state legislature and attract more candidates to run for office. State legislative challengers also strategically run more often in the most winnable districts, and by running more often against incumbents of the governor's and legislative majority party during bad economies, challengers give voters more opportunities to hold these legislators collectively accountable for their poor management of the state economy. However, even under the most favorable conditions for challenger entry, such as when district partisanship is more balanced or during poor economies, the predicted levels of challenger entry in state legislatures fall short of that found in Congress.

Even if one is satisfied with levels of challenger entry in state legislative elections, there is reason to be concerned about accountability in state legislatures: challengers' decision-making strongly considers national political conditions. For example, Republican challengers are more likely to emerge when a Democrat is in the White House, especially when this Democrat is unpopular. This strategy improves challengers' electoral prospects (a subject addressed in chapter 7). However, it does little to establish an electoral connection between what legislators do in office and their competition in elections. Such strategies do little to solve the moral hazard problem posed by representative government. If legislators recognize that national forces dictate whether they face competition, they could become less concerned about their own state-level policymaking's electoral consequences.

As put by Jacobson and Kernell in their discussion of Congressional challenger entry: "V. O. Key felt it necessary to argue in his last book that 'voters are not fools.' Neither, we contend, are politicians." (Jacobson and Kernell 1983, 19). This chapter affirms that Jacobson and Kernell's contention applies to challengers in state legislative elections. However, returning to Obama's reflection of his own non-foolish pB versus C calculation, the future Illinois state senator noted that being "a state senator was not a glamorous post," highlighting that "most people had no idea who their state legislators were" (Obama 2020, 24). The following chapter will begin to assess the extent to which Key's argument applies to voters and whether this future Illinois legislator's beliefs about voters were right.

Appendix

TABLE A.3.1 **Relationship between challenger entry and political variables by party**

	Chamber majority	Not chamber majority	Governor's party	Not governor's party
Ideological distance	0.592[*]	0.549[*]	0.627[*]	0.372[*]
	(0.082)	(0.097)	(0.084)	(0.089)
Ideological distance squared	−0.118[*]	−0.153[*]	−0.161[*]	−0.041
	(0.045)	(0.052)	(0.046)	(0.050)
Party loyalty	−0.004[*]	−0.000	−0.003[*]	−0.001
	(0.001)	(0.001)	(0.001)	(0.001)
Change in annual log of Q2 state personal income	−1.497[*]	0.011	−1.364[*]	−0.570
	(0.297)	(0.423)	(0.321)	(0.375)
Legislator salary (in thousands of 2010 dollars)	0.000	0.004[*]	−0.000	0.006[*]
	(0.001)	(0.001)	(0.001)	(0.001)
Legislative staff per member	−0.005	−0.036	−0.056[*]	−0.005
	(0.017)	(0.018)	(0.018)	(0.020)

	Chamber majority	Not chamber majority	Governor's party	Not governor's party
Session length	−0.000	−0.000	−0.000	−0.000
	(0.000)	(0.000)	(0.000)	(0.000)
Public-finance campaign option	0.097	0.554*	0.733*	0.041
	(0.093)	(0.109)	(0.110)	(0.098)
Logged average amount to win race	0.279*	0.189*	0.304*	0.249*
(state-year average)	(0.036)	(0.046)	(0.039)	(0.043)
Term limits enacted	0.209	−0.040	0.341*	−0.259
	(0.108)	(0.124)	(0.116)	(0.141)
Redistricted district	−0.097*	−0.019	−0.136*	0.011
	(0.024)	(0.031)	(0.025)	(0.028)
Distance to capital (logged)	−0.041*	−0.081*	−0.044*	−0.068*
	(0.010)	(0.012)	(0.011)	(0.011)
Incumbent-party pres. vote	−0.029*	−0.029*	−0.028*	−0.029*
	(0.001)	(0.001)	(0.001)	(0.001)
Previous incumbent-party vote	−0.009*	−0.009*	−0.009*	−0.010*
share	(0.001)	(0.001)	(0.001)	(0.001)
Seat previously contested	0.231*	0.178*	0.230*	0.173*
	(0.041)	(0.056)	(0.044)	(0.050)
Minority-party seat share	−0.183	1.098*	0.104	0.515*
	(0.176)	(0.233)	(0.187)	(0.214)
District size (logged)	−0.034	0.005	−0.052	−0.000
	(0.063)	(0.080)	(0.065)	(0.079)
Terms served	−0.008*	−0.011*	−0.008*	−0.010*
	(0.003)	(0.005)	(0.004)	(0.004)
Freshman incumbent	−0.043	−0.040	−0.068*	−0.006
	(0.024)	(0.033)	(0.026)	(0.029)
Chamber leader	−0.087*	−0.165*	−0.154*	−0.067
	(0.043)	(0.057)	(0.047)	(0.049)
Midterm appointee	0.030	0.255*	0.045	0.234*
	(0.073)	(0.092)	(0.076)	(0.088)
Woman legislator	0.058	0.005	0.044	0.040
	(0.033)	(0.046)	(0.035)	(0.041)
Woman legislator x Democratic	−0.025	0.121*	0.007	0.056
Party member	(0.045)	(0.058)	(0.048)	(0.052)
Nonwhite legislator	0.016	0.057	0.013	0.056
	(0.072)	(0.101)	(0.074)	(0.097)
Nonwhite legislator x Democratic	−0.065	−0.150	−0.123	−0.070
Party member	(0.082)	(0.110)	(0.083)	(0.104)
Member of the Democratic Party	−0.040	−0.043	−0.092*	−0.113*
	(0.035)	(0.039)	(0.030)	(0.032)
Member of chamber-majority party			0.158*	0.196*
			(0.026)	(0.025)
Member of governor's party	0.006	0.037		
	(0.029)	(0.037)		
Member of governor's party x state	−0.030	−0.006		
midterm	(0.038)	(0.051)		
Member of president's party	0.121*	0.100*	0.158*	0.044
	(0.026)	(0.035)	(0.029)	(0.032)

continues

	Chamber majority	Not chamber majority	Governor's party	Not governor's party
Member of president's party x federal midterm	0.245*	0.121*	0.262*	0.192*
	(0.037)	(0.050)	(0.041)	(0.045)
Midterm election (federal)	−0.016	−0.097*	−0.065*	−0.085*
	(0.029)	(0.040)	(0.032)	(0.035)
Midterm election (state)	0.037	0.020	0.022	0.005
	(0.035)	(0.034)	(0.025)	(0.027)
Off-year election	−0.074	−0.028	0.074	−0.220
	(0.351)	(0.292)	(0.337)	(0.390)
State senator	−0.133*	−0.013	−0.122*	−0.094
	(0.053)	(0.068)	(0.054)	(0.071)
Constant	0.136	0.019	−0.174	−0.305
	(0.583)	(0.682)	(0.586)	(0.747)
N	25,757	14,679	21,820	18,616
Log-likelihood	−13,854.9	−7,747.3	−11,822.5	−9,740.2

This table reports the results of probit regressions in which the outcome of interest is whether an incumbent state legislator faced a major-party challenger. Columns indicate party of incumbent legislator. Standard errors are in parentheses; *$p < 0.05$.

TABLE A.3.2 **Relationship between challenger entry and political variables by party**

	President's party	Not president's party	President's party	Not president's party
Ideological distance	0.554*	0.486*	0.548*	0.481*
	(0.092)	(0.082)	(0.092)	(0.082)
Ideological distance squared	−0.107*	−0.112*	−0.105	−0.112*
	(0.054)	(0.044)	(0.054)	(0.044)
Party loyalty	−0.001	−0.003*	−0.001	−0.003*
	(0.001)	(0.001)	(0.001)	(0.001)
Change in annual log of Q2 state personal income	−1.811*	−0.842*	−1.824*	−0.684*
	(0.355)	(0.344)	(0.355)	(0.345)
Pre-primary presidential approval			−0.006*	0.010*
			(0.001)	(0.001)
Legislator salary (in thousands of 2010 dollars)	−0.001	0.003*	−0.001	0.003*
	(0.001)	(0.001)	(0.001)	(0.001)
Legislative staff per member	−0.024	−0.046*	−0.025	−0.048*
	(0.018)	(0.017)	(0.018)	(0.018)
Session length	0.000	−0.001*	0.000	−0.001*
	(0.000)	(0.000)	(0.000)	(0.000)
Public-finance campaign option	0.773*	0.072	0.765*	0.091
	(0.111)	(0.095)	(0.110)	(0.096)
Logged average amount to win race (state-year average)	0.374*	0.179*	0.305*	0.292*
	(0.041)	(0.041)	(0.043)	(0.043)
Term limits enacted	0.078	0.014	0.027	0.061
	(0.109)	(0.126)	(0.108)	(0.131)
Redistricted district	−0.172*	0.046	−0.101*	−0.064*
	(0.028)	(0.026)	(0.031)	(0.029)

	President's party	Not president's party	President's party	Not president's party
Distance to capital (logged)	−0.065*	−0.046*	−0.066*	−0.047*
	(0.011)	(0.010)	(0.011)	(0.010)
Incumbent-party pres. vote	−0.031*	−0.024*	−0.032*	−0.024*
	(0.001)	(0.001)	(0.001)	(0.001)
Previous incumbent-party vote share	−0.009*	−0.009*	−0.009*	−0.010*
	(0.001)	(0.001)	(0.001)	(0.001)
Seat previously contested	0.187*	0.218*	0.192*	0.217*
	(0.048)	(0.045)	(0.048)	(0.045)
Minority-party seat share	−0.058	0.244	−0.071	0.231
	(0.197)	(0.193)	(0.197)	(0.193)
District size (logged)	−0.002	0.023	0.057	−0.069
	(0.071)	(0.068)	(0.072)	(0.070)
Terms served	−0.005	−0.013*	−0.005	−0.012*
	(0.004)	(0.004)	(0.004)	(0.004)
Freshman incumbent	−0.064*	−0.005	−0.065*	0.004
	(0.028)	(0.027)	(0.028)	(0.027)
Chamber leader	−0.129*	−0.109*	−0.129*	−0.106*
	(0.049)	(0.047)	(0.049)	(0.047)
Midterm appointee	0.180*	0.079	0.169*	0.112
	(0.085)	(0.078)	(0.085)	(0.078)
Woman legislator	0.009	0.088*	0.011	0.086*
	(0.036)	(0.041)	(0.036)	(0.041)
Woman legislator x Democratic Party member	0.073	−0.032	0.073	−0.029
	(0.051)	(0.050)	(0.051)	(0.050)
Nonwhite legislator	−0.107	0.155	−0.111	0.154
	(0.081)	(0.084)	(0.082)	(0.085)
Nonwhite legislator x Democratic Party member	−0.012	−0.201*	−0.002	−0.197*
	(0.090)	(0.091)	(0.090)	(0.091)
Member of the Democratic Party	−0.192*	0.031	−0.188*	0.049
	(0.030)	(0.028)	(0.030)	(0.028)
Member of chamber-majority party	0.225*	0.179*	0.227*	0.182*
	(0.025)	(0.024)	(0.025)	(0.024)
Member of governor's party	0.064*	−0.004	0.074*	0.021
	(0.032)	(0.031)	(0.032)	(0.031)
Member of governor's party x state midterm	0.012	−0.143*	0.002	−0.165*
	(0.044)	(0.042)	(0.044)	(0.042)
Midterm election (federal)	0.199*	−0.120*	0.215*	−0.146*
	(0.027)	(0.026)	(0.027)	(0.026)
Midterm election (state)	0.028	0.068*	0.035	0.080*
	(0.036)	(0.034)	(0.036)	(0.034)
Off-year election	0.075	−0.228	0.109	−0.295
	(0.338)	(0.314)	(0.331)	(0.329)
State senator	−0.200*	−0.087	−0.200*	−0.098
	(0.060)	(0.059)	(0.060)	(0.060)
Constant	−1.134	0.234	−0.752	−0.444
	(0.641)	(0.617)	(0.641)	(0.633)
N	19,882	20,554	19,882	20,554
Log-likelihood	−10,297.4	−11,239.3	−10,285.8	−11,206.6

This table reports the results of probit regressions in which the outcome of interest is whether an incumbent state legislator faced a major-party challenger. Columns indicate party of incumbent legislator. Standard errors are in parentheses; *$p < 0.05$.

CHAPTER FOUR

Who Represents You in the Legislature?

After candidates determine whether to run for office, voters—at least those who have a choice of candidates—decide how to cast their ballots. In the search for accountability in state legislatures, this decision brings us to Powell's second condition for accountability: voters must "know who is responsible for making policy" (Powell 2000, 51). Satisfying this condition is important to American voters and fundamental for elections' ability to create incentives for representation. In 2018, 95 percent of voters told the Pew Research Center that it was somewhat or very important that voters are knowledgeable about candidates and issues (Doherty, Kiley, and Johnson 2018). When solving the moral hazard problem posed by representative government, it would be seemingly difficult for a voter to punish a state legislator who does a bad job if the voter did not know who their state legislator was. However, as we will see below, most voters do not know who represents them in state capitols.

Before taking this statement to write off the typical voter as stupid, I ask readers to ask themselves who their state legislators are. I suspect many readers—if not most—cannot answer this question. This exercise is not intended to make one feel dumb but rather illustrate that even those who read books devoted to state legislative elections at times lack the information some may feel necessary to hold their state legislator accountable.[1] The many political offices a voter potentially needs to learn about in the complicated American federal system can lead to fatigue and a lack of overall political awareness (Nicholson 2003; Wolak 2009). Given that the typical voter does not have the same motivation to learn about state legislative politics as readers of this book, it is then unsurprising—but troubling—that the American electorate is not well equipped to punish legislators who perform poorly.

To assess the extent to which voters know who is responsible for making policy, the first part of this chapter shows that approximately 40 percent of voters cannot regularly identify which party controls their state legislature, and far fewer know who their state representative is. Such findings are concerning. While the American electorate is largely uninformed about their state legislatures, voters are not fools—to reinvoke V. O. Key's famous phrase. Many voters make educated guesses concerning who represents them in the state capitol, which likely makes them more capable of holding their representatives accountable. But even when making educated guesses, voters still know less about their state legislature than they do about Congress or their governor.

The second part of this chapter addresses whether a typically prescribed solution for low levels of political knowledge—increasing media coverage of state government—is a likely or feasible remedy to help voters know who is responsible for making policy. Unfortunately, state governments have long faced a severe visibility problem that appears to be getting worse. A third fewer reporters reside at state-capitol press bureaus than at the turn of the century. Even if this declining trend reverses itself, news coverage of state government will be unlikely to reach a normatively satisfying number of voters. Under an improbable hypothetical scenario in which the number of statehouse reporters is tripled, voters would still be less likely to identify the party that controls the state house than the US House. Therefore, many voters enter the voting booth with little information, and there does not appear to be a clear and feasible way to change American legislative elections to ensure voters know who is responsible for making policy.

Who Is Your State Legislator?

Concerns regarding citizens' knowledge of political affairs have been long debated by democratic theorists ranging from Aristotle to Thomas Jefferson (Hochschild 2010). Some take a dimmer view of voters' capabilities, characterizing the unattainable democratic ideal of an "omnicompetent, sovereign citizen" as bad just in the same sense that "it is bad for a fat man to try to be a ballet dancer" (Lippmann 1993, 39). Others counter that voters can make reasonable decisions with little information (e.g.,

Lupia 2015). The true answer likely lies somewhere between these two viewpoints. Even with these disagreements, most agree that voters need some information about who represents them for there to be meaningful electoral accountability.

Political scientists have largely come to a consensus that "most citizens are politically uninformed" (Delli Carpini and Keeter 1997), but political scientists know surprisingly little themselves about whether voters know who represents them in the state legislature. Most studies of state-level political knowledge focus on gubernatorial politics (e.g., Jaeger, Lyons, and Wolak 2017; Lyons, Jaeger, and Wolak 2013; Squire and Fastnow 1994). Meanwhile, research concerning voters' knowledge of their state legislator is relatively sparse and somewhat dated. Delli Carpini and Keeter (1997), for example, report that 28 percent of voters knew who their state legislator was in 1966. Studying three Oklahoma state legislative districts in the early 1980s, Songer (1984) found that 25 percent of voters could name their state representative. In a 1988 survey, Patterson, Ripley, and Quinlan (1992, 320) found that 28 percent of Ohioans could "name their state representative or legislator's party affiliation." In a 1990 survey, Delli Carpini, Keeter, and Kennamer (1994) find that less than half of Virginians could identify the majority parties of the Virginia House of Delegates or Senate.[2]

To provide an updated understanding of whether voters know who their state legislator is, I asked voters the straightforward question: Who represents you in the state legislature?

I asked this question on one national survey and two state-level surveys. The national survey was part of the 2018 Cooperative Election Study (CES). Each election year, the CES asks over thirty thousand Americans questions about American politics, and teams of social scientists ask subsamples of these respondents customized questionnaires or survey modules. Shortly before and after the 2018 election, over eight hundred voters answered a customized questionnaire focused on their knowledge and opinions concerning state politics.

These CES findings are valuable to understanding voters' knowledge of who represents them in legislatures, but in a methodological aside, I warn readers that results may overestimate the typical American's political knowledge. CES respondents are typically more educated and politically interested than the average American, and respondents who participate in online studies are more likely to be politically informed (Burnett 2016; Liu and Wang 2014). There is also evidence that respondents "cheat" when answering political knowledge questions on online surveys (B. Smith, Clifford, and Jerit 2020). When asked who their state representative was, one respondent honestly stated: "I can google it." The following findings then likely provide overestimates of citizens' knowledge.

The Center for the Study of Democratic Institutions at Vanderbilt University also generously allowed me to place questions concerning state legislators on their phone surveys of Tennessee voters in May 2012 and December 2013. As described in greater detail below, these state-level surveys shed light on how voters' knowledge of their federal and state legislators differs. Specifically, I asked voters to recall their federal and state legislators' names, identify their federal and state legislators' names from lists, and identify the party that controlled the US House and the state house. All survey findings presented in this and subsequent chapters are weighted to reflect more representative samples of the United States or Tennessee.

Recall of Legislators' Names

The CES asked a national sample of voters: "Even if you had to guess, who is your current representative in [Insert State Legislature Lower Chamber Name]?" Respondents answered this question online a month prior to the 2018 election, during many state representatives' reelection campaigns. Respondents typed their answers in a text form, and research assistants coded responses' accuracy. To my knowledge, this was the first national survey to assess voters' ability to recall their state legislator's name in at least the last fifty years.

Eleven percent of voters accurately recalled their state representative's name, 31 percent gave an incorrect answer, 18 percent of voters explicitly stated they did not know, and 38 percent refused to answer the question, leaving the text field blank.[3] Few voters then know who their state legislator is, but many incorrect answers were not random guesses and were often rooted in state politics. Instead of their state representative's name, approximately 4 percent of voters gave either the name of their state senator or governor. Voters' beliefs about who their state representative was then, at times, at least in the ballpark of state politics. Voters more often confused their state-level and federal legislators. 13 and 5 percent of voters, respectively, gave the name of their US House representative or one of their two US senators, suggesting the American federal system complicates the electorate's ability to satisfy Powell's first condition for accountability.

It is problematic for the prospects for accountability in state legislatures if an overwhelming majority of voters do not know who represents them in the state legislature. But how bad is this compared to what voters

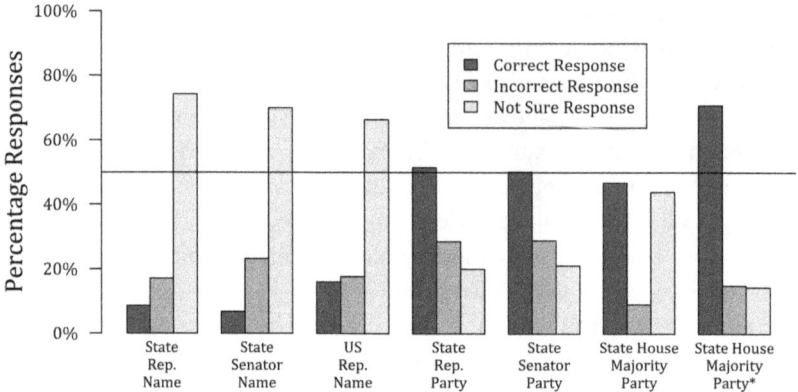

FIGURE 4.1. Percentages of Tennessee voters who could recall the names of their US House representative, state senator, or state representatives from memory. Respondents also identified which party controlled the Tennessee state house, but half of respondents were not explicitly given a 'not sure' response option (*).

know about Congress? Unfortunately, analyses of the CES prevent fair comparisons of voters' ability to name their state and federal legislators, as CES respondents saw their US senator and US House representatives' names in other survey questions. Such exposure would almost certainly increase the likelihood a voter could recall these federal legislators' names compared to their state legislators' names, exacerbating found differences in voters' knowledge of federal and state politics.

To make fairer comparisons of voters' knowledge of their representatives in state and federal government, I asked Tennessee voters to recall from memory their US House representative, state senator, or state representative's names in May 2012. Approximately 16 percent of Tennessee voters could recall their US House representative's name from memory. However, fewer than 10 percent of voters could recall either their state senator's or state representative's names (figure 4.1, first three sets of bars). Tennessee voters are then almost twice as likely to recall their federal legislators as they are to recall their state legislators.

Identification of Legislators' Names

When asked to identify instead of recalling their legislators' names in December 2013, Tennessee voters again demonstrated more knowledge about federal politics. Voters identified their legislator from a list of five names. One name was their legislator, three names were other legislators from the same chamber (e.g., US House or Tennessee House of Representatives), and the fifth name was either Warren Miller or Donald Stokes, two prominent political scientists. Figure 4.2 shows that 22 percent of voters could identify their state representative, 22 percent could identify their state senator, and 38 percent could identify their US House representative. Together, these surveys indicate that 22 percent or fewer voters could recall or identify their state legislator's name when voters had a one in five chance to get the identification question correct.[4] Such levels of voter knowledge are slightly lower than those reported in prior work, which suggested that approximately a fourth of voters knew who their state legislator was.

Identification of the Majority Party in the Legislature

Remembering names is difficult (Hollander 2014), and knowing an individual legislator's name may be an unnecessarily high standard for accountability (e.g., Lupia 2006). To make politics easier for voters, parties can famously impose "great political simplicity" on the American government (Schattschneider 1942, 53). While most Tennessee voters did not know who their legislator was, most voters knew to which party their state

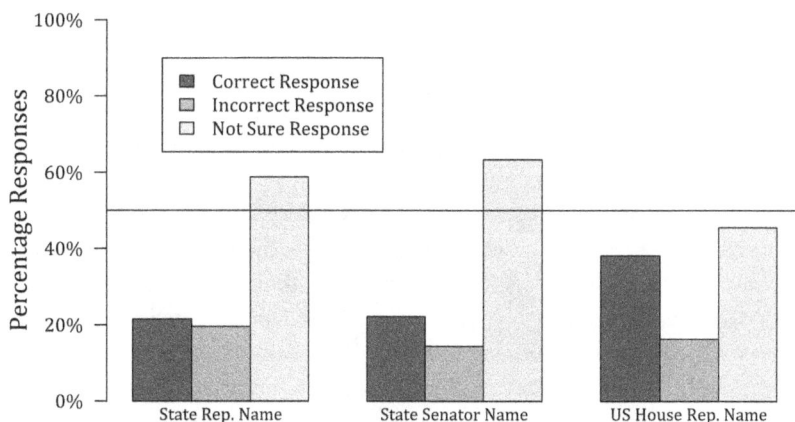

FIGURE 4.2. Percentages of Tennessee voters who could identify their US House representative, state senator, or state representatives from a list of five names.

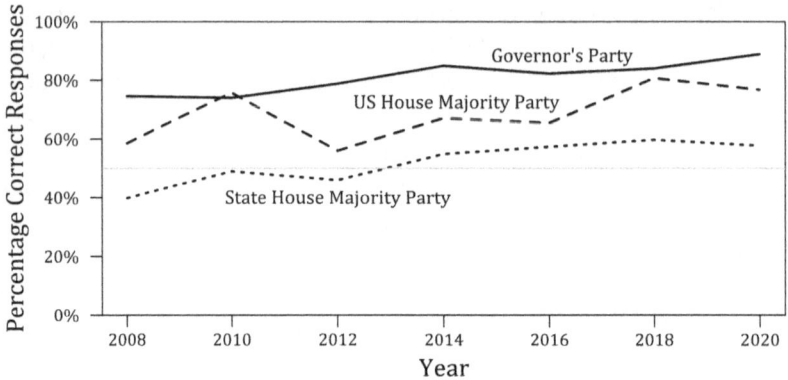

FIGURE 4.3. Percentages of registered voters from the 2008 to 2020 Cooperative Election Studies who gave correct responses regarding which party controls their governorship, the US House, or their state house.

representative or senator belonged. 52 and 50 percent of Tennessee voters accurately identified the party of their state representative or state senator (figure 4.1, fourth and fifth sets of bars). Fewer Tennesseans, however, knew which party had a majority of seats in their state house. In 2012, 47 percent believed Republicans (the correct answer), 9 percent stated Democrats, and 43 percent chose a provided "not sure" option. Tennessee voters seem to be slightly less informed about their state government than most Americans. Figure 4.3 illustrates the nationwide percentage of voters who could correctly identify which party controlled their governorship (solid line), the US House (dashed line), or their state house (dotted line) using responses to CES from 2008 through 2020. In 2012, a year before I asked Tennesseans which party controlled their legislature, approximately 46 percent of Americans correctly identified the party with the most seats in their legislature's lower chamber.

With party labels appearing on nearly every state legislative ballot, these statistics concerning which party controls the state house are more promising for the prospects for accountability than those concerning who your state legislator is. A voter only needs to know if their representative is a Republican or Democrat and electorally punish or reward accordingly. Still, it is disconcerting that fewer than half of voters across the country or in Tennessee could correctly answer "Which party had more seats in their state house of representatives?" in 2012. This question only has two reasonable answers. Theoretically, a respondent would have been more likely to correctly identify their legislator's party by flipping a coin with a donkey on one side and an elephant on the other.

Before concluding that the above figures merely add to the consensus that voters know little about politics, it is important to look at more than only the 2012 election. Fewer than half of voters could identify their state house majority party in 2008, 2010, and 2012, but at least 55 percent of voters could identify their state house majority party in the 2014 to 2020 surveys (figure 4.3). Such higher levels of knowledge presumably should increase the likelihood that voters hold their state legislators and their parties accountable for poor performance, a subject addressed in chapter 7. But why do surveys suggest that more voters knew which party controlled their state legislature in 2020 than in 2008? To begin to answer this question, it is helpful to consider how surveys are conducted — specifically, who is taking the survey and what respondents were asked.

Focusing on the first question, a greater percentage of 2020 CES respondents knew which party controlled their state legislature than did 2012 respondents, but the voters who responded to the 2012 CES are not the same voters who responded to the 2020 CES. Individual voters may be becoming more knowledgeable. But a possible alternative explanation for the increase in correct responses could be that 2020 respondents are simply more attuned to politics than 2012 respondents were. If this were the case, it could explain why levels of voter knowledge also increased concerning both federal and state politics during this time (figure 4.3, dashed and dotted lines). We then cannot be sure whether any specific voter was more knowledgeable about state politics in 2020 than in 2012. To empirically study whether such changes in knowledge occur and what causes them, the below investigation of the importance of media evaluates how the *same* voters become more knowledgeable over time, by examining those who responded to multiple CES surveys over different years.

For the second question — "What are respondents asked?" — it is important to consider how response options shape respondents' answers. Here, let us revisit findings concerning Tennessee voters knowing who their legislator was. Voters demonstrated higher levels of political knowledge when asked to identify instead of recalling their legislator's name, consistent with research that shows knowledge-recall questions are more difficult than recognition questions. Voters' responses also were not completely random. Remember, when identifying their state legislator, one of the five given names respondents could choose from was Warren Miller or Donald Stokes. Respondents then had a 1 in 5 chance of picking one of these political scientists. But only one (of 989) respondent did so. "Incorrect" respondents, while wrong, at least overwhelmingly chose the name of someone who served in the legislature.

Focusing on CES question wording and response options, CES respondents were given a "not sure" option when asked which party controlled different political institutions. In 2012, 11 percent provided an incorrect response, and 42 percent were not sure. Providing a respondent to a survey a "not sure" option gives him an easy out to a question when he is uncertain of the answer, but this "not sure" option will not be available in the voting booth. Survey research suggests "not sure" respondents are more likely to provide correct answers if given closed-item responses forcing them to give a definitive answer (e.g., Mondak 2000; see also Luskin and Bullock 2011). To investigate whether this phenomenon also happens with questions about state legislatures, I asked Tennessee voters which party had a majority of seats in the Tennessee state house but did so in two different ways. I asked all respondents the same question but explicitly gave half the respondents the options of "Democrats," "Republicans," and "not sure." The other half of respondents only received the options of "Democrats" or "Republicans."

Tennesseans' survey responses provide reason to be more optimistic about the voter. The final two sets of bar graphs in figure 4.1 suggest that uncertain or "not sure" voters make educated guesses about who represents them in state government when forced to do so. Recall that when explicitly given a "not sure" response option, 47 percent responded Republicans (the correct answer), 9 percent stated Democrats, and 43 percent chose the "not sure" option. In other words, one voter gave an incorrect answer for approximately every five voters who gave a correct answer. When respondents were only given "Republican" and "Democrat" options, 70 percent responded Republicans, 14 percent responded Democrats, and 14 percent voluntarily responded "not sure." Again, for every voter who gave an incorrect answer, five voters gave a correct answer. When removing the "not sure" option, the ratio of correct to incorrect responses then remained the same, but the number of correct responses disproportionately increased. If "not sure" respondents were to not have the "not sure" option and blindly guess which party controlled their state house, we should theoretically expect half these respondents to say "Republican" and the other half to say "Democrat," creating a one-to-one ratio of correct and incorrect responses. Instead, the observed ratio was five new correct responses for each new incorrect response. The disproportionate increase in correct answers suggests that "not sure" voters in Tennessee — a traditionally Republican state — when forced to guess tended to correctly state that Republicans controlled the state legislature.

It is preferable for voters to know who is responsible for making policy rather than be "not sure who is responsible for making policy," but the above point is an important one that I hope resonates with readers. Tennesseans — like many Americans — know relatively little about their state legislature, but Tennesseans at least seem to *try* to make reasonable guesses concerning who represents them in the legislature when they do not know for sure. Analyses in chapter 7 will build on this point and show that voters at times try to hold their state legislator accountable, even if they do not necessarily know who is responsible for making policy (figure 7.4).

Americans' Interest in State Legislatures

Americans' lack of political knowledge is particularly prevalent at the state legislative level (figures 4.1 to 4.3). But why is this the case? A good starting point to address this question are the first sentences of V. O. Key's textbook *American State Politics: An Introduction*:

> The American people are not boiling with concern about the workings of their state government. In the competition for public interest and attention the governments of the American states come off a poor second-best against the performance of the finished professionals who operate in Washington. (1956, 3)

Key's characterization of voters' interest in state government relative to other levels of government is over sixty years old but still appears to hold today. In the 2018 CES, 13 percent of voters stated they more closely followed "what is going on in government and public affairs" pertaining to their local government (i.e., town or city council) than state government, and 38 percent of voters more closely followed the federal government than state government. These differences in survey responses support Key's above characterization, but survey respondents sometimes give more socially desirable answers and overstate how closely they follow state government (Galais, Blais, and Bowler 2014). Hinting at this performance of social desirability, less than 3 percent of respondents who said

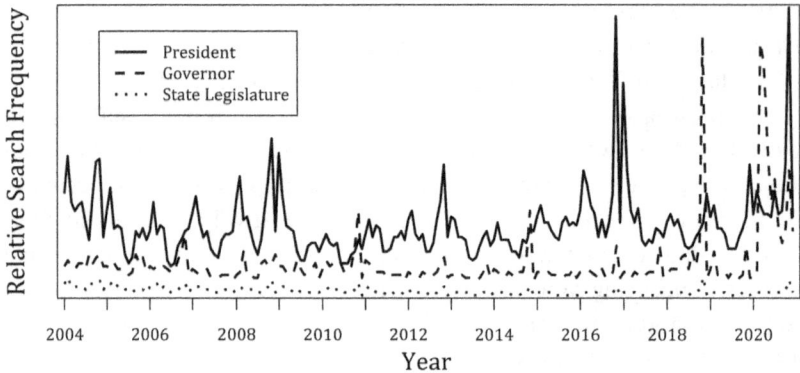

FIGURE 4.4. Monthly relative search frequency on Google for terms related to "president," "governor," and "state legislature."

they followed news about their state government "most of the time" could recall their state representative's name.

A more objective way to gauge Americans' concern with particular aspects of government is to examine what types of information about politics they seek. Google publishes its users' search terms through its Google Trends service. Using these data, figure 4.4 illustrates the relative search volume by month for the topics of "president," "governor," and "state legislature" from 2004 through 2020.[5] This figure's scale is normalized to the maximum search volume for the term "president" shortly before the 2016 presidential election.

Google searches reaffirm Key's textbook assertion that Americans are overwhelmingly more interested in "the finished professionals who operate in Washington," particularly before presidential elections. National politics almost always dominated voters' interests during the examined time period. Only immediately before the 2010 midterm election, 2018 midterm election, and the start of the COVID-19 pandemic, when many state governors enacted public health safety protocols, did Americans make more searches concerned with gubernatorial politics (figure 4.4, dashed line) than with the president (figure 4.4, solid line) or Congress (not shown). Meanwhile, relative search volume for the state legislature (figure 4.4, dotted line) never exceeded that for president, governor, or Congress and has declined by at least a third on average from 2004 to 2020.

Media Coverage of State Legislatures

Surveys reaffirm Americans' relatively low interest in state politics compared to federal politics and other subjects. A national 2009 Yale University survey, for instance, found that over twice as many voters reported they very closely followed national politics as followed state politics, and over three times as many respondents said they followed the weather forecast very closely as did for state politics (Leiserowitz, Maibach, and Roser-Renoug 2009). Learning about the weather is not hard for Americans. Individuals can open the newspaper or turn on the local television news to learn if it is supposed to rain tomorrow. In turn, over 75 percent of Americans interested in the weather report that it is "very easy" to stay informed about the weather from local news, with another 20 percent finding it "somewhat easy" (Pew Research Center 2019b). Even those not particularly interested in the weather learn about it from the news. A sports fan who watches the local television news to learn sports scores will likely have to sit through the weekly forecast before the sports anchor takes over.

Given that few Americans actively pursue information about state politics, many voters likely learn what they know about their state government in the same way many sports fans learn about the weather: without actively seeking it. This type of information acquisition relates to Anthony Downs's idea of "accidental" or by-product learning. Given the high costs associated with learning about politics, Downs argues that "the acquisition of any nonfree political information data whatever is irrational," and voters often learn about politics as a by-product of other activities (Downs 1957, 239). For example, voters may not follow energy markets, but they learn something about oil prices when filling up their car's gas tank.

Applying the idea of by-product learning to the media, Markus Prior (2007) shows how a particular media environment can have varying educational effects on different sets of voters. Specifically, Prior compares political learning during the "broadcast only" era of television to political learning after the advent of cable television. During the broadcast era, the nightly network news was the only show on television in the evenings. Some Americans watched TV news to learn about politics and current events, but others tuned in to be entertained. During the broadcast-only era, these entertainment seekers were exposed to political events of the day and experienced by-product learning despite not actively seeking information about politics.

The advent of cable television, however, changed viewers' media choices and consequently their overall levels of political learning. No longer constricted by a media environment that only offered the network news in the evening, politically interested viewers could change the channel to CNN. Entertainment seekers, meanwhile, could watch ESPN. CNN viewers continued to receive information about government and public affairs, but by watching SportsCenter instead of the network news, ESPN viewers had fewer opportunities to acquire political knowledge as a by-product of watching television. Through a series of experiments and surveys, Prior's research shows that voters with preferences for entertainment who had access to cable or additional media choices were less knowledgeable about politics than those who only had access to broadcast channels.

Characteristics of voters are thus critical for political learning via the media, but for voters to have the opportunity to learn about state politics from the media—even as a by-product—the media must cover state politics. In the 1970s, William Grommley found that newspapers devoted less than 18 percent of political news coverage to state and local politics, creating "a severe visibility problem" for state governments (Grommley, quoted in Rozell 2003, 138; see also Wolfson 1985 and Roeder 1994, 34). More recently, voters indicated on the 2018 CES whether "the press does a good job reporting on" different levels of government. By margins of 16, 22, and 25 percent, voters reported that the press does a better job reporting on the governor, Congress, and local government than on their state legislature, indicating that the severe visibility problem for state house news has not gone away, even in the eyes of voters.

Studies conducted by the Pew Research Center and the *American Journalism Review* likewise help affirm that state government still has a severe visibility problem.[6] These organizations documented the number of statehouse reporters since the 1990s. Altogether, approximately 1,761 full- and part-time reporters covered state government in 2022, and figure 4.5 provides a breakdown across states.[7] Larger states and those with longer legislative sessions often have more reporters, but the media's presence in the fifty state capitols remains relatively small, even with part-time reporters. Over 6,800 individuals are credentialed to cover the single legislature of Congress (Mitchell, Holcomb, and Weisel 2015), while the National Football League issued over 5,200 media credentials for Superbowl 56 (Krutzsch, email message to author, May 22, 2022).

When asked where they heard about their state legislative election, 60 percent of voters from the 2018 CES named television news. Similarly,

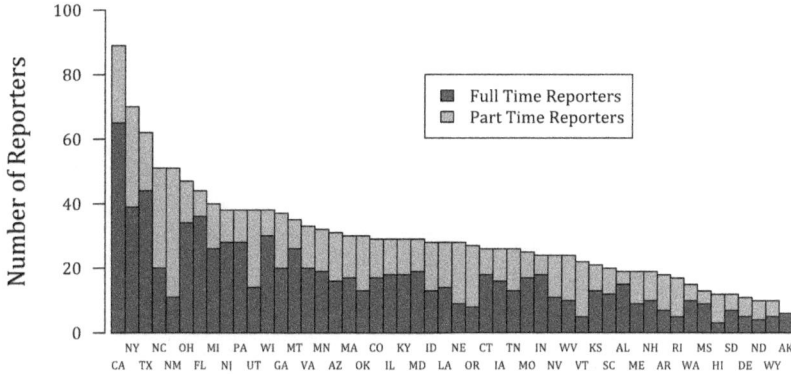

FIGURE 4.5. The number of full-time and part-time reporters devoted to state government by state as of 2022.

Pennsylvania Republican legislative caucus spokesman Stephen Miskin stated, "A lot of people still get their news from T.V." But when describing local television news stations' presence in Harrisburg, Miskin continued, "they're not here" (quoted in Enda, Matsa, and Boyles 2014). Miskin's characterization of Pennsylvania television stations' viewership and coverage of state politics reflects that of the country. Most Americans get their news from television (Mitchell et al. 2016). Americans also watch local television news (70 percent) more often than network (61 percent) or cable news (38 percent) (Jurkowitz and Mitchell 2013). Even with the rise of digital media, more Americans still report getting their local news from TV (Pew Research Center 2019b). Local television stations then have audiences to inform about state politics, but few stations invest substantial resources to cover state government. In 2013, 86 percent of local television stations did not have a reporter devoted to covering state government, and there were no full-time television statehouse reporters in eighteen states.

Local TV news stations also produce disproportionately fewer stories on state legislative politics than on other government levels. Leading up to the 2002 and 2004 elections, Erika Fowler, Ken Goldstein, Matthew Hale, and Martin Kaplan, in coordination with the Lear Center, measured the proportion of local television news stories devoted to different political campaigns (E. F. Fowler et al. 2007; Kaplan, Goldstein, and Hale 2003 and 2005).[8] In 2004, the presidential election dominated local news stations' attention, receiving over 60 percent of coverage (figure 4.6). There was

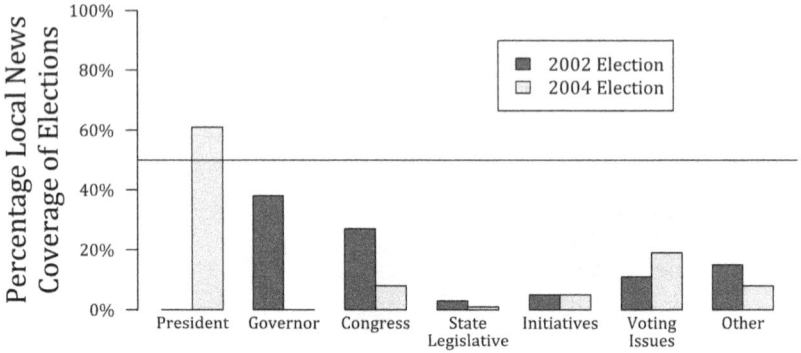

FIGURE 4.6. Percentages of local news stories devoted to different types of political campaigns in the 2002 and 2004 elections.

more coverage of state politics in the preceding midterm election when 38 percent of stories focused on gubernatorial contests. Nevertheless, even when presidential candidates were not on the ballot, only 3 percent of local television election news stories were devoted to state legislative elections. This figure dropped to 1 percent in 2004.[9] Fowler again found in 2012 that presidential campaigns received at least 60 percent of local news coverage, and lower ballot races—including both state legislative and city races—received less than 5 percent of local news coverage (E. F. Fowler 2018).

Local news stories about state legislative politics, however, appear to be more in-depth. Kaplan, Goldstein, and Hale note that "it was stories about state assembly, mayors and regional offices that were the longest; stories about these races had an average length of around 120 seconds." The authors continue, however, that "unfortunately, these three offices where longer stories did appear accounted for less than one-and-a-half percent of all stories" (2005, 13–14). Legislators appear aware of this lack of coverage, as less than half of state legislators who responded to the National Candidate Study agreed with the statement, "The news media in my area pay close attention to whether elected officials are serving the public interest."

The consolidation of local news stations compounds the problem of a lack of local political stories. Forty-seven percent of Americans reported that their local news media mainly cover an area other than the one where they live (Pew Research Center 2018). Focusing on the disparity between national and local news, Gregory Martin and Joshua McCrain (2019; see also Hopkins 2018) find that the 193 local news stations owned by the

Sinclair Broadcast Group more often reported on national politics than other local news stations and provided a third less coverage of local politics. Given that voters tend to rate issues as more important if they are covered by the news (Kinder and Iyengar 1989), a lack of local television news stories is likely partly responsible for the above-documented voters' relative lack of interest in state politics.

Despite television news' limited coverage of state legislative elections, 20 percent more voters indicated that they heard about their state legislative election from television news than did from newspapers. Such high reported voter exposure to television news is perhaps surprising since the print media covers state politics more than any other journalistic medium. In 2022, there were approximately 60 percent more state house newspaper reporters than local television reporters (Shearer et al. 2022). Even if voters do not indicate they get their state legislative news from newspapers, the number of newspaper reporters is important for television news as newspapers influence other local media content (Arnold 2006).

Regrettably for accountability in state legislatures, there have been severe cuts to state house newspaper reporting. Across all newspapers examined by the Pew Research Center, the number of full-time newspaper reporters dropped from 374 in 2014 to 245 in 2022, a 34 percent decline. To look at a longer time period, the Pew Research Center compared the number of full-time newspaper reporters found at 194 newspapers examined by the *American Journalism Review* in earlier studies. Pew found that there were 368 full-time reporters in 2003, 281 reporters in 2009, 250 reporters in 2014, and 206 reporters in 2022, reflecting a 44 percent decline in the number of full-time newspaper reporters in less than twenty years (Worden, Matsa, and Shearer 2022).[10] In 2013, 70 percent of newspapers did not have a reporter devoted to covering state government (Enda, Matsa, and Boyles 2014).

Political scientists repeatedly show that local newspapers' decline has implications for voters' behavior. Danny Hayes and Jennifer Lawless (2021, 88) provide evidence that "newspaper readers know more about their city and school officials and are more likely to vote, attend meetings, and even participate in other forms of local activism than nonreaders." Newspaper closures associate with depressed turnout in presidential and congressional elections (Gentzkow, Shapiro, and Sinkinson 2011), and after studying newspaper closures from 2009 to 2013, Joshua Darr, Matthew Hitt, and Johanna Dunaway (2018) find that a newspaper closure in a county leads to a 1.9 percent decrease in split-ticket voting between the president and US Senate. Marc Trussler (2020) similarly shows that access to high-speed internet—which provides readier access to preferred national than local news (Hopkins 2018)—decreases split-ticket voting in US House elections. Such findings indicate that media can help voters learn more about different political actors, make decisions based on local politics, and potentially separate "its choices of presidential and state candidates" (Key 1964, 307), which is important in a time of increasingly nationalized politics.

For readers further interested in the decline of newspaper reporting at the state house, I recommend the *American Journalism Review*'s series of articles from the 1990s and the first decade of the 2000s (Dorroh 2009; Layton and Dorroh 2002; 2003; Layton and Walton 1998; Lisheron 2010; Stepp 2004; Walton 2000) along with the Pew Research Center's 2014 and 2022 reports on the subject. The *American Journalism Review* provided arguably the best coverage of the decline of state house newspaper reporting, but in a sad irony, the *American Journalism Review* itself ended its own publication in 2015. From the *American Journalism Review*, I want to highlight Charles Layton and Mary Walton's (1998, 44) description of Jim Mitzelfeld, an enthusiastic young reporter for the *Detroit Free Press*—an account that illustrates the influence a statehouse reporter can have on accountability in state legislatures.

> One day [Mitzelfeld] heard that the governor had frozen the legislature's check-writing authority. It pricked his curiosity. "I was sort of skeptical it would even get in the paper. But I thought, 'Well, I'll ask somebody in the administration about this.' And it was in the course of working on this story that a source, in a phone interview—after failing to answer several questions clearly—said 'Well, there are rumors.'
>
> I said, 'What rumors?'
>
> 'Well, there are rumors that someone in the legislature is writing checks out to cash.'
>
> So immediately I said, 'Whoa! That's a big story if that's true.'"
>
> After two weeks of digging into state computer records, scrutinizing lists of processed checks and chasing other leads, [Mitzelfeld] established that staff people in the House Fiscal Agency, an arm of the legislature, had been writing fat checks to themselves and their colleagues. The fraudulent checks totaled $1.8 million.
>
> Only hours after the story broke, the governor called for a criminal investigation. It was front page news for the next two weeks. Five people eventually went to prison.

For a while, Mitzelfeld was golden. But Detroit's enthusiasm did not last. He would propose an enterprise story that might take two weeks' work, and editors would turn it down. In time, he says, they even seemed bored with the follow-ups on the bogus checks. "At two months out, we were having to fight the battle all over again."

In 1994, Mitzelfeld was awarded the Pulitzer Prize for beat reporting. But by then he was no longer a newspaper reporter. "I got a sense that a lot of what I didn't like about my job at that paper was happening at other papers," he says, "and that's part of why I got out."

After Mitzelfeld's reporting, Michigan state representative Stephen Shepich resigned from office and was convicted of receiving fraudulent travel reimbursement (Freedman 2013).

With the departures of newspaper reporters, nonprofit organizations have filled some of the empty seats in state capitols' press bureaus.[11] Nonprofit reporters made up 20 percent of statehouse reporters in 2022, up from 6 percent in 2014. Nonprofits valuably often offer free news stories to the public and republication in other news outlets, particularly in more-rural areas. For instance, in Iowa, despite the *Oelwein Daily Register* no longer being able to send their own reporter to Des Moines, the 5,920 citizens of Oelwein could still get news coverage of state politics. The *Oelwein Daily Register* was able to publish stories written by the *Iowa Capital Dispatch*, a nonprofit media outlet. The *Iowa Capital Dispatch* is partly funded by the national organization *States Newsroom*, which supports nonprofit reporting in twenty-seven states as of 2022. However, even Chris Fitzsimon—the director of *States Newsroom*—acknowledges that nonprofits cannot replace legacy papers, nor should they try. When speaking to the Pew Research Center, Fitzsimon specifically noted that many nonprofits rely on students or volunteers who have less institutional knowledge of the legislature and its history (Fitzsimon 2022). In 2022, 11 percent of statehouse reporters were students or volunteers.

While many excellent statehouse reporters like Mitzelfeld now work for nonprofits, the inexperience issue Fitzsimon highlights is a growing problem in state government news reporting. According to the former executive director of the National Association of State House Reporters, Tiffany Shackelford, "We are also seeing reporters who have been in these states for 20-some years taking buyouts or getting cut and being replaced by 22-year-olds . . . These may be talented reporters, but they don't have the institutional knowledge. And the statehouse beat is one of the most complex in the nation" (E. Smith 2009). Inexperienced state-house press corps compound problems created by state legislative term limits (e.g., Kousser 2005). As noted by one Michigan statehouse reporter, ". . . partly because of term limits, there's less long-lasting, there are fewer long-lasting relationships between the media and elected officials and so there's a little more distrust, a little more wariness" (quoted in Cooper and Johnson 2006, 21). If a trusted source did not tell Mitzelfeld "that someone in the legislature is writing checks out to cash," State Representative Shepich might not have been convicted and resigned. The following analyses show that the decline in statehouse reporters has implications for voters' knowledge, but it is important to recognize that reporters like Mitzelfeld help hold American legislators accountable, even if most voters do not pay attention.

Increasingly Partisan and Polarized State Legislatures

Since the 1990s, there has been a decline in the number of reporters covering state government, likely making it harder for voters to know who is responsible for making policy. However, during this time, there have also been substantial changes in the partisan makeup and polarization of state legislatures that may make it easier for voters to identify who controls their state government (Parry et al. 2022; Shor and McCarty 2022). For instance, in 2002, different parties controlled the upper and lower state legislative chambers in fourteen states. By 2020, this figure drops to two states. During this time, the average seat share for a chamber majority party grew from 62 percent to 67 percent. Unified legislatures with larger chamber majorities likely send stronger signals to voters about which parties control their state legislature, help provide "clarity of responsibility" (e.g., Fiorina 1995), and make it easier to "know who is responsible for making policy."

State legislatures have also become increasingly polarized. For readers interested in state legislative polarization, I recommend the extensive work by Boris Shor and Nolan McCarty (2011; 2022; McCarty 2019; see also Masket 2019). Using data collected by Shor and McCarty, figure 4.7 plots the median ideal points, which reflect state legislators' ideological representation, of Democrats and Republicans in state legislatures from 2001 to 2020. The solid lines are the loess curves for these points. During this time period, the difference between state legislative Democrats'

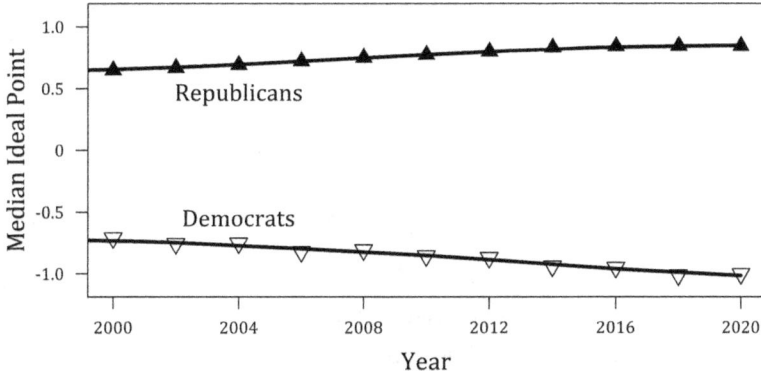

FIGURE 4.7. Increasing polarization in state legislatures as indicated by median roll call ideal points of Republican and Democratic state legislators across the United States.

and Republicans' ideologies has grown by almost 30 percent. Such growing polarization can help voters distinguish and identify differences between their state legislative parties as it does at the national level (Fortunato and Stevenson 2021; Levendusky 2009; see also Lyons, Jaeger, and Wolak 2013).

Unified legislatures, large majorities, and polarization likely make it easier for voters to know or even guess which party controls their legislature. For example, recall that "not sure" Tennesseans more often guessed that Republicans controlled their state house. With Tennessee more recently being a Republican state, these guesses suggest that many voters are not blind to political conditions within their states. For instance, earlier in this chapter, I asked readers to ask themselves who their state legislator is, which is a straightforward but potentially difficult question. I suspect more readers could tell me which party controls the Massachusetts state legislature, even if they do not live in Massachusetts, simply given the state's political reputation.

Do Voters Learn under Different Political Conditions and from the Media?

Having documented how little knowledge and interest voters have regarding their state legislature, I investigate what determines voters' knowledge of their legislature and if an increased media presence is a plausible solution to voters' lack of knowledge. For my study, I use responses from the 2010, 2012, and 2014 CES surveys to estimate the likelihood a voter could identify the majority party in his legislature as a function of the media and political conditions within his state. I focus on the 2010 to 2014 surveys because they include a set of respondents who answered each survey.

My central independent variables of interest are state-level media and political conditions. I measure voters' potential exposure to news coverage about their legislature in two ways. First, I use the logged number of full-time reporters (newspaper only) identified by the *American Journalism Review* in 2009 or full-time reporters (newspaper, digital, or television) identified by the Pew Research Center in 2013. When studying gubernatorial politics, Lyons, Jaeger, and Wolak (2013) show that increased media coverage by newspapers influences the likelihood that voters can correctly name their governor. While the numbers of reporters do not directly capture levels of media coverage, they reflect the resources the media devotes to state politics. My analyses also account for a state's population, as more populous states tend to have more media outlets. An individual reporter in California may reach more voters than a reporter in Delaware.

Second, I investigate the extent to which voters who live closer to the capital are more knowledgeable about state government. When describing local television's coverage of Missouri state politics over his forty-year career as a reporter, Bob Priddy told the *Columbia Journalism Review*

> Other than the television stations here in Central Missouri, in Columbia and Jefferson City, we almost never see anybody from the metropolitan areas, from Kansas City or St. Louis or Springfield for that matter, come up here to do any kind of live coverage or even have stringers to do things for them from the Capitol. The general feeling, I think, is that this isn't sexy enough for television and this isn't really the kind of thing they want to make the investment in, because it's 125 miles or so from either of our big metropolitan areas, St. Louis and Kansas City. (Lee 2015)

Dan Hopkins (2018; see also Alvarez 2010; Delli Carpini, Keeter, and Kennamer 1994) finds that "newspapers located in state capitals provide substantially more state-level coverage than others." Following Priddy's intuition and Hopkins's empirical findings, if the media helps promote political knowledge, I expect voters to be more likely to identify their state house majority party if more reporters cover the state house or if a voter lives closer to the capital.

To investigate the importance of state political conditions, I account for whether a voter was in a state with a unified government, larger legislative majority parties, longer-serving majority parties, and ideological distance or polarization between the state parties. States' differing legislative institutions also impact public opinion of state legislatures (Hamman 2006; Kelleher and Wolak 2007; Konisky and Ueda 2011; Richardson Jr., Konisky, and Milyo 2012; Squire 1993). Using an index measure of professionalism in a study of seven states, Peverill Squire finds that people are less likely to pay attention to more professionalized legislatures. One reason Squire posits for this finding is that "people can focus better on more amateur legislatures because they have shorter sessions, and consequently receive more in-depth news coverage" (Squire 1993, 483–84). To investigate this specific proposition across a more extensive set of states, I estimate the relationship that length of legislative sessions, size of legislative staff, and legislator salary have with voters' ability to identify the majority parties in their state legislature.[12] At the individual level, my analyses control for a respondent's strength of partisanship, gender, age, education, and income (Delli Carpini and Keeter 1997; Luskin 1990; Lyons, Jaeger, and Wolak 2013). Table A.4.2 provides summary statistics of the variables used in these analyses.

To assess the relationship between the above variables and political knowledge, I estimate a series of statistical models where the dependent variable is whether a voter correctly identified the party that controls their state house or state senate. Probit estimates are available in table 4.1. Using these estimates, table 4.2 presents differences in the average predicted probability of a voter correctly identifying their state house majority party given a change in an independent variable. As an example of how to interpret this table, the fourth row shows the difference in the probability that a voter correctly identifies their state house majority party associated with a 10 percentage point increase in the state house majority's size. The increases in these probabilities found in the 2010, 2012, and 2014 surveys are 0.040, 0.058, and 0.080. These differences in probabilities indicate that voters in states with larger legislative majorities are more likely to know which party is in charge of the legislature and, therefore, whom to reward or blame for good or bad policymaking.

Evidence repeatedly suggests that the media helps educate voters about their legislature. Voters in states with more full-time statehouse reporters

TABLE 4.1 **Identification of state legislative majority parties**

	2010 state house	2012 state house	2014 state house	2010 state senate	2012 state senate	2014 state senate
Number of full-time reporters at statehouse (logged)	-1.405* (0.361)	0.167 (0.382)	-1.290* (0.408)	-1.663* (0.357)	-1.744* (0.406)	-0.242 (0.416)
Number of full-time reporters at statehouse (logged) x state population (logged)	0.093* (0.023)	0.004 (0.024)	0.088* (0.026)	0.118* (0.022)	0.120* (0.026)	0.020 (0.026)
Respondent distance from capital (in hundreds of kms)	-0.045* (0.007)	-0.037* (0.007)	-0.038* (0.007)	-0.053* (0.006)	-0.047* (0.007)	-0.043* (0.007)
Polarization	0.217* (0.027)	0.100* (0.025)	0.124* (0.027)	0.345* (0.033)	0.237* (0.024)	0.292* (0.026)
Divided state government	-0.343* (0.023)	-0.370* (0.025)	-0.422* (0.029)	-0.372* (0.025)	-0.322* (0.028)	-0.435* (0.031)
Majority-party size	1.116* (0.195)	1.634* (0.188)	2.231* (0.184)	2.853* (0.192)	1.866* (0.172)	2.785* (0.169)
Years current majority party in power (logged)	0.003 (0.015)	-0.031* (0.015)	0.047* (0.013)	-0.109* (0.014)	-0.081* (0.019)	-0.066* (0.018)
New chamber majority	-0.075 (0.045)	-0.301* (0.042)	0.120* (0.049)	-0.034 (0.074)	-0.696* (0.044)	0.023 (0.062)
Session length (in hundreds of days)	-0.001* (0.000)	0.001* (0.000)	-0.000 (0.000)	0.000 (0.000)	0.000 (0.000)	-0.002* (0.000)
Legislative staff per member	0.010 (0.005)	-0.010 (0.006)	-0.001 (0.006)	0.033* (0.005)	0.022* (0.006)	0.047* (0.007)
Legislator salary (in thousands of 2010 dollars)	0.002* (0.000)	-0.000 (0.000)	-0.000 (0.000)	-0.001* (0.000)	-0.002* (0.000)	-0.001* (0.000)
Respondent party extremity	0.136* (0.009)	0.078* (0.009)	0.110* (0.009)	0.135* (0.009)	0.070* (0.009)	0.111* (0.009)
Female respondent	-0.466* (0.019)	-0.392* (0.019)	-0.446* (0.019)	-0.470* (0.019)	-0.355* (0.019)	-0.414* (0.019)
Nonwhite respondent	-0.139* (0.024)	-0.107* (0.024)	-0.186* (0.025)	-0.136* (0.024)	-0.067* (0.024)	-0.145* (0.025)
Age (in years)	0.010* (0.001)	0.008* (0.001)	0.008* (0.001)	0.011* (0.001)	0.008* (0.001)	0.010* (0.001)
Education: high school degree	0.002 (0.056)	0.214* (0.060)	0.077 (0.068)	-0.031 (0.057)	0.241* (0.058)	0.112 (0.067)
Education: some college	0.283* (0.056)	0.558* (0.060)	0.424* (0.068)	0.265* (0.056)	0.564* (0.059)	0.445* (0.067)
Education: two-year college	0.279* (0.060)	0.565* (0.063)	0.421* (0.071)	0.249* (0.061)	0.592* (0.062)	0.422* (0.070)
Education: four-year college	0.450* (0.055)	0.793* (0.061)	0.635* (0.068)	0.437* (0.056)	0.787* (0.059)	0.653* (0.067)
Education: postgrad degree	0.601* (0.058)	0.936* (0.063)	0.797* (0.070)	0.592* (0.059)	0.922* (0.062)	0.811* (0.069)

TABLE 4.1 (*continued*)

	2010 state house	2012 state house	2014 state house	2010 state senate	2012 state senate	2014 state senate
Income: $30,000–$70,000	0.085* (0.023)	0.106* (0.022)	0.134* (0.022)	0.103* (0.023)	0.101* (0.022)	0.147* (0.022)
Income: $70,000–$100,000	0.258* (0.028)	0.220* (0.036)	0.283* (0.037)	0.255* (0.029)	0.221* (0.036)	0.274* (0.035)
Income: above $100,000	0.380* (0.029)	0.304* (0.029)	0.315* (0.028)	0.383* (0.029)	0.314* (0.030)	0.362* (0.029)
State population (logged)	-0.333* (0.058)	-0.142* (0.067)	-0.324* (0.071)	0.090 (0.064)	0.143 (0.076)	-0.082 (0.076)
District size (logged)	0.015 (0.037)	-0.007 (0.026)	-0.014 (0.025)	-0.626* (0.052)	-0.671* (0.055)	-0.239* (0.055)
Constant	3.206* (0.791)	-0.240 (0.993)	2.732* (1.069)	2.816* (0.794)	3.201* (1.062)	1.178 (1.063)
N	50,407	47,563	47,058	50,456	47,576	47,151
Log-likelihood	-28,122.4	-30,093.5	-24,853.3	-27,348.3	-29,712.4	-24,304.2

This table reports the results of probit regressions in which the outcome of interest is whether a voter correctly identified the party with the majority of seats in their state house or state senate. Samples drawn from the 2010, 2012, and 2014 Cooperative Election Studies. Standard errors are in parentheses; $*p < 0.05$.

or who live closer to the capital (and thus are more likely to be exposed to news about state politics) were more knowledgeable about their state government. If each state had ten additional reporters, there would be at least a 0.014 increase in the predicted probability that a voter could correctly answer the question "Which party has a majority of seats in the state house?" (table 4.2, first row). The impact of additional reporters is slightly more substantial in more populous states.[13] For example, using findings from the 2014 CES, if every state were as populous as California, ten additional reporters would result in a 0.043 increase in the probability that a voter could correctly identify their state house majority party, but if every state were as populous as Delaware, the comparable change would be a decrease of 0.014 (t-statistic of difference 1.28). Additionally, if every voter lived 100 kilometers closer to the capital (table 4.2, second row), the probability that a voter could correctly identify their state house majority party would increase by at least 0.013. Under the assumption that there is more media coverage of state politics in states with more reporters or in areas closer to the capital, these findings suggest that one way to improve voters' knowledge of state politics is by increasing media coverage of state politics.

Little media attention is only part of the explanation for why voters know so little about their state legislatures. Voters also respond to political

TABLE 4.2 **Media and political variables' relationship with voter knowledge**

Variable	Change in variable value	Change in probability		
		2010	2012	2014
Full-time reporters	10 more reporters	+0.014	+0.043*	+0.020*
		(0.008)	(0.005)	(0.006)
Distance to capital	Respondent 100 kilometers closer to capital	+0.016*	+0.013*	+0.013*
		(0.002)	(0.002)	(0.002)
Divided government	All unified to all divided	-0.121*	-0.131*	-0.150*
		(0.008)	(0.009)	(0.010)
Majority-party size	Increase of majority-party seat share by 10 percent	+0.040*	+0.058*	+0.080*
		(0.007)	(0.007)	(0.007)
New majority	Chamber majority party changed in most recent election	-0.026	-0.107*	+0.042*
		(0.016)	(0.015)	(0.017)
Polarization	Standard-deviation increase in polarization	+0.045*	+0.021*	+0.026*
		(0.006)	(0.005)	(0.006)

This table reports the differences in average predicted probabilities of voters correctly identifying their state house majority party with changing variable values listed in the second column. Standard errors are in parentheses; $*p < 0.05$.

signals, which are not always clear. Consistent with the notion that divided government can obfuscate "clarity of responsibility," the probability of voters correctly identifying their state house majority party is at least 0.121 lower in states with divided government (table 4.2, third row). Clearer signals also help voters know which party controls their legislature. When a legislative majority is 10 percent larger, voters are at least 0.040 more likely to know which party controls their state house (table 4.2, fourth row). However, the evidence is less consistent that new legislative majorities decrease voter knowledge of the legislature.

Polarization is often considered bad for governing, but statistical analyses suggest that state legislative polarization appears to help voters know who is responsible for making policy. Voters living in states with polarized state legislatures were more likely to correctly identify their majority parties. At the extremes, if all legislatures' polarization were equivalent to that of the least polarized legislature in 2012 (Rhode Island), the predicted probability of a voter identifying their state house majority party would be 0.43. However, if all legislatures were as polarized as the most polarized legislature (California), the comparable probability would rise to 0.51, all else equal.[14]

Individual characteristics of voters are some of the strongest predictors of voters' knowledge of the legislature.[15] Rich, educated, and partisan voters are more likely to know who is responsible for making policy (table 4.3). Differences between informed and uninformed voters could have important policy implications, especially if informed voters differ from the typical voter. When comparing correct voters' demographics and policy preferences to those of the full sample within the 2012 CES, correct voters were approximately 8 percentage points more likely to be strong partisans, 6 percentage points more likely to have incomes above $100,000, and 3 percentage points more likely to have health insurance. Likely related to these demographic differences, such correct voters were also 3 and 2 percentage points more likely to support extending President Bush's tax cuts and repealing the Affordable Care Act. At the state level, a greater percentage of correct voters favored spending cuts rather than raising taxes to balance state government budgets. If taxes were to be used to balance state budgets, correct voters were more likely to favor sales taxes instead of income taxes, when sales taxes typically are regressive and have a greater impact on low-income citizens (Tax Policy Center 2020).

Such disparities in policy preferences are significant because state legislators may have stronger electoral connections with correct voters than with the whole electorate. In chapter 7, I show that correct voters are more likely to hold their state legislators accountable than incorrect voters. This stronger electoral connection increases legislators' incentives to represent voters with different views than the broader electorate. For example, suppose correct voters are more likely to hold state legislators accountable but less likely to support legislators who pass legislation that expands public health care. In that case, legislators would have less incentive to enact such reforms, even if more voters want them.

TABLE 4.3 **Individual-level variables' relationship with voter knowledge**

Variable	Change in variable value	Differences in predicted probabilities		
		2010 CES	2012 CES	2014 CES
Family income	$30k–70k to over $100k	+0.105*	+0.072*	+0.063*
		(0.010)	(0.010)	(0.009)
Education	High school to four-year college degree	+0.161*	+0.212*	+0.201*
		(0.009)	(0.009)	(0.009)
Party extremity	Independent to strong Dem / Rep	+0.145	+0.083*	+0.117*
		(0.010)	(0.009)	(0.009)

This table reports the differences in average predicted probabilities of voters correctly identifying their state house majority party with changing variable values listed in the second column. Standard errors are in parentheses; $*p < 0.05$.

What Happens If Political Conditions and
Media Coverage Change?

Voters are more knowledgeable about state politics in states where more reporters cover that state's government. These correlations, however, do not necessarily imply that voters learn from the media. Instead, the positive relationships between statehouse reporters and political knowledge may result from media outlets hiring more reporters because audiences in certain states are already more interested in state government. Similarly, the above findings do not necessarily imply that unified government or more polarized legislatures cause voters to be more likely to know which party controls their legislatures, as voters in these states may systematically differ from voters in other states. To partly rule out these alternative explanations for the relationship between the media and political knowledge, it is helpful to examine the extent to which the same voters learn, over time, who controls their state house.

To conduct such an investigation, I conduct a panel analysis using the subset of voters who responded to both the 2010 and 2014 CES. A key advantage of a panel research design is that it permits researchers to identify better how changes in the independent variable—media coverage of the state legislature—impact changes in the dependent variable—voters' knowledge of the state legislature—while individual characteristics of voters (e.g., income or education) remain relatively fixed between the 2010 and 2014 elections. Such a research design can lead to more robust causal inferences than those found in cross-sectional studies (Visser, Krosnick, and Lavrakas 2014). Danny Hayes and Jennifer Lawless (2017) use a similar approach to show that increasing local news coverage of congressional elections led to voters being more able to rate their US House incumbent, ideologically place their congressional candidate, and express a vote preference.

The general framework of the below panel study resembles the above analyses of individual election years, but differences in the sample and variable measurement are worth consideration. Voters who participate in the CES panel have higher levels of political interest than the typical CES respondent. Less informed voters also typically drop out of panel surveys at disproportionate rates (see Hillygus and Snell 2018 for a review). For instance, on the 2014 CES, 53 percent of all voters correctly identified their state house majority party, but the comparable figure for voters within the panel is 71 percent (see online appendix for further details). Readers should then consider that panel findings shed more light on how the media shapes knowledge of the more politically engaged rather than the whole electorate.

My panel analyses focus on *changes* that occur between the 2010 and 2014 surveys. For example, the dependent variable takes a value of +1 if a voter was correct in identifying the state house majority party in 2014 but incorrect in 2010 (reflecting improved knowledge); 0 if the voter was correct or incorrect in both years (reflecting no change in knowledge); and -1 if a respondent was correct in 2010 but incorrect in 2014 (reflecting worse knowledge).[16] State-level independent variables also capture change. For example, a key independent variable of interest is the change or difference in logged newspaper reporters from 2009 to 2013. If voters learn from greater media coverage of state government, I expect that increases in newspaper reporters will increase voters' knowledge of state politics. Similarly, I account for whether there was a change from a unified to a divided government from 2010 to 2014 rather than whether there was a divided government in 2014. Again, the logic is that voters may be more likely to identify their state house majority party in 2010 under unified government, but it may be more difficult for them to identify the state house majority party in 2014 if under divided government. I also account for the degree of increase in state legislative party polarization and for whether legislative parties increased the size of their majorities. I estimate the relationship between changes in voter knowledge and these independent variables using an ordered probit regression (table A.4.3).

Panel study findings reaffirm that voters appear to update their information about the state legislature as political conditions change and that they learn more when there is more media. With the onset of unified government and when chamber majorities increase their seat shares by a standard deviation (approximately 9 percent), the probability that a voter can identify their state house majority party respectively increases by 0.073 and 0.038. Meanwhile, if a new party recently took the majority in the state house, the probability that a voter can identify this party as the majority party falls by 0.063. Voters are then not blind to state politics. In light of the increased number of states with unified legislatures with larger majorities, such statistical findings likely partly explain the observed increase in voter knowledge from 2008 to 2020 (figure 4.3). Meanwhile, findings concerning the impact of increased polarization are in the expected direction but do not meet conventional levels of statistical significance.

My panel study also helps reaffirm the media's impact on political knowledge. Increases in the number of statehouse reporters lead to voters knowing more about their state legislature. Specifically, a standard-deviation increase in the change-in-reporter variable, which is roughly equivalent to three more reporters, results in a 0.046 increase in the probability that a voter who was incorrect in 2010 became correct in 2014 or increased their knowledge. A similar change in reporters also led to a 0.028 decrease in the likelihood that a correct voter in 2010 would give an incorrect response in 2014. Together, these findings show that voters respond to the media and changes in political contexts to update their political knowledge, increasing the likelihood that voters will know who is responsible for making policy.

Is More Media the Solution to the Lack of Voter Knowledge?

Differences in media coverage across and within states are then partly responsible for differences in voters' knowledge, but even if every state made considerable increases to the size of its press corps, voters would still likely know less about their state legislature than they do about other levels of government. To illustrate this finding, figure 4.8 uses responses from the full 2014 CES sample to plot the predicted probability that a voter could identify their state house majority party if their state had different numbers of full-time reporters devoted to covering the state house (solid black line). The horizontal dashed line represents the probability that CES respondents could identify the majority party of the US House. Even if the number of reporters devoted to the state government in every state were equivalent to that of Texas—the state with the most reporters at this time—voters would still be predicted to be less likely to identify their state house majority party as they were the US House majority party.

Unfortunately for prospects for accountability, most states are unlikely to experience this type of growth in news coverage any time soon. Supplying all state capitols with Texas levels of media coverage would require more than *tripling* the number of newspaper, digital, and television reporters devoted to state government nationwide. Given that so few states have populous press corps, changing the media landscape to make these types of meaningful differences in state political knowledge is not very feasible. It would necessitate considerable resources to dramatically reverse the recent cuts to statehouse news reporting—in a time when newspaper circulation and advertising revenues declined by more than 60 percent from

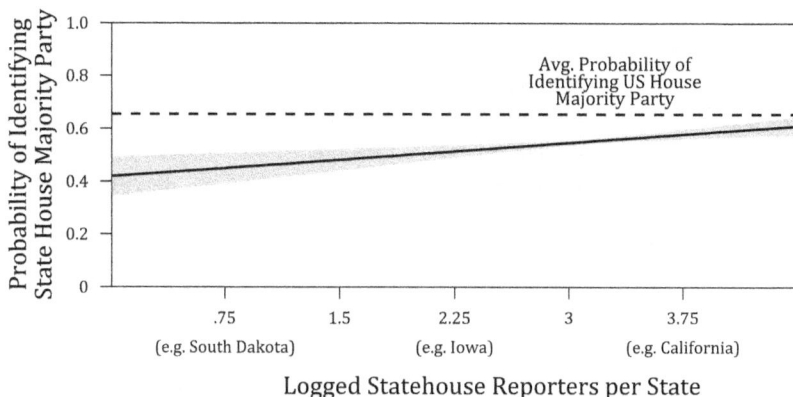

FIGURE 4.8. Predicted probability of a voter correctly identifying their state house majority party if there were different numbers of state house reporters in their state.

2001 to 2020 (Pew Research Center 2021). Such changes are then, unfortunately, unlikely achievable.

Recap

At the heart of this chapter is a fundamental question for statehouse democracy: Do voters know who represents them in the legislature? The answer is: many do not (figures 4.1, 4.2, and 4.3). This answer is troubling. When offering a defense of voters' competence, Lupia (2006, 232) makes the important point that "until critics can offer a transparent, credible, and replicable explanation of why a particular set of facts is necessary for a particular set of socially valuable outcomes, they should remain humble when assessing the competence of others." I do not claim that voters are incompetent or *must* know who their legislator is. Still, for the socially valuable outcome of holding those in power accountable, it is likely necessary that voters know their legislator's name, party, or the party that controls the legislature.

Both citizens and elites are responsible for the paltry levels of information about state politics within the American electorate. Voters seem to care relatively little about state politics. If web searches are an accurate indication of concern (figure 4.4), the founders' assertion that "the prepossessions of the people . . . will be more on the side of the State governments, than of the federal government" did not survive the test of time

(Madison 1788, *Federalist* no. 46). The founders and the political elites who followed also deserve blame for voters not knowing who is responsible for making policy. Voters more often recognize who is in power when signals are clear, such as when there is a unified state government. However, the founders constructed a complicated system with a tradition of bicameralism, where voters are also responsible for knowing who makes policy at the local, state, and federal levels. Such complexity sometimes leads voters to confuse their federal and state legislators.

The founders also stressed the media's importance for a healthy democracy. Thomas Jefferson preferred to have "newspapers without government" over "government without newspapers." Jefferson would likely be troubled by the recent decline of statehouse reporting, leading us closer to state legislatures without newspapers. The decline of the statehouse reporter is discouraging to prospects for accountability. Reporters themselves are neither a necessary nor sufficient condition for voters to "know who is responsible for making policy," as a voter's ballot or a candidate's political campaign could convey this information.[17] This chapter shows that voters are not blind to state politics and that more reporters lead to more informed voters—a result that is generally good for democracy. However, the media's impact on voter knowledge has its limits. Even if every capitol had fifty statehouse reporters, over a third of voters would still be unable to identify which party controls their legislature (figure 4.8).

Voters not knowing much about their state legislature is worrisome for accountability, but what may be more concerning is legislators' awareness of how uninformed voters are. When asked by the National Candidate Study, 49 percent of state legislators said they did not believe voters knew which party held the majority of seats in their state senate, and only 15 percent agreed with the statement that "voters know who in government to blame for policies they do not like." If most legislators do not believe voters know whom to punish for bad policymaking, what electoral incentive do legislators have to produce good policy? As the following chapters focus on the electoral implications of state legislators' and parties' own behavior, the answer again appears to be: not much.

Appendix

Predictors of Tennessee State House Knowledge

Using the May 2012 Vanderbilt poll, I investigate the relationship between individual-level and contextual variables and Tennesseans' ability to recall their state house member's name and party. I evaluate whether men, older, nonwhite, and more educated voters can identify their legislator's party more often. To account for respondents' political interests, my analyses include a measure of a respondent's strength of partisanship using a folded seven-point scale and an individual's responses to "How closely do you follow news about the Tennessee state legislature and governor?"

I also account for whether a legislator was of the same party as the voter, a freshman member, or a Republican. Main findings do not change when accounting for the specific number of years served or for whether the legislator was a member of party leadership. Legislators can also build their brand name by advertising during campaigns and position-taking during legislative sessions (Mayhew 1974). I therefore account for how much a legislator raised in campaign contributions in the previous election and for the number of bills or resolutions sponsored by the legislator from 2011 to 2012.

Findings concerning voters' knowledge of governors suggest that voters in electorally competitive states are more informed (Lyons, Jaeger, and Wolak 2013). Similarly, voters who live in a particularly Republican area may experience less state legislative electoral competition or recognize that their legislator is more likely to be Republican. My analyses, therefore, account for the district-level presidential vote share for the state legislator's party, whether the sitting state legislator faced a major-party challenger in the previous election, and how much a legislator raised in campaign contributions.

I investigate the role of the media in two ways. First, like the analyses in table 4.1, my study accounts for a survey respondent's distance from the state capital. Second, I estimate the relationship between how often a state legislator was mentioned in the four major Tennessee newspapers and their constituents' ability to recall or identify their name. Using the *Memphis Commercial Appeal, Knoxville News Sentinel, Tennessean,* and *Chattanooga Times*'s online archives, research assistants identified every Tennessee state senator or representative's newspaper mention from January 2011 to May 2012. If increased media coverage of state legislators contributes to more knowledgeable state legislative electorates, I expect a positive relationship between these variables.[18]

Statistical analyses in table A.4.1 suggest that more-partisan voters or those who report that they closely follow state government are more likely to recall their state legislator's name and party. Meanwhile, there is little evidence that increased media coverage increases voters' knowledge of who their legislators are. Neither voters who live closer to the capital nor who have state legislators mentioned more in the newspaper are more likely to recall their state legislator's name. Surprisingly, voters were less likely to recall representatives who position-take or sponsor more legislation.

Instead, there is evidence that voters are better able to identify their legislator's name if that legislator spent more on their most recent campaign and if that campaign was previously contested. Statistical analyses also suggest that increases in presidential vote share for the incumbent's party increase the probability that voters can identify their state representative's party and state legislator's name (t-statistic of difference 1.81). Similarly, voters are more likely to identify their legislator's party if she is Republican. Living in partisan districts or states then seems to help voters identify their representative's partisanship.

TABLE A.4.1 **Tennesseans' knowledge of their state legislators**

	State rep. name recall	State rep. party recall	State legislator identification
Number of newspaper mentions (logged)	-0.035	-0.008	0.041
	(0.062)	(0.054)	(0.052)
Respondent distance from capital (in hundreds of miles)	-0.044	0.062	0.117
	(0.101)	(0.079)	(0.088)
Total bills and resolutions sponsored (logged)	-0.900*	0.063	0.040
	(0.294)	(0.224)	(0.188)
Amount campaign raised (logged)	-0.011	-0.018	0.154*
	(0.101)	(0.087)	(0.057)
Seat previously contested	0.090	-0.097	0.350*
	(0.181)	(0.138)	(0.128)
District-level presidential vote for legislator's party	0.003	1.339*	1.428
	(0.870)	(0.634)	(0.789)
Republican legislator	0.040	0.597*	-0.201
	(0.248)	(0.186)	(0.236)
Freshman legislator	-0.290	0.207	-0.175
	(0.208)	(0.171)	(0.157)
Nonwhite legislator	-0.496	-0.293	-0.419
	(0.476)	(0.283)	(0.325)
Respondent follows state news	0.204*	0.401*	
	(0.075)	(0.060)	
Respondent party extremity	0.093	0.013	0.028
	(0.087)	(0.063)	(0.079)
Respondent-legislator same party	0.297*	0.691*	0.193
	(0.148)	(0.125)	(0.129)
Female respondent	-0.343*	-0.449*	-0.217
	(0.138)	(0.108)	(0.113)

TABLE A.4.1 *(continued)*

	State rep. name recall	State rep. party recall	State legislator identification
Respondent nonwhite	-0.554*	-0.092	-0.385*
	(0.244)	(0.152)	(0.189)
Respondent age	0.006	0.003	0.018*
	(0.004)	(0.003)	(0.004)
Respondent education	-0.022	0.048	0.054
	(0.038)	(0.029)	(0.030)
Constant	3.070	-2.822	-5.185*
	(2.037)	(1.554)	(1.299)
N	737	737	829
Log-likelihood	-139.9	-301.1	-346.9

This table reports the results of probit regressions in which the outcome of interest is whether a voter correctly recalled their legislator's name from a list, recalled their legislator's party, or identified their state legislator from a list. Standard errors are in parentheses; *$p < 0.05$.

TABLE A.4.2 **Summary statistics for chapters 4 and 7**

Variable	Min.	Max	Median	Mean	SD
Number of full-time reporters at statehouse (logged)	0.00	4.19	2.94	2.92	0.68
Respondent distance from capital (in hundreds of kms)	0.00	19.93	1.47	1.92	1.71
Divided state government	0.00	1.00	0.00	0.35	0.48
Majority-party size (state house)	0.50	0.92	0.63	0.63	0.08
Logged years current majority party in power (state house)	0.69	4.93	2.64	2.54	1.03
New chamber majority (state house)	0.00	1.00	0.00	0.10	0.30
Polarization (state house)	0.52	3.37	1.69	1.81	0.54
Majority-party size (state senate)	0.50	1.00	0.63	0.64	0.09
Logged years current majority party in power (state senate)	0.69	4.93	2.89	2.74	1.05
New chamber majority (state senate)	0.00	1.00	0.00	0.09	0.29
Session length (in hundreds of days)	40.00	518.30	146.97	180.66	110.94
Legislative staff per member	0.35	17.55	5.52	7.15	4.83
Legislator salary (in thousands of 2010 dollars)	0.00	236.64	56.97	78.42	57.41
Follows gov. and public affairs only now and then	0.00	1.00	0.00	0.11	0.31
Follows gov. and public affairs some of the time	0.00	1.00	0.00	0.25	0.44
Follows gov. and public affairs most of the time	0.00	1.00	1.00	0.58	0.49
Education: high school degree	0.00	1.00	0.00	0.25	0.43
Education: some college	0.00	1.00	0.00	0.24	0.43
Education: two-year college	0.00	1.00	0.00	0.10	0.30
Education: four-year college	0.00	1.00	0.00	0.25	0.43

continues

TABLE A.4.2 (*continued*)

Variable	Min.	Max	Median	Mean	SD
Education: postgrad degree	0.00	1.00	0.00	0.14	0.34
Income: $30,000–$70,000	0.00	1.00	0.00	0.41	0.49
Income: $70,000–$100,000	0.00	1.00	0.00	0.11	0.32
State population (logged)	13.24	17.43	16.07	16.01	0.89
State legislative approval	-2.00	2.00	0.00	-0.01	1.55
Presidential approval	-2.00	2.00	1.00	0.09	1.74
Party ID (7-pt)	-3.00	3.00	0.00	0.26	2.25
Democratic governor	0.00	1.00	0.00	0.46	0.50
Democratic Party seat share	0.13	0.92	0.46	0.49	0.15
Democratic state house majority	0.00	1.00	0.00	0.44	0.50
Correct state house majority party	0.00	1.00	1.00	0.55	0.50

Summary statistics of variables used in the main survey analyses in chapters 4 and 7. The online appendix provides more detail about these measures.

TABLE A.4.3 **Voter knowledge panel analyses**

	Knowledge change
Difference in reporters	2.796
	(1.548)
Difference in reporters x state population (logged)	-0.161
	(0.097)
Distance from capital	-0.011
	(0.018)
Difference in polarization	0.313
	(0.209)
Difference in divided government	-0.144[*]
	(0.035)
Difference in majority-party size	1.166[*]
	(0.274)
New majority	-0.263[*]
	(0.100)
Logged years current majority party in power	-0.092[*]
	(0.027)
Difference in session length	0.000
	(0.001)
Difference in staff	0.176[*]
	(0.037)
Difference in salary	0.001
	(0.002)
Respondent party extremity	0.076[*]
	(0.015)
Female respondent	-0.126[*]
	(0.035)
Nonwhite respondent	-0.015
	(0.047)
Age (in years)	-0.003[*]
	(0.001)
Education: high school degree	0.071
	(0.090)

	Knowledge change
Education: some college	-0.005
	(0.090)
Education: two-year college	0.208*
	(0.097)
Education: four-year college	0.050
	(0.090)
Education: postgrad degree	-0.001
	(0.090)
Income: \$30,000 — \$70,000	-0.085
	(0.051)
Income: \$70,000 — \$100,000	-0.073
	(0.053)
Income: above \$100,000	0.005
	(0.054)
State population (logged)	-0.038
	(0.054)
District size (logged)	-0.093*
	(0.041)
cut1	-3.314*
	(0.676)
cut2	-1.064
	(0.678)
N	25,101
Log-likelihood	-18,332.8

This table reports results of ordered probit regressions in which the outcome of interest is whether a voter correctly updated their information regarding which party had a majority of seats in their state house.

Samples drawn from the 2010, 2012, and 2014 Cooperative Election Studies. Standard errors are in parentheses; *p < 0.05.

CHAPTER FIVE

What Do Voters Think about in State Legislative Elections?

The previous chapters cast doubt that state legislative elections fulfill Powell's conditions for accountability. A third of state legislative incumbents win reelection without facing any opposition candidate, depriving millions of citizens of the "fair opportunity" to vote against policymakers (chapter 3). Moreover, at least 40 percent of voters do not know which party controls the state house, and fewer voters know who their legislator is, indicating that many voters do not "know who is responsible for making policy" (chapter 4). These figures shake confidence that elections create incentives for desirable policymaking in American state legislatures, but in our search for accountability, what ultimately matters is whether legislators, even if answering to poorly informed electorates, have an electoral motivation to act in their constituents' interests.

The National Candidate Study found that only 15 percent of legislators believe most voters know whom to blame for policymaking. The reality is that some voters do know whom to blame or reward. The behavior of these perhaps more exemplary voters in coordination with the challengers who run for office may be enough to create electoral incentives for good policymaking (Erikson, Wright, and McIver 1993). While the previous chapters cast a shadow on the prospects for accountability in state legislatures, they also bring to light some of the conditions surrounding elections that can promote favorable conditions for accountability. When there is a poor economy, more challengers run against incumbent state legislators, allowing voters to hold their state legislators accountable, and when more reporters are devoted to the state government, voters more often know which party controls their legislature. Hope for accountability in state legislatures then is not lost. However, optimism will be dashed if the number of "meaningful" votes in legislative elections is so paltry that legislators have little or no electoral incentives to represent their constituents.

To assess whether enough "meaningful votes" exist, chapters 6, 7, and 8 more directly focus on the relationship between voter behavior and election outcomes and address the question: do voters electorally reward or punish state legislators for their own performance? The answer to this question is yes, but electoral connections in state legislatures are underwhelming.

Before dissecting thousands of elections into dependent and independent variables for regressions in the following chapters, this chapter pumps the statistical brakes and lets voters speak for themselves about their behavior in state legislative elections. Specifically, in a survey conducted before and after the 2018 election, I asked voters what they liked and disliked about their state legislative candidates and let them freely respond. To my knowledge, this is the first nationwide survey where voters provided open-ended responses about their thoughts about state legislative elections. Voters were not forced to agree or disagree with preset categories to indicate whether they thought the economy, an issue, or partisanship was central to their decision-making in state legislative elections. Instead, they could give responses ranging from those that recognize effort (e.g., "He is willing to work hard") to those invoking ideological concerns, as when calling a Texas Democratic state legislative candidate a "brain-dead [liberal]!"

In this chapter, descriptive analyses of voters' own words and survey responses help set the stage for other questions and findings in this book. For example, chapter 6 addresses whether voters hold their state legislators individually accountable for their performance, investigating questions such as whether voters support state legislative candidates who share their ideological views, or whether voters punish legislators for unpopular roll-call votes. The present chapter begins to answer these questions by reporting how voters view their state legislative candidates' ideologies and why they liked the candidate they supported. Similarly, chapter 7 addresses whether voters hold their state legislators collectively accountable for their party's performance, similar to the idea of responsible party government. I show that state legislative parties are most likely to be held responsible for issues voters find the most important, but national politics is an even more important factor in state legislative elections. The present chapter lays the foundation for these analyses by highlighting what issues voters found most important in state legislative elections and how some voters think about federal politics when expressing their likes and dislikes of state legislative candidates.

I find that almost a third of voters do not have much opinion about any of their state legislative candidates. When asked if they could remember anything their state legislator has done for their district, over 75 percent of voters said "no" or "don't know." When describing what they like or dislike about their state legislative candidates, almost a third of voters did not have an opinion of either their Democratic or Republican candidate. Other voters referenced representation on issues, candidates' ideologies, and personal interactions with their legislators. However, more voters mentioned federal politics than knew who their state legislator was (chapter 4). An overwhelming majority of voters know state legislative Democrats are more liberal than state legislative Republicans, but less than 60 percent of voters know if their state parties are more liberal or conservative than the federal parties. Few voters having opinions—or sometimes confused opinions— about their state legislative candidates is not reassuring for the electoral foundation of statehouse democracy.

What Did You Like or Dislike about Your State Legislative Candidates?

To better understand voters' considerations in state legislative elections, I asked over six hundred voters who responded to the 2018 CES: "Was there anything in particular you liked about the [Democratic/Republican] candidate in the election for the [name of lower state legislative chamber]?" and "Was there anything in particular you disliked about the [Democratic/Republican] candidate in the election for the [name of lower state legislative chamber]?," where "Democratic/Republican" was replaced by the party they reported voting for or against. Voters could freely type responses in a text box. A team of three research assistants independently coded each response into general categories, such as whether a response mentioned a particular issue, political party, or candidate trait.

Many voters simply did not have opinions about their state legislative candidates. When asked if there was anything particular a voter liked or disliked about a candidate, the most popular response was "no" (figure 5.1, first set of bars). Specifically, 43 percent of respondents gave a "no" response when indicating their likes of a candidate, 39 percent gave a "no" response when indicating their dislikes of a candidate, and 32 percent gave a "no" response to *both* questions. If a voter were to reward or punish an individual legislator, one would presume that voters would like or dislike

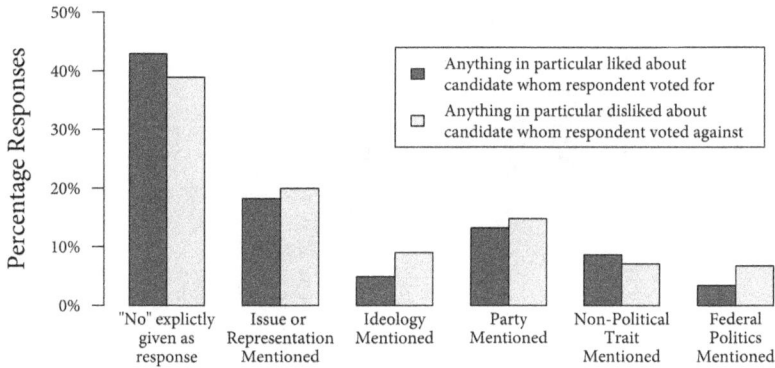

FIGURE 5.1. Percentages of subject areas voters mentioned when expressing their likes and dislikes of state legislative candidates.

something about the candidates they vote for or against, but this is not the case for a substantial number of voters in state legislative elections.

The demographics of voters who gave substantive responses to what they liked and disliked about their state legislative candidates differed from voters who gave "no" answers. As in findings from chapter 4 concerning voters who knew which party controlled their state legislature, voters who gave "no" responses had less income and education. Strong partisans were at least 10 percent more likely to identify what they liked and disliked about their state legislative candidates than weak partisans or independents, and donors to state political campaigns were 30 percent more likely to identify likes and dislikes. Similar to the takeaways from chapter 4, such findings suggest that state legislators may have a greater incentive to cater to more-affluent or more-partisan voters, as these voters are more likely to formulate opinions about state legislative candidates.

Issues

Voters often did not have much of an opinion about their state legislative candidates. Still, two-thirds gave *some* reason for liking or disliking at least one of their state legislative candidates. Over 20 percent of voters mentioned a specific issue or representation (figure 5.1, second set of bars). In a separate survey question, 5 percent of voters indicated they had contacted their state legislator within the last year "to advocate an issue position."[1] When stating their likes and dislikes of state legislative candidates,

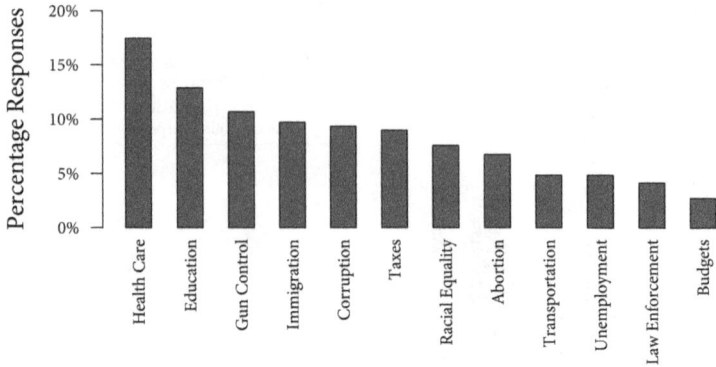

FIGURE 5.2. Percentages of issues voters identified as most important when deciding how to vote in their 2018 state legislative election.

education, health care, and taxes were the more frequently mentioned issues. One West Virginian voter stated they liked their Democratic candidate because this candidate's "views on education and healthcare align with mine." Multiple voters said they supported candidates because they were a "strong supporter of the NRA," but other voters opposed candidates because they "were anti-choice, pro-gun, and against the teachers when they were on strike here."

With some voters emphasizing health care and others highlighting the importance of gun rights, open-ended responses indicate that voters have different issue priorities. To better distinguish voters' priorities, the survey asked all voters to rate: "how important certain issues are in your decision to vote for your representative in [state legislature name]" on a scale from 0 to 100, where higher values indicate an issue is more important to a voter. When considering a predetermined set of twelve issues, voters again rated health care, education, and guns as their top issues when voting in state legislative elections (figure 5.2).[2] Voters, meanwhile, placed less priority on issues that often occupy much of state legislators' time, such as budgets or transportation/infrastructure. As discussed in chapter 7, issue importance is a critical ingredient for some of the most substantial evidence of collective accountability in state legislatures. Building on the concept of "issue publics" (Krosnick 1990b), a voter's approval of how the state legislature handled that voter's most important issue partly determines how a voter will vote in a state legislative election.

Ideology

Almost 10 percent of voters invoked ideological terms such as "conservative," "liberal," or "extremist" when indicating their likes and dislikes of state legislative candidates. Such ideological considerations are central to the assumptions that underlie theories of elections, particularly the median voter theorem. Chapter 6 walks through this theorem in greater detail, but its underlying logic again is that legislators anticipate voters will cast ballots based on the ideological proximity between the voter and the candidate. Such voter behavior theoretically encourages legislators to support policies that ideologically align with the voters' interests. Consistent with this prediction, when describing why they voted for a Republican state legislative candidate, one Republican Illinois voter stated, "He was just slightly closer ideologically to me than the Democrat."

This Republican voter's ideological reasoning for liking a state legislative candidate reflects asymmetries between Republican and Democratic voters. Focusing predominantly on federal politics, Matt Grossman and David Hopkins (2016) argue that the Republican party is more ideologically oriented, and the Democratic Party is more organized around groups. Grossman and Hopkins (2016, fig. 2.6) show that Republican voters are more likely to use ideological terms when expressing their likes and dislikes of the two major political parties. Similarly, at the state legislative level, I find that almost 15 percent of Republican voters' likes and dislikes of state legislative candidates included ideological terms. Meanwhile, less than 3 percent of Democrats and independents used ideological terms to describe state legislative candidates. Democratic voters were also more likely to mention specific "groups," but the difference between Democratic and Republican voters in this respect is less than 1 percent and does not meet conventional levels of statistical significance.

Voters' ideological characterizations of state legislative candidates also reflect Americans' rising "affective polarization," or growing dislike of those from the other party (see Iyengar et al. 2019 for a review). Five and 9 percent of voters, respectively, used ideological terms to describe the likes of the state legislative candidate they supported or dislikes of a candidate they voted against (figure 5.1). However, partisan asymmetries again emerge. Only 2 percent of Democrats used ideological terms to describe candidates they liked or disliked. Meanwhile, 9 percent of Republican voters used ideological terms to describe candidates they liked, and 20 percent of Republican voters used ideological terms to describe candidates they disliked.

One Republican respondent described a candidate for the state legislature as "[a] liberal communist democrat!" Another respondent disliked a Democratic candidate because she was a "total left wing liberal with untold amounts of money living in her castle ready to tell the plebes how to live." Some of the partisan asymmetries and affective polarization found in national politics also seem to emerge in state legislative politics.

Do Voters Know State Legislators' Ideologies?

Voters report that ideology matters when they vote for their state legislator, but these reports seem to be in tension with chapter 4's findings. If an overwhelming majority of voters do not know who their state legislator is, should one expect the typical voter to know state legislators' ideological positions?

Such a question leads to a classic "test" of voters' competence (e.g., Converse 1964, 19): placing American political candidates and parties as more liberal or conservative than one another. If voters believe state legislative Republicans are more conservative than state legislative Democrats, it provides reassurance that voters can use party labels to more meaningfully cast ideological ballots in state legislative elections. To investigate whether voters hold this knowledge, I asked voters to place their Democratic state house candidate, Republican state house candidate, state legislative Democrats, state legislative Republicans, Congressional Democrats, and Congressional Republicans on a liberal to conservative scale ranging from 0 to 100, where 100 was more conservative. Following previous tests of voter competence, I compare these placements to see if voters can accurately place the ideological positions of these parties relative to one another. Analyses in the next chapter will use these placements to study the relationship between perceived candidate ideology, voter ideology, and state legislative vote choice (table 6.1).

Providing reassurance that voters can identify differences between candidates and parties, 89.4 percent of voters placed their Republican state house candidate as more conservative than their Democratic state house candidate.[3] 91.0 percent of voters correctly identified that the Republican party was more conservative than the Democratic party in their state legislature, which is true in every state (Shor and McCarty 2011). This percentage is comparable to the 90.6 percent of voters who placed the Republican party as more conservative than the Democratic party in Congress. These percentages do not necessarily imply that voters have a comprehensive understanding of what their state legislative parties stand for. Nevertheless, they suggest that an overwhelming majority of voters recognize broad ideological differences between their state legislative parties and can make partly informed ideological decisions at the ballot box.

Knowing Democrats are more liberal than Republicans may be an easy test for voters, particularly in an era of increasingly polarized politics (figure 4.7). A more difficult test is whether voters can accurately see differences between their state and federal legislative parties. This test may be challenging in an era of nationalized state politics. In *The Increasingly United States*, Dan Hopkins (2018, 159) studies state party platforms since 1918 and shows that "state parties are increasingly talking about the same issues nationwide," often taking their cues from the national political parties (Hopkins 2018, 143; see also Paddock 2005). It then may only be reasonable for a voter who pays attention to these platforms to struggle to distinguish the ideological positions of their national and state parties. For example, Hopkins's study of voters' open-ended responses to surveys describing national and state parties shows "that voters today *perceive* the state parties as highly similar to their national affiliates" (Hopkins 2018, 168). If this is the case in state legislative politics, ideological differences between candidates and parties may get lost, limiting how meaningful ballots cast in state legislative elections are.

I find that voters' perceptions of Congressional and state legislative parties are similar but not exactly the same. When comparing a voter's placement of Congressional Democrats and their state's state legislative Democrats on 0 to 100 scales, the average absolute value of the difference was 8.7. The comparable figure for state legislative Republicans is 10.1. These differences are slightly less than half the magnitude of the standard deviation of the 0 to 100 placements measures. Voters who perceive their national party as more liberal also view their state party as more liberal. The correlation between voters' 0 to 100 placement of Congressional Democrats and their state's state legislative Democrats is 0.78. The comparable correlation for the Republican parties is 0.71.[4]

These correlations are strong but not perfect, implying that voters see some differences between their national and state parties—but how accurate are these perceptions? To answer this question, I determine whether a voter thought their state legislative Democratic (Republican) party was more liberal than the Democrats (Republicans) in Congress. I then assess these subjective evaluations' accuracy by comparing voters' perceptions to objective measures of federal and state legislators' ideologies derived from legislators' roll-call voting behavior (Shor and McCarty 2011). These roll-call measures indicate that the average California Democratic state legislator in 2018 was more liberal than the average Congressional Democrat. However, the average Alabama Democratic state legislator was more conservative than the average Congressional Democrat. With this objective information, I evaluate whether a voter who said California state legislative Democrats are more liberal than Congressional Democrats is correct. I refer to whether a voter knows this information as correctly relatively placing a political party.

Fifty-seven percent of voters knew their state legislative Democratic party was more liberal than Congressional Democrats, and 52 percent knew their state legislative Republican party was more conservative than Congressional Republicans. At first, these percentages may appear only slightly better than coin-flip guesses, but not all voters are randomly guessing, at least not when placing the Democratic party. After simulating random guesses using the true distribution of Congressional and state legislative parties' ideology, I find random guesses would have resulted in 29 percent of voters correctly relatively placing their state legislative Democratic party. Meanwhile, 50 percent of voters would have correctly relatively placed their state legislative Republican party.[5] Twenty-eight percent more voters (57 versus 29 percent) then correctly identified whether their state legislative Democrats were more liberal than Congressional Democrats than would have if they randomly guessed, which is encouraging for the prospect that voters can meaningfully cast ideological ballots. It is less encouraging that voters did not do much better than random guessing when trying to place the federal and state Republican parties (52 versus 50 percent).

Overall, only 32 percent of voters correctly placed both of their state legislative parties relative to the federal parties. All voters then again are not blind to state politics, but many voters' limited awareness of ideological differences across the federal system raises questions about how meaningful state legislators' ideologies can be in state legislative elections. If a standard for effective democracy in the American states is that voters know that Democratic state legislators are more liberal than Republican state legislators, voters appear well equipped to cast ideology-driven ballots. But if the standard is that a voter needs to recognize state legislators' ideology well enough to identify differences across levels of the American federal system, we may have some cracks in the foundation of statehouse democracy.

The Personal Vote

Ideology may not be the only reason voters like or dislike their state legislators. Despite one voter's belief that their Democratic state legislator lives in a "castle ready to tell the plebes how to live," some voters had personal connections to their elected officials. When describing the state legislative candidate they voted for, one voter expressed, "I personally know him to be an ethical, family man," and another stated, "Hard working and we know him personally. He will do a good job." Traits such as a candidate's ethics, hard work, and honesty were mentioned by at least 15 percent of voters in at least one of their responses. Nine percent of voters mentioned a nonpolitical trait when indicating what they liked about a candidate they supported, and 7 percent mentioned a nonpolitical trait when describing what they disliked about a candidate they opposed.

These characterizations relate to the classic political science concept of the "personal vote," which has its roots in political science research conducted in the 1970s by David Mayhew (1974) and Richard Fenno (1978). Fenno specifically focused on members of Congress developing a home-style or personal relationship with their constituents in their pursuit of re-election. Mayhew advanced the argument that members of Congress "credit claim" in pursuit of reelection. A member of Congress credit claims to "generate a belief in a relevant political actor [the voter] that one [the legislator] is personally responsible for causing the government ... to do something that the actor [voter] considers desirable" (Mayhew 1974, 52).

Surveys of state legislators repeatedly provide evidence that state legislators believe the personal vote is important. In 2014, the National Conference of State Legislatures asked over 1800 legislators, "How much time do you spend on each of the following activities?" Legislators could respond on a 1 to 5 scale representing "hardly at all" to "a great deal." The average response for "making sure district gets money/projects" was a 3.1, and the average score for "helping constituents with problems" was a 4.0. By comparison, the average score for "campaigning/fundraising" was only 2.6 (National Conference of State Legislatures 2017). Legislators further believe such efforts to help their districts will benefit them at the ballot box. When asked by the National Candidate Study, 76 percent of state legislators agreed with the statement, "Voters reward incumbents who deliver meaningful benefits to them and their communities, such as after a disaster or important new roads."

Some voters can identify instances where their state legislator did something for them or their district. When answering the open-ended question: "Do you happen to remember anything special that your representative in the [lower chamber name] has done for this district or people in this district while he or she has been in the state legislature? If so, what has this legislator done?" One voter indicated, "When I called his office because

I had a problem, within days it was taken care of." Another voter praised their representative for speaking about gun rights at the local high school after the Parkland school shootings in Florida. Voters also commended their representatives for bringing "development grants" or "state money" to their local communities, and when asked about their representative, one environmentally concerned voter expressed, "Small as it seems, he got us more public litter cans."

State legislators can credit claim for constituency service and even litter cans, but the above examples of voters' recalling things representatives have done for their district are more the exception than the rule. When asked if they could remember anything their representative had done for their district, 78 percent of voters explicitly answered this question "no" or with some version of "don't know." Such findings again raise concern for accountability in state legislatures. It is difficult for a voter to reward a state legislator for service to the district if an overwhelming number of voters do not know if their state legislator has done anything for their district. However, this concern assumes state legislators do things for their district, which not everyone agrees with. As put by one voter when answering the question of what their state legislator has done: "For us? Zero, zilch, Nada, Nothing! For their friends? Everything!! (At OUR Expense!)" Overall, it appears that even if state legislators attempt to cultivate a personal vote, they are not very successful.[6]

Collective Accountability and Party Balancing

Expecting voters to know what their legislators did for their districts may be too much. The optimistic authors of *Statehouse Democracy* even find it unreasonable to "expect the typical U.S. voter to respond to politicians' everyday political posturing or specific roll call votes" (Erikson, Wright, and McIver 1993, 4). As described in chapter 1, instead of evaluating individual actions, voters may instead follow a system of collective accountability, where voters hold legislators accountable for their political parties' actions. Responses from the 2018 CES support the idea that some voters think in this collective, partisan manner. Over 20 percent of voters mentioned a candidate's party at least once when expressing either a like or dislike of their state legislative candidates. When answering why they liked a Republican candidate, one voter stated: "D's won't correct the problems their policies have created. Maybe and it's a big maybe, the Republicans can undo some of it without creating a mess of their own." Similarly, when indicating why they disliked a candidate, one Democratic voter straight-forwardly stated: "He was a Republican, and the House needed to change."

When considering the role of parties in electoral accountability, most scholars focus on parties facilitating a system of responsible party government, where voters punish or reward members of a political party for bad or good performance. Such focus aligns with the perspective that elections solve a moral hazard problem and is a central focus of chapter 7. As discussed in chapter 1, an alternative view is that elections allow voters to "engage in electoral balancing—voting against the party in power in order to achieve more moderate policies" (Caughey and Warshaw 2022, 92). Again, the balancing argument is typically employed to explain the onset of divided government and why the president's party loses seats in midterm elections. Voters "balance" the party in the White House by voting against the president's party in congressional midterm elections in hopes of producing a divided federal government.

Balancing explains some election outcomes, but in a methodological aside, it is important not to interpret evidence in support of balancing—or most any other theory—as evidence that necessarily *proves* that theory. The same evidence can be consistent with multiple explanations. For example, the evidence most often presented for balancing is, again, that the president's party does worse in federal elections. One interpretation of this correlation is that voters balance or consciously vote against the president's Congressional co-partisans to create a divided government. However, this empirical finding could also be explained by different voters turning out in these elections, such as in the theory of surge and decline (e.g., A. Campbell 1960). It is then useful to take different approaches to the same question to see how much evidence there is for a particular theory.[7]

Most studies of state-level balancing, for example, very reasonably focus on election results to see if voters cast ballots against the governor's party in state legislative elections. Another approach, however, is to simply ask voters themselves if they agree with the statement: "I prefer when one political party controls the governorship and a different political party controls the legislature," which is the underlying assumption of state-level balancing. I am unaware of any study that asked voters this question, and when responding to the 2018 CES, only 13 percent of voters agreed with the statement. Among these state-level balancing voters, only 6 percent reported voting for governor and state house candidates of different parties in the 2018 election. By comparison, 10 percent of voters who said they did not prefer balancing split their tickets. However, in states without a gubernatorial election—where we should expect to see more balancing—34 percent of state-level balancers voted against the governor's party in their state house election. Meanwhile, only 19 percent of self-described non-balancers voted against the governor's party.[8] More voters then appear to balance in state midterm elections, but less than 5 percent of all voters (13 percent times 34 percent) say they will balance and actively engage in state-level balancing in these midterms. At least when asking voters themselves, state-level balancing appears to occur but is relatively rare.

It is more often argued that voters support political parties as part of a system of collective accountability that resembles responsible party government's reward-and-punishment framework. In this system, voters punish parties when they do a bad job, thereby creating incentives for political parties and their members to do good jobs. Party labels on the ballot simplify this form of collective accountability, but American federalism introduces a complication. When parties share the same brand name at the state and federal level, party labels potentially confuse voters and raise the possibility of misattribution of responsibility across levels of government, a subject addressed in greater detail in chapter 7. Recall that 18 percent of voters named a federal legislator when asked who their state legislator was (chapter 4), and more than 10 percent of voters mentioned *federal* politics when indicating what they liked or disliked about their *state* legislative candidates.

Further showing how presidential politics looms large with voters even within state legislative politics, mentions of President Trump alone exceeded the combined number of statements concerning candidates' demographics (e.g., "I love having a woman of color"), religious affiliation (e.g., "good morial [*sic*] and Christen [*sic*] man!!!"), and involvement in the local community (e.g., "yes, I personally have met the candidate and I like his policies and involvement in my community"). Some presidential mentions reflected policy or ideological concerns. One Democratic voter did not like a Republican state legislative candidate because "He supports Trump policies," and a Republican voter disliked their Democratic candidate because "She didn't back the president." However, most responses had little to do with legislators' own policy positions. When commenting on what they liked and disliked about their state legislative candidates, one voter indicated that "Donald Trump has turned me 100% against any Republican." In turn, an Ohio Republican state legislative candidate did not receive this voter's support.

Voting for or against a state legislative candidate because of what a voter thinks of President Trump is a form of collective accountability, as the behavior of a member of the Republican party in federal office has implications for a member of the Republican party in a state legislature. A concern, however, is that state legislators have little control over any president's behavior, so if a federal politician's actions determine a voter's vote in a state legislative election, what incentive do state legislators have to consider voters' interests? If state legislators are held to account for all their — even federal — party members' actions, this type of accountability does little to solve the moral hazard problem posed by representative government. Instead, it severs the electoral connection between what a state legislator does himself and his own electoral fate.

Recap and What's Next

The findings in this chapter demonstrate that some voters like or dislike something about their state legislative candidates, and most voters have some idea of their state legislative candidates' and parties' ideological positions. Unfortunately, many voters neither identify anything they like or dislike about their state legislative candidates nor remember anything their state legislator has done for their district. Lacking such information and not knowing who represents them in the legislature are seemingly substantial obstacles for voters knowing who is responsible for making policy and for elections' ability to serve as an accountability mechanism in state legislatures.

Not all voters need to know everything about their legislators for elections to provide some accountability. The following chapters more directly address the question: do voters hold state legislators accountable for their own performance? Analyses in chapter 6 study the extent to which voters hold their legislators individually accountable by studying the relationship between legislators' individual actions, such as roll-call votes, and their electoral fates. Turning the focus to collective accountability in chapter 7, I show how objective and subjective measures of performance (e.g., growth in the state economy or voters' approval of the state legislature) relate to legislative election outcomes. In chapter 8, I study how voters in primary elections respond to legislators' ideological representation and loyalty to their party.

Together, these chapters offer the most substantial evidence that legislators face electoral punishment for their representation and when voters disapprove of the legislature's performance. However, the relationships I find between how a legislator performs in office and elections are small, do not match those found at the federal level, and are too weak to meaningfully threaten most incumbents' reelection. Instead of being primarily determined by their own performance at the state house, legislators' elections are dominated by politics at the White House. So, while the analyses in the following chapters help provide a "Yes" answer to the question of whether elections hold state legislators accountable for their own performance, this "yes" answer has some serious qualifications — qualifications that cast doubt that *meaningful* electoral accountability exists in most state legislatures.

CHAPTER SIX

Accountability for Representation

"Out of Step" but Mostly Still in Office

When saying what they liked and disliked about their state legislative candidates, voters often noted the importance of candidates' issue positions (figure 5.1). It is then unsurprising that some candidates stress their stances on policy in campaigns, as was done when Democrat Betsy Holland challenged incumbent Republican Beth Beskin in the contest for the 54th Georgia state house district in 2018. Holland's campaign highlighted her own gun ownership along with concerns for Georgians' health care and infrastructure, stating, "Traffic in this town is miserable—I'm not telling you anything you don't experience every day!" (Andrews 2018). Despite most voters being unaware of who their state legislator is (chapter 4) or what their legislator does (chapter 5), at least one voter knew Holland's positions, reporting on the 2018 CES that they liked Holland because: "Betsy Holland is for gun control, wants to expand Medicaid, wants to expand infrastructure spending, etc." This voter's support helped Holland defeat the incumbent Beskin with 51.7 percent of the vote and become the first Democrat to represent Georgia's 54th state house district in over a decade.

A voter's focus on Holland's issue positions provides hope for the search for accountability in state legislatures. A central responsibility of state legislators is to represent their districts, and by supporting the candidate that agreed with her on the issues, this particular voter creates incentives for the newly elected Holland to act in the voter's interest. Otherwise, Holland risks losing her job. Across the country, other voters similarly reported on the 2018 CES that they liked their respective state legislative candidates because the candidate "was a moderate," "has a proven record of supporting issues I'm in favor of," or "has done a fine job representing her constituents." Others disliked their candidates because: "He is an extremist and isn't for the people"; the candidate voted "in favor of funding cuts to much needed programs for seniors and the poor" and "was unresponsive to constituents." Some voters then consider what individual legislators do when casting their ballots for state legislators. However, the electorate's lack of knowledge about their state legislators leaves it unclear whether enough citizens cast ballots based on how their legislator represents their district for elections to be meaningful accountability mechanisms.

In this chapter, I add clarity and investigate how election outcomes relate to three aspects of state legislators' individual performance in the legislature: state legislators' ideological representation, state legislators' decisions on single roll-call votes, and state legislators' effectiveness. Together, my analyses offer the most evidence that state legislators' individual behavior has implications for their own elections. Still, there is a lot left to be desired for accountability in state legislatures. Voters' behavior in state legislative elections relates to voters' subjective perceptions of their candidates' ideologies as well as to objective measures of ideological representation, individual roll-call votes, and effectiveness—findings that are promising for accountability. However, the strength of these district-level electoral connections is often smaller than that found in federal elections. Of greater concern, factors unrelated to legislators' own behavior, such as district partisanship and whether a legislator is a member of the president's party in a midterm election, have stronger relationships with the outcomes of legislative elections than a legislator's ideological representation of their district.

Voters are partly responsible for meager electoral connections in state legislatures, but political elites, such as challengers and the media, are again central players. Whether a challenger runs changes reelection probabilities more than do voters' responses to incumbents' representation. Additionally, when there is less media coverage, state legislators are less likely to be punished for poor representation. So, if the question is whether incumbents are held individually accountable for their legislative behavior, the answer is "Yes, electoral connections exist." But this "yes" answer deserves serious qualification.

The Median Voter Theorem

When the Republican incumbent Beth Beskin campaigned against Betsy Holland in the Georgia 54th state house district—a district where the

Democratic presidential candidate Hillary Clinton won 54 percent of the vote in 2016—Beskin stressed her "balanced perspective" and "reputation for working across the aisle and being an independent thinker" (Catts 2018). Beskin's strategy to emphasize a moderate approach reflects many state legislative candidates' beliefs about achieving electoral success. For instance, when responding to the National Candidate Study, 40 percent of state legislators said: "Moderate candidates and politicians win significantly more votes."

Both Democrats and Republicans often adopt strategies like Beskin's. When seeking the seat for the 134th Texas state house district in 2016, Democratic challenger Ben Rose told the *Houston Chronicle* that his campaign's challenge was informing voters that the incumbent Sarah Davis "is not a moderate" and "right there in lockstep with the Republican establishment" (R. Elliott 2016). Buttressing this point in a separate interview, Rose said Davis was "out of step on guns," opposed expanding Medicaid in Texas, and was "the only representative in the whole state house—with all the crazy characters that exist there—to vote against the Muslim appreciation day" (Kuffner 2016). Davis responded to Rose's comments by stating: "I always have a primary opponent who says I'm not conservative enough, and I win. And then I always have a Democrat who says I'm too conservative. And I win" (R. Elliott 2016). Ultimately the "too conservative" message did not appear to resonate as Davis—the most moderate Republican in the Texas House (Shor and McCarty 2011)—defeated Rose in the general election.

Beth Beskin stressing her "balanced perspective" or Ben Rose calling Sarah Davis "out of step" are campaign tactics emphasizing an individual state legislator's perhaps undesirable representation for a particular district. Such strategies may seem obvious even to casual observers of politics but are rooted in theories of political science, particularly the median voter theorem. The median voter theorem predicts that candidates have an electoral incentive to provide ideologically moderate representation. The theorem was notably formalized by Duncan Black (1958) but gained more attention from political scientists following Anthony Downs' (1957) book *An Economic Theory of Democracy*.

Drawing from Black's and Downs's work, the spatial model helps illustrate the logic behind the theorem. Let figure 6.1 represent a district with nine voters. For simplicity, the numbers in this figure represent voters' ideal points in a discrete policy space (e.g., a voter can take a position of 1 or 2, not 1.5). A voter will more likely support candidates with positions closer to her ideal point. For example, a voter with an ideal point

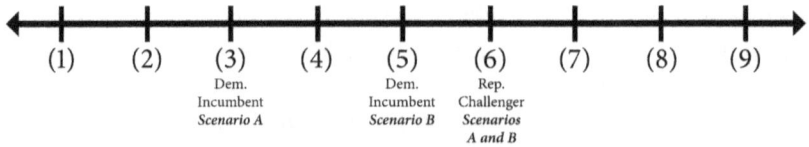

FIGURE 6.1. The above line represents a hypothetical district of nine voters with a Democrat incumbent and a Republican challenger. In Scenario A, the incumbent takes an ideological position of 3, and in Scenario B, she takes a position of 5. The Republican challenger takes the position of 6 in both scenarios.

of 3 will support a candidate who is at 4 over a candidate who is at 6. In this example, if the voter is indifferent between two candidates (i.e., the same distance from each of the two candidates), the voter will support the incumbent (e.g., for her experience). The candidate who receives the majority of votes (in this case, at least five) wins the election.

First, consider Scenario A, where a Democratic incumbent seeks re-election and has an ideological position of 3. Her Republican challenger has an ideological position of 6. If voters support the candidate whose ideal point is closest to their own, the Democratic incumbent receives the support of Voters 1 through 4, and the Republican challenger receives the support of Voters 5 through 9. With five of nine voters' support, the Republican challenger wins the election. Here, the pivotal voter is the median or middle voter: Voter 5. With the choice of an incumbent at 3 versus a less ideologically distant challenger at 6, Voter 5 supports the challenger—giving this Republican candidate the necessary fifth vote to win the election.

In Scenario A, the Democratic incumbent loses the election. However, a fundamental assumption underlying the notion that elections solve a moral hazard problem via electoral accountability is that incumbents typically do not enjoy losing. To avoid such a fate, the incumbent can change her ideological position or representation to obtain more electoral support. Now consider Scenario B, where the incumbent's ideal point is 5. As in Scenario A, Voters 1 through 4 support the Democratic incumbent, and Voters 6 through 9 support the Republican challenger. The new decision Voter 5 faces is between supporting a candidate whose ideal point is at 5 (the incumbent's new ideological position) versus 6 (the challenger's position). Voter 5 will then support the more ideologically proximate incumbent, and the incumbent receives the necessary fifth vote to be reelected.

The simple differences between outcomes for Scenarios A and B illustrate a critical theoretical point: elections can pressure the incumbent to provide representation favorable to the median voter or majority of his district. Such median voter theorem predictions underlie canonical explanations of representation and legislative behavior (e.g., Krehbiel 1998), but it is unlikely that each legislator represents the median voter in their district. Recall that thousands of state legislators represent very similar districts but provide very different types of representation (figure 1.2). At least some of these legislators must then be—to use Ben Rose's words—"out of step" (see also Canes-Wrone, Brady, and Cogan 2002). Party obligations, interest groups, and personal policy preferences may be responsible for two legislators providing different types of representation to the same type of district, but the central concern here is understanding whether elections offer enough incentive to counter these forces and encourage state legislators to represent their district.

Political scientists repeatedly find that members of Congress have such electoral incentives. Brendan Nyhan and coauthors (2012) show that members of Congress who voted for the Affordable Care Act, also called Obamacare, in the first decade of the 2000s were less likely to be reelected. Austin Bussing and coauthors (2020) similarly provide evidence that Republicans who voted to repeal and replace Obamacare in 2017 faced punishment in the 2018 elections, and Gary Jacobson (1993; 2013) shows that Democrats who supported major health care reforms or deficit reductions in the 1990s or financial reforms in the first decade of the 2000s also received fewer votes. Expanding the focus beyond individual votes to summary measures of ideological representation, Brandice Canes-Wrone and coauthors find that ideologically extreme members of the US House are less likely to be reelected (Canes-Wrone, Brady, and Cogan 2002). When employing measures of ideology based on campaign contributions instead of roll-call votes, there is evidence that levels of individual accountability have decreased in more-recent elections (Bonica and Cox 2018; Utych 2020; see also Canes-Wrone and Kistner 2020; Barber 2022). Even with these decreases, studies of Congress generally support the proposition that some degree of district-level accountability exists at the federal level.

Fewer challengers, less media coverage, and lower levels of voter knowledge (chapters 3, 4, and 5), however, create obstacles for state legislative accountability that are less present in federal elections. In turn, one cannot assume that findings from congressional elections will translate to subnational state legislatures. If such predictions do not apply to state legislative elections, it brings into question whether theories of legislative behavior predicated on an "electoral connection" or on the median voter theorem necessarily apply to state legislatures. More importantly, for American democracy, it means that legislators have little incentive to represent their constituents.

Do Voters Cast Ideological Ballots?

That voters care about candidates' ideological positions is a critical assumption that underlies the median voter theorem. Supporting this assumption at the federal level, James Adams and coauthors (2017) provide evidence that voters' subjective views of candidates' ideology relate to their vote choices in congressional elections. At the state legislative level, voters repeatedly referenced ideology when stating what they liked and disliked about state legislative candidates (figure 5.1), but to my knowledge, no research provides empirical support for the assumption that an individual voter is more likely to cast a ballot for the state legislative candidate whom they think has ideological views similar to their own.

To determine whether support for such an assumption exists, I follow prior work on Congress (Adams et al. 2017) and evaluate how voters' perceptions of their own ideology and state legislative candidates' ideologies relate to vote choice (see chapter 5 for detail about these ideological placements). Specifically, I subtract the absolute distance between a voter's self-placed ideology and their perception of their Republican candidate's ideology from the absolute distance between the same voter and their Democratic candidate to create a *relative ideological-distance* measure. As an example, if the voter placed herself at 50, the Democratic candidate at 35, and the Republican candidate at 60, the distance between the voter and the Democratic candidate is 15; the distance between the voter and the Republican candidate is 10; and the difference of these distances is 5, where the voter is closer to the Republican candidate than the Democratic candidate. This distance measure grows when a voter becomes more ideologically distant from their Democratic candidate compared to their Republican candidate.[1]

I then estimate the relationship between a voter's support for a Democratic candidate in their state house election and their relative ideological distance (table 6.1). To support the presumptions underlying the median voter theorem, the voter should be less likely to support the Democratic

TABLE 6.1 **Voters' perceived representation and vote choice**

	Candidate distance	Party distance	Candidate and party distance
Relative Ideological Distance — candidates	−0.031*		−0.021*
	(0.005)		(0.004)
Relative Ideological Distance — state parties		−0.015*	−0.001
		(0.005)	(0.004)
Party ID (7-pt)	0.525*	0.351*	0.312*
	(0.066)	(0.071)	(0.082)
Change in annual log of state real disposable income	2.474	−2.546	−0.993
	(4.417)	(6.646)	(7.270)
Presidential approval		0.435*	0.386*
		(0.093)	(0.098)
Governor approval		0.291*	0.243*
		(0.096)	(0.089)
State legislative approval		−0.037	0.025
		(0.121)	(0.123)
Female respondent	−0.264	−0.227	−0.346
	(0.247)	(0.186)	(0.230)
Nonwhite respondent	0.423	0.523*	0.525*
	(0.218)	(0.208)	(0.257)
Age (in years)	0.003	0.010	0.006
	(0.006)	(0.007)	(0.007)
Education: high school degree	0.462	0.537	0.568
	(0.457)	(0.478)	(0.571)
Education: some college	0.432	0.270	0.326
	(0.452)	(0.472)	(0.515)
Education: two-year college	0.421	0.465	0.406
	(0.339)	(0.357)	(0.419)
Education: four-year college	0.402	0.500	0.434
	(0.391)	(0.487)	(0.488)
Education: postgrad degree	0.462	0.208	0.218
	(0.378)	(0.372)	(0.424)
Income: $30,000 — $70,000	0.243	0.546	0.327
	(0.247)	(0.343)	(0.359)
Income: $70,000 — $100,000	1.243*	1.131*	1.326*
	(0.463)	(0.452)	(0.517)
Income: above $100,000	−0.083	0.461	0.145
	(0.312)	(0.368)	(0.400)
Session length (in hundreds of days)	0.001	0.002*	0.001
	(0.001)	(0.001)	(0.001)
Legislative staff per member	−0.010	−0.051	−0.029
	(0.028)	(0.030)	(0.037)
Legislator salary (in thousands of 2010 dollars)	0.004*	0.005*	0.004
	(0.002)	(0.002)	(0.003)
District size (logged)	−0.260	−0.152	−0.251
	(0.168)	(0.178)	(0.197)
Constant	2.218	−0.054	1.705
	(1.812)	(1.783)	(2.004)
N	516	593	504
Log-likelihood	−73.9	−73.6	−60.1

This table reports probit regression results in which the outcome of interest is whether a voter supported the Democratic state house candidate. Sample drawn from the 2018 Cooperative Election Studies. Standard errors are in parentheses; *$p < 0.05$.

candidate as this distance grows. Analyses additionally account for a voter's partisanship, race, age, gender, education, and income, and for growth in the state's economy. My models also include a voter's approval of the state legislature, governor, and president, subjects related more to collective accountability, which I more fully discuss in chapter 7.[2]

The coefficient on the relative ideological-distance measure is of central interest in supporting the assumption that legislators' ideology relates to vote choice. It captures the relationship between vote choice and voters' perceptions of state legislators' ideology. The negative sign on this coefficient indicates that as voters perceive themselves to be more distant from the Democratic candidate than the Republican candidate, voters become less likely to vote for the Democratic candidate (table 6.1, first column). Such behavior creates incentives for state legislators to ideologically represent more voters, as was the case when moving from Scenario A to Scenario B in the above explanation of the median voter theorem. We see a similar pattern in voters' reported behavior when only considering a voter's perceived distance from the state parties. Voters who perceive themselves to be more distant from the state legislative Democratic party than the state legislative Republican party are less likely to vote for the Democratic candidate (table 6.1, second column).

Voters, however, appear to care more about their perceived ideology of candidates rather than their perceived positions of state parties' ideology. To illustrate this, I conduct an analysis that considers a voter's relative ideological distance from both their state legislative candidates and parties (table 6.1, third column). Using these estimates, figure 6.2 shows the predicted probability of a voter supporting a Democratic candidate as they become ideologically distant from either the candidates (solid line) or state parties (dashed line). If there is no difference between how a voter perceives the ideological positions of the Democratic and Republican candidates (figure 6.2, zero point on the x-axis), the predicted probability of a voter supporting a Democratic state house candidate in the 2018 election—which was the best election year for Democrats in a decade—was approximately 0.580. However, if this same voter perceived the Democratic candidate to be 10 points more conservative on the 0 to 100 scale, this voter would become 0.027 less likely to support the Democratic candidate (figure 6.2, solid line). This is less than half the impact of a voter identifying as a "Republican" rather than a "strong Republican."[3] Meanwhile, there is little if any relationship between vote choice and a voter's relative ideological distance from their state parties (figure 6.2,

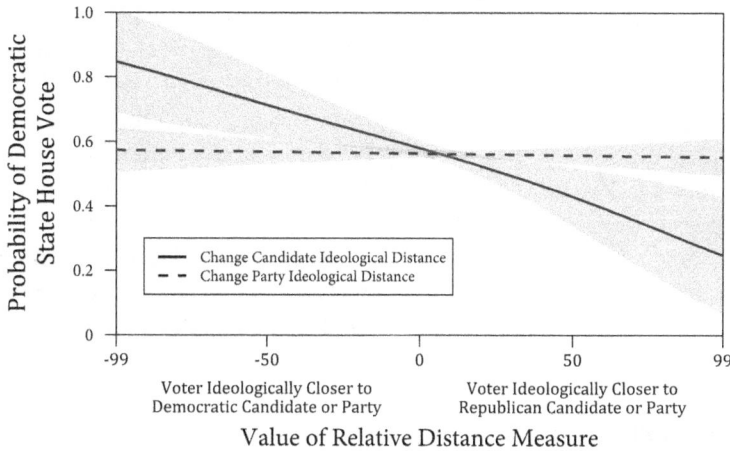

FIGURE 6.2. Predicted probability of a voter supporting a Democratic state house candidate associated with the perceived ideological distance between the voter and their state legislative candidates or parties.

dashed line) when we also account for state legislative candidates' ideology. This result is similar to Hopkins's finding that state party ideology has little relationship with gubernatorial election outcomes (Hopkins 2018, fig. 7.8).

That voters are more likely to report voting for candidates they perceive to be ideologically proximate to them is good news for the search for individual accountability in state legislatures. In another methodological aside, it is again important to recognize the limitation of surveys and reconsider the extent to which voters' reported perceptions of state legislative candidates are accurate. Recall that less than a third of voters could correctly place both of their state legislative parties relative to the federal parties (chapter 5). Political science research additionally shows that voters often "project" their own views onto the perceptions of candidates they like or support (Achen and Bartels 2016, ch. 10; Conover and Feldman 1982; Granberg and Brent 1980; see also Krosnick 1990a). In projection, a voter first chooses a candidate to support, then "projects" their (the voter's) ideology onto the candidate, and finally decides what this candidate's ideology is. If this is the case, the correlation between vote choice and ideological distance then may exist because vote choice impacts the perception of a candidate's ideology and not because ideological distance impacts vote choice.

Fully unpacking the implications of projection on analyses of survey data is beyond this book's scope, but I encourage readers to consider biases when reading this or other work. Measurement poses difficulties for all scientists. Such challenges are why this and the following chapters include analyses where the key independent variables are measured subjectively by looking at voters' beliefs (e.g., voters' views of candidates' ideology or their approval of the legislature) and objectively (e.g., roll-call votes or state economic growth). Few—if any—variables will be perfectly measured or without bias, but my aim is to provide a thorough search for accountability in state legislatures with the best measures we have.

Accountability for Ideological Representation

Voters appear to act upon their beliefs about candidates' ideology. However, voters' perceptions of state legislative politics do not always reflect reality (chapter 5), leading to the question: does state legislators' actual ideological representation have implications for their elections? To better establish whether such an electoral connection exists, I expand upon my and others' research (Rogers 2017; Birkhead 2015; Hogan 2008; Caughey and Warshaw 2022) and evaluate the relationship between objective measures of ideological representation and election outcomes. To objectively measure ideological representation, I again use legislators' estimated ideological distance from their districts, as described in chapter 2. Following the assumptions underlying the median voter theorem, I expect that as the ideological distance between a legislator and their constituency grows, a legislator should experience less electoral success. Also as discussed in chapter 2, research on US House elections additionally finds evidence that voters both reward and punish legislators for voting with their party more (Carson et al. 2010). To assess whether voters exhibit such behavior to punish state legislators for such "party loyalty," my statistical models include a measure of the percentage of votes in which a legislator voted with a majority of their party.

My analyses also build on previous chapters' findings to better understand elites' role in the accountability process. I describe these analyses in greater detail below, but in a brief preview, I first follow chapter 3's findings and examine the extent to which the likelihood of incumbents winning reelection is attributable to challenger versus voter behavior. Second, I build on chapter 4's findings and investigate how the number of reporters covering state government associates with the extent to which voters reward and punish legislators.

For my statistical models, the conceptual dependent variable of interest is election outcomes, which I empirically measure in two different ways. First, I evaluate the relationship between representation and vote share (table A.6.1). Second, I assess the relationship between representation and reelection (table A.6.2), as some incumbents may care little if they receive 51 percent or 91 percent of the vote, as long as they keep their job (Milyo 2001). Each analysis focuses on districts where an election only elected a single legislator across forty-eight states from 2001 to 2020. When studying the relationship between representation and vote share, I only focus on races where the incumbent faced a major-party challenger, and I estimate a linear, multilevel model with fixed effects for years and random effects for states. To study the relationship between representation and reelection, I examine all races where the incumbent sought reelection and survived the primary but conduct separate analyses of races where the incumbent faced a major-party challenger. For my reelection analyses, I estimate a probit model with random effects for states.

Losing Votes for Ideological Representation

Returning to the Georgia 54th state house district, Betsy Holland edged incumbent Beth Beskin by less than 2 percent of the vote. A slight shift in vote share could then have changed who won this electoral contest. Promising for the health of statehouse democracy, good representation appears to increase incumbents' electoral success, albeit to a small degree. State legislative incumbents, on average, receive approximately 62 percent of the vote when seeking reelection against a challenger. If an incumbent's estimated ideological distance increases by a standard deviation, predicted incumbent vote share would fall by approximately 0.81 percent, all else equal (table 6.2, first row). As detailed below, this change in incumbent vote share is far smaller than the 6.6 percent vote-share change associated with a 13 percent change in district partisanship (table 6.2, fifth row). Still, it is larger than the 0.32 percent vote-share change associated with an incumbent whose campaign raises $100,000 instead of $75,000 when their challenger only raises $50,000 (table 6.2, sixth row). Although there are diminishing impacts for increasingly unrepresentative behavior, as indicated by the *ideological distance squared* variable's negative coefficient in table A.6.1. Increasing ideological distance by one standard deviation

TABLE 6.2 **Predicted changes in incumbent vote share and probability of reelection**

Variable	Change in variable value	Change in incumbent vote share *Contested races*	Change in probability of reelection *All races*	Change in probability of reelection *Contested races*
Ideological distance	Increase of 1 standard deviation	−0.806* (0.046)	−0.011* (0.001)	−0.014* (0.002)
Party loyalty	Increase of 13 percent	0.066 (0.060)	+0.005* (0.001)	+0.003 (0.002)
Democratic woman legislator	Man to woman	−0.400* (0.123)	−0.006 (0.003)	−0.006 (0.006)
Republican woman legislator	Man to woman	+0.652* (0.139)	−0.004 (0.003)	−0.003 (0.005)
District partisanship	Increase of 13 percent	+6.632* (0.053)	+0.017* (0.001)	+0.024* (0.001)
Campaign fundraising advantage	Increase of $25,000	+0.323* (0.008)		+0.000* (0.000)
Reporters	Increase of 12 reporters	+0.420* (0.142)	−0.001 (0.002)	+0.002 (0.003)

This table shows differences in incumbent vote share or probability of reelection associated with changing the variable value listed in the second column. Standard errors are in parentheses; *$p < 0.05$.

decreases vote share by 0.81 percent, but a three-standard-deviation increase results in a predicted loss of approximately 0.92 percent.

My analyses also suggest that voters' perceptions of representation differently impact the electoral prospects of men and women legislators. Recall that voters sometimes perceive women politicians to be more liberal (e.g., McDermott 1997; see chapter 2 for more discussion), which could influence their electoral prospects. Similar to some studies of US House elections (see Lawless 2015 for a review), I do not find that women legislators receive fewer votes than men legislators, all else equal. However, there are important differences by party. Democratic women state legislators receive 0.40 percent fewer votes than their Democratic men counterparts. Meanwhile, Republican women legislators receive 0.65 percent more votes than their Republican men counterparts, all else equal. Such behavior is consistent with the general prediction that voters will electorally reward more "moderate" incumbents, as they are voting against women Democrats, who voters may think are more liberal in an already more liberal party. And they are more likely to support women Republicans, who voters may think are more liberal in the more-conservative party.

Voters appear to respond to incumbents' representation, both perceived and actual. But is this a satisfying amount of accountability? An empirical benchmark for accountability in state legislatures laid out at the beginning of this book was whether electoral connections in state legislatures matched that found in Congress. To contrast accountability across subnational and national legislatures, I create comparable ideological-distance measures for state legislators and US House members and relate these measures to incumbent vote share.[4] These analyses are similar to those above but only account for variables common to Congress and state legislatures (e.g., district-level presidential vote but not state legislative professionalism).

The dashed and solid lines in figure 6.3 respectively indicate a US House or state legislative incumbent's predicted vote share for different levels of representation. Moving from the left to the right of this figure reflects worsening representation on the part of incumbents. Consistent with prior comparisons of the incumbency advantage (J. M. Snyder Jr. and Ansolabehere 2002), incumbents' predicted vote shares are higher in federal elections, and consistent with prior work on accountability, legislators who provide worse representation do worse in elections. Moving from the left to the right of figure 6.3, a standard-deviation change in ideological distance results in a 1.13 percent change in Congressional vote share, and a two-standard-deviation change results in a 1.88 percent change in vote share. These changes are similar in magnitude to the findings of other

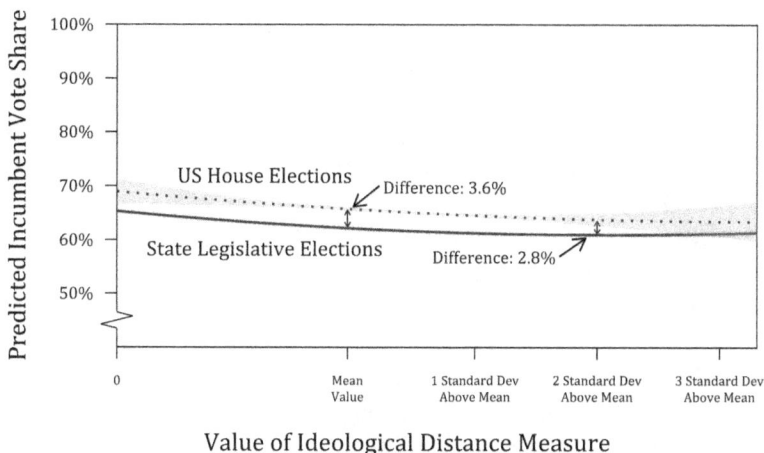

Value of Ideological Distance Measure

FIGURE 6.3. Predicted vote share for US House and state legislative incumbents as incumbents provide worse representation of their districts (moving from left to right along the x-axis).

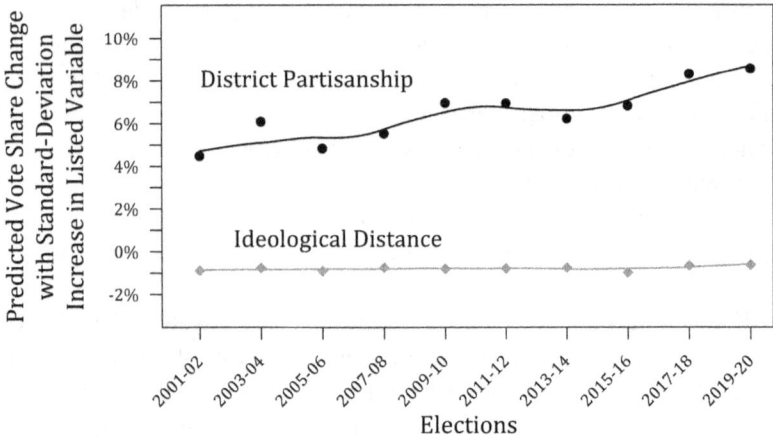

FIGURE 6.4. Predicted differences in vote share associated with a standard-deviation change in the ideological-distance or district-partisanship measures.

recent studies of congressional elections (e.g., Tausanovitch and Warshaw 2018).[5] Meanwhile, comparable changes in state legislative representation result in more minor 0.86 and 1.19 percent changes in vote shares, respectively. Neither members of Congress nor state legislators pay a substantial price for poor representation, but the price is higher in Congress. Such differences between federal and state elections are not encouraging if our accountability benchmark is electoral connections found in congressional elections. But if we have a lower standard, we may be okay.

Political scientists debate whether there has been a decline in the levels of individual accountability in US House elections (Bonica and Cox 2018; Utych 2020; Canes-Wrone and Kistner 2020). When studying state legislative elections, I find little evidence of a substantial decline from 2001 to 2020. To illustrate this, I reconduct the analyses presented in the first column of table A.6.1 but do so separately for pairs of election years (i.e., 2001 to 2002 or 2003 to 2004). The grey diamonds in figure 6.4 represent the predicted change in incumbents' vote share associated with a standard-deviation change in the ideological-distance measure. The grey line represents the loess curve for these predictions, each of which is statistically distinguishable from zero. In no election does a standard-deviation change in ideological distance result in a predicted vote-share change of greater than 1 percent.

In addition to incumbents' individual behavior, voters appear to respond to state-level conditions in state legislative elections. For example, consistent with prior findings concerning state-level balancing, the governor's state legislative co-partisans receive approximately 0.30 percent fewer votes than legislators unaffiliated with the governor's party (t-statistic of difference 1.93).[6] Meanwhile, there is little evidence that legislators who oversee weak economies receive fewer votes on Election Day, even when only considering legislators affiliated with the state house majority or governor's parties (see online appendix). Such findings indicate that state legislators who are members of the parties in power in state government have limited electoral incentives to stimulate the state economy.

Losing Reelection: Challengers or Voters?

The above representation findings are the most substantial evidence that I am aware of that state legislators' individual behavior matters for how many votes they receive at the ballot box. However, are these changes in vote share meaningful enough to determine who represents Americans in state legislatures? Again, returning to the contest for the 54th Georgia state house district, where the margin of victory was 1.7 percent of the vote, Beskin's estimated ideological distance was slightly better than the national average (0.68 versus 0.72). If her ideological distance had been a standard deviation lower, her predicted vote share would have increased by 1.2 percent, edging her closer—but still 0.5 percent away from victory.[7] A typical change in representation would then have not changed the outcome of this particular race. If Beskin's ideological distance had been 0, reflecting "perfect" representation, her vote share would have increased by approximately 2.5 percent, which would have been enough to secure her reelection to the 54th District.

This Georgia example shows that voters can threaten an incumbent's reelection prospects. Still, a legislator is unlikely to provide perfect representation, and few state legislative contests are decided by less than 1.7 percent of the vote. From 2001 to 2020, reelection-seeking state legislative incumbents, on average, received approximately 62 percent of the vote when facing a challenger and were successful in 91 percent of general elections (figure 2.1).[8] Together, healthy election margins but small losses in voter share raise the questions: Does ideological representation impact legislators' actual reelection instead of just vote share? And if so, how worried should unrepresentative incumbents be about losing their jobs?

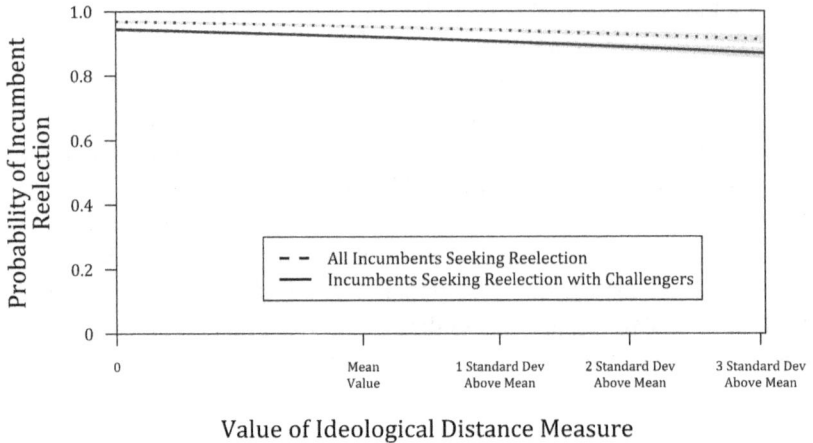

FIGURE 6.5. Predicted probability of state legislative incumbents' reelection in all races and in races with a challenger, as incumbents provide worse representation of their districts (moving from left to right along the x-axis).

Promising for accountability, the answer to the first question is: yes. More concerning for accountability, the answer to the second question is: not very worried. To illustrate these findings, the dotted line in figure 6.5 plots the predicted probability of an incumbent being reelected (y-axis) at different levels of ideological distance (x-axis) across all races where the incumbent appeared in the general election (see table A.6.2 for estimates). Moving from the left to the right of figure 6.5—which reflects incumbents providing worse representation—the dotted line indicates that an incumbent's probability of reelection falls as he provides worse representation. Across the 2001 to 2020 elections, a standard-deviation increase in ideological distance reduces the probability of an incumbent winning reelection by 0.011, and a three-standard-deviation increase reduces this probability by 0.038.[9]

Unrepresentative incumbents having lower reelection probabilities is additional evidence that there is some accountability in state legislatures for ideological representation. However, remembering what we learned in previous chapters, other political actors potentially influence these estimates. For example, challengers' responses to ideological representation may play a more substantial role in election outcomes than voters' responses. To help us understand how challengers may be more

responsible than voters, consider two scenarios. In the first scenario, all
incumbents face a challenger, but voters randomly cast their ballots. Here,
every incumbent—regardless of their representation—should have the
same likelihood of reelection. In a second scenario, less representative
incumbents more often faced challengers, as we know is the case (figure 3.4), and voters again randomly cast their ballots. In this second scenario, less representative incumbents will be more likely to lose because
they were the ones more likely to face a challenger. Voters likely do not cast
random ballots, but the second scenario indicates that challenger rather
than voter behavior can explain the decreasing dashed line in figure 6.5.

To partly disentangle the extent to which unrepresentative incumbents
lose reelection is due to challengers' versus voters' behavior, I reconduct
my analyses (table A.6.2, column 1) but only consider races where the
incumbent faced a challenger (table A.6.2, column 3). Unsurprisingly,
the average predicted probability of incumbent reelection is lower when
considering contested races (figure 6.5, solid line) instead of all races
(figure 6.5, dotted line). However, the predicted probability of reelection
decreases at an ever-so-slightly-greater rate when only considering races
with challengers compared to races with and without challengers. When
considering all races, a standard-deviation increase in ideological distance
associated with a 0.011 decrease in the probability of incumbent reelection. When only considering races with a challenger, the comparable decrease in probability is 0.014. If voters randomly cast their ballots, there
should be no difference between these two probabilities, but this slight
0.003 difference at least suggests voter behavior could contribute to the
increased likelihood of the defeat of unrepresentative incumbents, albeit
to a statistically uncertain and small degree. This difference, however, is
far smaller than the 0.034 increase in the probability that an incumbent
faces a challenger associated with a standard-deviation change in ideological distance (table 3.1). Voters then respond some to legislators' representation, but a key reason why unrepresentative state legislators lose
on Election Day is that challengers decide to run against unrepresentative
legislators more often, giving voters "a fair opportunity to cast a meaningful vote for or against the policymakers."

Balancing and District Partisanship

While political elites' decisions are important for accountability in state
legislatures, most voters' behavior is certainly not random. If voters cast

random ballots, there should be no difference between the impact other variables have on reelection probabilities when considering all races (table A.6.2, first column) versus contested races (table A.6.2, third column). For example, the impact of a 13 percent change in district partisanship on incumbent reelection grows from 0.017 to 0.024 when considering contested races instead of all races (table 6.2, fifth row). Similarly, in federal midterm elections, members of the president's party are 0.077 more likely to lose in contested races but only 0.052 more likely to lose in all races. These differences suggest that incumbents who lose in partisan districts and during federal midterm elections are not just losing because challengers run against them but because voters are helping kick them out of office.

Voters' behavior may not be random, but the above comparisons suggest voters respond to national politics when voting in state legislative contests. Such nationalization is not unique to state politics. Recall, Gary Jacobson (2021, 503, fig. 4; 2015) documents the "extremely close connection between presidential and congressional voting," where the bivariate correlation between district-level congressional and presidential vote is 0.80 in the 2000 election and 0.95 in the 2016 election.[10] There is a similar but less substantial strengthening of the relationship between presidential vote and ballots cast in state legislative elections. When examining all contested state legislative races, the correlation between the district-level vote for the state legislature and president was 0.72 in the 2000 election. Meanwhile, the comparable correlation in 2016 was 0.84.[11]

To more systematically understand how the relationship between district partisanship and vote choice has changed, it is useful to return to the above analyses that examine pairs of election years separately. The black dots in figure 6.4 represent the predicted change in state legislative incumbents' vote share associated with a 13 percent or standard-deviation increase in the district-level presidential vote for the incumbent's party. In the 2001–2002 elections, a standard-deviation increase in presidential vote resulted in a 4.5 percent predicted change in incumbent vote share. However, in the 2019–2020 elections, a similar increase in the presidential vote is associated with an 8.6 percent predicted change in incumbent vote share.[12] In light of evidence that voters' partisanship at the federal and state levels are increasingly aligned (Caughey and Warshaw 2022; Hopkins 2018), such findings suggest that the role of voters' more nationalized partisanship has almost doubled in twenty years.

National influences again emerge when considering whether voters engage in "federal-state balancing" in state legislative elections. In the

2001 to 2010 federal midterm elections, a president's-party state legislative incumbent received approximately 0.7 percent less vote share than
an incumbent unaffiliated with the president's party. In the 2011 to 2020
elections, the comparable difference grew to 4.5 percent. Returning to
Georgia's 54th District, the negation of this midterm "punishment" and
the associated predicted 4.5 percent swing in vote share would have been
more than enough to keep the Republican Beskin in office. Instead, she
was sent home on Election Day.

There are multiple explanations for why the president's party does
worse in midterm elections. However, the most common explanations do
little to instill confidence that this type of voter behavior is good for accountability in state legislatures. For example, more-partisan voters may
turn out in midterm elections (e.g., A. Campbell 1960). Such an explanation only underscores partisanship's importance for state legislative
elections, but legislators have little control over whether an election is in
the midterm. Another explanation is that voters are trying to balance the
federal and state levels of government (e.g., Erikson, Folke, and Snyder
2015), but balancing is also potentially troublesome for solving the moral
hazard problem posed by representative government, as when an election
occurs and which party occupies the White House are out of a state legislator's hands. Altogether, it is concerning that whether an election takes
place in the presidential election year or the *federal* midterm ultimately
appears to be one of the most significant factors for *state* legislators' electoral fates, at least in my judgment.

The Media Shining Light on Ideological Representation

Accountability for state legislators' representation is relatively weak (e.g.,
figure 6.3), but how can it be improved? As documented in my prior work
(Rogers 2017), the relationship between legislators' representation and
their vote shares is more pronounced in more-competitive districts, such
as those where the incumbent's party received less than 60 percent of the
vote. Findings are similar when examining elections from 2001 to 2020.[13]
Returning to Powell's requirements for accountability, more challengers
are another solution to provide more accountability, as they give voters
more fair opportunities to hold their legislators responsible for poor representation. Powell also posits that for accountability to exist, voters must
know who is responsible for making policy, and to increase voters' knowledge, we again can look to political elites. Recall chapter 4 shows that
voters are more informed about their state legislature in states with more

media devoted to state politics, suggesting media coverage is a potential solution to the meager amount of accountability in state legislatures.

Drawing from what we know about congressional elections, the media can impact legislative elections in at least two ways. First, the media helps legislators establish a personal vote with their districts, and second, the media brings poor representation to voters' attention. Focusing on the former and as discussed in chapter 5, the legislators could build their "personal vote" through activities such as "credit claiming" or "position-taking." Snyder and Stromberg (2010, 359), for example, posit that representatives who are covered more by local media may "have a greater incentive to work for their constituency, for example, by considering constituency (rather than party or personal) interest in voting and by engaging in pork barrel politics." Consistent with this expectation, Snyder and Stromberg find that when a greater proportion of a newspaper's readership is in a Congressional district, which relates to how much that newspaper covers a particular member of Congress, the incumbency advantage for that member of Congress increases (see also Canes-Wrone and Kistner 2020; Cohen, Noel, and Zaller 2011; Peterson 2019; Prior 2006). The media also appears to play a helping hand in getting state legislative incumbents more votes. For each additional twelve reporters in a state, incumbents' predicted vote shares increase by approximately 0.26 percent (table A.6.1, second column). The impact of the media, however, appears to have decreased over time. From 2001 to 2010, an additional twelve reporters associated with a predicted 0.51 increase in incumbent vote share (t-statistic of difference 1.77), but from 2011 to 2020, twelve additional reporters associated with a 0.20 increase in incumbent vote share (t-statistic of difference 0.95).

The media, on average, increases incumbents' vote shares, but does the media help voters hold ideologically unrepresentative incumbents accountable? The answer to this question again appears to be that the media's impact has diminished in more-recent elections. The second column of table A.6.1 presents statistical analyses where I estimate ideological distance's relationship with vote share conditional on the number of reporters devoted to covering state government and a state's population, and the online appendix presents comparable analyses for the 2001 to 2010 and 2011 to 2020 time periods. Using these analyses, table 6.3 presents predicted changes in vote share associated with a standard-deviation change in ideological distance. The first row of this table presents these predicted changes in vote share if every state had two statehouse reporters, as was the case in South Dakota in 2013. The second row of this table

TABLE 6.3 **Predicted change in vote share in states with different numbers of reporters**

	2001–2010	2011–2020	2001–2020
2 reporters	0.163	−0.970*	−1.286*
	(0.307)	(0.321)	(0.176)
43 reporters	−2.189*	−0.740*	−0.695*
	(0.350)	(0.158)	(0.126)

This table reports the predicted change in vote share associated with a standard deviation increase in the ideological-distance metric when there are different numbers of reporters in a state.

presents predicted changes in vote share if every state had forty-three statehouse reporters, as was the case in California in 2013.

When focusing on the 2001 to 2010 elections, I find that a state legislator faces little—if any—electoral punishment for poor representation when there are only two reporters in a state. However, when there are forty-three reporters, a standard-deviation increase in ideological distance associates with a 2.2 percent loss in vote share, all else equal (table 6.3, first column). Such findings suggest reporters were critical for individual accountability in state legislative elections during this decade. However, when we turn to elections from 2011 to 2020, reporters appear to make a negligible difference in whether voters hold their legislators accountable. If every state had either two or forty-three reporters, a standard-deviation increase in ideological distance associated, respectively, with a 1.0 or 0.7 percent loss in vote share, all else equal (table 6.3, second column). The differences of these differences are not statistically distinguishable from zero, but together these estimates suggest that increases in reporters, at least in terms of number, have not meaningfully promoted individual accountability in more-recent elections.[14] Findings are similar when only focusing on newspaper reporters instead of all reporters, suggesting that the transition to more nonprofit or digital news outlets (see chapter 4 for discussion) is unlikely responsible for this decline (see online appendix). Overall, it appears that the media is becoming a less promising solution to remedy the low levels of individual accountability in state legislatures.

Accountability for Individual Roll-Call Votes

The above tests of the median voter theorem's important prediction provide some, but not overwhelming, evidence that ideologically representative state legislators will do better in elections. Instead of caring whether their representative is too liberal or too conservative, Americans may be concerned about an individual legislator's specific votes or how effective a legislator is. When asked what they liked or disliked about their state legislative candidates, over twice as many respondents to the 2018 CES mentioned a specific issue rather than their candidates' overall ideology. Hoping to capitalize on such concerns in the 54th Georgia state house district, Holland criticized the Georgia state legislature for passing HB 918, which lowered state income taxes. However, Beskin repeatedly highlighted her support of HB 918 along with her opposition to guns on college campuses, telling a local Atlanta newspaper: "I've voted each vote deliberately and after much thought. I made sure I voted for the best interest of all of my constituents" (Ruch 2018).

Beskin's expressed concerns for constituents' views are not unique, particularly when legislators take votes on more-salient issues. One such issue that frequented state legislative agendas in the first two decades of the 2000s was the question of how to define marriage (National Conference of State Legislatures 2015). For instance, in 2009, most Maine Democratic legislators supported a bill legalizing same-sex marriage (LD 1020), and Republicans opposed the bill. However, a few legislators broke party lines to vote with what they thought were their constituents' views on this policy matter. Republican Senator Christopher Rector supported the bill, and on the day of the vote, spoke extensively about how he "tried to listen as carefully and as thoughtfully as possible" to his Senate district, stating:

> In the end the constituent responses that I have received are overwhelmingly on one side of this issue and I believe my first responsibility is to reflect the views of the vast majority of my constituents. As the Senator from Knox County, I will therefore be casting my vote in favor of L.D. 1020. (Maine State Legislature 2009)

Democratic Senator Troy Jackson took a similar approach when deciding how to vote on same-sex marriage. When LD 1020 was introduced, Jackson told the *Ellsworth American*: "I'm undecided right now . . . I've got to hear from my constituents" (Ouellette 2009). After listening to constituent opinion, Jackson explained his nay vote on the Senate floor:

> I said this before, this vote for me was extremely tough. It's something I've worried about since before we even got in here. I voted the way I did and I have

to live with that. As the Senator from Knox, Senator Rector, said, he voted the way with his constituents, a majority of them, did and I vote the way I thought the majority of my constituents did. (Maine State Legislature 2009)

When state legislators know their constituencies' opinions, it can result in better representation. Daniel Butler and David Nickerson (2011), for example, find that when they informed New Mexico state legislators of polling data that showed their constituents favored spending all of a $400-million surplus in the state government budget, these legislators were more likely to support spending the surplus on a tax rebate. After listening to their own constituents in Maine, Senator Rector supported LD 1020, and Senator Jackson opposed the measure, but these senators may need a hearing aid. When put to a statewide referendum vote, only 43 percent of Rector's district supported same-sex marriage, and 42 percent of Jackson's district opposed it. Senators Jackson and Rector were not alone in being out of step with the majority of their districts. 108 of 181 Maine state legislators voted *against* the majority opinion of their district on LD 1020.

Rector and Jackson's misperception of constituent opinion is unfortunately common in state legislatures. Using findings from the National Candidate Study, David Broockman and Chris Skovron (2018) find state legislators misjudged their constituents' views on same-sex marriage by 7 percent, abortion by 9 percent, and gun control by 18 percent, generally with a conservative bias. Legislators may try to represent their constituents' opinions when legislators know those opinions, as shown by Butler and Nickerson, but legislators often misperceive their constituents' preferences, as shown by Broockman and Skovron. Such misperceptions have troubling implications for representation, particularly if state senators like Rector and Jackson unintentionally misrepresent their constituents' interests.[15] However, the lack of issue-specific public opinion measures at the state legislative district level makes it difficult to investigate whether there are electoral ramifications for incorrectly assessing public opinion and casting unpopular roll-call votes.

Some states, however, have veto referendum elections where voters can veto legislation adopted by the legislature before it becomes a law. The results of these elections provide measures of public opinion on state legislation — and thereby legislators' roll-call positions — on the *exact* bill adopted by the state legislature. Results from referenda and initiative elections have shed light on whether state legislators vote consistently with their constituents' preferences (e.g., Gerber 1996; Giger, Kluver, and Witko 2019; Snyder 1996), but I am unaware of research outside of my own that utilizes referenda to determine whether voters reward or punish state legislators for their positions on particular pieces of legislation.

The veto-referenda considered here address a range of issues state legislatures wrestled with in the last twenty-five years, such as same-sex marriage, collective bargaining, and the legalization of marijuana. As it is important to be concerned about biases in studies that use subjective measures of representation (e.g., table 6.1), readers should be conscious of biases that employ more objective measures in this study. For example, the veto-referenda considered here are not randomly selected. Only twenty-three states have veto referendum, and only thirteen at times provide the necessary data to create district-level referendum election results. The appendix provides descriptions of the bills, the dates the referenda elections took place, and statewide support for each bill (table A.6.3). Nineteen of the considered thirty-nine referenda took place outside the general election, affecting turnout and who expresses their opinions on bills. Some referenda were concerned with more-prominent issues, such as same-sex marriage in Maine and collective bargaining in Ohio. However, other referenda likely made fewer headlines, such as those concerned with building a casino in Central Valley, California, or changing regulations for hunting Alaskan wolves or Michigan doves.

All bills were not about wolves or doves, and the bills facing veto referendum often received much greater attention than the typical state legislative bill, presumably increasing the likelihood that voters would hold legislators accountable for unpopular votes. Over $1 million was spent on at least three-fourths of referenda considered, and over $10 million was spent on a third of the referenda considered. However, there was considerable variation in spending. In 2012, campaigns spent over $17 million on a same-sex marriage referendum in Washington but spent less than $40,000 on a medical-marijuana initiative in Montana. Supplementary analyses suggest that the prominence of the referendum, as indicated by campaign spending, does little to alter results. I focus here on cross-state results and refer readers to Rogers (2017) for more micro-level analyses of accountability for specific bills that faced a veto referendum.

Voters vetoed seventeen of thirty-nine considered bills, and approximately 38 percent of roll calls cast by contested, reelection-seeking legislators did not represent their district's majority opinion, suggesting there are an ample number of legislators to hold accountable. To assess whether voters hold legislators responsible for individual roll-call votes, I estimate the relationship between the percentage of voters in a state legislative district who supported an incumbent's roll-call position and contested incumbents' vote shares in their first election following their roll-call vote. I again focus on electoral contests where only one candidate was elected. For comparability across studies, analyses in the first column of table 6.4 employ a model similar to that in the third column of table A.6.1, and analyses in the second through fourth columns include more legislator-specific controls, such as their affiliation with the governor's party, but for different time periods.[16]

I find that voters hold state legislators accountable for their individual roll-call votes, but relationships are once again weak. Using results from the first column of table 6.4, figure 6.6 illustrates the predicted incumbent vote share as an incumbent's roll-call position becomes increasingly popular within her district. This figure has a limited vertical or y-axis for presentation purposes, while the horizontal or x-axis reflects the range of voters' public opinion on considered roll-call votes. As more voters approve of a legislator's roll-call vote, that legislator receives a greater percentage of the vote. A standard-deviation or 13 percent change in public opinion associates with a 0.82 percent change in incumbent vote share, which is comparable to the change in vote share associated with a standard-deviation change in the ideological-distance measure in the above analyses.

Voters responding to specific roll-call votes provide even more evidence that electoral connections exist in state legislatures, but it is again important to consider how meaningful these relationships are and how they change over time. When considering a shift in public opinion equivalent to the true observed range of public opinion on roll-call votes (i.e., with 7 to 91 percent of voters supporting a legislator's roll-call vote), analyses predict a legislator would gain 5.3 percent in vote share. Five percent is not 0 percent but a move from 7 percent approval to 91 percent approval reflects an extraordinary change in public opinion. When accounting for a fuller set of variables, such as a legislator's seniority or affiliations with the chamber majority party, the relationship between public opinion and legislator vote share weakens. Instead of a 0.8 percent change in vote share, a 13 percent change in public support for a bill associated with a 0.5 percent change in vote share.

Legislators also appear to need to worry less about an unpopular roll call than they did in earlier elections. Statistical analyses in the third and fourth columns of table 6.4 are similar to that in the second but separately

TABLE 6.4 **District opinion on incumbent's roll call and vote share**

	2001–2020	2001–2020	2001–2010	2011–2020
District support for bill	0.063*	0.036*	0.053*	0.022*
	(0.009)	(0.008)	(0.013)	(0.011)
Ideological distance	−2.555*	−3.062*	−4.824*	−0.842
	(1.041)	(0.972)	(1.543)	(1.173)
Ideological distance squared	0.662	0.513	0.980	−0.105
	(0.476)	(0.443)	(0.741)	(0.518)
Party loyalty	0.006	0.036*	0.025	0.050*
	(0.014)	(0.015)	(0.021)	(0.020)
Change in annual log of Q4 state personal income		0.951	24.825*	9.934
		(5.224)	(9.826)	(8.017)
Redistricted district		−0.448	−2.032	−0.475
		(0.408)	(1.066)	(0.551)
Distance to capital (logged)		0.090	0.148	−0.009
		(0.110)	(0.179)	(0.131)
Incumbent contribution advantage	0.523*	0.784*	0.610*	0.849*
	(0.053)	(0.062)	(0.093)	(0.077)
Incumbent-party presidential vote	0.574*	0.594*	0.500*	0.627*
	(0.014)	(0.013)	(0.023)	(0.016)
Previous incumbent-party vote share	0.143*	0.130*	0.319*	0.086*
	(0.013)	(0.012)	(0.024)	(0.014)
Seat previously contested	3.086*	2.911*	8.314*	1.613*
	(0.574)	(0.536)	(0.924)	(0.616)
Terms served		0.083	−0.124	0.078
		(0.091)	(0.152)	(0.107)
Freshman incumbent	−0.754*	−0.421	−0.014	−0.545
	(0.235)	(0.272)	(0.388)	(0.355)
Chamber leader		1.340*	2.066*	−0.209
		(0.471)	(0.584)	(0.699)
Midterm appointee		0.999	−0.372	1.503
		(0.926)	(1.309)	(1.206)
Woman legislator		−0.231	−0.145	−0.207
		(0.367)	(0.574)	(0.435)
Woman legislator x Democratic Party member		−0.290	−0.240	−0.503
		(0.469)	(0.692)	(0.590)
Nonwhite legislator		−1.609	−1.923	−1.233
		(0.956)	(1.286)	(1.275)
Nonwhite legislator x Democratic Party member		2.187*	3.112*	1.551
		(1.020)	(1.398)	(1.357)
Member of the Democratic Party	0.637*	0.730*	−5.188*	1.581*
	(0.238)	(0.269)	(0.574)	(0.383)
Member of chamber-majority party		−2.560*	0.288	−4.146*
		(0.279)	(0.400)	(0.532)
Member of governor's party		−2.474*	−1.516*	−2.110*
		(0.321)	(0.466)	(0.464)
Member of president's party	0.738*	−1.747*	−7.431*	−0.954
	(0.297)	(0.345)	(0.587)	(0.590)
Midterm election (federal)	7.663*	6.302*	2.489	1.815*
	(0.894)	(0.990)	(1.559)	(0.717)
Midterm election (state)		−0.652	−0.788	−1.790*
		(0.427)	(0.571)	(0.713)
Member of the president's party x federal midterm	−5.139*	−2.995*	0.884	−4.644*
	(0.452)	(0.466)	(0.715)	(0.693)

TABLE 6.4 (*continued*)

	2001–2020	2001–2020	2001–2010	2011–2020
Member of the governor's party x		0.281	1.615*	2.447*
state midterm		(0.465)	(0.648)	(0.749)
State senator		−2.588*	−2.315*	−2.766*
		(0.320)	(0.502)	(0.413)
Constant	11.377*	14.300*	8.850*	14.608*
	(1.922)	(2.081)	(3.057)	(2.656)
N	2,385	2,379	1,107	1,272
Log-likelihood	−7,289.0	−7,085.1	−3,239.4	−3,706.0

This table reports the results of a linear regression in which the outcome of interest is incumbent vote share in state house elections. Standard errors are in parentheses; *$p < 0.05$.

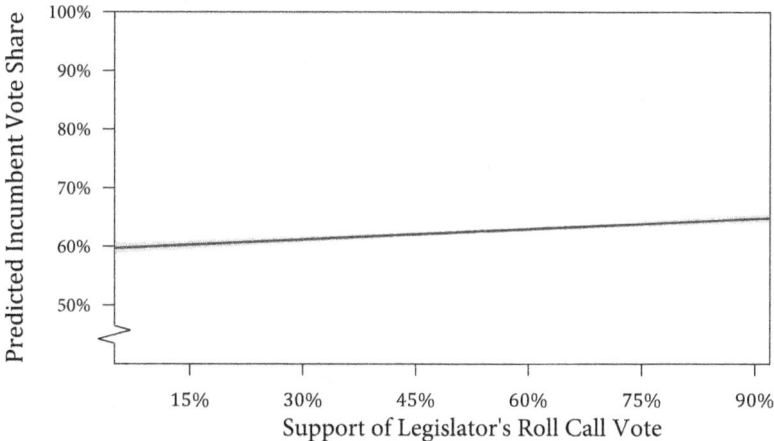

FIGURE 6.6. Predicted vote share for incumbents as the popularity of their individual roll-call vote increases (moving from left to right along the x-axis).

examine the 2001 to 2010 and 2011 to 2020 elections. From 2001 to 2010, a standard-deviation or 13 percent change in public opinion associates with a 0.7 percent change in vote share. However, the comparable estimate for the 2011 to 2020 elections is only 0.3 percent. Are incumbents held accountable for their representation on key issues? Again, the answer is: yes. Nevertheless, legislators must be overwhelmingly out of step with their districts before they must seriously worry about losing their job.

Accountability for Legislative Effectiveness

Voting on bills is one of the most important components of a legislator's representation, but bills do not magically appear. Legislators draft legislation, shepherd bills through committees, and build coalitions to secure final passage. Beth Beskin expressed pride in sponsoring HB 820, which led to a referendum on whether caps on city property taxes should change. After multiple town halls, HB 820 passed both chambers of the Georgia state legislature, and reflecting on her efforts in the state house, Beskin later told the *Atlanta-Journal Constitution*: "I think I've been an effective legislator" (Kass 2018).

State legislators who can effectively craft legislation and pass bills will likely be able to provide more for their constituents. In turn, voters may care more about whether their legislator can get something done than whether their representative is a perfect delegate in their roll-call behavior. Gerard Miquel and James Snyder (2006) begin to shed light on the electoral implications of state legislator effectiveness in their study of the North Carolina state legislature. Specifically, Miquel and Snyder utilized legislative effectiveness scores produced by the North Carolina Center for Public Policy Research (NC Center) to better understand what types of North Carolina legislators were "effective." The NC Center regularly surveyed North Carolina legislators, lobbyists, and journalists. As described by the NC Center:

> These three groups are asked to rate each legislator's effectiveness on the basis of participation in committee work, skill at guiding bills through committees and in floor debates, and general knowledge or expertise in specific fields. The survey respondents also are asked to consider the respect that legislators command from their peers, as well as his or her ethics, the political power they hold (by virtue of office, longevity, or personal skills), their ability to sway the opinions of fellow legislators, and their aptitude for the overall legislative process. (NC Center 2016)

Using survey responses, the NC Center ranked each North Carolina legislator's "effectiveness" in the state house and state senate. Miquel and Snyder discover that committee chairs and majority-party members tend to be more effective, and "legislators who are more effective in their first term in office . . . are promoted more quickly to powerful positions in the chamber" (Miquel and Snyder 2006, 349). Effective legislators also more often won higher office. State Senator Kay Hagan, for example, was named "one of North Carolina's Ten Most Effective Senators" three sessions in a row before being elected to the US Senate.

Political candidates and commentators also bring legislators' effectiveness to voters' attention. State Senator Jeff Tarte boasted on his campaign website that the "North Carolina Center for Public Policy Research . . . selected me as the "Top Freshman Senator" from 15 new Senators" (Tarte 2019), and in the endorsement editorial "The Best Choices for N.C. House and Senate," the *Charlotte Observer* observed:

> Voters in this district should seek change. Republican Jim Gulley has spent 12 years in Raleigh representing this district, which includes Matthews, Mint Hill and areas of east Charlotte. Yet he consistently ranks near the bottom in effectiveness. In fact, his rating by the nonpartisan, non-profit N.C. Center for Public Policy Research has gone down, not up, during his last two terms. Critics in his district complain he has not been accessible or visible to constituents. (Onge 2008)

Some then believe legislators' effectiveness matters for elections, but do voters hold legislators accountable for being ineffective? Studying elections from 1978 to 2000, Miquel and Snyder find that a standard-deviation increase in a legislator's effectiveness ranking (approximately thirty-four ranking positions) results in a 10 percent decrease in the likelihood a legislator is challenged and a 6 percent increase in the likelihood of reelection. Miquel and Snyder appropriately note that such findings should be interpreted as the impact of "relative legislative performance" and not raw effectiveness, as the NC Center only provides rankings of legislators compared to their peers (Miquel and Snyder 2006, 352).[17] Despite this limitation, Miquel and Snyder's findings are evidence that what legislators do in office matters for their elections.

Miquel and Snyder's study tells us more about electoral accountability for state legislators' effectiveness than any research to date but faces generalizability or external validity limitations by focusing on a single state. In some ways, North Carolina is similar to other states. Like state legislative incumbents across the country, North Carolina incumbents overwhelmingly win reelection. From 2004 to 2016, 95 percent of incumbents who sought reelection won, and in contested races, incumbents received approximately 58 percent of the vote on average. In other ways, it is difficult to generalize results from North Carolina to other legislatures, particularly in the time period Miquel and Snyder studied. Before 2002, most North Carolina legislative districts were multi-member districts, and as put by Miquel and Snyder, "[t]he heavy use of first-past-the-post multi-member districts in the North Carolina legislature complicates the study of electoral outcomes" (Miquel and Snyder 2006, 368). For instance, fewer incumbents will likely go unopposed, and having different numbers of major-party candidates within a district makes it more challenging to estimate the direct relationship between a legislator's effectiveness and vote share across districts. Measures of a legislator's ideological representation and levels of campaign spending were also not readily available until the late 1990s, precluding their inclusion in Miquel and Snyder's analyses.

To overcome some of these limitations and provide an updated examination of the extent to which legislators have an electoral incentive to be effective, I study how a legislator's effectiveness relates to election outcomes in two ways. First, I follow Miquel and Snyder and evaluate how a North Carolina legislator's effectiveness ranking relates to state legislative competition and election outcomes. Second, to broaden my analyses, I utilize State Legislative Effectiveness Scores (Bucchianeri, Volden, and Wiseman 2020) for state legislators across the country to assess how effectiveness relates to election outcomes for a broader set of states, which I describe in greater detail below.

Accountability for Effectiveness in North Carolina

In my first study of legislative effectiveness, I update Miquel and Snyder's analyses of North Carolina through the 2016 election, the last year the NC Center published legislator effectiveness scores. I specifically examine how a North Carolina legislator's effectiveness ranking relates to state legislators' vote share (table 6.5) and reelection (table 6.6). Unlike Miquel and Snyder, I focus on a time period when North Carolina exclusively had single-member state legislative districts.[18] Similar to Miquel and Snyder, I invert the NC Center's effectiveness rankings, such that higher values reflect a relatively more effective legislator. Analyses in the first and third columns of tables 6.5 and 6.6 aim to follow Miquel's and Snyder's statistical model, where I account for whether a legislator was a majority-party member or served as a chair or vice-chair of a "power" committee.[19] For comparability across analyses within this chapter, the second and fourth columns add controls similar to those in tables A.6.1. I separate analyses

TABLE 6.5 **North Carolina legislator effectiveness and vote share**

	State reps.— Miquel and Snyder model	State reps.	State senators— Miquel and Snyder model	State senators
Relative legislator effectiveness	0.024	−0.028*	0.131*	0.128*
	(0.015)	(0.012)	(0.047)	(0.046)
Power committee chair	0.138	−0.183	−0.646	−1.264
	(1.224)	(0.938)	(1.283)	(1.050)
Power committee vice chair	−0.321	−0.604	−0.880	−0.718
	(0.924)	(0.718)	(1.324)	(1.055)
Ideological distance		2.128		2.857
		(3.990)		(3.937)
Ideological distance squared		−2.175		−1.867
		(2.786)		(2.011)
Party loyalty		0.043		−0.011
		(0.038)		(0.045)
Incumbent-party presidential vote	0.546*	0.506*	0.606*	0.531*
	(0.036)	(0.032)	(0.046)	(0.050)
Previous incumbent-party vote share		0.165*		0.195*
		(0.043)		(0.083)
Seat previously contested		5.011*		5.767
		(1.836)		(3.270)
Incumbent contribution advantage		1.589*		−0.692
		(0.192)		(0.501)
Member of president's party		−5.114*		−7.324*
		(0.668)		(1.108)
Member of chamber-majority party	−0.797	−1.037	−0.205	−6.129*
	(0.872)	(0.708)	(1.125)	(1.221)
Terms served	−0.025	−0.007	−0.093	−0.191
	(0.150)	(0.142)	(0.177)	(0.155)
Member of the Democratic Party		2.666*		5.865*
		(0.693)		(1.018)
Freshman incumbent		−0.631		0.610
		(0.848)		(0.948)
Midterm election (federal)		−0.677		−0.634
		(1.089)		(1.424)
Constant	28.623*	13.604*	23.837*	17.784
	(2.328)	(5.024)	(3.040)	(9.219)
N	323	322	172	171
Log-likelihood	−1,056.4	−946.3	−530.7	−479.5

This table reports the results of a linear regression in which the outcome of interest is incumbent vote share in North Carolina state house elections from 2004 to 2016. Columns 1 and 3 follow the model previously used by Miquel and Snyder. Columns 2 and 4 follow models presented in table A.6.1. Standard errors are in parentheses; *$p < 0.05$.

for state house and state senate members, as the effectiveness rankings are published separately for these chambers. The least effective state house member ranking is 120, but the least effective state senator's ranking is 50.

My updated study provides stronger evidence that North Carolina state senators' effectiveness meaningfully impacts state senators' legislative election outcomes than effectiveness does for state representatives.

TABLE 6.6 **North Carolina legislator effectiveness and incumbent reelection**

	State reps.—Miquel and Snyder model	State reps.	State senators—Miquel and Snyder model	State senators
Relative legislator effectiveness	0.002	−0.005	0.126*	0.118
	(0.006)	(0.007)	(0.050)	(0.074)
Power committee chair	1.017	1.283	−1.569	−2.059
	(0.762)	(0.848)	(1.169)	(1.336)
Power committee vice chair	0.266	0.706	0.446	2.007
	(0.395)	(0.486)	(2.077)	(111.003)
Ideological distance		−2.874		−0.548
		(2.256)		(4.612)
Ideological distance squared		1.411		1.329
		(1.677)		(2.171)
Party loyalty		−0.018		0.108
		(0.019)		(0.081)
Incumbent-party presidential vote	0.108*	0.131*	0.209*	0.276*
	(0.017)	(0.025)	(0.062)	(0.136)
Previous incumbent-party vote share		0.099*		0.427
		(0.032)		(0.287)
Seat previously contested		3.624*		14.661
		(1.484)		(10.517)
Incumbent contribution advantage	0.817*	0.730*	−0.380	−0.187
	(0.143)	(0.167)	(0.400)	(0.588)
Member of president's party		−1.124*	−3.984*	−10.538
		(0.384)	(1.313)	(5.807)
Member of chamber-majority party	−0.522	−0.842*	−0.701	−2.070
	(0.335)	(0.405)	(1.095)	(2.511)
Terms served	−0.113	−0.175	−0.174	−0.224
	(0.059)	(0.097)	(0.116)	(0.182)
Member of the Democratic Party		0.470		−1.293
		(0.490)		(2.070)
Freshman incumbent		0.185		−1.007
		(0.464)		(1.509)
Midterm election (federal)		−0.537		−0.171
		(0.328)		(1.058)
Constant	−4.329*	−10.724*	−5.723	−52.363
	(0.986)	(3.293)	(3.857)	(32.026)
N	684	681	286	286
Log-likelihood	−57.8	−44.7	−16.7	−11.8

This table reports the results of probit regressions. The outcome of interest in the first two columns is whether an incumbent faced a major-party challenger. The outcome of interest in the final four columns is whether an incumbent won reelection. Standard errors are in parentheses; *$p < 0.05$.

Suppose a state senator increased their relative effectiveness by fourteen ranks (approximately a standard deviation). In that case, statistical analyses suggest that such a change would result in a 1.8 percent increase in a North Carolina senator's vote share (table 6.5, columns 3 and 4), which is comparable to the change associated with a 3.4 percent change in district partisanship. Similarly, when using Miquel and Snyder's set of controls, I find that such an increase in a state senator's ranking associates with a 0.04 increase in the probability of reelection (table 6.6, column 3). When using a fuller set of controls, I find a positive association between senators' effectiveness and reelection, but estimates do not reach conventional levels of statistical significance (table 6.6, column 4). Results are less conclusive when studying state representatives. There is little evidence that legislative effectiveness positively relates to state representatives' vote share or reelection probabilities (table 6.5 and 6.6, columns 1 and 2).

Accountability for Effectiveness in State Legislatures

North Carolinians reward state senators for effectiveness, but it is less clear that state house members' effectiveness matters in elections. So once again, the answer to whether incumbents are held accountable for their own behavior is a qualified yes, at least in North Carolina. But what about the rest of the United States?

Unfortunately, most states are unlike North Carolina and did not have a Center for Public Policy Research that produced individual effectiveness ratings for state legislators.[20] More fortunately, Craig Volden and Alan Wiseman established the Center for Effective Lawmaking, which helps the media, citizens, and political scientists to evaluate American legislators' effectiveness. Volden and Wiseman define effectiveness as "the proven ability to advance a member's agenda items through the legislative process and into law" (Volden and Wiseman 2014, 18) and developed a legislative effectiveness score (LES) for nearly every member of Congress since the 1970s. An LES reflects more than just the number of bills a legislator passes. The LES captures the substance of bills and whether a legislator's bill received any action in committee, any action beyond committee, whether it passed in its respective home chamber, and whether the bill became law (Volden and Wiseman 2014, 24). Political scientists have used the LES to study gender politics, lobbying, social networks in Congress, and legislative organization, among other topics (e.g., Battaglini, Sciabolazza, and Patacchini 2020; Clarke 2020; Egerod 2021; Volden, Wiseman, and Wittmer 2013).

The Center for Effective Lawmaking generously shared their state legislator's effectiveness scores (SLES) for usage within this book. Volden, Wiseman, and Peter Bucchianeri created the SLES using a similar methodology as for their Congressional scores, but at least one key aspect is worth highlighting: scores for single legislative sessions are not directly comparable across states and chambers. To better ensure comparability across legislators within states, I use a measure developed by Volden and Wiseman that classifies legislators' effectiveness relative to an expected benchmark, based on a legislator's seniority, majority-party status, and chair positions. Using this benchmark, legislators are then classified as being above, below, or meeting expectations. I hereafter refer to this measure as a legislator's *SLES ratio*. Within the main text, I focus on comparisons between legislators' SLES ratios and election outcomes within each state. The appendix presents similar results that compare legislators across states or use legislators' raw SLESes instead of SLES ratios (table A.6.4). These analyses provide less evidence of accountability than those presented in the main text.

I evaluate the relationship between a legislator's SLES ratio in each legislative session and their vote share in the next election. My analyses again account for a legislator's partisanship, ideological distance, party loyalty, freshman status, district partisanship, previous competition, and chamber, as well as for the state economy and for whether an election occurred in the midterm. I conduct a separate linear regression for each of the forty-six states considered. For clarity in presentation, I do not present full statistical results but instead plot the predicted vote-share change for a state legislator whose effectiveness was below expectations instead of meeting expectations in figure 6.7. If voters hold state legislators accountable for not effectively moving bills through the legislative process, we should expect these estimates to be less than zero (figure 6.7, vertical gray line).

Analyses of forty-six states again provide limited evidence that voters across the country hold state legislators accountable for their legislative effectiveness. Evidence of electoral punishment for legislative ineffectiveness meets conventional levels of statistical significance only for legislators from Delaware, North Dakota, Kentucky, Maine, and Iowa. A Delaware legislator whose legislative behavior is "below expectations" is expected to receive 2 percent fewer votes than a legislator who "meets expectations" (figure 6.7, bottom of the graph). Not all voters punish legislators for their ineffectiveness. Statistical analyses suggest that Tennessee state legislators who perform below legislative effectiveness expectations receive 1 percent greater vote shares than legislators who meet expectations (figure 5.7, top of the graph).

In the forty other examined states, we are statistically uncertain whether voters hold legislators accountable for their effectiveness. Returning to North Carolina, a North Carolina legislator whose legislative behavior is

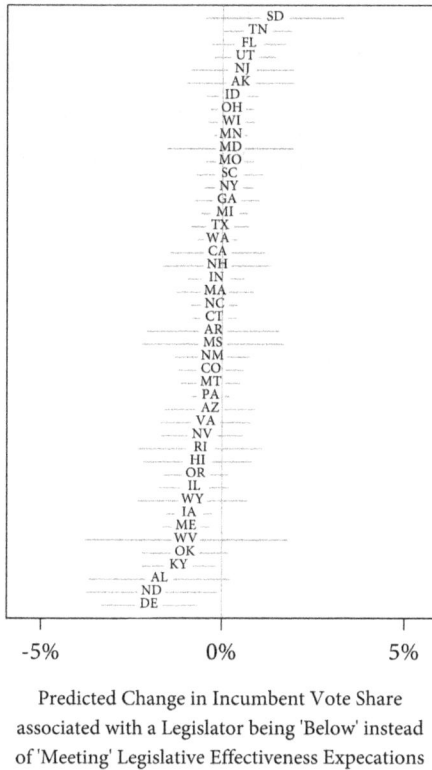

-5%   0%   5%

Predicted Change in Incumbent Vote Share
associated with a Legislator being 'Below' instead
of 'Meeting' Legislative Effectiveness Expecations

FIGURE 6.7. Predicted vote-share differences associated with a legislator failing to meet instead of meeting legislator-effectiveness expectations.

"below expectations" is predicted to receive 0.2 percent fewer votes than a
legislator who "meets expectations." However, this estimate has considerable
uncertainty (t-statistic of difference 0.65). When ignoring the uncertainty of
estimates, analyses suggest that voters punish state legislators for ineffectiveness in thirty states and reward ineffective legislators in sixteen states.

It is not immediately clear why voters in some states hold state legislators accountable for their legislative effectiveness and voters in other
states do not. The Pearson's R correlations between vote-share differences
presented in figure 6.7 and an index measure of professionalism (Squire
2017) is only 0.14, and the correlation between vote-share differences and
the measure of reporters devoted to state government is only 0.11. When
regressing the vote-share differences presented in figure 6.7 on state-level

variables, there are not systematic relationships between these differences and measures of legislative professionalism or the number of reporters devoted to covering state government. As we learn more about state legislators' effectiveness, I look forward to future research to better identify what institutions promote accountability for legislators' effectiveness.

A lack of a statistically significant relationship again does not imply that voters do not hold their state legislators accountable, nor that state legislative elections do not meet our empirical standards for electoral accountability. For instance, in a comparable study of US House elections, I find little relationship between an incumbent US House member's vote share and LES score (table A.6.4). There can be other explanations for the above "null" results. My analyses focus on single states, using smaller samples and less powerful tests. I also do not measure voters' opinions concerning legislators' effectiveness or what voters would like legislators to do. Reporters or politicos who responded to NC Center surveys may have assessed a particular legislator as being the best at getting a bill through a committee, producing a stronger NC Center ranking for that legislator, but such a ranking does not mean that a legislator has effectively provided what some constituents might want, such as bringing money or litter cans to their district.[21] Given that few voters can identify what a legislator has done for their district (chapter 5), this explanation is unlikely but possible. Nevertheless, at least across the types of effectiveness considered here, there is not much evidence that voters hold their state legislators accountable for their effectiveness in most states.

Recap

In our search for accountability in state legislatures, analyses in this chapter offer four different studies of the relationship between legislators' individual behavior in the legislative chamber and voters' behavior at the ballot box. These studies provide evidence that legislators' actions have some implications for their electoral success. Voters report punishing state legislators they perceive to be ideologically distant from them. Legislators who fail to represent their districts on a broad ideological dimension or cast unpopular roll-call votes fare worse on Election Day. And legislators who fail to meet expectations for their effectiveness receive fewer votes, at least in a handful of states. These changes in electoral outcomes indicate that some poorly performing legislators have something to fear on Election Day.

An overwhelming number of legislators, however, have little to worry about when representing their individual districts in the legislature, which is troubling. No study that examined actual election results predicted that a standard-deviation change in ideological representation or standard-deviation change in the popularity of a roll-call vote would result in more than a 2 percent change in vote share or .02 change in probability of re-election. And an overwhelming number of states fail to produce evidence that voters hold legislators accountable for their effectiveness at getting bills through the legislative process. Electoral connections for state legislative representation then exist, but returning to our empirical standards for accountability, they are typically weaker than those found in Congress.

These discouraging findings may not surprise some. It simply may be too much to "expect the typical U.S. voter to respond to politicians' everyday political posturing or specific roll call votes" (Erikson, Wright, and McIver 1993, 4), especially when there is so little media coverage of state politics. To find evidence of accountability, we then may need to lower expectations and consider a simpler way to solve representative government's moral hazard problem. Recall, Schattschneider famously wrote that parties impose "great political simplicity on the most complex governmental system of the world" (Schattschneider 1942, 53) by helping voters hold their elected officials and their parties collectively accountable for their performance. Such simplified accountability is quite possible in state legislatures, particularly when chapter 4 shows that more voters know which party runs their legislature than know who their legislator is. Chapter 4, however, also provides evidence that voters have more interest in national than state politics. Building on this finding, the following chapter shows that all politics are not local at the state legislative ballot box.

Appendix

TABLE A.6.1 **Ideological distance from district and incumbent vote share**

	State leg.	State leg.	State leg.	US House
Ideological distance	−5.446[*]	9.164	−5.821[*]	−5.558[*]
	(0.327)	(6.136)	(0.334)	(2.769)
Ideological distance squared	1.809[*]	1.550[*]	1.932[*]	1.390
	(0.171)	(0.176)	(0.174)	(1.576)
Party loyalty	0.005	0.005	0.001	−0.003
	(0.005)	(0.005)	(0.004)	(0.010)

continues

	State leg.	State leg.	State leg.	US House
Change in annual log of Q4 state personal income	−0.258 (2.089)	0.175 (2.090)		
Incumbent contribution advantage	1.124* (0.026)	1.123* (0.026)	0.622* (0.020)	0.657* (0.031)
Incumbent-party pres. vote	0.510* (0.004)	0.511* (0.004)	0.521* (0.004)	0.477* (0.011)
Previous incumbent-party vote share	0.173* (0.004)	0.172* (0.004)	0.178* (0.004)	0.281* (0.014)
Seat previously contested	4.898* (0.193)	4.878* (0.193)	4.974* (0.195)	7.105* (0.513)
Freshman incumbent	−0.276* (0.102)	−0.277* (0.102)	−0.885* (0.092)	−0.497* (0.246)
Member of the Democratic Party	0.549* (0.102)	0.503* (0.102)	0.628* (0.086)	−0.331 (0.173)
Midterm election (federal)	1.577* (0.225)	1.545* (0.225)	−0.109 (1.156)	6.893* (0.406)
Midterm election (state)	0.208 (0.134)	0.226 (0.134)		
Member of president's party	−0.834* (0.112)	−0.848* (0.112)	−0.785* (0.114)	−0.034 (0.233)
Member of president's party x federal midterm	−3.501* (0.160)	−3.482* (0.160)	−3.815* (0.161)	−6.154* (0.322)
Logged full-time reporters	0.567* (0.192)	9.557* (2.208)		
Ideological distance x reporters		−7.206* (2.160)		
Ideological distance x reporters x state pop.		0.501* (0.139)		
Ideological distance x state pop.		−1.025* (0.411)		
Reporters x state pop.		−0.617* (0.144)		
Legislator salary (in thousands of 2010 dollars)	0.015* (0.003)	0.015* (0.003)		
Legislative staff per member	0.045 (0.056)	0.043 (0.056)		
Session length	−0.003* (0.001)	−0.003* (0.001)		
Public-finance campaign option	0.210 (0.337)	0.196 (0.336)		
Logged average amount to win race (state-year average)	−0.905* (0.182)	−0.894* (0.181)		
Term limits enacted	−0.301 (0.334)	−0.299 (0.329)		
Redistricted district	0.738* (0.165)	0.734* (0.165)		
Distance to capital (logged)	0.045 (0.041)	0.038 (0.041)		
State population (logged)	0.423 (0.299)	1.766* (0.483)		
Minority-party seat share	−1.794* (0.794)	−1.982* (0.796)		

	State leg.	State leg.	State leg.	US House
District size (logged)	−0.460	−0.471		
	(0.288)	(0.287)		
Terms served	0.085*	0.085*		
	(0.016)	(0.016)		
Chamber leader	0.744*	0.742*		
	(0.191)	(0.191)		
Midterm appointee	0.311	0.314		
	(0.299)	(0.299)		
Woman legislator	0.652*	0.644*		
	(0.139)	(0.139)		
Woman legislator x Democratic Party member	−1.052*	−1.027*		
	(0.185)	(0.185)		
Nonwhite legislator	−0.101	−0.067		
	(0.312)	(0.312)		
Nonwhite legislator x Democratic Party member	1.184*	1.118*		
	(0.348)	(0.348)		
Member of chamber-majority party	−1.130*	−1.152*		
	(0.088)	(0.088)		
Member of governor's party	−0.260*	−0.264*		
	(0.113)	(0.113)		
Member of governor's party x state midterm	−0.304	−0.324*		
	(0.158)	(0.157)		
Off-year election	0.923	1.020		
	(1.068)	(1.057)		
State senator	−2.694*	−2.686*		
	(0.256)	(0.256)		
Constant	24.514*	5.562	18.683*	11.410*
	(3.429)	(6.562)	(1.242)	(1.746)
N	21,683	21,683	21,811	3,145
Log-likelihood	−68,394.1	−68,370.3	−69,473.0	−9,090.9

This table reports the results of a linear regression in which the outcome of interest is incumbent vote share in state house or US House elections from 2001 to 2020. Standard errors are in parentheses; *p < 0.05.

TABLE A.6.2 **Ideological distance from district and incumbent reelection**

	Incumbents seeking reelection with and without a challenger	Incumbents seeking reelection with and without a challenger	Incumbents seeking reelection with a challenger	Incumbents seeking reelection with a challenger
Ideological distance	−0.366*	3.058	−0.347*	3.972
	(0.042)	(1.958)	(0.048)	(2.223)
Party loyalty	0.005*	0.005*	0.002	0.002
	(0.002)	(0.002)	(0.002)	(0.002)
Change in annual log of Q4 state personal income	−0.120	−0.064	0.125	0.187
	(0.591)	(0.592)	(0.668)	(0.669)

continues

	Incumbents seeking reelection with and without a challenger	Incumbents seeking reelection with and without a challenger	Incumbents seeking reelection with a challenger	Incumbents seeking reelection with a challenger
Incumbent contribution advantage			0.290* (0.014)	0.289* (0.014)
Incumbent-party pres. vote	0.055* (0.002)	0.055* (0.002)	0.063* (0.002)	0.063* (0.002)
Previous incumbent-party vote share	0.020* (0.001)	0.020* (0.001)	0.020* (0.002)	0.020* (0.002)
Seat previously contested	0.485* (0.067)	0.489* (0.067)	0.644* (0.083)	0.651* (0.083)
Freshman incumbent	−0.109* (0.034)	−0.109* (0.034)	−0.119* (0.039)	−0.118* (0.039)
Member of the Democratic Party	−0.072* (0.035)	−0.075* (0.035)	−0.086* (0.040)	−0.089* (0.040)
Midterm election (federal)	0.242* (0.050)	0.242* (0.050)	0.258* (0.058)	0.257* (0.058)
Midterm election (state)	0.049 (0.045)	0.049 (0.045)	0.066 (0.052)	0.066 (0.052)
Member of president's party	−0.154* (0.040)	−0.152* (0.040)	−0.155* (0.047)	−0.155* (0.047)
Member of president's party x federal midterm	−0.662* (0.058)	−0.662* (0.058)	−0.714* (0.067)	−0.714* (0.067)
Logged full-time reporters	0.714 (0.428)	1.121 (0.695)	0.286 (0.437)	1.021 (0.753)
Ideological distance x reporters		−0.562 (0.712)		−0.944 (0.804)
Ideological distance x reporters x state pop.		0.048 (0.046)		0.075 (0.052)
Ideological distance from district x state pop. (logged)		−0.254 (0.132)		−0.317* (0.151)
Reporters x state pop.	−0.048 (0.028)	−0.083 (0.045)	−0.017 (0.029)	−0.075 (0.049)
Legislator salary (in thousands of 2010 dollars)	0.001 (0.001)	0.001 (0.001)	0.002* (0.001)	0.002* (0.001)
Legislative staff per member	0.005 (0.012)	0.004 (0.012)	−0.001 (0.010)	−0.001 (0.010)
Session length	−0.001 (0.000)	−0.001 (0.000)	−0.000 (0.000)	−0.000 (0.000)
Public-finance campaign option	−0.115 (0.086)	−0.109 (0.086)	−0.001 (0.075)	0.004 (0.074)
Logged average amount to win race (state-year average)	−0.165* (0.047)	−0.167* (0.047)	−0.255* (0.046)	−0.258* (0.046)
Term limits enacted	0.061 (0.063)	0.058 (0.063)	0.046 (0.052)	0.045 (0.052)
Redistricted district	0.104* (0.036)	0.108* (0.036)	0.052 (0.041)	0.055 (0.041)
Distance to capital (logged)	−0.011 (0.014)	−0.012 (0.014)	−0.014 (0.016)	−0.016 (0.016)
State population (logged)	0.172 (0.091)	0.350* (0.130)	0.019 (0.090)	0.250 (0.139)

	Incumbents seeking reelection with and without a challenger	Incumbents seeking reelection with and without a challenger	Incumbents seeking reelection with a challenger	Incumbents seeking reelection with a challenger
Minority-party seat share	−0.729[*]	−0.731[*]	−0.347	−0.351
	(0.226)	(0.226)	(0.226)	(0.225)
District size (logged)	0.188[*]	0.198[*]	0.193[*]	0.206[*]
	(0.083)	(0.083)	(0.081)	(0.081)
Terms served	0.004	0.004	0.004	0.005
	(0.006)	(0.006)	(0.007)	(0.007)
Chamber leader	0.760[*]	0.758[*]	0.630[*]	0.629[*]
	(0.107)	(0.107)	(0.117)	(0.117)
Midterm appointee	0.755[*]	0.757[*]	0.653[*]	0.661[*]
	(0.132)	(0.133)	(0.145)	(0.146)
Woman legislator	−0.063	−0.063	−0.029	−0.028
	(0.047)	(0.047)	(0.052)	(0.052)
Woman legislator x Democratic Party member	−0.016	−0.015	−0.027	−0.026
	(0.063)	(0.063)	(0.072)	(0.072)
Nonwhite legislator	−0.122	−0.114	−0.112	−0.103
	(0.094)	(0.095)	(0.108)	(0.109)
Nonwhite legislator x Democratic Party member	0.048	0.042	0.143	0.135
	(0.111)	(0.111)	(0.134)	(0.134)
Member of chamber-majority party	−0.189[*]	−0.190[*]	−0.184[*]	−0.187[*]
	(0.030)	(0.030)	(0.035)	(0.035)
Member of governor's party	0.026	0.024	−0.009	−0.012
	(0.038)	(0.038)	(0.043)	(0.043)
Member of governor's party x state midterm	−0.091	−0.091	−0.097	−0.097
	(0.055)	(0.055)	(0.063)	(0.063)
Off-year election	0.148	0.151	0.108	0.117
	(0.142)	(0.142)	(0.122)	(0.121)
State senator	−0.146[*]	−0.156[*]	−1.170[*]	−1.176[*]
	(0.072)	(0.072)	(0.087)	(0.088)
Constant	−5.344[*]	−7.816[*]	−3.061[*]	−6.314[*]
	(1.142)	(1.796)	(1.124)	(1.939)
N	39,227	39,227	21,683	21,683
Log-likelihood	−5,326.3	−5,323.0	−4,175.5	−4,172.1

This table reports the results of a probit regression in which the outcome of interest is incumbent reelection in state legislative elections from 2001 to 2020. Standard errors are in parentheses; *$p < 0.05$.

Descriptions of bills that faced veto-referendum

State	Bill	Date of referendum	Issue description	Statewide support of bill
AK	SB 21	8/19/2014	Provide tax incentives for oil drilling	53%
AZ	SB 1431	11/6/2018	Expand state-scholarship eligibility for all public school students	35%
CA	SB 2	11/2/2004	Require medium-to-large businesses to provide health care coverage	49%
CA	SB 903	2/5/2008	Permit 5500 additional slot machines at certain Native American casinos	56%
CA	SB 174	2/5/2008	Permit 5500 additional slot machines at certain Native American casinos	56%
CA	SB 175	2/5/2008	Permit 5500 additional slot machines at certain Native American casinos	56%
CA	SB 957	2/5/2008	Permit 5500 additional slot machines at certain Native American casinos	56%
CA	AB 277	11/4/2014	Allow North Fork Tribe to build a casino in Central Valley	39%
CA	SB 270	11/8/2016	Prohibit single-use plastic bags at grocery stores and introduce fee for recycled bags	53%
CA	SB 10	11/3/2020	Replace cash bail with risk assessments for detained suspects awaiting trial	44%
CO	SB 42	11/3/2020	Give CO electoral votes to presidential candidate who wins national popular vote	52%
ID	S 1108	11/6/2012	Limit agreements between teachers and school boards and end issuance of renewable contracts	43%
ID	S 1110	11/6/2012	Establish teacher pay for performance based on test scores	42%
ID	S 1184	11/6/2012	Increase technology spending in schools, with the ability to offset costs using teacher salaries	33%
MD	HB 1368	11/7/2006	Require voter registration regulations	71%
MD	SB 167	11/6/2012	Allow undocumented immigrants to pay in-state college tuition	59%
MD	HB 438	11/6/2012	Permit same-sex marriage	52%
ME	LS 1196	11/8/2005	Prevent sexual discrimination in employment, housing, and education	55%
ME	LD 2247	11/4/2008	Repeal soda tax to pay for health care program	35%
ME	LD 1020	11/3/2009	Permit same-sex marriage	47%
ME	LD 1376	11/8/2011	Repeal same-day voter registration	39%
ME	LD 1646	6/12/2018	Establish ranked-choice voting	46%
ME	LD 798	3/3/2020	Create vaccination exemptions	73%
MI	PA 269	11/5/2002	Eliminate straight party ticket	40%
MI	PA 160	11/7/2006	Authorize dove-hunting season	31%
MI	PA 4	11/6/2012	Authorize governor to establish city manager upon state finding financial emergency	47%
MI	PA 520	11/4/2014	Allow establishment of wolf-hunting seasons and designate wolf as game animal	45%
MI	PA 21	11/4/2014	Allow Natural Resources Commission to designate game species and hunting seasons	36%
MT	SB 424	11/6/2012	Enact a medical-marijuana program	57%
ND	SB 2370	6/12/2012	Change the North Dakota University mascot	67%

State	Bill	Date of referendum	Issue description	Statewide support of bill
OH	HB 545	11/4/2008	Limit interest rates on short-term loans to 28%	64%
OH	SB 5	11/8/2011	Limit collective bargaining for state employees	39%
SD	RL- 12	11/2/2010	Expand smoking ban	64%
WA	ESSHB 2295	11/2/2004	Authorize creation of charter schools	41%
WA	SB 5726	11/6/2007	Allow consumers to collect trip damages from their insurance company	57%
WA	SB 5688	11/3/2009	Grant domestic partners all rights, responsibilities, and obligations granted to married couples	53%
WA	SB 6239	11/6/2012	Permit same-sex marriage	54%
WA	M-1000	11/5/2019	Allow affirmative action policies in public employment	51%
WA	SB 5395	11/3/2020	Require sexual education in schools	58%

TABLE A.6.4 **Legislator effectiveness and incumbent vote share**

	State leg.	State leg.	US House
State legislative effectiveness ratio	0.001		
	(0.068)		
Session legislative effectiveness score		−0.070	−0.087
		(0.044)	(0.058)
Ideological distance	−5.993*	−5.951*	−5.864*
	(0.373)	(0.369)	(2.773)
Ideological distance squared	2.023*	1.999*	1.539
	(0.197)	(0.195)	(1.578)
Party loyalty	−0.006	−0.001	0.000
	(0.005)	(0.004)	(0.011)
Incumbent-party pres. vote	0.511*	0.513*	0.476*
	(0.004)	(0.004)	(0.011)
Previous incumbent-party vote share	0.179*	0.176*	0.283*
	(0.005)	(0.005)	(0.014)
Seat previously contested	4.897*	4.768*	7.148*
	(0.214)	(0.211)	(0.514)
Incumbent contribution advantage	0.652*	0.651*	0.657*
	(0.023)	(0.022)	(0.031)
Member of president's party	−1.313*	−1.329*	−0.078
	(0.128)	(0.127)	(0.236)
Member of the Democratic Party	0.868*	0.869*	−0.373*
	(0.092)	(0.091)	(0.175)
Freshman incumbent	−0.798*	−0.855*	−0.519*
	(0.100)	(0.099)	(0.247)
Midterm election (federal)	−0.228	−0.178	6.850*
	(1.168)	(1.167)	(0.407)
Member of president's party x federal midterm	−3.396*	−3.373*	−6.071*
	(0.177)	(0.176)	(0.328)
Constant	20.002*	19.829*	11.290*
	(1.288)	(1.274)	(1.751)
N	18,380	18,679	3,144
Log-likelihood	−58,593.9	−59,552.2	−9,086.7

This table reports the results of a linear regression in which the outcome of interest is incumbent vote share in state house or US House elections from 2001 to 2018. Standard errors are in parentheses; *p < 0.05.

CHAPTER SEVEN

The Electoral Impact of Party Performance

All Politics Are Not Local

In 1935, a twenty-two-year-old Boston College senior ran for city council on the platform of "Cambridge jobs for Cambridge people." As one in a field of sixty candidates, the local newspaper did not even mention the college student's name, which would later become iconic in American politics. After narrowly losing the election, this young politician reflected on advice from his father—Thomas P. O'Neill Sr.—a former city councilmember himself:

> During the campaign, my father had left me to my own devices, but when it was over, he pointed out that I had taken my own neighborhood for granted. He was right: I had received tremendous vote [*sic*] in the other sections of the city, but I hadn't worked hard enough in my own backyard. "Let me tell you something I learned years ago," he said. "All politics is local." (O'Neill and Novak 1987, 26)

The junior Thomas O'Neill—better known as "Tip"—listened to his father and was subsequently elected to the Massachusetts state house one year later.

The notion that "all politics is local" has a long history in state legislative politics. The Founding Fathers believed that "[a] local spirit will infallibly prevail much more in the members of Congress, than a national spirit will prevail in the legislatures of the particular States" (Madison 1788, *Federalist* no. 46; see also *Federalist* no. 45). Modern-day party organizations also emphasize the importance of "local" politics. Before the 2010 elections, the executive director of the Democratic Legislative Campaign Committee — the national organization devoted to electing Democratic state legislators — said: "We work on state legislative races all the time, and we work closely with individual campaigns and leaders to run the best race possible; personalizing campaigns, localizing them" (Rothman 2010; see also Fiddler 2016 and Housman 2020).

The fatherly advice that "all politics is local" may have helped elect Tip O'Neill to the state legislature. If so, perhaps sons should listen to their fathers more often. But as many mothers can attest, fatherly advice is not always right. Localized electoral success does not seem to fit the previous chapter's findings, which show that legislators' own actions have limited implications for their elections. Nor does localized electoral success fit with figure 1.1, which shows voters knowing more about national politics (chapters 4 and 5) and voters increasingly voting against the president's party in midterm elections (chapter 6).

The previous chapters cast doubt on the notion that all politics are local, but they also show that local state conditions matter in state legislative elections. For instance, reconsider findings concerning challenger entry (chapter 3). State legislative incumbents more often face challengers when the state economy is weak (figure 3.5). Like challengers, voters may also assess conditions in their state and hold state parties and their members responsible for their collective performance, similar to the idea of responsible party government. Consistent with this form of state-level accountability, this chapter shows that voters who subjectively approve of the state legislature more often vote for the party in control of the legislature, particularly when they approve of how the legislature handles the issue a voter finds most important. More informed voters additionally drive this electoral connection, which supports the idea of the "miracle of aggregation," an argument put forth by prior studies of state politics that I describe in greater detail below.

Regrettably, the weight of the evidence in this chapter is again less promising for accountability in state legislatures. Instead of serving as a referendum on state legislators' own actions, state legislative elections are dominated by national politics. State legislative seat changes are driven more by national political conditions than state political conditions, and voters' opinions of the president have three times the predicted impact on state legislative election outcomes as does their approval of the state legislature. Misinformation further plagues accountability in American state legislatures. Some voters reward the minority instead of the majority party in the legislature even when they approve of the legislature's performance. While these voters may be *trying* to hold the state legislative party they believe to be in power responsible, such misinformed behavior at times reduces electoral accountability in state legislatures.

Responsible State Party Government

For accountability, Powell requires voters to "know who is responsible for making policy." Given the paltry number of voters who know who their legislator is (chapter 4) or what they do (chapter 5), it is then less surprising that legislators' individual behavior has little impact on legislative election outcomes (chapter 6). Powell's knowledge requirement, however, does not imply that every voter needs to know every detail about politics for *some* electoral accountability to exist.

Collecting detailed information about their state legislator may make little sense for an individual voter, especially when they can rely on "heuristics" (e.g., Lupia 2006). A heuristic is an information shortcut a less informed individual can use to make a decision as if they were more fully informed. As an example, consider that I know a restaurant reviewer has similar tastes to my own. If this reviewer likes a new restaurant, I can more confidently rely on the reviewer's recommendation as a shortcut to determine where to eat my next meal without thoroughly researching the restaurant's menu. In politics, party labels are one of the most common types of heuristic. In the context of roll-call voting addressed in the previous chapter, consider a situation where there is a bill a voter likes, and it is known that the state Republican party passes this bill. Even if a voter does not know who their state legislator is, the ballot will tell the voter which state legislative candidate is a member of the Republican party. On Election Day, the voter can then reasonably use this party label as a "shortcut" to know which candidate or party to reward for passing their favored bill.

Not every roll-call vote goes down party lines (e.g., Dancey and Sheagley 2013), but with information about who is in power and how things are going, political parties and labels can establish a system of collective accountability consistent with theories of retrospective voting (Fiorina 1981; Key 1966). Austin Ranney describes such a system in *The Doctrine of Responsible Party Government*:

> . . . the people decide whether to approve of the general direction the party in power has been taking—in short, whether their wants are being satisfied. If the

answer is yes, they return that party to power; if the answer is no, they replace
it with the opposition party. (Ranney 1954, 12)

Applying the idea of responsible party government to states, members of a
state legislative party need to seek voters' approval to avoid being replaced.
Such a system of accountability helps address the moral hazard problem
posed by representative government. The threat of being removed from
power provides party members an electoral incentive to produce policies
favorable to voters. Otherwise, they and their co-partisans are out of a job.

Political scientists have long pointed to political parties as saviors of
American democracy. E. E. Schattschneider famously wrote that parties impose "great political simplicity on the most complex governmental system
of the world" (Schattschneider 1942, 53). The American Political Science
Association later amplified this admiration of parties by issuing a report,
partly drafted by Schattschneider, stating: "Party responsibility means the
responsibility of both parties to the general public, as enforced in elections"
(APSA 1950, 17). To meet Powell's condition that voters "must know who
is responsible for making policy," a system of responsible party government
only requires voters to know which party controls the legislature. More
voters know which party controls their legislature than know who their
legislator is, and this enlarged set of voters could better hold parties and
their members collectively accountable than individually accountable. For
instance, when asked what they liked about their Democratic state legislative candidate, one respondent to the CES stated, "There was nothing about
the candidate. I voted more based on the actions of the Democratic party."

Simplifying party labels can be attractive shortcuts in low-information
elections such as those for the state legislature. But returning to another
piece of fatherly wisdom, shortcuts often come at some cost in quality, particularly when boiling down "the most complex governmental system of the
world."[1] For example, even though the Democratic or Republican parties
control nearly all state legislative chambers across the country, what it means
to be a state legislative Democrat or Republican differs across the United
States (Shor and McCarty 2011). Within the American federal system, where
national parties share the same labels as state parties, it is difficult for many
voters to be cognizant of their state parties' ideological nuances (chapter 5;
Hopkins 2018).

We already know voters' perceptions of parties' ideology matter relatively little in state legislative elections (table 6.1). Nevertheless, voters can
still employ shortcuts or heuristics within a responsible party government

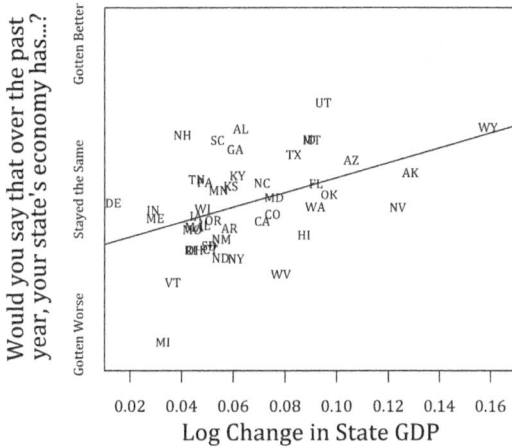

FIGURE 7.1. Relationship between how a state economy actually performed and voters' subjective assessment of their state economies in 2006.

framework. Instead of focusing on the ideological positions of state parties, voters can base their votes on how parties performed while in power. But this leads to a new question: do voters know how their parties performed?

To shed light on this question, a helpful first step is to compare how a state actually performed against how voters viewed its performance. Figure 7.1 compares an objective measure of state economic strength—the annual log change in state GDP (x-axis)—to the mean state-level response of voters to the question: "Now thinking about your state's economy, would you say that over the past year, your state's economy has ... Gotten better, stayed the same, gotten worse?" (y-axis, CES 2006).[2] The positive slope of the best-fit line indicates that voters' subjective opinions about the state of the economy reflect objective measures of the economy. For example, Michiganders recognized their state's weak economy, and Wyomingites recognized their state's strong economy.[3] Across all states, the correlation between the objective and subjective measures is 0.48. Voters then likely have some awareness of whether their state economy got better or worse, but what is critical for responsible party government is how voters responded to these economic changes on Election Day. And here, we encounter an accountability puzzle.

Theories of responsible party government and retrospective voting assert that when the economy does well, the party in power should do better in elections. But this does not appear to be the case. Figure 7.2's left panel

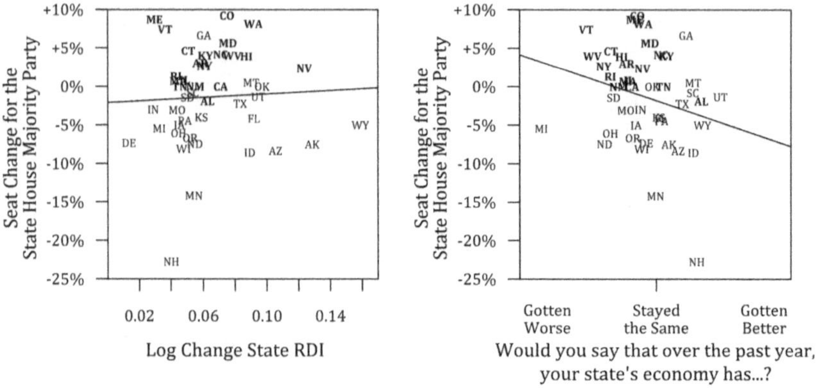

FIGURE 7.2. Relationships between how the state economy actually performed (left panel, x-axis) or voters' subjective assessment of their state economy in 2006 (right panel, x-axis) and how the state house–majority party performed in the 2006 election (y-axis on each panel). Bolded state abbreviations indicate where the Democratic party had a majority in the state house.

shows that the relationship between changes in state real disposable income and seat change for the state house majority party is near zero, and the right panel shows that in states where voters thought the economy had gotten better, the state house majority party more often lost seats. Returning to the examples of Michigan and Wyoming, where Republicans had unified control of these states' legislatures, theories of retrospective voting predict voters would punish Michigan Republicans for their weak economy but reward Wyoming Republicans for their strong economy. Instead, each Republican state party lost 5 percent of state house seats.

Republican defeats were common in 2006. Republicans lost state house seats in thirty-eight legislatures nationwide in addition to losing control of the US House and Senate. Such national trends in state elections reflect the nationalization of state politics. As discussed in chapter 5, Dan Hopkins argues that "voters today perceive state parties as highly similar to their national affiliates" (Hopkins 2018, 168), an assessment that fits the conceptualization of voter behavior where "voters use the same criteria to choose candidates across the federal system" (Hopkins 2018, 3).[4] Hopkins's argument largely focuses on political parties' ideological positions and voters' perceptions of these positions, but we know voters' perceptions of state parties' ideological positions matter relatively little for voters' behavior in state legislative elections (figure 6.2; see also Hopkins 2018, figure 7.8).

These meager relationships between voters' perceptions of their state legislative parties' ideologies and voting behavior do not imply that "nationalized" perceptions of state parties are not meaningful for state legislative elections. One can extend Hopkins's "same criteria" argument beyond parties' ideology to parties' performance. Specifically, voters could rely on the performance of more-recognized party figureheads when formulating opinions about the performance of more-obscure state-level partisan actors (Kahneman and Frederick 2002; Tversky and Kahneman 1974; see also Gabaix and Laibson 2005). For example, 20.8 percent of respondents to the 2008 Cooperative Election Study (CES) were "not sure" if they approved of their state legislature. However, only 1.6 percent of respondents were "not sure" whether they approved of President Bush. Nearly every voter then had some evaluation of a Republican political actor, albeit at the federal level.

If voters with undefined views of the state legislature heuristically turn to their more accessible evaluation of the president when deciding how to vote in a state-level election, such behavior would be an attribution error. An attribution error occurs when a voter assigns responsibility to one political actor for a policy outcome under another political actor's control. Michael Sances (2017; see also Malhotra and Kuo 2008; Gomez and Wilson 2008; Arceneaux and Stein 2006) provides a nice example of such errors. Sances studies the electoral impact of local tax increases that voters enacted themselves and finds voters more often voted against incumbent presidential candidates if their town experienced a tax increase. Since a presidential candidate has little control over tax increases implemented by voters, punishing the candidate for such policies does little to solve the moral hazard problem posed by representative government.

Attribution errors are often found in federalist systems across the world (Anderson and Ward 1996; Leigh and McLeish 2009; Rodden and Wibbels 2011; see also Erikson and Filippov 2001; Kedar 2006; Leon 2012; Martins and Veiga 2013). With multiple layers of government, it is not always clear whom to reward for good times or blame for bad times (Arceneaux 2005), and in turn, co-partisans across different levels of government frequently experience similar electoral fates.[5] For instance, Chubb (1988) finds that the president's party is more successful in both gubernatorial and state legislative elections when the national economy is strong. Stein (1990) and Carsey and Wright (1998) similarly provide evidence that presidential approval associates with gubernatorial election outcomes, and Berry, Berkman, and Schneiderman (2000) find that presidential approval relates to the likelihood that an incumbent state legislator is reelected. Such relationships between presidential politics and state election outcomes again challenge the claim that "the electorate often manages to make an effective separation of its choices of presidential and state candidates" (Key 1964, 307). More importantly, if voters make attribution errors and electorally punish state-level political actors for the president's actions and not their own, elections will do little to motivate legislators' own actions. Why would a state legislator change his behavior in fear of voters if his behavior does not dictate his own election?

Attribution errors also complicate a prominent argument concerning the effectiveness of American state elections. Acknowledging that a typical voter does not follow state politics, the authors of *Statehouse Democracy* argue that all voters do not need to be informed for there to be accountability in state legislatures. Instead, the "collective outcomes, including election results, can be driven by a relatively small number of actors, not just those who are 'typical,'" through a process known as the "miracle of aggregation" (Erikson, Wright, and McIver 1993, 4; see also 247–50 and Caughey and Warshaw 2022, 161–62).

Writing at approximately the same time, Benjamin Page and Robert Shapiro more thoroughly present the idea of the "miracle of aggregation" in *The Rational Public*. Grappling with bleak findings that individual Americans do not hold stable political opinions over time (e.g., Converse 1964), Page and Shapiro acknowledge that individual opinions as expressed on surveys may change. Page and Shapiro, however, build on the logic of Condorcet's jury theorem and argue that such change is random and "simple statistical reasoning indicates that those errors will tend to cancel each other out when the opinions of individuals are aggregated" (Page and Shapiro 1992, 16). Unstable individual attitudes, as measured by surveys, are then less troublesome for the health of democracy, as long as errors randomly cancel out.

To understand how the idea of the "miracle of aggregation" can apply to elections, again consider a district of nine voters. Assume three voters are well-informed and make normatively desirable decisions in elections, but the remaining six are uninformed and randomly cast ballots. Most of the electorate is then uninformed, as is common in state legislative elections, but this district must still determine whether to let an incumbent stay in office. For purposes of this example, assume the incumbent supported an unpopular bill that outlawed owning kittens. If the six uninformed voters randomly cast their ballots, three of these voters should support the feline-hating incumbent, and the other three voters should support the pro-kitten challenger, effectively canceling each other out. The election will then be determined by the remaining well-informed voters who punish the incumbent for his anti-kitten position, thereby holding this incumbent accountable.

A successful miracle then requires at least two divine things. First, some voters must be informed, which we know is the case as at least half of voters generally know which party controls their state legislature (figure 4.3). Second, voting errors among the less informed must be unbiased and random. As put by Erikson, Wright, and McIver:

> Even when citizens vote for the "wrong" candidate (in the sense that with a lot more information and study, they would vote differently), such errors will tend to cancel out so that in the end the full electorate will often behave very much, although not exactly, as it would have had individuals had much better information and were less error prone in their decision making. (Erikson, Wright, and McIver 1993, 250)

Suppose the miracle of aggregation applies to state legislative elections. In that case, some voters being uninformed is then less worrisome for accountability because—again as put by Erikson, Wright, and McIver—"some important individuals do pay attention, with consequences that can extend to the ballot box" (Erikson, Wright, and McIver 1993, 4). I do not dispute that *some* voters pay attention to state legislatures (chapter 4), but it is less clear whether *enough* pay attention for state legislators to face meaningful consequences at the ballot box and that "errors will tend to cancel out," particularly if attribution errors are systematically biased (e.g., by national politics).

Together, retrospection and responsible party government simplify the accountability process for voters in a complex form of government, but it is largely unknown what cost accountability in state legislatures pays for simplification. To continue my search for such accountability, I study the electoral impact of state legislative parties' performance in two ways. First, I examine how objective measures of performance, such as growth in the state economy, relate to state legislative election outcomes. I expect that elections reward the party in control of the legislature for good policy outcomes. However, objective performance measures do not always translate into subjective assessments of government performance (De Boef and Kellstedt 2004), and voters may evaluate legislatures using differing criteria (chapter 5). Therefore, I also examine how voters' subjective approval of the legislature relates to their individual vote choice in state legislative elections. These individual-level analyses allow us to discern which voters (e.g., those who are more informed) drive state legislative elections' outcomes, as predicted by the miracle of aggregation.

Accountability and Objective Measures of Performance

The meager relationship between the state economy's growth and state legislatures' election outcomes (figure 7.2, left panel) suggests that strong economies did little to help reelect state legislators in 2006. However, state real disposable income is just one way to measure the economy, let alone state legislators' performance, and 2006 is a single election year. To more broadly assess whether elections reward legislative majority parties for good policy outcomes, I study how various measures of government performance associated with party seat changes in state legislatures in the 1972–2020 elections.

My analyses resemble previous work (e.g., Chubb 1988) but differ in at least two key respects. First, most prior research fails to consider the party in control of the state legislature, leaving it relatively unknown whether the majority parties in the state legislature have electoral incentives to produce good policies. Therefore, I assess the electoral success of the state house majority party in addition to the governor's party and president's party to establish whether voters reward legislative parties independent of their affiliation with the president. Second, previous research primarily explores how electoral outcomes vary with changes in the economy. But state legislatures are responsible for a plethora of policy outcomes, ranging from education to health care to law enforcement. Thus, I also evaluate whether voters reward state legislatures for economic growth as well as for other policy outcomes, as described below in greater detail.

My dependent variable is the proportion change in state house seats for the Democratic party with observations at the state-year level. I focus on state house elections as state senate elections often have staggered terms, but the appendix presents comparable results for state senate elections (table A.7.2). My central independent variables capture different areas of policy performance. Main analyses focus on annual changes in logged real disposable income. To capture the reward or punishment for the party in control of the state house, I estimate the relationship between seat change and policy performance conditional on whether the Democratic party controlled the state house. Under theories of retrospective voting, I would expect to find that a Democratic state house majority party would gain seats during a robust state economy.

State legislatures are, of course, responsible for more than steering a good economy. Education expenditures, for example, are the second-largest appropriation in state budgets, and state governments are responsible for a third of nonfederal public safety spending (Barnett 2011). Prior work studying local levels of government provides evidence that voters engage in retrospective voting for policy performance in areas such as education (C. R. Berry and Howell 2007) and crime (Arnold and Carnes 2012). It again would be wrong to claim there is overwhelming evidence of accountability in local elections, but I am aware of more evidence of local-level accountability than state legislative accountability. If one finds that voters at times hold members of Congress and mayors accountable for objective measures of performance, why not state legislators?[6]

To expand my search for accountability beyond economic measures of performance, I follow studies of accountability in local levels of government and Dynes and Holbein's (2020) study of policymaking. Specifically, I evaluate the relationship between election outcomes and twenty-five different measures that capture a state's policies or performance concerning the economy, inequality, education, taxes, health care, the environment, and crime. Most data come from the Correlates of State Policy Project Database (Grossmann, Jordan, and McCrain 2021). Unfortunately, not all measures are available for all years of the study, which I designate in table 7.2 below. Table A.7.1 provides summary statistics for variables used in these seat-change analyses, and I refer readers to the Institute for Public Policy and Social Research at Michigan State University for fuller descriptions of these variables.[7]

In addition to how state parties perform, surges in partisan turnout could impact state legislative elections' outcomes. State legislative parties who recently experienced electoral success also may hold an increased number of vulnerable seats and be "exposed" (Oppenheimer, Stimson, and Waterman 1986).[8] My analyses, therefore, account for changes in a state's congressional vote, a state legislative party's seat change in the previous election, whether the Democrats controlled the state house, and whether the election occurred in the midterm. I estimate the relationships between these variables and party seat changes using ordinary least-square regressions with state fixed effects and clustered standard errors by state.

Theories of political accountability predict electorates will punish or reward their state legislators for how they perform. The results in table 7.1 suggest otherwise: there is little relationship between the state economy and seat changes for the state house majority party. The coefficient on the interaction term of "change in logged state RDI x state house maj. party" indicates whether the party in control of the state house gains seats with economic growth, and estimates are in the unexpected negative direction and statistically indistinguishable from zero (table 7.1, column 1). These null findings persist even when accounting for the strength of the national economy (table 7.1, column 2), examining only presidential election years (table 7.1, column 3), federal or state midterm election years (table 7.1, columns 4 and 5), unified state governments (table 7.1, column 7), and more-professional legislatures (table 7.1, column 7). Together, it appears that the lack of a relationship between seat change and the economy in 2006 (figure 7.2) is not a one-off instance.

Seat change for the governor's party in the state house additionally has little relationship with the strength of the state economy. The statistical analyses in the second column of table 7.1 capture the extent to which state legislative elections relate to non-state legislative actors' performance. Specifically, they account for which party controlled the governorship in a state or the presidency along with the national economy. The coefficient on the interaction term of "change in logged state RDI x gov. party" indicates whether the governor's party gains state house seats with economic growth, and like the results concerning the state house majority party, estimates are in the unexpected negative direction and statistically indistinguishable from zero. Such findings are perhaps surprising in light of findings from chapter 3. Recall, during bad economies, incumbent state legislators who were members of the governor's party were more likely to face challengers (figure 3.5). However, even with these increased levels of competition, the governor's state legislative party does not systematically lose more seats during state-level economic downturns (table 7.1). Similar to the state-level balancing results in chapter 6, statistical analyses do not provide strong evidence that the governor's party systematically loses seats in the state midterm election. Together these legislative and gubernatorial findings do not provide much evidence that "all state legislative politics" are local, at least not in regard to the economy.

Nor is there much evidence that state parties are rewarded for good outcomes in policy areas such as education and health. To demonstrate this, I replicate the model presented in the first column of table 7.1, but I make

TABLE 7.1 **State and national economic performance and state house seat change**

	1972–2020	1972–2020	Presidential elections	Federal midterm elections	State midterm elections	Unified state govt.	Professional legislatures
Change in logged state RDI	-0.150 (0.117)	0.069 (0.218)	0.145 (0.204)	-0.068 (0.527)	0.098 (0.295)	0.128 (0.307)	-0.135 (0.348)
Change in logged state RDI x state house maj. party	-0.157 (0.213)	-0.010 (0.224)	0.289 (0.321)	-0.119 (0.315)	0.518 (0.369)	-0.203 (0.325)	-0.300 (0.353)
Change in logged state RDI x gov. party		-0.239 (0.306)	-0.338 (0.307)	-0.294 (0.566)	-0.444 (0.366)		0.052 (0.355)
Change in logged state RDI x pres. party		-0.046 (0.226)	0.014 (0.374)	-0.318 (0.383)	-0.209 (0.367)	-0.044 (0.291)	0.134 (0.333)
Change in logged national RDI		-1.030* (0.305)	-0.722* (0.201)	-1.805* (0.765)	-1.176* (0.302)	-1.176* (0.352)	-0.880 (0.472)
Change in logged national RDI x state house maj. party		-0.106 (0.266)	-0.490 (0.347)	0.180 (0.540)	-0.872 (0.477)	0.133 (0.405)	-0.009 (0.426)
Change in logged national RDI x gov. party		0.310 (0.360)	0.049 (0.351)	1.327 (0.877)	0.725* (0.457)		0.340 (0.485)
Change in logged national RDI x pres. maj. party		2.340* (0.370)	1.626* (0.464)	3.871* (0.741)	1.768* (0.588)	1.911* (0.473)	1.794* (0.555)
State house majority party dummy	-0.030* (0.008)	-0.035* (0.010)	-0.035 (0.019)	-0.040* (0.015)	-0.023 (0.011)	-0.038* (0.011)	-0.028* (0.013)
Governor party dummy		-0.008 (0.008)	-0.012 (0.019)	-0.023 (0.015)	-0.011 (0.010)	-0.017 (0.014)	
President party dummy		-0.077* (0.013)	-0.064* (0.015)	-0.147* (0.017)	-0.070* (0.013)	-0.089* (0.013)	-0.083* (0.019)
Previous Democratic seat change	-0.204* (0.048)	-0.258* (0.056)	-0.284* (0.120)	-0.100* (0.040)	-0.147* (0.041)	-0.390* (0.110)	-0.322* (0.071)
Statewide congressional vote change	0.252* (0.047)	0.140* (0.039)	0.121* (0.033)	0.153* (0.064)	0.244* (0.050)	0.167* (0.044)	0.207* (0.056)

continues

TABLE 7.1 **(continued)**

	1972–2020	1972–2020	Presidential elections	Federal midterm elections	State midterm elections	Unified state govt.	Professional legislatures
Federal midterm election		0.001				-0.013*	-0.019
		(0.011)				(0.006)	(0.016)
Federal midterm x pres. party		-0.039*					-0.015
		(0.013)					(0.018)
State midterm election		-0.006	-0.053	-0.018		-0.009	-0.018
		(0.010)	(0.029)	(0.026)		(0.011)	(0.016)
State midterm x gov. party		0.003	0.017	-0.005		0.013	0.008
		(0.010)	(0.024)	(0.023)		(0.011)	(0.015)
State midterm x state house maj. party		0.009	0.021	0.002			0.007
		(0.008)	(0.017)	(0.031)			(0.011)
Constant	0.001	0.041*	0.054	0.087*	0.018	0.064*	0.058*
	(0.004)	(0.013)	(0.030)	(0.013)	(0.010)	(0.012)	(0.023)
Observations	1092	1082	554	528	510	659	567
R^2	0.224	0.359	0.347	0.454	0.343	0.418	0.388

This table reports the results of linear regressions in which the outcome of interest is state-level state house seat change for the Democratic party. Standard errors are in parentheses; *$p < 0.05$.

the following change. Instead of testing for the relationship between seat change and changes in real disposable income, I substitute measures of other state policy outcomes, as summarized in the leftmost column of table 7.2. I interact each of those measures (e.g., the poverty rate) with an indicator variable that captures whether Democrats controlled the state house. Each row in table 7.2 reports the coefficient on the interaction term of this "state house majority party x performance" measure. Since the dependent variable in each analysis is seat change for Democrats in the state house, the coefficients for these interaction terms reflect the relationship between these policy measures and seat change for the state house majority party. If voters hold state house majority-party members collectively accountable for their performance in these policy areas, we should expect these coefficients to be positive and statistically distinguishable from zero.

TABLE 7.2 **State policy performance and state house majority party seat change**

	Policy area	Years	Estimate	N
Economy	State GDP	1972–2020	0.003 (0.004)	1092
	State unemployment	1978–2016	0.007 (0.005)	874
	Consumer price index	1972–2010	0.000 (0.005)	870
	Housing price index	1978–2010	−0.003 (0.006)	741
Inequality	Gini coefficient	1972–2012	−0.008 (0.005)	914
	Poverty rate	1982–2016	0.002 (0.005)	788
	Prop. of food-insecure individuals	2004–2016	0.009 (0.007)	309
Taxes	Max state tax rate	1980–2020	−0.006 (0.006)	919
	State income tax as percentage of AGI	1980–2020	0.004 (0.005)	898
Crime	Violent crime rate	1972–2014	−0.003 (0.005)	959
	Robbery crime rate	1972–2014	−0.012 (0.006)	959
	Property crime rate	1972–2014	−0.001 (0.005)	959
	Car theft rate	1972–2014	0.002 (0.005)	959
	Murder rate	1972–2014	−0.009 (0.005)	959

continues

TABLE 7.2 (*continued*)

	Policy area	Years	Estimate	N
Education	SAT score	1988–2020	−0.010 (0.005)	749
	High school graduation rate	2004–2006	0.003 (0.011)	88
	High school dropout Rate	2004–2008	0.009 (0.009)	117
	School attendance rate	1988–2008	0.001 (0.005)	482
Environment	Residential-sector energy prices	1972–2016	−0.006 (0.006)	1003
	Co2 emissions	1972–2016	−0.003 (0.005)	870
Health care	Health spending per capita	1994–2008	−0.013 (0.006)	352
	Individuals w/o health insurance (logged)	2002–2010	0.001 (0.009)	221
Family	Divorce rate	1978–2004	0.001 (0.007)	508
	Abortion rate	1978–1992	0.003 (0.010)	336
	Birth rate	1994–2008	0.001 (0.006)	352

This table reports the OLS coefficient for the interaction term of state house majority party and the indicated policy measure from a linear regression where the outcome of interest is state-level state house seat change for the Democratic party. Standard errors are in parentheses; $*p < 0.05$.

Regrettably, for our search for accountability, changes in a state's GDP, unemployment rate, consumer price index, or housing prices relate little to outcomes in state legislative elections (table 7.2, first four rows). Nor do I find evidence that a state's performance regarding economic inequality, taxes, crime, education, the environment, health care, or family issues has any bearing on whether the state house majority party picked up any seats in the next election. Readers should be cautious that state legislatures have more power over some policy areas (e.g., taxes) than others (e.g., divorce rates) and some estimations include relatively few elections. A lack of a statistically significant finding again does not imply there is no relationship, but there is not a whole lot of evidence that elections reward the state legislative party in charge of the state house, even if that state legislature successfully implements effective policies. Findings are similar when examining the relationship between policy performance and governor's party seat change in the state legislature (table A.7.3).

Whereas state parties' performances seem to have little electoral relevance, national economic conditions are a driving force in state legislative elections. When the national economy grows by 2 percent, the analysis predicts a 2.8 percent seat change for the president's party in state house elections (table 7.1, column 2). National forces reach state legislatures in both presidential and midterm elections but are stronger in midterm elections (table 7.1, columns 3 and 4). In the midterm, a 2 percent change in the national economy associates with a predicted 5.7 percent change in seats for the president's state legislative co-partisans. Consistent with earlier findings concerning federal-state balancing (tables 3.1, A.6.1, and A.6.2), statistical analyses predict the president's party will lose 8 percent of its seats, all else equal, during a midterm election. Considerable portions of state legislators' electoral fates are then largely beyond legislators' own control, even when presidential candidates are not on the ballot.

While national conditions appear to play an important role in state legislative elections, the relationship between the national economy and seat change for the president's party in state legislatures has varied over time. To illustrate these differences, I reconduct the regression analysis presented in the second column of table 7.1 for twenty-year intervals of elections (e.g., 1960 to 1980, 1962 to 1982 . . . 2000 to 2020). The black circles in figure 7.3 reflect the predicted seat change for the president's party associated with 2 percent growth in the national economy, and the black line represents the loess curve of these points. Solid circles (i.e., those filled in black) indicate that a predicted seat-change estimate is statistically distinguishable from zero.

The relationship between presidential and state legislative politics is strongest during the Kennedy, and Johnson administrations, weaker during the Ford, Carter, Reagan, and Bush administrations, and grows again during the Clinton, Bush, and Obama presidencies. Specifically, the predicted seat change for the president's party following an additional 2 percent national economic growth was 2.7 percent in elections from 1960 to 1980 (t-statistic of difference 4.16); 2.2 percent in elections from 1980 to 2000 (t-statistic of difference 2.67); and reached a high of 4.4 percent in elections from 1992 to 2012 (t-statistic of difference 3.98). The 1970s and 1980s' dip in the association between national politics and state elections coincides with an era of weaker federal parties (Rhode 1991).[9] The resurged relationship between national politics and state legislative elections in the 1990s and the first decade of the 2000s is similar to the "rebound" found in more-recent gubernatorial elections (Hopkins 2018, 45). More-recent state legislative elections, however, suggest this rebound may be waning. When studying the 2000 through 2020 elections, 2 percent economic growth

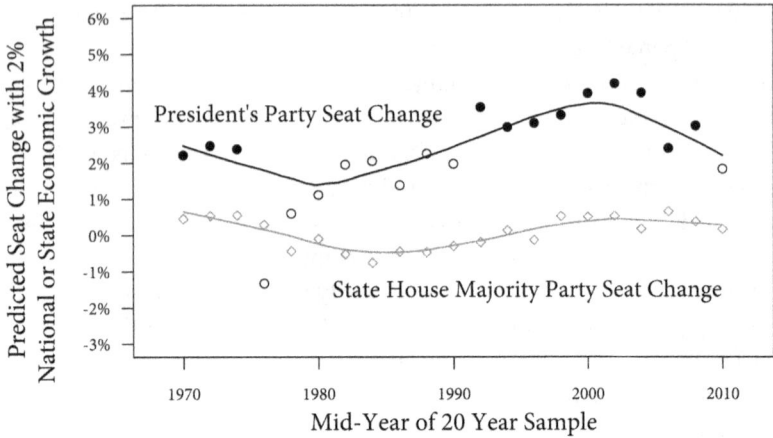

FIGURE 7.3. Predicted state-legislative seat change associated with 2 percent economic growth for state house–majority and president's party, using estimates from regressions that span twenty years. Solid dots or diamonds indicate estimate is statistically distinguishable from zero.

associates with only a 2.2 percent seat change for the president's party (t-statistic of difference 1.81). Also reflecting a surge and decline of national political influence, statistical analyses suggest that the president's party would respectively lose 11 percent, 5 percent, and 8 percent of seats in midterm elections in the 1960 to 1980, 1980 to 2000, and 2000 to 2020 elections.

National conditions' relationship with state legislators' electoral fates may temporally vary, but elections over the last sixty years produce little evidence that the state economy associates with the electoral fates of members of the state house majority party. The diamonds in figure 7.3 indicate the predicted seat change for the state house majority party associated with a 2 percent growth in the state economy. Predicted seat change never exceeds 1 percent, and no estimates meet conventional levels of statistical significance. The strongest estimated relationship between state economic growth and seat change for the party in control of the state house over a twenty-year period occurs in elections from 1996 to 2016, where 2 percent growth in the state economy associates with a 0.7 percent seat gain for the state house majority party (t-statistic of difference 1.17). When conducting similar analyses of seat change for the governor's party, the strongest estimated relationship emerges in elections from 1964 to 1984, where a 2 percent growth in the state economy associates with a 0.6 percent seat gain for the governor's party (t-statistic of difference 0.97); again, no seat-

change estimate reaches conventional levels of statistical significance. Together, these national and state-level findings suggest that the nationalization of state politics has ebbed and flowed, but state conditions consistently
appear to be unimportant for seat change in state legislatures.

Accountability and Subjective Measures of Performance

Elections do not appear to hold state legislative parties accountable for
policy performance, at least not against objectively measured state-level
policy outcomes. However, it is again helpful to take a methodological aside
and recognize limitations to using objective measures of performance when
making conclusions about accountability. Voters may evaluate their legislators for criteria beyond those considered above (figure 5.1), and objective measures of policy performance do not always perfectly translate into
subjective judgments (figure 7.1). Prior work shows that multiple factors,
such as a state's policy liberalism and economy, can weigh upon voter's
assessment of their legislature's performance (Langehennig, Zamadics, and
Wolak 2019), and voters can place greater weight on specific issues when
voting for their state legislator (figure 5.2). For instance, one voter may approve of their legislature for their management of the economy but care
little about education policy, while another voter may care about education and not the economy. The above analyses also assume voters know
which party controls their state legislature, which is not always the case
(figure 4.3).

To overcome these limitations, I investigate whether individuals report
voting for the state house majority party when they believe the legislature
is doing a good job. I again use nationally representative surveys conducted
by the Cooperative Election Study from 2008 to 2020. Before the election,
voters indicated if they approved of their legislature's performance, and
after the election, the same voters indicated how they voted in a state legislative election. Using these ratings, I estimate how state house vote choice
varies as a function of voters' approval ratings of their state legislature,
governor, and president while accounting for a respondent's party identification, gender, race, age, education, and income.[10]

I evaluate the relationship between a voter's approval of the state legislature and vote choice using probit analyses that employ survey weights
to create a more representative sample (table 7.3). For clarity in presentation, table 7.4 presents the differences in the predicted probabilities of
a vote for the state house majority party candidate if a voter "strongly

TABLE 7.3 **State legislative, gubernatorial, and presidential approval and state house vote choice**

	2008	2010	2012	2014	2016	2018	2020
State legislative approval	0.082*	0.099*	0.072*	0.059*	0.111*	0.064*	0.048*
	(0.026)	(0.022)	(0.022)	(0.023)	(0.027)	(0.025)	(0.017)
Governor approval	0.126*	0.072*	0.101*	0.176*	0.142*	0.144	-0.025
	(0.023)	(0.029)	(0.017)	(0.018)	(0.023)	(0.023)	(0.017)
Presidential approval	0.307*	0.422*	0.452*	0.359*	0.379*	0.514*	0.629*
	(0.017)	(0.021)	(0.018)	(0.018)	(0.012)	(0.019)	(0.013)
Party ID (7-pt)	0.521*	0.479*	0.456*	0.472*	0.422*	0.461*	0.454*
	(0.018)	(0.018)	(0.014)	(0.012)	(0.012)	(0.012)	(0.010)
Female respondent	0.031	0.010	-0.127*	0.098*	0.080*	-0.038	-0.009
	(0.030)	(0.025)	(0.039)	(0.034)	(0.027)	(0.033)	(0.038)
Nonwhite respondent	0.354*	0.195*	0.148*	0.150*	0.229*	0.393*	0.250*
	(0.063)	(0.054)	(0.062)	(0.066)	(0.054)	(0.042)	(0.064)
Age (in years)	-0.002	-0.004*	-0.001	-0.004*	0.002	-0.003*	-0.004*
	(0.001)	(0.001)	(0.001)	(0.001)	(0.001)	(0.001)	(0.001)
Education: high school degree	-0.082	-0.074	-0.052	-0.007	-0.002	-0.058	-0.036
	(0.105)	(0.129)	(0.109)	(0.105)	(0.066)	(0.115)	(0.146)
Education: some college	-0.132	-0.126	0.010	-0.094	0.019	-0.090	-0.079
	(0.099)	(0.144)	(0.107)	(0.118)	(0.072)	(0.118)	(0.134)
Education: two-year college	-0.211	-0.122	0.047	-0.003	-0.039	-0.198	0.017
	(0.109)	(0.129)	(0.112)	(0.128)	(0.082)	(0.107)	(0.138)
Education: four-year college	-0.132	-0.104	-0.032	0.024	-0.011	-0.070	-0.095
	(0.093)	(0.120)	(0.108)	(0.101)	(0.074)	(0.112)	(0.140)
Education: postgrad degree	-0.026	-0.049	-0.004	0.081	0.093	-0.066	0.019
	(0.110)	(0.134)	(0.112)	(0.119)	(0.084)	(0.106)	(0.145)
Income: $30,000–$70,000	-0.033	-0.010	-0.013	-0.091*	-0.072*	-0.038	-0.051
	(0.040)	(0.035)	(0.039)	(0.039)	(0.034)	(0.041)	(0.041)

	(1)	(2)	(3)	(4)	(5)	(6)	(7)
Income: $70,000—$100,000	-0.059	-0.180*	-0.151*	-0.071	-0.091	-0.003	-0.110*
	(0.043)	(0.059)	(0.058)	(0.073)	(0.060)	(0.060)	(0.053)
Income: above $100,000	-0.099	-0.157*	-0.130*	-0.171*	-0.132*	-0.108*	-0.064
	(0.056)*	(0.037)	(0.054)	(0.053)	(0.036)	(0.043)	(0.048)
Session length (in hundreds of days)	-0.001*	-0.000	-0.000	0.000	-0.000	0.000	0.000
	(0.000)	(0.000)	(0.000)	(0.000)	(0.000)	(0.000)	(0.000)
Legislative staff per member	-0.012*	-0.004	-0.014*	-0.020*	-0.014*	-0.003	-0.006
	(0.004)	(0.008)	(0.005)	(0.006)	(0.005)	(0.005)	(0.006)
Legislator salary (in thousands of 2010 dollars)	0.002*	0.001	0.001	-0.000	0.000	0.000	0.001*
	(0.000)	(0.001)	(0.001)	(0.000)	(0.000)	(0.000)	(0.000)
Democratic governor	-0.040	0.026	0.015	0.019	0.025	0.009	-0.122*
	(0.032)*	(0.051)	(0.065)	(0.057)	(0.060)	(0.055)	(0.049)
Democratic state house majority	-0.177*	-0.003	0.037	0.112	-0.100	-0.188*	-0.139
	(0.031)	(0.082)	(0.083)	(0.082)	(0.093)	(0.084)	(0.090)
Democratic Party seat share	1.444*	0.837*	0.866*	0.607*	1.179*	1.081*	0.910*
	(0.149)	(0.309)	(0.333)	(0.268)	(0.406)	(0.292)	(0.291)
Divided state government	-0.125*	0.029	0.033	-0.040	-0.022	-0.037	0.074
	(0.030)	(0.046)	(0.058)	(0.048)	(0.046)	(0.048)	(0.039)
Polarization (state house)	-0.097*	0.023	0.094*	0.074*	0.106*	0.007	-0.008
	(0.027)	(0.036)	(0.041)	(0.035)	(0.033)	(0.033)	(0.030)
Constant	-0.481*	-0.111	-0.195	-0.102	-0.778*	-0.313*	-0.383*
	(0.105)	(0.193)	(0.184)	(0.179)	(0.170)	(0.149)	(0.190)
N	20,208	31,863	30,939	28,851	35,879	37,898	40,497
Log-likelihood	-4,179.9	-5,822.8	-7,047.6	-6,359.6	-7,864.7	-4,879.7	-5,071.1

This table reports the results of probit regressions in which the outcome of interest is whether a voter voted for the Democratic candidate in their state house elections. Samples drawn from the Cooperative Election Studies. Standard errors are in parentheses; *$p < 0.05$.

TABLE 7.4 **State legislative approval's relationship with state house vote choice**

Sample	2008	2010	2012	2014	2016	2018	2020
All voters	+0.043*	+0.048*	+0.035*	+0.030*	+0.060*	+0.021*	+0.015*
	(0.013)	(0.010)	(0.010)	(0.011)	(0.014)	(0.009)	(0.005)
Correct voters	+0.092*	+0.085*	+0.064*	+0.056*	+0.074*	+0.041*	+0.017*
	(0.020)	(0.011)	(0.014)	(0.013)	(0.014)	(0.011)	(0.007)
Not sure voters	+0.004	+0.002	−0.002	+0.007	+0.024	+0.001	+0.003
	(0.016)	(0.017)	(0.013)	(0.015)	(0.015)	(0.009)	(0.006)
Incorrect voters	−0.023	−0.038	+0.031	−0.067*	+0.042	−0.049*	+0.047*
	(0.015)	(0.022)	(0.020)	(0.034)	(0.026)	(0.015)	(0.013)

This table reports the differences in average predicted probabilities of a voter supporting the state house majority party associated with adjusting a voter's approval rating of the state legislature from "strongly disapprove" to "strongly approve." Standard errors are in parentheses; *$p < 0.05$.

approves" of the state legislature instead of "strongly disapproves." After presenting the strength of the relationships between state legislative approval and vote choice from 2008 to 2020, I focus on the 2018 election, where I asked a more extensive set of questions pertaining to state legislative elections to show that accountability in state legislatures depends on voters' issue priorities and knowledge.

Promisingly for accountability in state legislatures, voters' assessments of the state legislature relate to their decisions in state legislative elections in each election considered. The probability of voting for a state house majority party candidate increases by up to 0.060 when voters strongly approve of their legislature instead of strongly disapprove (table 7.4, "All voters" row). The relationship between approval and vote choice was most substantial in 2016 but weakest in 2020. State legislative parties and their members then have *some* electoral incentive to perform well, thereby helping solve the moral hazard problem posed by representative government.

State legislators' electoral fates are additionally subject to voters' assessments of the governor. Table 7.5 is similar to table 7.4 but reports the differences in the predicted probability of voting for a state legislator of the governor's party when voters strongly approve instead of strongly disapprove of the governor. In every considered election except the 2010 and 2020 elections, the relationship between governor approval and state house vote choice is stronger than that found between state legislative approval and vote choice. Such findings complement those concerning challengers' strategies in elections. Recall from chapter 3 that challengers more often run against the governor's state legislative co-partisans during bad economies. Findings in table 7.5 generally indicate that the governors' state legislative co-partisans are more difficult to beat when voters are happy with the governor's performance.

To situate state legislative findings within a broader American political context, I conduct a comparable study of US House elections.[11] Similar to conclusions concerning individual representatives' ideological representation (figure 6.3), analyses of voters' subjective assessments of Congress and their state legislature provide evidence of stronger electoral accountability in congressional elections than in state legislative elections. A voter strongly approving instead of strongly disapproving of the US Congress results in an 0.074 change in the probability that they will vote for a member of the US House majority party (figure 7.4, dotted line). Meanwhile,

TABLE 7.5 **Governor's approval's relationship with state house vote choice**

Sample	2008	2010	2012	2014	2016	2018	2020
All voters	+0.070*	+0.035*	+0.052*	+0.100*	+0.082*	+0.051*	−0.008
	(0.015)	(0.015)	(0.009)	(0.011)	(0.013)	(0.010)	(0.005)
Correct voters	0.068*	+0.029	+0.054*	+0.108*	+0.084*	+0.054*	−0.014*
	(0.022	(0.015)	(0.011)	(0.013)	(0.013)	(0.010)	(0.007)
Not sure voters	+0.050*	+0.039*	+0.061*	+0.072*	+0.06*	+0.029*	+0.002
	(0.017)	(0.015)	(0.014)	(0.020)	(0.013)	(0.010)	(0.007)
Incorrect voters	+0.117*	+0.058*	+0.007	+0.108*	+0.112*	+0.089*	−0.008
	(0.017)	(0.025)	(0.022)	(0.023)	(0.031)	(0.024)	(0.010)

This table reports the differences in average predicted probabilities of a voter supporting the governor's party in state legislative elections associated with adjusting a voter's approval rating of the governor from "strongly disapprove" to "strongly approve." Standard errors are in parentheses; $*p < 0.05$.

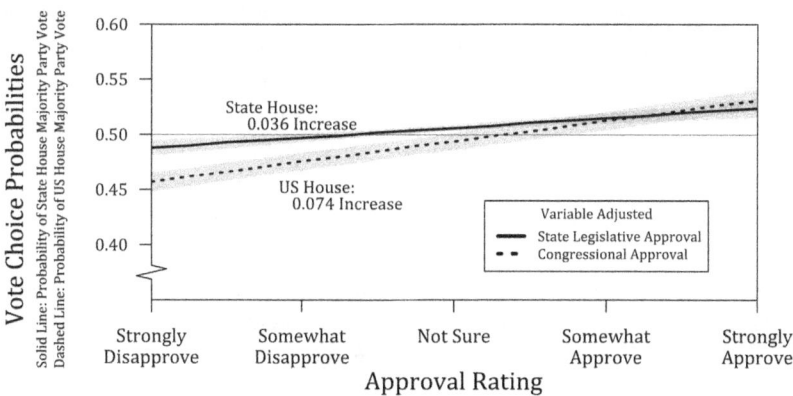

FIGURE 7.4. Predicted probability of voting for a member of the majority party in the US House or state house, associated with a voter's approval rating of Congress or their state legislature.

a voter strongly approving instead of strongly disapproving of their state legislature results in a 0.036 predicted change in the probability that they will vote for a member of the state house majority party (figure 7.4, solid line).[12] Electoral connections then exist in state legislatures. But if our standard is the level of accountability in federal elections, state legislative elections again fail to meet this benchmark.

Why So Little Evidence of Collective Accountability?

The relationships between voters' approval ratings and vote choice help provide a "yes" answer to the question of "do elections hold state legislators accountable for their own performance?" But the above results still raise at least two questions. First, why didn't we detect these relationships when studying objective measures of performance (tables 7.1 and 7.2)? Second, why are the relationships so weak (figure 7.4)? To answer these questions, it is helpful to return to issues raised earlier in this book. Specifically, we will find that detecting evidence of accountability in state legislatures will partly depend on what voters know about state legislative elections (chapter 4) and what issues they care most about (chapter 5).

Accountability for Issues Voters Care About

Objective measures of policy performance, such as indicators for economic or education outcomes, have little relationship with electoral change in state legislatures (table 7.2), suggesting a lack of collective accountability for how the legislature addresses particular policy issues. Voters, however, care about different issues (figure 5.2). As a sports fan may care more about Olympic gymnastics than about track and field, a voter could care more about whether the legislature provides funding to build good roads than about whether it invests in schools. Social psychologist Jon Krosnick nicely applied this reasoning to voting behavior when forming hypotheses concerning the importance of "issue publics" — groups of people who follow an issue particularly closely — stating: "The impact of a policy attitude on a citizen's candidate preference should depend on the personal importance of the policy attitude to voter" (Krosnick 1990b, 62).

Studies of electoral behavior offer mixed evidence of whether issue importance matters in shaping voters' decision-making. Studying the 1968, 1980, and 1984 elections, Krosnick finds a stronger association between voters' issue positions and evaluations of presidential candidates on issues that voters find important (see also Aldrich and McKelvey 1977; Granberg and Holmberg 1986; Visser, Krosnick, and Simmons 2003). Other political scientists find less evidence that issue importance affects voter behavior (Hinckley, Hofstetter, and Kessel 1974; Leeper and Robison 2018; Niemi and Bartels 1985). In their study of the 1980 to 2008 presidential elections, Thomas Leeper and Joshua Robison, for example, conclude that "issue importance has a small, but highly variable, influence over voter decision-making," and as characterized by Robert Johns (2010, 146), the empirical evidence concerning issue publics and voting is "surprisingly patchy."

To assess whether voters hold their state legislators accountable for their performance on certain issues, I asked 2018 CES respondents to approve of "how the [insert state legislature name here] is handling the following issue" for twelve different issues. Using these approval ratings, I employ a statistical model similar to that presented in table 7.3. The dependent variable is still state house vote choice, but the key independent variable of interest is a voter's issue-level approval, such as their approval of the state legislature's handling of education or health care. I then calculate the differences in the predicted probability of voting for the state house majority party associated with a voter strongly approving instead of disapproving of a legislature's performance on an individual issue and report these differences in table 7.6.[13]

There is little statistical association between vote choice and voters' "issue-level approval" ratings across each of the twelve considered issues.

TABLE 7.6 **Issue-specific state legislative approval's relationship with state house vote choice**

Issue	Change in probability	Issue	Change in probability
Unemployment	−0.038	**Gun control**	−0.029
	(0.041)		(0.029)
Health care	+0.017	**Immigration**	−0.006
	(0.041)		(0.039)
Transportation	−0.075	**Taxes**	−0.014
	(0.028)		(0.035)
Education	−0.013	**Corruption**	+0.015
	(0.024)		(0.039)
Abortion	+0.028	**Law enforcement**	−0.002
	(0.027)		(0.031)
Racial equality	+0.002	**Budgets**	+0.031
	(0.035)		(0.038)
		Most important issue	+0.145*
			(0.027)

This table reports the differences in average predicted probabilities of a voter supporting the state house majority party in state legislative elections associated with adjusting a voter's approval rating of the state legislature's performance from "strongly disapprove" to "strongly approve" for the listed issue. Standard errors are in parentheses; *$p < 0.05$.

Such results are consistent with other findings in this book. Recall, there were meager relationships between the popularity of state legislators' individual roll-call votes and election outcomes (figure 6.6), and objective measures of a state legislature's performance on issues such as the economy, education, or health care do not systematically relate to majority-party seat change in state legislatures (table 7.2). Together, these analyses provide scant evidence that voters hold legislators accountable for their performance on specific issues.

However, none of these analyses account for whether voters cared about the economy, education, or health care policies. Thus, to investigate the importance of issue importance or "issue publics," I utilize the issue-importance rankings detailed in chapter 5. Specifically, I identify which issue a voter indicated was most important to them and examine the relationship between vote choice and a voter's approval of the legislature for this particular issue. In other words, for one observation, a voter's state legislative approval rating could be the voter's issue-level approval of the state legislature's handling of abortion. For another observation, it could be the voter's issue-level approval of the state legislature's handling of immigration, depending on whether the voter indicated abortion or immigration was the most important issue in their decision to vote for their state representative.

When only considering the approval ratings for the issue a voter indicated was most important to their state legislative vote, a more promising accountability picture emerges. A voter strongly approving instead of strongly disapproving of how their state legislature handled the most important issue to that voter increases the likelihood of voting for the state house majority party by 0.145 (table 7.5, bottom right cell). This relationship between how voters perceive the legislature to perform on their most important issue and vote choice is the strongest piece of evidence offered by this book that voters provide collective accountability in state legislative elections. It is over twice as strong as any relationship found between overall state legislative approval and vote choice. Failing to account for voters' priorities in state legislative elections is then at least one reason prior analyses reveal so little accountability in state legislative elections.

A "Miracle" Muddled by Misinformation

When voters care more about a particular issue, their assessment of the legislature's handling of that issue shapes state legislative elections' outcomes. We, however, know that the typical voter neither cares nor knows much about state legislative politics. And this lack of knowledge is another reason why we find voters largely fail to hold state legislators collectively accountable.[14]

To illustrate the role misinformation plays in state legislative elections, the bottom three rows of table 7.4 present the predicted change in the probability of vote choice associated with a voter strongly approving instead of strongly disapproving of the legislature for three distinct groups of voters: those who correctly identified their state house majority party, those who were not sure which party controlled the state house, and those who incorrectly identified the state house majority party (e.g., a voter indicated the Republicans had a majority of seats when Democrats did).

Voters who correctly identified which party controlled their state house were generally the most likely to hold that party accountable for its performance (table 7.4, "Correct voters" row). In the 2018 election, approximately 60 percent of voters were informed or knew which party controlled their state house, 31 percent stated they were not sure, and 9 percent incorrectly identified the state house majority party. Figure 7.5 illustrates the predicted probability that correct and incorrect voters supported a candidate of the state house majority party under different levels of state legislative approval in the 2018 election. The probability that an informed voter who strongly disapproved of the legislature would vote for the state house majority party was .514. If this same voter instead strongly approved of the legislature's performance, this probability rises to .555 (figure 7.5, solid line). This .041 increase suggests that state legislative parties have an electoral incentive to gain these voters' approval.[15]

Misinformation, however, muddles accountability in state legislatures. While there is consistently a positive relationship between state legislative approval and vote choice among correct voters, there is the opposite relationship between approval and vote choice among voters who incorrectly identified their state house majority party in the 2014 and 2018 elections. When an incorrect voter strongly disapproved of the state legislature in 2018, the predicted probability this voter supported the state house majority party was .581. If this voter instead strongly approved of the legislature, the comparable probability falls to .532 (figure 7.5, dotted line). Taken together, the solid and dotted lines in figure 7.5 indicate that when the state legislature performs well, informed voters who correctly identify the state house majority party electorally reward the party in power, but misinformed voters at times punish the incumbent party even when the state legislature has done a good job in the eyes of the voter.

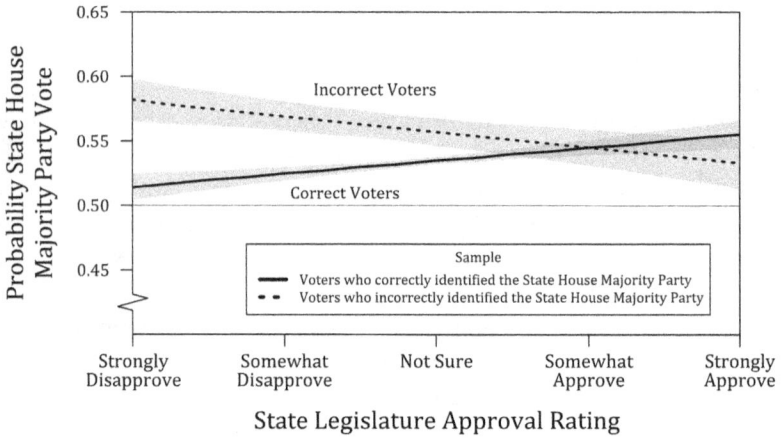

FIGURE 7.5. Predicted probability of voting for a member of the state house–majority party, associated with a voter's approval rating of the state legislature among voters who correctly and incorrectly identified the state house–majority party.

The counteracting relationships presented in figure 7.5 help further explain the weak electoral connections in state legislatures and cast doubt that miracles of aggregation ameliorate accountability concerns. Misinformed voters at times try to hold legislative parties accountable by voting for or against the party they *believe* to be in power, but their mistaken attribution ultimately punishes the parties that are *actually* in power for doing a good job. In other words, voters seem to *try* to hold their state legislators accountable but being misinformed undermines their efforts. Some voters may recognize that the state economy is weak (figure 7.1) but blame the wrong party. For a miracle of aggregation to succeed, "typical" voters' errors need to be random and cancel out. Instead, voters' errors are not random but can result from somewhat rational behavior detrimental to accountability in state legislatures.

Misattribution in a Complicated Federal System

Voter behavior in state legislative elections further appears to be shaped by attribution errors rooted in national politics. Survey data provide overwhelming evidence that national politics dominate state legislative elections. Table 7.7 is similar to table 7.4 but presents the predicted impact of strongly approving instead of disapproving of the president's performance on vote choice in state legislative elections. Presidential approval's influence (table 7.7, first row) is always more substantial than state legislative approval in predicting vote choice (table 7.4, first row). Figure 7.6 illustrates the remarkable relative impact of presidential to state legislative approval in 2018. As voter approval of the president or state legislature grows, the predicted probabilities of voting for these parties' candidates increase, but changes in presidential approval have over three times the impact of comparable shifts in state legislative approval.[16] In earlier work (Rogers 2016), I provide a similar study of New Jersey and Virginia state

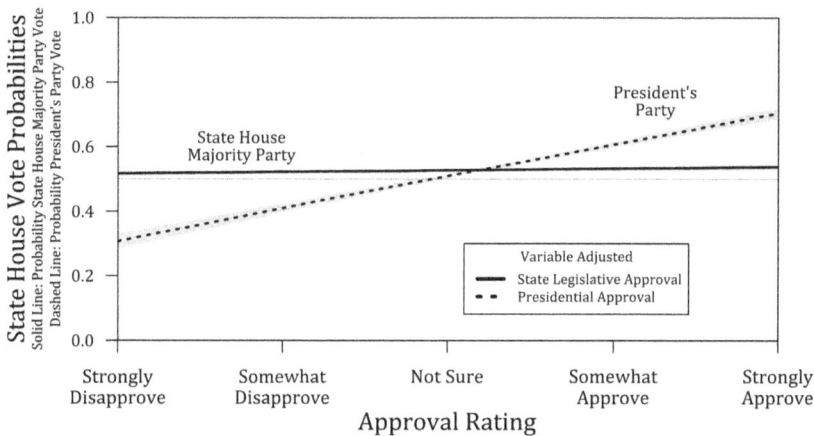

FIGURE 7.6. Predicted probability of voting for a member of the president's party or state house–majority party, associated with a voter's approval of the president or state legislature.

TABLE 7.7 **Presidential approval's relationship with state house vote choice**

Sample	2008	2010	2012	2014	2016	2018	2020
All voters	+0.221*	+0.357*	+0.398*	+0.277*	+0.332*	+0.396*	+0.544*
	(0.015)	(0.021)	(0.019)	(0.016)	(0.013)	(0.020)	(0.018)
Correct voters	+0.201*	+0.362*	+0.439*	+0.268*	+0.328*	+0.407*	+0.572*
	(0.021)	(0.028)	(0.027)	(0.021)	(0.025)	(0.024)	(0.017)
Not sure voters	+0.226*	+0.323*	+0.355*	+0.284*	+0.304*	+0.396*	+0.525*
	(0.026)	(0.026)	(0.026)	(0.028)	(0.021)	(0.030)	(0.033)
Incorrect voters	+0.233*	+0.344*	+0.418*	+0.243*	+0.355*	+0.256*	+0.440*
	(0.038)	(0.077)	(0.050)	(0.038)	(0.035)	(0.036)	(0.046)

This table reports the differences in average predicted probabilities of a voter supporting the president's party in state legislative elections associated with adjusting a voter's approval rating of the president from "strongly disapprove" to "strongly approve." Standard errors are in parentheses; *p < 0.05.

legislative elections, which occur in the "off-year" separate from presidential or congressional elections. I find presidential approval has a more considerable impact on state legislative vote choice than state legislative approval in elections dating back to the 1970s.

The strong relationship between presidential approval and state legislative vote choice has implications for the "miracle of aggregation" explanation of state legislative election outcomes. Again, voters' errors do not appear to be random but instead are the systematic result of their perceptions of national politics. Even more "exemplary" voters exhibit a national politics bias. In each considered election, the relationship between presidential approval and vote choice is comparable if not larger among correct (table 7.7, "Correct voters" row) than incorrect voters (table 7.7, "Incorrect voters" row). Misattribution errors ultimately undermine elections' ability to solve the moral hazard problem in state legislatures. Legislative parties, after all, have little control over the president's performance. These results clearly rebel against the fatherly wisdom that "all politics is local."

Recap

In the search for accountability in state legislatures, this chapter's findings add to the growing evidence that levels of meaningful electoral accountability are meager at best. Fortunately, when evaluating subjective evaluations of the legislature's performance, I find that voters more often support the party in control of the legislature when they approve of the legislature's performance, particularly on the issue most important to individual voters. There is, however, little evidence that objective measures of state-level performance have any relationship with seat change for the parties in control of the state legislature, and state legislative electoral connections are again weaker than those in US House elections.

Errors made by voters are partly responsible for these discouraging relationships. Misinformed voters who are upset with the legislature at times punish the party they believe is in power rather than the party that is actually in power. Otherwise stated, these voters punish the party in power for doing a good job. Voters' attribution errors further compound problems for establishing collective accountability across the different levels of the American federal system. Presidential approval has three times the impact on state house vote choice that state legislative approval does, even when only considering the issues voters say are most important to their state legislative vote, swamping out the impact of state legislators' own actions on their elections. "Miracles of aggregation" then are not divine enough to reach heavenly levels of accountability in state legislative elections.

If national politics dominate state legislative elections, they become "second-order" elections analogous to European Parliament elections, in which votes are cast "on the basis of facts in the main political arena of the nation" (Reif and Schmitt 1980, 9). Second-order elections are unlikely to serve elections' first-order purpose—to hold state legislators accountable for their own performance. If the president's actions drive state legislative elections' outcomes, state legislators lack strong incentives to represent their constituents' interests. Why should a legislator work to stimulate the economy or gain his constituents' approval if a voter's Election-Day decision is not based on his own performance? Without this electoral connection, the moral hazard problem posed by representative government once more rears its ugly head.

To this point, our search for accountability suggests that poorly performing legislators have little to fear come Election Day. But this finding does not mean that representation and performance have no impact on legislators' likelihood of reclaiming office. The general election is not the only way for voters to kick legislators out of the legislature. Legislators can also be voted out in the primary election or choose to leave the legislature voluntarily. For instance, three of the four Republican senators critical to legalizing same-sex marriage in New York in 2011 were forced from the legislature by 2014 largely due to internal party controversy and primary elections. The fourth Republican was Senator James Alesi, who retired after casting the decisive vote for legalizing same-sex marriage. When discussing his decision not to seek reelection, Alesi told the *New York Times* that "If I'm in the general election, there's no question I'll win the seat" (Eligon 2012) but thought that the district's support was not enough, later stating "I've gotten a lot of support from Democrats and the gay community, but unfortunately they can't vote in a Republican primary" (Lovett 2012). Were Alesi's fears of losing a primary election warranted? I turn to this question about accountability in the primary election in the next chapter.

Appendix

TABLE A.7.1 **Summary statistics**

Variable	Min.	Max	Median	Mean	SD
Democratic party state house seat change	−0.636	0.711	0.000	−0.004	0.094
Change in logged state RDI	−0.173	0.343	0.024	0.024	0.030
Change in logged national RDI	−0.020	0.073	0.023	0.023	0.020
State house majority party dummy	0.000	1.000	1.000	0.564	0.496
Statewide congressional vote change	−0.700	0.656	−0.002	−0.003	0.086
Governor party dummy	0.000	1.000	1.000	0.530	0.499
President party dummy	0.000	1.000	0.000	0.444	0.497
State midterm election	0.000	1.000	0.000	0.421	0.494
Federal midterm election	0.000	1.000	0.000	0.473	0.499
Professionalism (Squire)	0.027	0.659	0.181	0.210	0.125
State GDP	−0.310	13.884	0.061	0.439	2.052
State unemployment	−6.700	6.800	−0.400	−0.122	1.760
Consumer price index	−0.134	0.068	0.001	−0.001	0.026
Housing price index	−1.450	1.662	0.135	0.158	0.284
Gini coefficient	−0.092	0.121	0.006	0.006	0.018
Poverty rate	−6.900	9.600	0.000	−0.032	2.134
Prop. of food-insecure individuals	−7.993	10.450	−0.010	0.081	3.095
Max state tax rate	−14.500	4.500	0.000	−0.018	0.873
State income tax as percentage of AGI	−0.036	0.028	0.000	0.000	0.003
Violent crime rate	−0.944	0.840	0.023	0.050	0.171
Robbery crime rate	−5.968	1.080	0.022	−0.084	0.776
Property crime rate	−0.495	0.460	−0.001	0.018	0.122
Car theft rate	−0.680	5.865	0.002	0.010	0.245
Murder rate	−6.900	9.600	0.000	−0.044	1.361
SAT score (logged)	−0.186	0.137	0.003	0.002	0.038
High school graduation rate	−16.528	8.782	0.537	0.319	3.404
High school dropout rate	−3.800	2.700	−0.200	−0.131	0.931
School attendance rate	−10.843	9.758	0.025	0.074	1.482
Residential sector energy prices	−24.150	23.620	0.710	0.917	2.031
Co2 emissions	−0.322	0.547	0.027	0.029	0.084
Health spending per capita	0.032	0.308	0.111	0.112	0.033
Individuals w/o health insurance	−0.644	0.392	0.069	0.065	0.129
Divorce rate	−3.230	3.100	−0.100	−0.106	0.506
Birth rate	−0.192	0.296	0.007	0.010	0.064

Summary statistics of variables used in chapter 7's seat-change analyses.

TABLE A.7.2 **State and national economic performance and state senate seat change**

	1972–2020	1972–2020	Presidential elections	Federal midterm	State midterm	Unified state govt.	Professional Legislatures
Change in logged state RDI	0.007 (0.106)	−0.264 (0.240)	−0.135 (0.283)	−0.326 (0.405)	−0.544 (0.362)	−0.177 (0.249)	−0.093 (0.580)
Change in logged state RDI x state senate maj. party	−0.166 (0.147)	0.049 (0.245)	0.328 (0.346)	−0.037 (0.434)	0.551 (0.426)	0.163 (0.566)	−0.470 (0.525)
Change in logged state RDI x gov. party		0.146 (0.250)	0.054 (0.350)	0.144 (0.382)	0.254 (0.379)	−0.034 (0.532)	0.129 (0.363)
Change in logged state RDI x pres. party		0.348 (0.273)	0.224 (0.368)	0.215 (0.471)	0.299 (0.376)	0.100 (0.263)	0.824* (0.339)
Change in logged national RDI		−0.315 (0.470)	0.131 (0.490)	−1.533 (0.949)	0.205 (0.754)	−0.585 (0.537)	−0.739 (0.935)
Change in logged national RDI x state senate maj. party		−0.126 (0.516)	−0.982 (0.513)	0.806 (0.792)	−0.414 (0.733)	0.137 (0.898)	0.781 (0.824)
Change in logged national RDI x gov. party		−0.370 (0.507)	−0.218 (0.501)	−0.009 (0.974)	−0.531 (0.715)	−0.626 (0.845)	−0.058 (0.688)
Change in logged national RDI x pres. maj. party		1.982* (0.517)	1.244* (0.602)	3.622* (1.039)	0.839 (0.651)	2.030* (0.608)	1.092 (0.569)
State senate majority party dummy	−0.042* (0.010)	−0.047* (0.013)	−0.032 (0.024)	−0.065* (0.022)	−0.045* (0.015)	−0.065* (0.018)	−0.060* (0.018)
Governor party dummy		−0.004 (0.008)	−0.017 (0.015)	−0.005 (0.016)	−0.004 (0.015)	0.019 (0.015)	−0.005 (0.011)
President party dummy		−0.068* (0.010)	−0.047* (0.014)	−0.140* (0.025)	−0.054* (0.017)	−0.085* (0.015)	−0.064* (0.011)
Previous Democratic seat change	−0.103 (0.055)	−0.140* (0.052)	−0.128 (0.069)	−0.076 (0.104)	−0.067 (0.054)	−0.155* (0.059)	−0.239* (0.054)
Statewide congressional vote change	0.159* (0.050)	0.055 (0.040)	0.026 (0.042)	0.085 (0.074)	0.140 (0.070)	0.070 (0.044)	0.040 (0.074)

continues

TABLE A.7.2 (*continued*)

	1972–2020	1972–2020	Presidential elections	Federal midterm	State midterm	Unified state govt.	Professional Legislatures
Midterm election		0.004				-0.014*	-0.000
		(0.006)				(0.006)	(0.012)
Federal midterm x pres. party		-0.044*					-0.027
		(0.012)					(0.016)
State midterm election		-0.013	-0.053	-0.047		-0.010	-0.014
		(0.010)	(0.040)	(0.033)		(0.010)	(0.019)
State midterm x gov. party		0.003	0.013	-0.006		-0.008	0.007
		(0.011)	(0.018)	(0.023)		(0.013)	(0.014)
State midterm x. state senate maj. party		0.012	0.027	-0.027		0.025	0.013
		(0.010)	(0.025)	(0.026)		(0.014)	(0.014)
Constant	-0.000	0.036*	0.055	0.056*	0.019	0.043*	0.042*
	(0.002)	(0.010)	(0.045)	(0.013)	(0.015)	(0.014)	(0.015)
Observations	957	949	489	460	447	582	515
R^2	0.126	0.230	0.195	0.348	0.212	0.249	0.253

This table reports the results of linear regressions in which the outcome of interest is state-level state senate seat change for the Democratic party. Standard errors are in parentheses; *$p < 0.05$.

TABLE A.7.3 **State house seat change for the governor's party as a function of state policy performance**

	Policy area	Years	Estimate	N
Economy	State GDP	1972–2020	0.001 (0.005)	1082
	State unemployment	1978–2016	0.002 (0.005)	865
	Consumer price index	1972–2010	−0.010 (0.005)	864
	Housing price index	1978–2010	0.013 (0.005)	735
Inequality	Gini coefficient	1972–2012	0.008 (0.005)	907
	Poverty rate	1982–2016	0.005 (0.005)	779
	Prop. of food-insecure individuals	2004–2016	0.011 (0.008)	306
Taxes	Max state tax rate	1980–2020	−0.006 (0.005)	909
	State income tax as percentage of AGI	1980–2020	0.000 (0.005)	888
Crime	Violent crime rate	1972–2014	0.007 (0.005)	951
	Robbery crime rate	1972–2014	0.001 (0.005)	951
	Property crime rate	1972–2014	−0.002 (0.005)	951
	Car theft rate	1972–2014	0.009 (0.005)	951
	Murder rate	1972–2014	0.009 (0.005)	951
Education	SAT score	1988–2020	−0.005 (0.005)	739
	High school graduation rate	2004–2006	0.002 (0.009)	88
	High school dropout Rate	2004–2008	0.005 (0.010)	117
	School attendance rate	1988–2008	0.005 (0.006)	476
Environ-ment	Residential sector energy prices	1972–2016	0.003 (0.005)	994
	Co2 emissions	1972–2016	0.002 (0.005)	863
Health care	Health spending per capita	1994–2008	−0.002 (0.006)	346
	Individuals w/o health insurance	2002–2010	0.002 (0.010)	219
Family	Divorce rate	1978–2004	0.003 (0.007)	504
	Abortion rate	1978–1992	−0.006 (0.010)	336
	Birth rate	1994–2008	0.004 (0.006)	346

This table reports the OLS coefficient for the interaction term of the governor's party and the indicated policy measure from a linear regression where the outcome of interest is state-level state house seat change for the Democratic party. Standard errors are in parentheses; *$p < 0.05$.

TABLE A.7.4 **State legislative and US House approval and vote choice**

	State house	US House
State legislative approval	0.079*	
	(0.016)	
Congressional approval		0.129*
		(0.007)
Governor approval	0.081*	0.089*
	(0.013)	(0.010)
Presidential approval	0.445*	0.420*
	(0.007)	(0.008)
Party ID (7-pt)	0.473*	0.382*
	(0.007)	(0.005)
Female respondent	0.015	0.027*
	(0.013)	(0.013)
Nonwhite respondent	0.209*	0.211*
	(0.038)	(0.032)
Age (in years)	−0.002*	−0.002*
	(0.000)	(0.000)
Education: high school degree	−0.048	0.028
	(0.049)	(0.038)
Education: some college	−0.068	0.018
	(0.055)	(0.043)
Education: two-year college	−0.080	−0.000
	(0.051)	(0.040)
Education: four-year college	−0.064	0.034
	(0.050)	(0.040)
Education: postgrad degree	0.015	0.124*
	(0.059)	(0.038)
Income: $30,000−$70,000	−0.048*	−0.019
	(0.015)	(0.017)
Income: $70,000−$100,000	−0.111*	−0.032
	(0.023)	(0.024)
Income: above $100,000	−0.133*	−0.046*
	(0.018)	(0.022)
Democratic state house majority	0.166*	
	(0.035)	
Democratic US House majority		0.095*
		(0.031)
Democratic governor	0.042	0.208*
	(0.028)	(0.030)
Democratic president	0.423*	0.285*
	(0.027)	(0.043)
Constant	−0.318*	−0.431*
	(0.055)	(0.058)
N	227,307	234,905
Log-likelihood	−42,653.4	−54,147.3

This table reports the results of a probit regression in which the outcome of interest is whether a voter voted for the Democratic candidate in their state or US House elections. Samples were drawn from the Cooperative Election Studies. Standard errors are in parentheses; *$p < 0.05$.

CHAPTER EIGHT

"Accountability" in Primary Elections

In the 1990s, thirty-two states adopted laws and constitutional amendments that defined marriage as a relationship between a man and a woman, but in the early twenty-first century a dozen state legislatures adopted laws recognizing same-sex marriages or civil unions (National Conference of State Legislatures 2015). One of these states was New York. The state senate voted against legalizing same-sex marriage 38–24 in 2009 but reconsidered a similar measure two years later. State Senator James Alesi voted against the 2009 bill, but he was the first Republican to support the new legislation in 2011. Alesi told the *New York Post,* "My vote is probably the most significant vote on this issue, because how I vote will send a message down the line" (Dicker 2011). Three other senate Republicans heard this message and broke party lines to help pass the Marriage Equality Act, 33–29. After the 2011 vote, visitors in the New York General Assembly chambers erupted into a victorious chant of "U.S.A.! U.S.A.!" (Blain and Lovett 2011), but not everyone shared this excitement, particularly not members of the Republican caucus.

The following year and less than two months after the *New York Times* published an article titled "State Senator Loses Support of Local G.O.P." (Eligon 2012), Alesi announced his retirement from the legislature, citing fears of the primary election: "The conservatives pretty much declared there would be trouble for the four senators" (Preston 2012). Alesi was right. The three other Republicans who supported the Marriage Equality Act sought reelection but faced party ire for their actions.

Senator Roy McDonald, for instance, defended his support of the Marriage Equality Act and broke party ranks by stating:

> You get to the point where you evolve in your life where everything is not black and white, good and bad, and you try to do the right thing. You might not like that. You might be very cynical about that. Well, fuck it, I don't care what you think. I'm trying to do the right thing. I'm tired of Republican-Democrat politics . . . They can take the job and shove it. (HeadCount 2011)

Unsurprisingly, party leaders did not receive McDonald's passionate words well. The vice chairwoman of the Wilton Republican Committee in McDonald's district stated: "If I said that to the person who hired me, I would be fired" (Eligon 2012). And indeed this is what happened. Republicans nominated county clerk Kathleen Marchione over McDonald in the 2012 Republican primary for McDonald's seat. Marchione went on to win the general election, like many other successful primary challengers. From 2001 to 2020, over 99 percent of the candidates who defeated an incumbent in the primary also won the general election.

The two other Republican supporters of the Marriage Equality Act only had marginally more electoral success than McDonald. Stephen Saland squeaked out his party's nomination 50.5 percent to 49.5 percent but lost a three-way general election race by fewer than 2,500 votes. In this general election contest, it likely was not helpful that Saland's primary challenger ran under the "Conservative" party label and received over seventeen thousand votes. The fourth Republican to support the Marriage Equality Act—Senator Mark Grisaniti—secured both his nomination and reelection in 2012.[1] Upset with Grisaniti's success, the President of the National Organization for Marriage stated, "We've defeated Republican after Republican who voted for gay marriage, and we will defeat Mark Grisaniti" (Vogel 2012), which conservatives did two years later in the Republican primary.

Grisaniti's defeat left no Republicans in the New York Senate who supported the Marriage Equality Act less than three years after its passage and one year before *Obergefell v. Hodges* would permit same-sex marriage nationwide. These Republican senators' political fates could serve as examples for other state legislators: If you buck the party line, there can be an electoral price to pay. But it is unclear whether the events around the Marriage Equality Act are exemplary or anecdotal.

At first glance, competitive state legislative primaries appear to be the exception rather than the rule. Figure 8.1 illustrates the levels of primary competition in US and state house elections from 1994 to 2020. Fewer than 20 percent of state house incumbents regularly face in-party primary challengers (figure 8.1, dashed black line). For 9 percent of state legislators, the

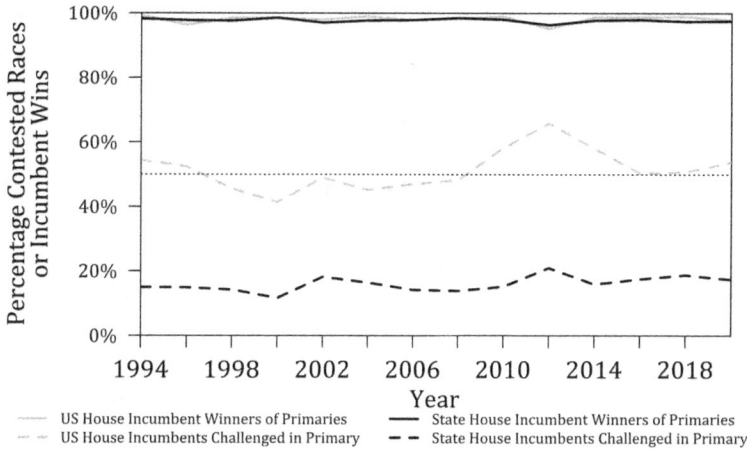

FIGURE 8.1. Percentages of US House and state legislative incumbents who faced a primary challenger or won their primary election.

primary challenger is the only competition incumbents face. Some competition can be better than no competition, but with so few in-party primary challengers, 98 percent of incumbents typically win their primaries (figure 8.1, solid black line). So few incumbent losses led one American politics textbook to characterize a state legislative primary to be "not unlike the common cold. It is a nuisance, but seldom fatal" (Bibby 2003, 172).

Ninety-eight percent is not 100 percent, and in the search for accountability in state legislatures, the Republican fatalities in the New York primary elections suggest that incentives for representation could exist in the party nomination process. Senator Alesi openly stated that he would not run for reelection because he thought he would lose the primary. Another New York Republican may have personally supported same-sex marriage but voted for the Marriage Equality Act to avoid electoral punishment. If this was the case, the threat of losing a primary election creates incentives for legislators to represent their party base. This incentive structure creates a form of accountability, as electoral sanction constrains legislators' behavior, but primary "accountability" in the absence of general election accountability could allow legislators to ignore most of their constituency and ultimately lead to more polarized legislatures.

In this chapter, I investigate the extent to which such primary "accountability" exists in state legislatures and study the rates at which incumbents

face challengers and win primary elections. Focusing on incumbents' ideological representation, I derive and test theoretical predictions regarding
when incumbents should face challengers and be successful in primary elections. Raising concerns for representation in state legislatures—at least for
the median voter—I find that more ideologically extreme and party-loyal
legislators face fewer primary challengers and more frequently win their
party's nomination. For Republicans, the relationship between ideological
extremity and competition in primary elections is at times stronger in more-
partisan districts but not consistently impacted by states' primary rules, such
as those that limit which voters can participate in a party's primary. Primaries then create electoral incentives for legislators' behavior, but these incentives entice many legislators to be loyal to their party rather than their
whole district, raising concerns for polarization and electoral connections
in state legislatures.

Incentives for Representation in Two-Stage Primary and General Elections

After Alesi voted for the Marriage Equality Act, he was confident he could
win the general election but concerned about the primary election. Alesi
is not alone in his fears of the primary electorate. In 2014, Sarah Anderson, Daniel Butler, and Laurel Harbridge-Yong (2020, table 4.2) asked
215 state legislators, "In general, if you were to make compromises on
policy, how much retribution would you face from voters?" and followed
up this question by asking which groups would be most likely to punish
state legislators for such compromise. Over twice as many state legislators
said that primary voters were "somewhat likely" or "very likely" to punish
them as compared to those who said general election voters were "somewhat likely" or "very likely" to punish them. Later, in the 2016 National
Candidate Study, almost 20 percent of Democratic state legislators and
38 percent of Republican legislators said they "feel more vulnerable to a
primary challenge than a general election loss" (Skovron 2018, 23).

The spatial model helps illustrate the logic behind Alesi's and other state
legislators' primary fears. Let figure 8.2 represent a moderate Republican
district with nine voters. For simplicity, I again assume a discrete policy space
where numbers indicate an individual's ideal point.[2] Voters 1–3 are registered Democrats; Voter 4 is an independent Democrat; Voters 5 and 6
are independent Republicans; and Voters 7–9 are registered Republicans.
Voters 1–4 participate in the Democrat primary; Voters 5–9 participate in

(1)   (2)   (3)   (4)   (5)   (6)   (7)   (8)   (9)

			Dem. Challenger Scenarios A, B, and C	Rep. Incumbent Scenarios A and B	Rep. Incumbent Scenario C		Rep. Primary Challenger Scenarios B and C	

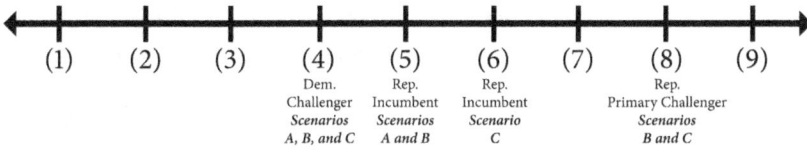

FIGURE 8.2. The above line represents a hypothetical district of nine voters with a Republican incumbent, Republican primary challenger, and Democratic challenger. See table 8.1 for election-outcome predictions.

TABLE 8.1 **Example outcomes of state legislative primary elections**

Scenario	Republican incumbent ideal point	Democrat challenger ideal point	Rep. primary challenger ideal Point	Moderate district (voters 1–9)		Conservative district (voters 4–9)	
				Winner Rep. primary	Winner General election	Winner Rep. primary	Winner General election
A	5	4	None	Incumbent (voters 5–9)	Incumbent (voters 5–9)	Incumbent (voters 5–9)	Incumbent (voters 5–9)
B	5	4	8	Primary challenger (voters 7–9)	Democrat challenger (voters 1–5)	Primary challenger (voters 7–9)	Primary challenger (voters 6–9)
C	6	4	8	Incumbent (voters 5–7)	Incumbent (voters 5–9)	Incumbent (voters 5–7)	Incumbent (voters 5–9)

This table shows the predicted outcomes of Republican primary elections in moderate and conservative districts based on the ideological positions of the Republican incumbent and primary challenger.

the Republican primary; and all voters participate in the general election. Below, I consider a more-conservative district where I remove Voters 1–3 from the district. In each district, I assume that voters support the most ideologically proximate candidate, and that, if indifferent between two candidates, a voter supports the candidate who shares their party affiliation. If indifferent between candidates of the same party, a voter supports the incumbent.[3] Following these assumptions, table 8.1 presents the outcomes of state legislative races in moderate and conservative districts where candidates' ideal points vary under three different scenarios: A, B, and C.

First, consider Scenario A, where only a Republican incumbent and one Democratic candidate run for a state legislative seat. With no intraparty competition, there is no primary election and only a general election. As discussed in chapter 6, the median voter theorem predicts that candidates have an electoral incentive to adopt a moderate—the median voter's— ideological position to maximize their chances of winning (e.g., Downs 1957). In figure 8.2, this ideological position is the ideal point of Voter 5.[4]

If the Republican incumbent takes this position in either the moderate or conservative district, he obtains the support of Voters 5–9 and wins the general election.

Now consider Scenario B, which features the same Republican incumbent and Democrat challenger, but in which there is also a conservative Republican candidate who is upset with the incumbent's representation (e.g., for his vote on the Marriage Equality Act). This upset Republican challenges the incumbent in the primary and positions himself at the ideologically conservative position of 8. In a moderate district, the incumbent's ideological position of 5 is optimal to beat the Democrat in the general election, as in Scenario A. But applying the median voter theorem's logic to primary elections suggests that an ideological position of 5 is not optimal for winning the Republican primary. Recall that Republican primary voters are Voters 5–9, making Voter 7 the median *primary* voter. When the incumbent takes an ideological position of 5, the incumbent only receives the support of Voters 5 and 6 in the primary. Meanwhile, the primary challenger receives support from Voters 7, 8, and 9 and wins the primary election.

In either the moderate or conservative district, the primary election outcome is the same when candidates take the positions laid out in Scenario B, as voters in the Republican primary election do not change when removing three Democrats. General election outcomes, meanwhile, differ. In the general election, the moderate district's median voter—Voter 5—prefers the Democratic challenger's ideal point of 4 to the Republican primary challenger's position of 8. Voter 5 then supports the Democratic challenger, and the Republican primary challenger loses. In the conservative district without Voters 1–3, Voter 6 becomes pivotal in the general election. This Republican voter supports the primary challenger over the Democratic challenger, and the primary challenger wins the general election. This result implies that primary challengers should theoretically foresee having the most primary election success against moderate same-party incumbents and general election success in partisan districts. These types of races should be the most competitive and attract primary challengers.

A primary challenger may like the ideological positioning of candidates in Scenario B—as it leads to his victory in the primary election—but in this scenario, the incumbent loses the primary contest. A fundamental assumption underlying theories of electoral accountability, however, is—again—that incumbents do not enjoy losing. Scenario C illustrates how the incumbent can avoid electoral defeat. In Scenario B, the incumbent lost the median primary voter—Voter 7—to the primary challenger. If the incumbent changes his ideal point from 5 to the more-conservative position of 6 and other candidates remain fixed, the incumbent wins Voter 7's support and his party's nomination. The incumbent also wins the general election with Voter 5's support in either the moderate or conservative district.

Electoral victory takes more than a candidate choosing to place himself at 5 or 6, but the simple differences between the outcomes of Scenarios B and C illustrate another important theoretical point: primary elections can alter the incentives for representation. When applied to the general election, the median voter theorem suggests that centripetal forces lead candidates to moderate positions. When similar logic is applied to primary elections, centrifugal forces instead lead candidates to more-extreme positions (Burden 2001). In the above example, the Republican incumbent has an incentive to provide more-conservative representation to ward off more-conservative primary competition. However, by doing so, the median voter of the moderate district does not receive her ideal representation. Returning to the moral hazard problem posed by representative government, a normatively desirable aspect of this theoretical prediction is that a legislator is "accountable" to someone, even if it is only his partisan base. However, primary elections can ultimately present incumbents, such as Alesi, with a trade-off. Providing more-moderate representation could result in more general election votes at the expense of primary votes. However, more-extreme representation attracts primary support at the expense of general election support.

If legislators change their representation to cater to primary voters, such behavior could underlie some of the increasing polarization in state legislatures (figure 4.4). When studying this polarization, Shor and McCarty (2022) highlight that, similar to Congress, state legislative polarization appears to be growing asymmetrically, where one party is becoming more extreme faster than the other party. While Republicans are becoming more extreme at a faster rate in Congress, Democrats are, however, becoming more extreme more quickly in state legislatures, especially from 2011 to 2020. There are many explanations for legislative polarization (see McCarty 2019 for a review). Research on state legislatures often focuses on whether different primary systems (e.g., closed primaries restricted to a particular set of primary voters) produce more-extreme legislators. Meanwhile, we know less about whether state legislators have an electoral incentive to provide more-extreme representation.

Related research on Congressional primaries suggests that such electoral incentives exist. Hall and Snyder (2015) provide evidence that more-extreme US House candidates are more successful in primary elections (see also Brady et al., 2007). When studying the Senate, Hirano and Snyder

(2014; see also Boatright 2014) found extreme US Senators more likely to be challenged in primary elections, but, once challenged, extreme Senators were no more likely to lose than moderates. Despite these federal-level findings, I am unaware of published analyses that examine how a state legislative incumbent's representation affects their primary competition outside of a single study of California. Gerber (2002) found moderates did better in state assembly elections under a "blanket" primary in 1998—where voters could select either Republican or Democratic candidates on the same ballot—than in a "closed" primary in 1996, where voters could only choose candidates from one party.[5]

To better understand the relationship between representation and primary competition, Jason Windett and I, along with devoted research assistants, collected state legislative primary election results from 1991 to 2015 from secretaries of states and boards of elections. I then extend this collection of election results through 2020 using data from the National Institute on Money in State Politics (2022), Handan-Nader, Myers, and Hall (2022), and state government websites.[6] Using these data, I investigate the relationship ideological representation has with challenger entry and incumbent success in primary elections. I further examine how relationships differ in partisan districts, the importance of a legislator's party loyalty, and whether found relationships differ in closed primaries. I expand upon the theoretical importance of closed primaries in greater detail below, but to briefly preview, moderate incumbents should theoretically be less electorally successful in a closed primary that restricts who can vote in a party's primary to registered voters. I conclude by evaluating whether state legislators have electoral incentives to represent the median voter in their district when considering the outcomes of both the primary and general elections.

The analyses in this chapter are similar to those in chapters 3 and 6 but focus on the primary instead of the general election. My dependent variable is whether an incumbent faced a primary opponent or won renomination. Most independent variables employed here are the same as those in previous chapters, with one notable difference. Spatial model predictions suggest incumbents will face less primary competition if their ideal point is closer to the median voter in their party primary (e.g., Cadigan and Janeba 2002). Testing this specific prediction requires ideological measures of primary voters within a district, which do not readily exist at the state legislative district level. I cannot then create an ideological-distance measure for primary elections similar to that used to study general elections. I

TABLE 8.2 **Predicted changes in probabilities of a primary challenger**

Variable	Change in variable value	Change in probability of challenger to ...	
		Democrat incumbents	Republican incumbents
State economy	Increase of 1 standard deviation (approx. 2 percent)	−0.001 (0.002)	−0.004* (0.002)
District partisanship	Increase of 1 standard deviation (approx. 13 percent)	+0.060* (0.004)	+0.045* (0.005)
Ideal point	Change of 1 standard deviation (more liberal for Dems.; more conservative for Reps.)	−0.028* (0.003)	−0.016* (0.004)
Gender	Man to woman	0.007 (0.006)	+0.028* (0.007)
Closed primary	All states have closed primary	−0.007 (0.012)	+0.028* (0.010)
Party loyalty	Increase of 12%	−0.015* (0.003)	−0.028* (0.003)

This table reports the differences in average predicted probabilities of an incumbent facing a primary challenger associated with changing the variable value listed in the second column. Standard errors are in parentheses; *$p < 0.05$.

then follow work on Congressional primary competition and estimate the direct relationship between the likelihood that an incumbent receives a primary challenger and legislators' ideology using legislators' ideal points (Shor and McCarty 2011). Since lower and higher ideal point values respectively represent more-extreme representation for Democrat or Republican incumbents, I estimate separate models for Democrats and Republicans. To facilitate substantive interpretations of probit estimates (table A.8.1), table 8.2 presents differences in predicted probabilities associated with changes in key independent variables of interest.

Challenger Entry in State Legislative Primaries

For electoral accountability, voters "must have a fair opportunity to cast a meaningful vote for or against the policymakers." Relatively few of these opportunities exist in general elections, and fewer exist in primary elections (figure 3.1). However, there are some common predictors of whether a state legislator will face a primary or general election challenger. Chamber leaders and freshmen legislators are at least 0.017 less likely to face general election and primary challengers. Additionally, Republican incumbents

Democrats   **Republicans**

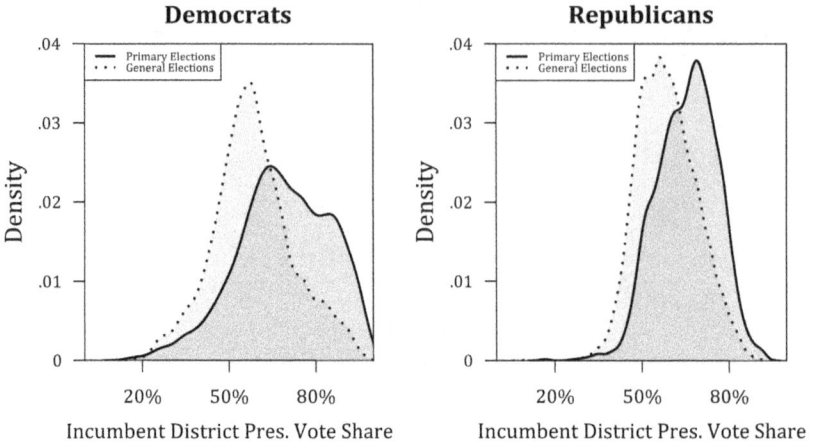

FIGURE 8.3. Distribution of state legislative incumbents who face a challenger in the primary or general election, by their district partisanship.

in both general and primary elections are more likely to face challengers when there is a weak economy. Two percent economic growth is associated with a 0.004 decrease in the probability of a contested Republican primary (table 8.2, first row). Republican incumbents then have both primary and general election incentives to avoid competition.

Primary challengers appear to be more concerned about politics than about the financial and time sacrifices they must make to serve in the state legislature.[7] For instance, increasing the seat share of the primary challenger's party by 10 percent increases the probability of a challenger by at least 0.011. Primary challengers are also much more likely to run in partisan districts. Figure 8.3 shows distributions of incumbents who faced a primary or general election challenger by the partisanship of the incumbent's district. In districts with a Democratic incumbent, the average presidential vote share for the incumbent's party was 69 percent when there was a primary challenger and 58 percent when there was a general election challenger (figure 8.4, left panel). In districts with a Republican incumbent, these respective percentages are 65 percent and 59 percent (figure 8.4, right panel).[8] Statistical analyses suggest that a 10 percent increase in the district-level presidential vote for the incumbent's party increases the probability of a primary challenger by at least 0.045 (table 8.2, second row). When comparing primary elections from 2001 to 2010 to those from 2011 to 2020, this statistical relationship has grown slightly, but differences do not meet conventional levels of statistical significance.

As district-level partisanship is an increasingly important part of who wins general elections (figure 6.4), running in a partisan district is theoretically a sensible strategy for primary challengers. For example, in the above Scenario B, the conservative challenger who defeated the incumbent in the primary lost the general election in the moderate district but won in the more conservative district. The incumbent is likely unhappy with losing his seat via the primary, but there is little the incumbent can do to change the partisanship of his district. However, theoretical predictions in Scenario C suggest that if the incumbent provides more-conservative representation, he can avoid electoral defeat in the primary. However, does the incumbent's representation matter for their competition in primary elections?

On average, Democratic state legislators who face primary challengers are slightly more conservative than Democratic state legislators who do not face primary challengers. The average ideal points for contested and uncontested Democrats are -0.83 and -0.86, which is consistent with general theoretical expectations. Meanwhile, Republican state legislators who face primary challengers are more conservative on average than Republican state legislators who get a pass in the primary. The average ideal points for contested and uncontested Republicans are 0.84 and 0.77. These Republican averages are perhaps surprising, but it is important to remember that representation's and district partisanship's impacts on challenger entry are likely interrelated. Primary challengers may often oppose conservative, Democratic state legislators, but this pattern may only emerge because these conservative Democrats represent more-conservative districts (figure 1.2). It is difficult to discern whether state legislators' representation has a meaningful relationship with primary election competition or if primary challengers simply run in more-partisan districts.

Statistical findings in table A.8.1 that account for both district partisanship and representation begin to disentangle this puzzle. For clarity in the presentation in my below discussion of changes in predicted probabilities, whenever I present changes to a Democratic legislator's ideal point, the change will *decrease* the Democrat's ideal point, thereby making Democrats more liberal. Similarly, my discussion of Republican legislators focuses on predictions following *increases* in Republicans' ideal points, thereby making Republicans more conservative. I find that a standard-deviation decrease in a Democratic incumbent's ideal point reduces the predicted probability of a primary challenger by 0.028. Similarly, a standard-deviation increase in a Republican incumbent's ideal point decreases the predicted probability of a primary challenger by 0.016 (table 8.2, third row). Across both parties, it appears that if incumbent legislators want to avoid primary challengers, they should provide more-extreme representation.

The direct relationship between legislators' ideology and competition in state legislative primaries then appears to be weaker in Republican than in Democratic contests. However, when evaluating the role of ideology in Republican primaries, district partisanship and gender stereotypes seem to play important roles in Republican contests. Statistical analyses in the second and fourth columns of table A.8.1 account for the relationship between a legislator's ideological representation and challenger entry conditional on their district's partisanship. Using these estimates, I find that in a district where the Republican party received 50 percent of the presidential vote, a standard-deviation increase in a Republican incumbent's ideal point decreases the predicted probability of a primary challenger by 0.004 (t-statistic of difference 0.87). However, in a district where the Republican party received 70 percent of the presidential vote, the comparable decrease is 0.023 (t-statistic of difference 5.27). Republicans' ideology then appears to matter more in more-partisan districts. Meanwhile, I do not find similar differences in Democratic challenger entry across more-marginal and partisan districts.

Ideological stereotypes also appear to shape intraparty competition in Republican primaries. Recall, prior work shows that voters perceive women candidates as more liberal than otherwise comparable men candidates (e.g., McDermott 1997), and Republican women US House incumbents, who are perceived to be more liberal, face more challengers in US House primaries than their Democratic counterparts (Lawless and Pearson 2008). In state legislative primaries, I similarly find that Republican candidates are 0.028 more likely to challenge Republican women state legislative incumbents, who are likely perceived to be more liberal, than men incumbents in primaries (table 8.2, fourth row). Again, I do not find gender differences between the rate of primary challengers across men and women Democratic state legislative incumbents.

Together, these findings again underscore the importance of representation for elites' behavior for accountability in state legislative elections. Legislators who want to avoid competition in the primary election have an electoral incentive to provide more ideologically extreme representation. This is a type of "accountability," as legislators' electoral fates are connected to their performance in office. However, these electoral incentives created by accountability in the primary counter those made by the threat of general election challengers, who less often run when the incumbent provides better representation of the median voter in the district (figure 3.4). As addressed in greater detail below, such counteracting forces are potentially troublesome for state legislators' overall electoral incentives for representation in state legislatures.

Incumbents Winning Primary Elections

If a legislator faces a challenger in their primary election, it raises the risk that they will lose their job. Overall, over 98 percent of incumbents win their primary election, suggesting that an overwhelming number of state legislators cruise to victory. However, 15 percent of incumbents who face a primary challenger lose their primary election, which is a greater percentage than the 9 percent of incumbents who face a major-party challenger and then go on to lose the general election (figure 2.1). Such differences may partly explain why over twice as many state legislators said that primary voters were "somewhat likely" or "very likely" to punish them as compared to those who said general election voters were to do the same. But are these fears of primary voters warranted?

To better understand who wins and loses state legislative primary elections, I conduct analyses similar to the above, but my dependent variable is whether an incumbent won their party's nomination. Similar to analyses in chapter 6, I examine races with and without a challenger to disentangle the extent to which incumbent loss in primary elections is attributable to challenger versus voter behavior. Probit estimates for these analyses are available in table A.8.2, and table 8.3 provides differences in the predicted probability of an incumbent's renomination associated with changes in central independent variables of interest.

Both Democratic and Republican state legislators are more likely to win their primary if they provide more-extreme representation. When considering all primaries that feature a Democratic incumbent, a standard-deviation decrease in legislator ideology increases the predicted probability that a Democratic incumbent wins renomination by 0.008. When considering races with a primary challenger, the difference in probabilities rises to 0.020 (table 8.3, third row). This 0.012 difference suggests that extreme incumbents' electoral success in primaries is partly attributable to primary voters rewarding more-liberal representation. Similarly, consistent with the assumption that voters perceive women candidates as more liberal, the probability of a women Democratic state legislator winning

TABLE 8.3 **Predicted changes in probabilities of incumbent renomination**

| | | Change in probability of renomination | | | |
| | | Democratic incumbents | | Republican incumbents | |
Variable	Change in variable value	All races	Contested races	All races	Contested races
State economy	Increase of 1 standard deviation (approx. 2 percent)	−0.000 (0.001)	−0.002 (0.005)	+0.000 (0.001)	−0.002 (0.004)
District partisanship	Increase of 1 standard deviation (approx. 13 percent)	−0.009* (0.002)	−0.005 (0.007)	−0.006* (0.002)	−0.004 (0.010)
Legislator ideal point	Change of 1 standard deviation (more liberal for Dems.; more conservative for Reps.)	+0.008* (0.001)	+0.020* (0.008)	+0.004* (0.002)	+0.007 (0.007)
Incumbent gender	Man to woman	+0.007* (0.002)	+0.045* (0.013)	−0.008* (0.004)	−0.014 (0.017)
Closed primary	All states have closed primary	+0.001 (0.003)	−0.007 (0.017)	−0.012* (0.005)	−0.037 (0.020)
Party loyalty	Increase of 12%	+0.005* (0.001)	+0.019* (0.006)	+0.007* (0.001)	+0.014* (0.007)

This table reports the differences in average predicted probabilities of an incumbent winning their primary election associated with changing the variable value listed in the second column. Standard errors are in parentheses; *$p < 0.05$.

renomination is 0.007 higher in all races and 0.045 higher in races with a challenger (table 8.3, fourth row). Together, these findings suggest that voters respond to the perceptions of candidates' ideology in Democratic primary elections.

Both perceived and actually conservative Republican state legislators also experience more primary success, but voters' role in these Republican defeats is less clear than in Democratic primaries. When considering all races, a standard-deviation increase in a Republican state legislator's ideology increases the probability of renomination by 0.004, which is smaller than the comparable relationship in Democratic races. And women Republican incumbents—who are likely perceived to be more liberal—are more likely to lose. Meanwhile, when I focus on the same relationships within Republican primaries with a challenger, more-liberal and women Republicans are more likely to lose, but estimates do not meet conventional levels of statistical significance.[9] Such weaker findings are somewhat surprising given that Republican voters tended to describe and think about their state legislators in more ideological terms (chapter 5, Grossman and Hopkins 2016).

These electoral incentives for extreme representation or "accountability" in the primary are discouraging if our goal is to have legislators represent the typical or median voter in their district. I address the relative electoral incentives created by primary and general elections at the end of this chapter, but such accountability for lack of extreme representation may be partly responsible for the asymmetric polarization in state legislatures. Recall, Democratic state legislators are becoming more extreme than Republicans at a faster rate (figure 4.7), and the above findings provide evidence that while both Republican and Democratic state legislators have an electoral incentive to provide extreme representation to win their primary elections, the incentives are greater for Democrats (table 8.3). While these findings do not establish that primaries cause state legislative polarization, a question that needs more study, they present a pattern of electoral incentives consistent with trends in state legislative representation. If primaries are responsible for such polarization, there are other consequences to consider. For instance, prior work finds that polarization leads to less well-functioning legislatures (e.g., Birkhead 2016) and voter distrust (e.g., Banda and Kirkland 2018). Such accountability in state legislative primaries could also be responsible for changes in representation in the federal government, as the next career step for many extremist state legislators is to run for Congress (Hall 2019; Thomsen 2017). The cracks in the electoral foundation of statehouse democracy then have implications beyond what happens at the state house.

Primaries as Partisan Affairs

Legislators' ideological representation and district partisanship appear to matter for who runs and ultimately wins primary elections, as in general elections. Primary elections, however, have distinct differences from general elections. They decide who will represent a *party* in the general election and, ultimately, the state legislature. Despite some progressive-era reformers' motivations to establish direct primaries to reduce party elites' power (see Ware 2002 for a detailed history), elites often use the primary process to put their chosen candidates in office. Recall that the Wilton County Republican Committee spoke out against New York State Senator Roy McDonald's vote on the Marriage Equality Act, partly leading to McDonald's defeat in the primary election. This elite-level behavior is not unique to New York. When surveying over a thousand local county party chairs across the country about candidate recruitment, David Broockman and coauthors found that party leaders were more likely to select candidates who were "more likely to stay loyal to the party if elected" by a 4-to-1 margin (Broockman et al. 2021, 733).

Political scientists have become increasingly focused on elites' role in nominations and have offered insights about their impact on federal elections. While oft-given advice is not to judge a book by its cover, political science book titles can frequently be telling, at least in this area of study. When studying who wins presidential party nominations, Marty Cohen and coauthors (2008) titled their book *The Party Decides*, and when looking at who wins Congressional nominations, Hans Hassell (2017) titled his book *The Party's Primary: Control of Congressional Nominations*. As suggested by their titles, these works argue that party elites strongly influence who runs and wins federal primary elections, often favoring candidates who will adhere to the party's positions. State legislative party leaders also often seek cohesiveness and conformity in the legislature. In turn, they tend to prefer candidates elected by their party's voters or who toe the party line. It, however, remains a question whether state legislators face different electoral consequences for only facing partisan primary voters or for being loyal to their party—circumstances that the next two sections of this chapter investigate.

Closed Primaries

We know challengers run more often in partisan districts (table 8.2) and lose more often in more-partisan districts (table 8.3). Together, these findings suggest that who votes in primaries matters for primary competition. Any voter may participate in a state legislative primary, but there can be restrictions on which party's primary a voter may participate in. According to the Council for State Governments, nine states have "closed primaries," which are restricted to registered party members, and voters in fifteen states can choose, on the day of the election, whether to vote in the Democrat or Republican primary. Most other states fall somewhere between these two extremes with differing degrees of openness. In some states, independent voters can participate in any primary, but "independents" must publicly declare whether they will participate in the Republican or Democrat primary in other states. Republican and Democratic primaries within a single state can have different rules, as the individual parties determine who can vote in their elections.

In a country that prides itself on being a free, fair, and open democracy, it may seem odd that some states restrict who can vote in elections. But for some legislators, it is open primaries that make little sense. As put by former Colorado State Senator Ted Harvey: "It's like saying the Mormon Church will get to choose who is going to be the Pope or allowing [New England Patriots football coach] Bill Belichick to decide who's going to be the quarterback for the Denver Broncos" (Greenblatt 2016). Just as football coaches' decisions impact teams' success, participation by nonparty members in a party's primary could have deflating effects on that party's ideological homogeneity.[10] Texas, for example, has an open primary system, and Republican legislator Patricia Harris told the *Texas Tribune*: "That's how I'd get elected a lot of times, is because my constituents that are Democrats vote in Republican primaries" (Sullivan 2015). With her crossover support in the primary, Harris was able to be one of the most liberal Republicans in the Texas house.

Concerns about crossover support in Republican primaries arose repeatedly in Montana. One race that prompted a call for significant change in primary rules was a primary contest between State Senator Scott Boulanger and State Representative Pat Connell in 2014. Before the election, Boulanger told the *Helena Independent Record* that "I represent the conservative Republicans . . . (Connell) represents the 20 percent of the Republicans who are trying to convince everyone that 80 percent of us are wrong" (Bureau and Lutey 2014). Connell, meanwhile, told the same newspaper that "I've listened to myself being called a RINO (Republican in name only) and a liberal, and that I might as well be a Democrat because I crossed the aisle. I guess that's great sound-bite politics, but . . . does it really matter who you're working with if you're getting something done?" Connell was more conservative than any Democratic legislator in Montana, making him more than a Republican in name only, but he was more liberal than Boulanger. With Montana's open primaries and only one candidate in the Democratic primary, voting for and electing a moderate in the Republican primary was probably attractive for many Democratic voters. If such crossover voting occurred, it was likely critical. Connell defeated Boulanger in the primary by a mere thirty-nine votes and went on to win the general election.[11]

Limiting primary contests to partisans may prevent the election of moderates, but as described by Tennessee State Senator Jeff Yarbro, "If we limit participation to people who are hardcore partisans, you're going to see the legislature get even more polarized and less responsive to the people that they represent" (Boucher 2015). Political science research may assuage some of Yarbro's concerns. At least within presidential primaries, the ideology of primary voters does not appear to vary much from that of the general election electorate, and the evidence is mixed that primary electorates in congressional elections are more extreme (Geer 1988; Sides et al. 2018; see also Hill 2015; Jacobson 2012). However, Caughey and Warshaw (2022, 46, 75) find that "ideological differences between Democrats and Republicans in the same state have grown," leading to their speculation that "the mass public has in turn reinforced and probably exacerbated partisan divergence among political elites."

While I am unaware of research that studies state-primary electorates, research by Christian Grose (2020; see also McGhee and Shor 2017) suggests that implementing the top-two primary in California produced more-moderate federal elected officials. Studying primary systems in nearly every state, my coauthors and I find little evidence that closed-primary systems produce more ideologically extreme state legislators (McGhee, Masket, Shor, Rogers, and McCarty 2014; see also Bullock and Clinton 2011). However, our research does not evaluate whether legislators in closed primaries have an electoral incentive to provide more-extreme representation. Legislators' ideology appears to matter in state legislative primaries. But does legislators' representation matter more if there are restrictions on who can vote in a primary?

Spatial model predictions suggest it should. Reconsider the scenarios in table 8.1. Each scenario originally had five voters participate in the Republican primary: two independent Republicans (Voters 5 and 6) and three registered Republicans (Voters 7, 8, and 9). To win the primary, the Republican candidate needed the median primary voter's support: Voter 7. The Republican incumbent could accomplish this by positioning himself at 6 (Scenario C). Now reconsider these examples but limit eligible Republican primary voters to registered Republicans: Voters 7–9. The pivotal voter in the Republican primary is now Voter 8, and to win this voter's support and the Republican nomination, the incumbent must take an even more conservative position of 8. Changing which voters can participate in primary elections then can theoretically influence who will win primary nominations.

Table 8.4 summarizes the conditional relationships of representation with primary challenger entry or incumbent renomination under different primary systems (see table A.8.3 for probit estimates). The first row of this table presents the impact of standard-deviation changes in representation when there is a not a closed primary, the second row presents these differ-

TABLE 8.4 **Impact of ideological representation changes under closed primaries**

Type of primary	Change in probability of challenger		Change in probability of victory			
	All races		All races		Contested races	
	Democrat	Republican	Democrat	Republican	Democrat	Republican
Not closed	−0.024*	−0.017*	+0.007*	+0.003	+0.020*	+0.000
primaries	(0.004)	(0.004)	(0.001)	(0.003)	(0.008)	(0.008)
Closed	−0.031*	−0.011	+0.009*	+0.008*	+0.023	+0.022
primaries	(0.006)	(0.007)	(0.002)	(0.003)	(0.013)	(0.013)
Difference	−0.008	+0.006	+0.002	+0.005	+0.002	+0.021
	(0.007)	(0.006)	(0.002)	(0.003)	(0.013)	(0.014)

This table reports the differences in average predicted probabilities of an incumbent facing a primary challenger or winning their primary election associated with changing an incumbent's ideal point by one standard deviation more liberal or conservative for Democrats and Republicans. Standard errors are in parentheses; *$p < 0.05$.

ences when there is a closed primary, and the third row presents the differences of these differences. For the question of whether closed primaries increase the importance of ideological representation, we are interested in the differences in the third row.

My analyses provide limited evidence that closed primaries electorally benefit more-extreme legislators, either in avoiding challengers or winning renomination. Across states with either open- or closed-primary systems, I generally find that more-extreme legislators face few challengers or more often win reelection. However, none of the differences between these differences in predicted probabilities across open- and closed-primary systems meets conventional levels of statistical significance. We then lack certainty that closed primaries change legislators' incentives to provide more extreme and polarized representation.

Party Loyalty

The lack of differences between open and closed primaries may assuage some Montana Republicans' concerns that open primaries would lead to the election of liberal Republican legislators. Montana Republican leadership's concerns, however, were not only ideological. When filing affidavits in a lawsuit to establish closed primaries, majority leaders Matthew Rosendale and Keith Regier named eighteen "dissident" Republican state legislators whom they rated as "distressingly low" in party loyalty (Clines 2015, O'Hara 2015). Rosendale expected that "this problem will get worse without significant changes in how the Republican Party nominates its candidates during elections" (Rosendale 2015). Such lawsuits reflect party leaders' intention to establish conformity in their parties, similar to how Republican party elites sought to replace incumbent state legislators with more-loyal partisans following incumbents' votes on same-sex marriage in New York.

Democratic elites take similar actions to remove disloyal Democratic state legislators from their ranks. One such case occurred following the 2015 Illinois General Assembly, where Democrats held seventy-one seats, enough to override a gubernatorial veto. After Illinois governor Bruce Rauner vetoed a bill that would remove the governor from negotiations with state union workers, a veto-override vote was held in the state house but failed. An upset Speaker of the House, Michael Madigan, placed blame on Democratic representative Ken Dunkin—who was absent from the vote—telling the press on the day of the vote that "Had Mr. Dunkin been here, there would have been 71 democrats [sic] voting to override" (Thomas 2015). To which the defiant Dunkin responded, "I don't work for Mike Madigan" (Schutz 2015). Two months later, Dunkin again made his independence from party leadership clear when he was the lone Democrat not to support an override of Governor Rauner's veto of legislation concerning childcare and services for the elderly. Defending his position, Dunkin told the *Chicago Tribune* he was not in Springfield to "be some robotic Democrat" (Geiger 2015).

Dunkin explained he was acting in Illinois voters' best interests, but he ultimately paid for breaking party lines. In the 2015 to 2016 session, Dunkin voted with a majority of his party 80 percent of the time, 7 percent lower than the average Illinois Democrat. In the 2016 Democratic primary, Juliana Stratton challenged Dunkin with the Illinois Democratic party establishment's support. She raised over $2.2 million and received the endorsements of the Illinois secretary of state, the Chicago Teacher's Union president, and even the president of the United States: Barack Obama. Once an Illinois state legislator himself, President Obama was not a fan of Dunkin (Schuba 2016). Obama gave a speech on bipartisanship to the Illinois General Assembly in 2016, during which Obama and Dunkin had the following exchange (Obama 2016; Zorn 2016):

> President Obama: "... And where I've got an opportunity to find some common ground, that doesn't make me a sellout to my own party."
> Ken Dunkin stands in the chamber and yells: "Heck, yeah!"
> President Obama: "That applies—" (laughter) "—Well, we'll talk later, Dunkin. You just sit down" (Applause and laughter).

Involving himself in Dunkin's Democratic state legislative primary, the president recorded a TV ad for Juliana Stratton and stated (Pearson 2016):

> Juliana will fight to get guns off our streets and fight for tougher penalties for violent offenders. I'm Barack Obama. I'm asking you to vote for Democrat Juliana Stratton for state representative.

To the pleasure of President Obama and Speaker Madigan, Stratton defeated the disloyal Dunkin in the primary with 68 percent of the vote.

Dunkin would likely tell progressive reformers that the establishment of the direct primary did not go far enough to limit party leaders' power over the nomination process. Even with Dunkin's defeat, it is unclear whether bucking party leadership has systematic electoral consequences for state legislators. I am unaware of an existing study that tests such a proposition, even within Congress.

When studying the relationship between party loyalty and challenger entry in state legislative primaries, I again find that elites respond to legislators' behavior. The shaded grey region at the bottom of figure 8.4 illustrates the distribution of party-loyalty scores for state legislators across the country. The solid and dashed lines reflect the relationship between Democrats' and Republicans' levels of party loyalty and the probability they face a challenger. A typical Republican state legislator votes with his

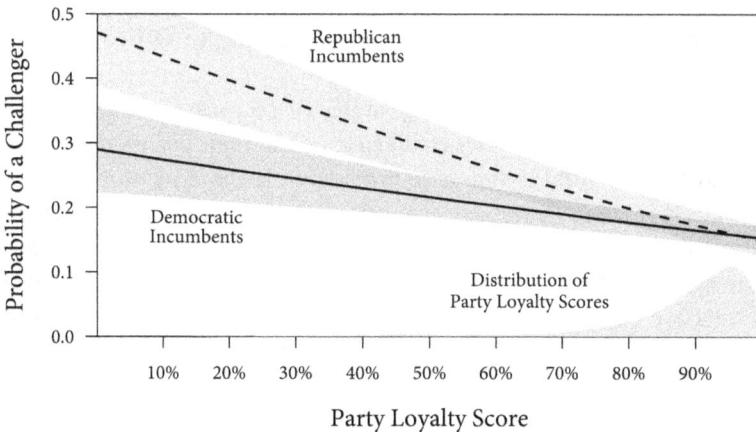

FIGURE 8.4. Lines represent the predicted probability of a primary challenger as a state legislator casts more roll-call votes with the majority of their party (moving from left to right along the x-axis).

party approximately 86 percent of the time, and the probability such an average legislator faced a challenger was 0.183. If this Republican instead voted with their party 76 percent of the time, reflecting approximately a standard-deviation decrease in the party-loyalty measure, this probability of a challenger rises to 0.209, suggesting that going against the party leadership is not electorally advisable, at least in the primary. On the Democratic side, if Representative Dunkin had voted with his party 12 percent more often, his predicted probability of facing a challenger would have fallen by 0.015 (table 8.2, final row).[12]

Disloyal incumbents are also more likely to lose their primary elections. In all races, a standard-deviation increase in party loyalty increases the probability of renomination by 0.005 for Democrats and 0.007 for Republican incumbents. When considering races with a challenger, these differences in probability grow to 0.019 and 0.015, suggesting that voters partly respond to how loyal legislators are to their party. A smart party leader, who reads books devoted to state legislative elections, can point to figure 8.4 to reassure a wavering state legislator to vote with the party, as party loyalty helps fend off primary competition. This leader can then turn back the pages to convince the wavering legislator that he will be more likely to win their primary (table 8.3) without being less likely to win the general election (table 6.2). For a legislator to stay loyal to the party may be smart primary politics, but such strategies lead a legislator to vote with his party more often than with the typical voter.

Representing the Median Voter and Returning to Office

Together, the representation findings in this chapter show that if state legislators want to avoid a primary challenger or win their party's nomination, they have an electoral incentive to provide more-extreme representation, particularly in more liberal or conservative districts. Such "accountability" in the primary again is potentially discouraging if our goal is to have legislators represent the typical or median voter in their district. We know legislators have electoral incentives to represent their district's median voter if they wish to avoid a major-party challenger (chapter 3) and ultimately win the general election (chapter 6). But how should a legislator interpret these earlier findings in this book in light of this chapter's findings? Is representing the median voter a sensible strategy if the legislator's ultimate goal is to win both the primary and general elections?

To shed light on this fundamental question for representative government, I conduct statistical analyses that evaluate the relationship between a legislator's ideological distance from their district—reflecting a legislator's representation of the median voter—and whether that legislator won *both* the primary and general elections (table 8.5). These analyses are similar to those in table A.6.2 but consider all legislators who appeared in the primary, including those who lost the primary election and did not appear in the general election.[13] This study therefore assesses whether legislators who provide better representation of the median voter in their district are more likely to return to office by surviving both the primary and general elections.

My analyses reveal that some legislators have electoral incentives to represent the median voter, but there are key differences across districts. When considering incumbents who sought reelection in a marginal district—one where the incumbent's party received 60 percent or less of the presidential vote—a standard-deviation increase in the ideological-distance measure associated with an 0.025 decrease in the predicted probability that a legislator would return to office. Such findings are consistent with the analyses from chapter 6 that show legislators have an electoral incentive

TABLE 8.5 **Representation and returning to office**

	All districts	Marginal districts	Safe districts
Ideological distance from district	−0.111	−0.674[*]	0.586[*]
	(0.083)	(0.111)	(0.140)
Ideological distance squared	0.037	0.162[*]	−0.182[*]
	(0.046)	(0.062)	(0.079)
Party loyalty	0.009[*]	0.006[*]	0.012[*]
	(0.001)	(0.002)	(0.002)
Legislator salary (in thousands of 2010 dollars)	0.003[*]	0.003[*]	0.002[*]
	(0.001)	(0.001)	(0.001)
Legislative staff per member	0.009	−0.005	−0.000
	(0.009)	(0.012)	(0.011)
Session length	−0.001[*]	−0.000	−0.001[*]
	(0.000)	(0.000)	(0.000)
Public-finance campaign option	−0.131	−0.186[*]	0.000
	(0.072)	(0.088)	(0.097)
Logged average amount to win race (state-year average)	−0.211[*]	−0.232[*]	−0.059
	(0.036)	(0.047)	(0.048)
Term limits enacted	0.056	0.085	0.102
	(0.052)	(0.066)	(0.059)
Distance to capital (logged)	−0.030[*]	−0.004	−0.062[*]
	(0.011)	(0.015)	(0.016)

continues

TABLE 8.5 (*continued*)

	All districts	Marginal districts	Safe districts
Incumbent-party pres. vote	0.027*	0.054*	−0.003
	(0.001)	(0.002)	(0.002)
Previous primary contested	−0.158*	−0.071	−0.277*
	(0.026)	(0.037)	(0.038)
District size (logged)	0.249*	0.256*	0.136*
	(0.051)	(0.068)	(0.066)
Terms served	−0.009*	0.008	−0.016*
	(0.004)	(0.006)	(0.006)
Freshman incumbent	−0.119*	−0.177*	0.041
	(0.028)	(0.036)	(0.047)
Chamber leader	0.751*	0.901*	0.556*
	(0.080)	(0.112)	(0.119)
Midterm appointee	0.716*	0.707*	0.617*
	(0.096)	(0.134)	(0.147)
Woman legislator	−0.045	−0.046	−0.003
	(0.024)	(0.033)	(0.040)
Nonwhite legislator	−0.186*	−0.089	−0.005
	(0.034)	(0.057)	(0.047)
Member of chamber-majority party	−0.120*	−0.200*	−0.072
	(0.023)	(0.031)	(0.042)
Member of governor's party	0.010	0.019	−0.037
	(0.029)	(0.038)	(0.049)
Member of president's party	−0.087*	−0.199*	0.043
	(0.030)	(0.041)	(0.046)
Midterm election (federal)	0.168*	0.213*	0.075
	(0.037)	(0.050)	(0.056)
Midterm election (state)	0.100*	0.061	0.109
	(0.036)	(0.046)	(0.061)
Off-year election	0.242*	0.208	0.271
	(0.117)	(0.145)	(0.138)
Redistricted district	−0.125*	−0.046	−0.176*
	(0.025)	(0.034)	(0.039)
Member of the president's party x federal midterm	−0.409*	−0.563*	−0.136*
	(0.042)	(0.058)	(0.066)
Member of the governor's party x state midterm	−0.106*	−0.043	−0.123
	(0.042)	(0.056)	(0.068)
State senator	−0.192*	−0.190*	−0.236*
	(0.041)	(0.053)	(0.056)
Constant	−0.861*	−1.495*	0.256
	(0.372)	(0.487)	(0.492)
N	40,181	18,223	21,958
Log-likelihood	−9,026.3	−5,283.2	−3,325.8

This table reports the results of a probit regression in which the outcome of interest is whether an incumbent who appeared in the primary election won the general election. Standard errors are in parentheses; $^*p < 0.05$.

to represent the median voter. However, I find the opposite relationship when considering safe districts—where the incumbent's party received at least 60 percent of the presidential vote. A standard-deviation increase in ideological distance associated with a 0.008 *increase* in the likelihood of returning to office. Such estimates are consistent with the findings of the present chapter, that legislators have an electoral incentive to provide extreme representation, particularly in more-partisan districts.[14] Across both marginal and safe districts, state legislators additionally have an electoral incentive to vote more often with their party, and the incentives for party loyalty are more substantial in safe districts.

These findings from safe districts underscore how "accountability" in the primary and corresponding electoral incentives to provide extreme representation are potentially troubling for representation in state legislatures, particularly in a country where most state legislative districts are fairly partisan (figure 2.3). This book documents many of the reasons why state legislators win and lose elections, but district partisanship is one of the strongest predictors of whether an incumbent will win the general election (figure 6.4). For instance, in a district where the incumbent's party received at least 60 percent of the presidential vote, incumbents win reelection 99 percent of the time. Legislators in such districts may recognize that they have the general election likely locked up and see the logic in trying to avoid a primary defeat by casting that more-extreme roll-call vote. This roll-call may result in a general election challenger (chapter 3) or a slight loss in incumbent vote share (chapter 6), but in a partisan district, this challenger or loss of vote is unlikely enough to kick an unrepresentative incumbent out of office. Legislators in more-marginal districts have greater reason to worry about such challengers or about the median voter, as they are less likely to return to office if they provide worse representation. However, these incumbents with reason to worry constitute a minority of state legislators (figure 2.4).

Recap

This chapter helps establish that state legislative primaries create more electoral connections between voters and legislators, offering a form of "accountability." Incumbent state legislators representing more-partisan districts face more competition. They can fend off some of this competition by providing more-extreme ideological representation or being loyal to their party in their roll-call voting. Such findings potentially lead to growing polarization in state legislatures and likely counter the motivations behind progressive-era reforms that established primaries to decrease party leaders' influence. A positive spin on these results is that legislators' behavior has implications for the elections. State legislators are held accountable to someone, creating some incentive to represent some part of the electorate instead of acting however they want without repercussion.

The presence of accountability to some part of the electorate may be a good spin, but good spin is not necessarily good for statehouse democracy. Such behavior may hold a legislator accountable but competes with our normative goal for the electoral process to create incentives for a legislator to represent the district's median voter. Some legislators still have this incentive, at least those who represent more-marginal districts. However, the combination of more-partisan districts and the increasing importance of partisanship in state legislative elections may make incumbents less fearful of the general election. In such cases, the above analyses troublingly reveal that a majority of legislators have an incentive to provide extreme representation. The electoral incentives primaries create for party loyalty compound this problem. Legislators may listen more to their party leadership than their whole district, perhaps out of fear that party leaders will work to support a future primary opponent, as done by Illinois Speaker Madigan with the help of the president of the United States. To be clear, very few legislators lose their primary elections. However, given the weak electoral connections in the general election, it then may be a sensible strategy for many legislators to focus on surviving the primary if they ultimately want to return to office. Together, the empirical regularities documented about primary and general elections in prior chapters raise concern that state legislative elections do not create desirable incentives for representation and indicate there are substantial cracks in the foundation of statehouse democracy, which I address in the next, and concluding, chapter.

Appendix

TABLE A.8.1 **Primary challengers**

	Democrats	Democrats	Republicans	Republicans
Legislator ideal point	0.284[*]	0.631[*]	−0.170[*]	0.360
	(0.042)	(0.113)	(0.038)	(0.191)
Party loyalty	−0.006[*]	−0.001	−0.011[*]	−0.002
	(0.001)	(0.004)	(0.001)	(0.006)
Closed primary	−0.034	−0.119	0.120[*]	0.225
	(0.057)	(0.232)	(0.045)	(0.220)
Change in annual log of Q2 state personal income	−0.205	−0.214	−1.040[*]	−1.031[*]
	(0.433)	(0.433)	(0.387)	(0.388)
Legislator ideal point x incumbent pres. Vote		−0.006[*]		−0.009[*]
		(0.002)		(0.003)
Party loyalty x incumbent pres. vote		−0.000		−0.000
		(0.000)		(0.000)
Legislator ideal point x closed primary		0.096		0.077
		(0.072)		(0.074)
Party loyalty x closed primary		0.002		−0.002
		(0.002)		(0.002)
Legislator salary (in thousands of 2010 dollars)	−0.002[*]	−0.002[*]	−0.004[*]	−0.003[*]
	(0.001)	(0.001)	(0.001)	(0.001)
Legislative staff per member	−0.013	−0.012	0.033[*]	0.035[*]
	(0.013)	(0.013)	(0.016)	(0.016)
Session length	0.000	0.000	0.000	0.000
	(0.000)	(0.000)	(0.000)	(0.000)
Public-finance campaign option	−0.052	−0.047	−0.340[*]	−0.323[*]
	(0.102)	(0.102)	(0.166)	(0.163)
Logged average amount to win race (state-year average)	0.066	0.066	−0.002	0.002
	(0.043)	(0.043)	(0.046)	(0.046)
Term limits enacted	−0.224[*]	−0.228[*]	0.085	0.067
	(0.087)	(0.086)	(0.091)	(0.089)
Distance to capital (logged)	0.032[*]	0.031[*]	−0.063[*]	−0.063[*]
	(0.012)	(0.012)	(0.014)	(0.014)
Incumbent-party pres. vote	0.020[*]	0.022[*]	0.014[*]	0.032[*]
	(0.001)	(0.006)	(0.001)	(0.009)
Previous primary contested	0.459[*]	0.455[*]	0.401[*]	0.401[*]
	(0.028)	(0.028)	(0.027)	(0.027)
Own-party seat share	0.949[*]	0.934[*]	0.508[*]	0.520[*]
	(0.207)	(0.206)	(0.214)	(0.213)
District size (logged)	0.041	0.041	0.119	0.108
	(0.071)	(0.071)	(0.073)	(0.072)
Terms served	0.009[*]	0.008[*]	0.012[*]	0.012[*]
	(0.004)	(0.004)	(0.005)	(0.005)
Freshman incumbent	−0.077[*]	−0.076[*]	−0.214[*]	−0.213[*]
	(0.035)	(0.035)	(0.032)	(0.032)
Chamber leader	−0.178[*]	−0.181[*]	−0.263[*]	−0.265[*]
	(0.062)	(0.062)	(0.060)	(0.060)
Midterm appointee	0.359[*]	0.364[*]	0.228[*]	0.220[*]
	(0.087)	(0.087)	(0.084)	(0.085)
Woman legislator	0.033	0.035	0.120[*]	0.122[*]
	(0.026)	(0.027)	(0.030)	(0.030)

continues

	Democrats	Democrats	Republicans	Republicans
Nonwhite legislator	0.174*	0.172*	0.025	0.028
	(0.033)	(0.034)	(0.069)	(0.069)
Member of chamber-majority party	−0.059	−0.063	0.055	0.056
	(0.046)	(0.046)	(0.048)	(0.048)
Member of governor's party	0.055	0.052	−0.057	−0.057
	(0.037)	(0.037)	(0.039)	(0.039)
Member of president's party	−0.069	−0.069	−0.057	−0.056
	(0.038)	(0.038)	(0.038)	(0.038)
Midterm election (federal)	−0.074	−0.077	−0.093*	−0.093*
	(0.041)	(0.041)	(0.043)	(0.043)
Midterm election (state)	0.047	0.045	−0.139*	−0.141*
	(0.044)	(0.044)	(0.042)	(0.042)
Off -year election	−0.250	−0.253	−0.117	−0.121
	(0.172)	(0.170)	(0.229)	(0.222)
Redistricted district	0.147*	0.141*	0.188*	0.189*
	(0.032)	(0.032)	(0.030)	(0.030)
Member of president's party x federal midterm	−0.037	−0.035	0.035	0.033
	(0.055)	(0.055)	(0.053)	(0.053)
Member of governor's party x state midterm	−0.060	−0.062	0.067	0.069
	(0.049)	(0.049)	(0.050)	(0.050)
State senator	0.025	0.027	0.038	0.045
	(0.061)	(0.061)	(0.058)	(0.058)
Constant	−3.253*	−3.414*	−2.072*	−3.149*
	(0.585)	(0.692)	(0.591)	(0.815)
N	19,352	19,352	19,908	19,908
Log-likelihood	−7,462.4	−7,455.2	−8,122.4	−8,116.3

This table reports the results of a probit regression in which the outcome of interest is whether an incumbent faced a primary challenger from 2001 to 2020. Standard errors are in parentheses; $*p < 0.05$.

TABLE A.8.2 **Representation and incumbent renomination**

	Democrats	Democrats— challenged races	Republicans	Republicans— challenged races
Legislator ideal point	−0.401*	−0.219*	0.157*	0.074
	(0.070)	(0.091)	(0.062)	(0.075)
Party loyalty	0.009*	0.008*	0.010*	0.005
	(0.002)	(0.003)	(0.002)	(0.003)
Closed primary	0.011	−0.036	−0.174*	−0.155
	(0.070)	(0.082)	(0.069)	(0.079)
Change in annual log of Q2 state personal income	−0.461	−0.491	0.370	−0.515
	(0.826)	(1.099)	(0.668)	(0.909)
Legislator salary (in thousands of 2010 dollars)	0.002*	0.002*	0.005*	0.003*
	(0.001)	(0.001)	(0.001)	(0.001)
Legislative staff per member	0.003	−0.008	−0.016	0.005
	(0.013)	(0.016)	(0.018)	(0.016)
Session length	−0.000	−0.000	−0.001	−0.001
	(0.000)	(0.000)	(0.000)	(0.001)

	Democrats	Democrats—challenged races	Republicans	Republicans—challenged races
Public-finance campaign option	−0.045 (0.104)	−0.228 (0.131)	0.230 (0.178)	−0.322 (0.211)
Logged average amount to win race (state-year average)	−0.147* (0.063)	−0.140 (0.078)	−0.060 (0.069)	−0.115 (0.081)
Term limits enacted	0.127 (0.074)	0.000 (0.085)	0.112 (0.096)	0.208* (0.094)
Distance to capital (logged)	−0.034 (0.021)	−0.002 (0.030)	−0.035 (0.024)	−0.082* (0.031)
Incumbent-party pres. vote	−0.013* (0.002)	−0.002 (0.003)	−0.007* (0.003)	0.001 (0.003)
Previous primary contested	−0.374* (0.050)	−0.102 (0.063)	−0.349* (0.046)	−0.135* (0.059)
Own-party seat share	−0.947* (0.289)	−0.481 (0.362)	−0.863* (0.338)	−0.754 (0.434)
District size (logged)	0.086 (0.087)	0.140 (0.103)	−0.006 (0.097)	0.142 (0.106)
Terms served	−0.023* (0.007)	−0.026* (0.009)	−0.015 (0.009)	−0.013 (0.012)
Freshman incumbent	0.016 (0.065)	−0.060 (0.085)	0.175* (0.056)	0.071 (0.076)
Chamber leader	0.603* (0.177)	0.692* (0.224)	0.694* (0.162)	0.737* (0.208)
Midterm appointee	0.478* (0.211)	0.820* (0.247)	0.426* (0.181)	0.664* (0.222)
Woman legislator	0.152* (0.053)	0.228* (0.069)	−0.115* (0.052)	−0.060 (0.070)
Nonwhite legislator	−0.103 (0.060)	0.031 (0.077)	−0.305* (0.105)	−0.450* (0.150)
Member of chamber-majority party	0.056 (0.082)	0.011 (0.106)	−0.004 (0.085)	0.103 (0.115)
Member of governor's party	−0.052 (0.065)	0.015 (0.087)	0.083 (0.067)	0.085 (0.092)
Member of president's party	0.053 (0.071)	0.012 (0.095)	−0.064 (0.067)	−0.145 (0.093)
Midterm election (federal)	0.016 (0.079)	−0.045 (0.105)	0.069 (0.078)	−0.025 (0.109)
Midterm election (state)	0.022 (0.084)	0.048 (0.111)	0.244* (0.078)	0.202 (0.106)
Off-year election	0.172 (0.145)	0.054 (0.170)	0.209 (0.215)	0.070 (0.207)
Redistricted district	−0.233* (0.057)	−0.196* (0.076)	−0.240* (0.051)	−0.185* (0.069)
Member of president's party x federal midterm	0.098 (0.102)	0.112 (0.138)	−0.021 (0.094)	0.020 (0.131)
Member of governor's party x state midterm	0.053 (0.091)	−0.010 (0.123)	−0.198* (0.091)	−0.229 (0.127)
State senator	−0.085 (0.079)	−0.087 (0.101)	−0.215* (0.076)	−0.279* (0.086)

continues

	Democrats	Democrats— challenged races	Republicans	Republicans— challenged races
Constant	3.207*	0.753	2.779*	0.986
	(0.698)	(0.862)	(0.724)	(0.783)
N	19,355	3,119	19,907	3,395
Log-likelihood	−1,828.8	−1,177.8	−2,258.4	−1,428.2

This table reports the results of a probit regression in which the outcome of interest is whether an incumbent won their primary election. Standard errors are in parentheses; *$p < 0.05$.

TABLE A.8.3 **Representation and incumbent renomination**

	Democrats	Democrats— challenged races	Republicans	Republicans— challenged races
Legislator ideal point	−0.510*	−0.178	−0.504	−0.171
	(0.194)	(0.263)	(0.326)	(0.422)
Party loyalty	0.004	0.003	−0.002	0.001
	(0.008)	(0.011)	(0.012)	(0.017)
Closed primary	−0.506	−0.585	0.500	0.894
	(0.394)	(0.503)	(0.440)	(0.577)
Change in annual log of Q2 state personal income	−0.448	−0.523	0.416	−0.421
	(0.828)	(1.101)	(0.670)	(0.912)
Legislator ideal point x incumbent pres. vote	0.002	−0.001	0.010	0.003
	(0.003)	(0.004)	(0.005)	(0.006)
Party loyalty x incumbent pres. vote	0.000	0.000	0.000	0.000
	(0.000)	(0.000)	(0.000)	(0.000)
Legislator ideal point x closed primary	−0.130	−0.018	0.144	0.215
	(0.124)	(0.155)	(0.123)	(0.151)
Party loyalty x closed primary	0.005	0.006	−0.009	−0.014*
	(0.004)	(0.005)	(0.005)	(0.006)
Legislator salary (in thousands of 2010 dollars)	0.002*	0.002*	0.005*	0.003*
	(0.001)	(0.001)	(0.001)	(0.001)
Legislative staff per member	0.002	−0.009	−0.014	0.008
	(0.013)	(0.016)	(0.018)	(0.017)
Session length	−0.000	−0.000	−0.001	−0.001
	(0.000)	(0.000)	(0.000)	(0.001)
Public-finance campaign option	−0.055	−0.222	0.219	−0.321
	(0.104)	(0.132)	(0.179)	(0.215)
Logged average amount to win race (state-year average)	−0.147*	−0.137	−0.060	−0.115
	(0.062)	(0.077)	(0.070)	(0.083)
Term limits enacted	0.132	0.002	0.120	0.213*
	(0.074)	(0.083)	(0.097)	(0.097)
Distance to capital (logged)	−0.036	−0.003	−0.033	−0.082*
	(0.021)	(0.030)	(0.024)	(0.032)
Incumbent-party pres. vote	−0.017	−0.008	−0.033*	−0.010
	(0.010)	(0.014)	(0.017)	(0.022)
Previous primary contested	−0.372*	−0.100	−0.349*	−0.135*
	(0.050)	(0.064)	(0.046)	(0.060)

	Democrats	Democrats—challenged races	Republicans	Republicans—challenged races
Own-party seat share	−0.953*	−0.484	−0.836*	−0.778
	(0.289)	(0.358)	(0.340)	(0.440)
District size (logged)	0.086	0.135	0.000	0.142
	(0.087)	(0.103)	(0.098)	(0.109)
Terms served	−0.022*	−0.026*	−0.016	−0.013
	(0.007)	(0.009)	(0.009)	(0.012)
Freshman incumbent	0.015	−0.062	0.175*	0.079
	(0.065)	(0.085)	(0.056)	(0.076)
Chamber leader	0.597*	0.684*	0.700*	0.740*
	(0.177)	(0.224)	(0.162)	(0.209)
Midterm appointee	0.503*	0.837*	0.452*	0.654*
	(0.214)	(0.250)	(0.184)	(0.227)
Woman legislator	0.153*	0.229*	−0.117*	−0.064
	(0.053)	(0.069)	(0.052)	(0.070)
Nonwhite legislator	−0.091	0.042	−0.297*	−0.439*
	(0.060)	(0.078)	(0.105)	(0.151)
Member of chamber-majority party	0.055	0.010	−0.007	0.104
	(0.082)	(0.105)	(0.085)	(0.116)
Member of governor's party	0.010	0.012	−0.117	−0.133
	(0.070)	(0.093)	(0.076)	(0.102)
Member of president's party	0.057	0.017	−0.065	−0.150
	(0.071)	(0.095)	(0.067)	(0.094)
Midterm election (federal)	0.023	−0.040	0.067	−0.028
	(0.079)	(0.105)	(0.078)	(0.110)
Midterm election (state)	−0.027	−0.051	−0.242*	−0.194
	(0.084)	(0.111)	(0.078)	(0.107)
Off-year election	0.180	0.062	0.202	0.056
	(0.144)	(0.169)	(0.216)	(0.213)
Redistricted district	−0.233*	−0.201*	−0.237*	−0.184*
	(0.057)	(0.076)	(0.052)	(0.069)
Member of the president's party x federal midterm	0.091	0.103	−0.018	0.031
	(0.102)	(0.138)	(0.094)	(0.132)
Member of the governor's party x state midterm	−0.061	0.005	0.194*	0.211
	(0.092)	(0.123)	(0.091)	(0.128)
State senator	−0.083	−0.083	−0.223*	−0.280*
	(0.080)	(0.101)	(0.076)	(0.088)
Constant	3.610*	1.343	4.452*	1.717
	(0.963)	(1.240)	(1.302)	(1.654)
N	19,354	3,119	19,907	3,395
Log-likelihood	−1,826.4	−1,176.9	−2,252.6	−1,423.5

This table reports the results of a probit regression in which the outcome of interest is whether an incumbent won their primary election. Standard errors are in parentheses; *$p < 0.05$.

CHAPTER NINE

The Cracking Foundation
of Statehouse Democracy

Two brothers—Earnest and Paul Liebmann—emigrated from Germany to the United States in 1902 and built the first ice-making plant in the Oklahoma territory (Zizzo 2001). Oklahoma became a state five years later, and in 1925, the state legislature made it illegal to sell ice from a new plant without a license. The rebellious brothers, however, built a new ice facility in Oklahoma City. In turn, the New State Ice Company—which had a monopoly on the Oklahoma City ice industry—sued the Liebmann family. This chilly controversy tested America's free-enterprise system during the Great Depression and eventually reached the US Supreme Court. The court thawed Oklahoma's icy situation and ruled in the Liebmann's favor, but Justice Louis D. Brandeis dissented, and in doing so, praised at least one aspect of the American federal system:

> It is one of the happy incidents of the federal system that a single courageous state may, if its citizens choose, serve as a laboratory; and try novel social and economic experiments without risk to the rest of the country. (New State Ice Co. v. Liebmann, 285 U.S. 262 [1932] [Brandeis, L. dissenting])

Lawmaking in the "laboratories of democracy" can lead to major changes in American lives. But experiments can go awry, and something, like an election, needs to hold the experimenters in check. The Massachusetts state legislature, for example, adopted "An Act Providing Access to Affordable Quality, Accountable Health Care" in 2006, which included a mandate that nearly every Massachusetts resident obtain health insurance. Less than four years after this state policymaking experiment, the US Congress and President Obama enacted the "Affordable Care Act," which included a similar mandate for all Americans. There was considerable disagreement regarding whether the Affordable Care Act was a "happy incident of the federalist system." Many voters punished their member of Congress for supporting the measure, serving as evidence that elections create incentives for representation in Congress (e.g., Nyhan et al. 2012). When constructing the American federal system, the founders expected elections would similarly help remove bad policymakers from office when something went wrong in the laboratories. But as the previous chapters show, not all appeared to have gone as planned on the electoral front. While American federalism can allow states to experiment "without risk to the rest of the country," the complexities introduced by a federalist system of government pose risks for those who live in those state laboratories.

In this concluding chapter, I review the key findings of this book and their implications for the study of American politics and, more importantly, for the state of American democracy. Madison, Hamilton, and others built the laboratories of democracy centuries ago but would be aghast if they saw how the labs are run now. States can and sometimes do produce representative policies, but actual electoral sanction itself is unlikely the cause. Can the system be meaningfully fixed? I am doubtful. But my judgment is not the final one. My analyses are extensive but not exhaustive. And as addressed below, I look forward to future studies of the "laboratories of democracy" that will identify how elections or other institutions can bring about more accountability. Providing evidence that such accountability-producing features of government can be feasibly achieved would be good news for the state of statehouse democracy.

Do Elections Hold State Legislators Accountable for Their Own Performance?

The central question addressed by this book is: Do elections hold state legislators accountable for their own performance. A "yes" answer to this accountability question reassures us that state legislative elections help solve the moral hazard problem posed by representative government. A "no" answer suggests that state legislators can be lazy, cater to special interests, and create bad policies with little fear of losing reelection. Fortunately, I find the answer to the above question to be: "Yes, there is evidence of electoral accountability in state legislative elections." Unfortunately, there are some serious caveats to this "yes" answer. The meager evidence of electoral accountability presented in this book is also the most substantial evidence—at least that I am aware of—that how state legislators perform has *any* implications for their own elections, which is troublesome for state-house democracy. Both elites and voters are responsible for the levels of electoral accountability in state legislatures. These political actors at times respond to state legislators' behavior, helping establish electoral connections between state legislators and those they represent, but the strength of these connections is limited.

The Role of Elites and Accountability in State Legislatures

A contribution of this book is demonstrating the extent to which challengers and the media enable voters to hold their legislators accountable. For instance, voters can only have the "fair opportunity" to throw an unrepresentative legislator out of office if there is another candidate to vote for, and legislative candidates provide such opportunities. Helping voters hold legislators collectively or individually accountable, general election challengers more often oppose incumbent state legislators when the economy is weak or a state legislator is ideologically distant from their constituents (chapter 3). In-party challengers also more often emerge when an incumbent state legislator is ideologically extreme or disloyal to their party, establishing a form of "accountability," at least to a legislator's party (chapter 8). Each of these behaviors develops more opportunities for critical electoral connections to exist between state legislators and voters. Without such opportunities, elections cannot be a credible solution to representative government's moral hazard problem, and this elite behavior helps provide that "yes" answer to this book's central question.

The media also helps us get to that "yes" answer by informing voters of "who is responsible for making policy." Few voters have the time, interest, or capacity to sit in the state capitol looking over the shoulder of their state legislator. Instead, voters must rely on media elites to disseminate what their state legislators are doing. Hopkins (2018) shows that there is more media coverage of state politics in geographic areas closer to the state capital, and chapter 4 shows that voters in these areas are more knowledgeable about their state legislature. Similarly, voters in states with greater numbers of reporters devoted to state government are more likely to identify their state house majority party. Voters, furthermore, appear to put this acquired knowledge to some use on Election Day. When more reporters cover state government, voters are likelier to cast ballots against unrepresentative state legislators (chapter 6).

Challengers and the media can positively impact the accountability process in state legislatures, helping provide that normatively desirable "yes" answer to our core question. Even with these reassuring relationships, one must not lose sight of the forest for the trees. Both challengers and the media are depressingly absent from state legislative politics (figures 2.1 and 4.5). Remember the distressing story of Emile Bruneau in chapter 2. Bruneau won reelection unopposed in both the primary and general elections in 1991, 1995, 1999, and 2003. Like Bruneau, over a third of state legislators regularly do not face either a primary or general election challenger. They win reelection just by signing up. The relatively low number of challengers in state legislative elections leaves millions of voters without a fair opportunity to cast a ballot against their state legislators. Such a hard problem does not look to be easily solved. Even if state governments enacted institutional changes to encourage more people to run for the state legislature, such as by providing public financing of campaigns or increasing state legislative salaries, state legislative competition would still not match that found in Congress. Regrettably, this problem has gotten more severe in recent years, as historical trends suggest that contestation levels in state legislatures are getting worse, not better (figure 3.1).

Like the dearth of state legislative challengers, the little news coverage and fewer reporters devoted to the state government exacerbate state legislatures' accountability problem. One cannot reasonably expect voters to be informed about their state legislature when media coverage of state legislators is hard to find (e.g., figure 4.6). Even among those who think local news about government and politics is important or interesting, only 30 percent think it is easy to stay very informed about these subjects (Pew Research Center 2019a). We are unlikely to see more coverage anytime soon. William Grommley claimed in the 1970s that state governments faced "a severe visibility problem," and that visibility problem continues decades later. A third fewer reporters reside at state-capitol press bureaus than at the turn of the last century, leaving fewer reporters to cover fifty state governments than cover a single Superbowl. Adding reporters is likely not sufficient or achievable to solve the accountability problem in state legislatures. Even tripling the number of reporters would likely not be enough to make people as informed about their state legislature as they are about Congress (figure 4.8).

The Role of Voters and Accountability in State Legislatures

Voters' behavior also plays a vital role in fostering electoral accountability, which at times proactively contributes to providing that "yes" answer.

For instance, some voters listen to the reporters who remain in state capitols. In turn, most voters know something about their state legislature, such as which party controls their state legislature (chapter 4). An overwhelming majority of voters know that Democratic state legislative parties are more liberal than Republican state legislative parties, and on this ideological dimension, most voters correctly relatively place at least one of their state parties against the corresponding Congressional party (chapter 5). Such findings indicate that some voters know who is responsible for making policy and thus are not blind to what is happening in the state legislature.

Voters also repeatedly act to provide state legislators electoral incentives to perform well. Focusing on individual accountability, they more often support legislators whom they perceive to be ideologically close to them and who provide better representation of their district (chapter 6). Furthermore, incumbent state legislators who vote more often with their party do better in primary elections (chapter 8). In regard to collective accountability, voters are more likely to support the state house majority party when they approve of the state legislature's performance, particularly on issues that a voter cares most about (chapter 7), thereby helping to establish a state-level system of responsible party government. These electoral connections suggest that legislators' own behavior matters, providing a "yes" answer to "Do elections hold state legislators accountable for their own performance?"

Despite some voters following state politics and responding to state legislators' performance, an alarming number do not. Over 40 percent of voters regularly cannot identify which party controls their state legislature, and over 80 percent of voters could not recall who their state legislator was. Such statistics suggest a disturbing number of voters do not know "who is responsible for making policy." Focusing on legislators' behavior, over 30 percent of voters did not identify something they liked or disliked about either of their state legislative candidates, and over 75 percent of voters could not identify something their state legislator did for their district. These statistics suggest that many voters may have difficulty casting "meaningful votes" in state legislative elections. News organizations could make knowing this information easier with more reporters, but the voter bears some responsibility, as many appear to do little to seek this information (figure 4.4).

Meaningful votes in state legislative elections are at times hard to find, leading to underwhelming electoral connections in state legislatures. Voters punish their state legislators less often than they punish their members of Congress for comparable changes in ideological representation (figure 6.3). This disparity in the frequency with which voters hold state and national lawmakers accountable for their behavior persists even when operating under a simpler system of responsible party government (figure 7.3). In fact, voters are more likely to punish state legislators for the president's actions than for the state legislature's performance (figure 7.4). Such misattribution of responsibility undermines the fundamental argument for elections controlling legislators' behavior. If legislators' own elections are not significantly tied to their own behavior, what electoral incentive do they have to behave?

Together, my findings do provide a "yes" answer to "Do elections hold state legislators accountable for their own performance?" However, the amount of accountability these elections provide is not enough to establish confidence that state legislative elections serve one of their primary purposes: to solve the moral hazard problem posed by representative government, at least in my judgment.

"The Electorate Acts as Reasonably and Responsibly as We Should Expect"

The voter certainly has limitations, as does any individual. Still, I want to be clear that my findings are not a condemnation of American voters. Instead, the lack of accountability stems in large part from the complex form of government in which the voter is asked to participate. To understand this distinction, it is useful to return to the long debate about voter competence and V. O. Key's famous assertion in *The Responsible Electorate*. Responding to what he characterized as a portrayal of voters as "obscene parodies of the models set up by democratic idealists," Key famously claimed that "voters are not fools." Not all shared Key's general view of "the responsible electorate." Writing at roughly the same time, Philip Converse (1964, 49) offered his own famous characterization of voters, stating that the "mass public contains significant proportions of people who, for lack of information about a particular dimension of controversy, offer meaningless opinions that vary randomly in direction." Key and Converse were not the first nor last to disagree about voters' competence. Some scholars agree with Key's overarching argument and rational-choice perspective (e.g., Fiorina 1981) more than others (Achen and Bartels 2016, 92). When considering Key's canonical statement, my findings appear more at home in the second camp rather than the first, but evidence in this book repeatedly supports Key's fuller argument that voters behave as reasonably as we might expect.

Key's statement that "voters are not fools" is attractive for its optimistic simplicity. Politics, however, can be dark and complicated. Neither Key nor his students were foolish enough to think simple statements gave full explanations. For example, in his study of the US Congress, one bright student of Key—David Mayhew—will forever be connected to his postulate: "Members of Congress are single-minded seekers of reelection." Mayhew's emphasis on electoral motivations helps scholars explain the behaviors of members of Congress and legislative politics, but it is too often lost that Mayhew recognized "that a complete explanation (if one were possible) of a congressman's or anyone else's behavior would require attention to more than just one goal" (Mayhew 1974, 15). Similarly, Key's fuller argument in *The Responsible Electorate* is too often overlooked and bears repeating:

> The perverse and unorthodox argument of this little book is that voters are not fools. To be sure, many individual voters act in odd ways indeed; yet in the large the electorate behaves about as rationally and responsibly as we should expect, given the clarity of the alternatives presented to it and the character of the information available to it. (Key 1966, 6)

Voters at times "act in odd ways" in state legislative elections—at least given normative expectations—but a perverse and unorthodox argument of this little book (*Accountability in State Legislatures*) is that voters behave "about as rationally and responsibly as we should expect," particularly given the "information available to it." Recall findings from chapter 4. Voters who were forced to guess which party controlled their state legislature more often than not made "reasonable" and correct guesses. Alternatively, reconsider findings from chapter 6. Voters who had more opportunities to receive news about their state legislator more often punished their state legislator for inadequate representation. And chapter 7 showed that voters who correctly identified the party in control of the state house were more likely to hold this party "responsible." Misinformed voters (i.e., those who incorrectly identified the party in control of the state house), however, at times punished the incumbent party even when they approved of the legislature's performance (figure 7.4). A misinformed electorate then appears to *try* to hold state legislative parties "responsible" but fails to do so given "the character of the information available to it."

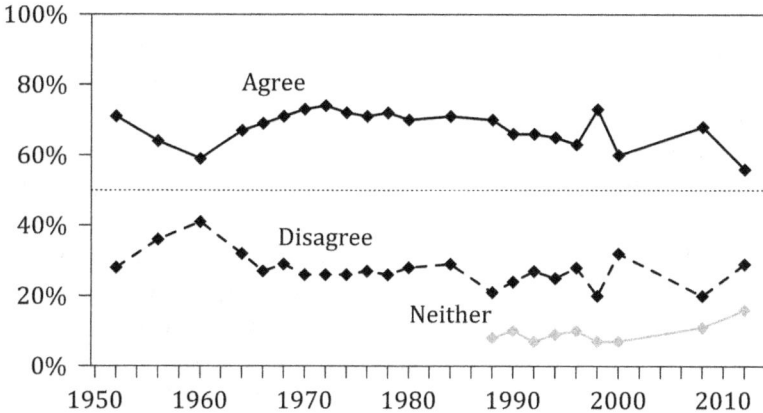

FIGURE 9.1. Percentages of ANES respondents who agreed or disagreed with the statement: "Sometimes politics and government seem so complicated that a person like me can't really understand what's going on."

American voters are not fools but are instead trapped in a complicated federal system. The idea that American politics is overly complex or that the voter cannot satisfy some idealistic form of democracy is not a statement made only by academics in their ivory-tower offices. Most voters are aware that politics is complicated. Since the inception of the American National Election Study (ANES), political scientists have regularly asked voters whether they agree with the statement: "Sometimes politics and government seem so complicated that a person like me can't really understand what's going on." Figure 9.1 plots the percentage of voters who agreed and disagreed with this statement and shows that voters regularly recognize that they participate in a system of government they do not understand. Over the past several decades, 60 percent of voters have consistently agreed that politics is so complicated that they cannot really understand what is going on.[1]

Voters become even more likely to think government is too complicated after being forced to think about state politics. I asked over four hundred voters the above "American politics is 'so complicated'" question both before and after they answered approximately twenty-five questions related to federal and state politics (e.g., those described in chapters 4, 5, and 6). Before answering these twenty-five questions, 39.3 percent of voters disagreed that politics was too complicated, but after doing so, only 36.1 percent disagreed with the statement (t-statistic of difference 1.92).

A 3 percent change in opinion is not huge. However, this shift in opinion occurred in less than ten minutes among the same voters, some of whom may have remembered their answer to the initial question.

The founders designed this "complicated" form of government for a country where they anticipated state-level affairs to loom much larger in citizens' lives. In *Federalist Paper* no. 45, James Madison (1788) argued that "the powers reserved to the several States will extend to all the objects which, in the ordinary course of affairs, concern the lives, liberties, and properties of the people." Continuing this state-centered argument in *Federalist Paper* no. 46, Madison (1788) wrote that it was "beyond doubt that the first and most natural attachment of the people will be to the governments of their respective States" and that "the prepossessions of the people . . . will be more on the side of the State governments, than of the federal government." In theory, a federalist system can promote such attachments, but Madison probably never envisioned a federal government that would collect over five times the amount of taxes as state governments. Nor did Hamilton foresee a country where he could travel from Washington, DC to New York to see a Broadway show in hours instead of days. And Jefferson—who would rather have had newspapers without a government than a government without newspapers—likely never expected Monticello and Jefferson City citizens to read the same political news on the same day, let alone receive this news via the internet.

The founders expected a "national spirit" would not meaningfully "prevail in the legislatures of the particular States" (Madison 1788, *Federalist* no. 46), but contemporary American society makes it unreasonable to expect the typical American voter to have Madison's envisioned attachment to the states. Here, I again encourage readers to read Dan Hopkins's (2018) aptly titled *Increasingly United States* for further evidence of the nationalization of American politics. Nationalized politics combined with the federal system makes the already "false ideal" set for voters even more out of reach in state legislative elections. An idealist form of democracy under a federal system asks nearly every voter to evaluate their president, US senator, US House representative, governor, lieutenant governor, attorney general, mayor, and school board official—to name a few—in addition to their state legislators. Even if the typical voter were "equipped to deal with so much subtlety, so much variety, so many permutations and combinations" (Lippmann 1993, 16), what reasonable voter would?

Can Madisonian attachments to state politics be revived (if they ever existed)?[2] I am doubtful. How should we expect voters to hold legislators

accountable when it is increasingly difficult to determine what a legislator is doing (chapter 4)? Even if information about state politics is made
available to voters, there is no assurance that all will use it. Few voters are
interested in politics, let alone state politics, and increased news coverage
does little good if no one reads it. Even in the event that voters do satisfy
Powell's condition for accountability—i.e., that voters "know who is responsible for making policy"—those voters still need a "fair opportunity"
to remove their legislator from office. Here, national politics again infuses
itself into the state politics scene, with challengers responding to national
conditions when deciding whether to run for office (chapter 3). Thus, the
lack of accountability in state legislatures is what we should continue to
regularly expect, given the nature of the American federal system.

Representation in the "Laboratories of Democracy"

Federalism is not all bad. Justice Brandeis reminds us of this with his concept of states as "laboratories of democracy." Federalism permits national,
state, and local governments to independently address issues and to ultimately have different policies for handling those issues (Scott 2011). Congress, for example, decides whether to authorize war with another nation,
and school boards determine whether to teach creationism alongside evolution. Suppose school board members in Kansas and Massachusetts establish differing curriculums based on their individual constituencies' preferences. In these cases, it *can* be a "happy incident of the federalist system"
that elected officials closer to the people have the opportunity to represent local public opinion.

   Political scientists have repeatedly provided evidence of such happy incidents or representation in states. Recall, Erikson, Wright, and McIver
found that in the 1970s and 1980s, "there exists a strong connection between opinion and policy, with liberal states producing liberal policies and
conservative states producing conservative policies" (Erikson, Wright, and
McIver 1993, back cover). The authors of *Statehouse Democracy* go as far
as to conclude from their analyses that "state opinion is virtually the *only*
cause of the net ideological tendency of policy in the state" (Erikson, Wright,
and McIver 1993, 81; emphasis in the original).[3] More recently, Devin Caughey and Christopher Warshaw examined millions of Americans' opinions
and discovered that "policy liberalism of state publics is a robust predictor
of future changes in the liberalism of state policies" from the 1930s into the

2010s (Caughey and Warshaw 2018). They conclude that their findings "on the whole paint a reassuring portrait of statehouse democracy" (Caughey and Warshaw 2018, abstract).

The reassuring picture of statehouse democracy depicted by these excellent studies of representation does not immediately appear to comport with the characterization I present. I do not dispute that, on average, liberal states produce liberal policies and conservative states produce conservative policies. Political scientists already provide substantial, albeit at times different, evidence for such claims. Instead, my concern is how we get these liberal and conservative policies. Or, more specifically, how do we get the policymakers? The findings of *Accountability in State Legislatures* cast a dark cloud of doubt on the founders' proposition that elections provide a meaningful "dependence on the people" to control the "angels" in American legislatures (Madison or Hamilton 1788) and highlight an unhappy incident of federalism: national politics' dominance of state legislative elections.

Elections have consequences, and nationalized subnational elections in a federal system can result in unrepresentative policymaking. For example, reconsider the Affordable Care Act. The passage of this bill and Barack Obama's unpopularity helped Republicans take control of the US House and twenty state legislative chambers in the 2010 elections. A consequence of nationalized state legislative politics in the 2010 elections was Republican legislatures' attempts to end liberal policies in liberal states. New Republican majorities in Wisconsin curtailed collective bargaining rights when most Wisconsinites opposed such action (Rasmussen Reports 2011). And in Minnesota—a state where most voters are pro-choice (St. Cloud State University 2009)—a newly elected Republican state legislature tried to restrict abortions, only to be stopped by a Democratic governor's veto. New legislative majorities that take office under today's nationalized politics can enact legislation out of step with their state electorates.

In a more comprehensive study of state-level policymaking, Jeffrey Lax and Justin Phillips examine thirty-nine state policies and find that policy only matches majority opinion 48 percent of the time. Even when 70 percent of a state's citizens favor a particular policy, that state has that policy only 57 percent of the time (Lax and Phillips 2011, 153). Caughey and Warshaw (2022, 5) offer a study of seventy-two policies from 1936 to 2020 and state that "in the short term, states often exhibit a democracy deficit, but over the long term, state publics tend to work their will." Specifically, they find that "average policy matches majority opinion 59% of the time" and that congruence increases at a rate of 3 percentage points per decade (Caughey and Warshaw 2022, 114, 128). If incongruent policies are unhappy incidents, it should *only* take over a century to rectify these mismatched policies. The process could likely be sped along if there were more meaningful electoral accountability in state legislatures.

But how did we get these mismatched policies in the first place? Research on representation in state governments provides evidence that these "unhappy incidents" could be more the fault of the legislature than the governor. Caughey and Warshaw with Yiqing Xu study the policy implications of Democrats versus Republicans controlling the governorship or state legislature in a state and find that legislative majorities are slightly more critical for the direction of policy than control of the governorship. They find that "barely electing a Democratic governor is estimated to increase change in Policy Liberalism by about 0.03" (Caughey, Warshaw, and Xu 2017, 1347), but "narrowly electing a Democratic house majority causes a 0.05 increase in Policy Liberalism" (Caughey, Warshaw, and Xu 2017, 1350). The legislature's importance for policymaking is reaffirmed by their panel analysis, which finds that "Democratic governors increase state Policy Liberalism by about 0.07, and Democratic control of the state house and senate increases it by 0.17 and 0.27 respectively" (Caughey, Warshaw, and Xu 2017, 1351).

Caughey and his coauthors emphasize that the magnitude of the effects "should not be overstated," but such findings are somewhat troubling in light of nationalized state legislative politics. They establish that even though more voters are familiar with their governor than with the state legislature (figure 4.3), the legislative branch is the more influential branch of state government for policymaking. Meanwhile, this book establishes that control of this influential branch is determined more by what happens at the White House than by what happens in the legislature. If legislators are routinely elected through misattribution of responsibility, their relative influence on policymaking may not signify that a healthy republic or well-functioning laboratory exists in each state.[4]

Not all readers will agree with my glass-half-empty conclusions. Looking at the glass half full, some argue that democracy in the American states, on average, results in good policymaking, particularly in the long term, and are more satisfied with the state of statehouse democracy. I am sympathetic to this argument. It is difficult to determine what the standards should be for elected officials and voters. Following the standards for accountability laid out at the beginning of this book, state legislative elections fall short of Powell's requirements that voters know who is responsible for policy-making and have a fair opportunity to punish the incumbent. Moreover, electoral connections in state legislatures also repeatedly fall short of those found in Congress (e.g., figure 2.1, figure 6.3, table A.7.3).

In the absence of meaningful electoral messages, state legislators may not work as hard (e.g., Fouirnaies and Hall 2022) or may respond to political actors other than voters, like activists or interest groups. These political actors already shape state representation and policymaking. Michael Barber (2016) shows that state legislators in states with higher individual campaign-contribution limits are more polarized, and interest-group lobbying shapes the state legislatures' agendas (e.g., Butler and Miller 2021) and state legislators' positions (e.g., Grose et al. 2022). Interest groups know that lobbying can be effective and fill the halls of state capitols with lobbyists, to the tune that there are over twenty-five times as many lobbyists registered with state governments (chapter 2) than reporters at state houses (chapter 4). Legislators even readily admit they listen to these interest groups. The National Candidate Study, for example, asked legislators, "When you aren't sure whether a new proposal would make good policy, which of the following are particularly important sources of information?" Legislators could choose multiple categories. Thirty-eight percent chose "think tanks or interest groups," but only 19 percent chose "the constituents you represent." Such findings are potentially concerning, as interest groups and activists do not always have the same goals as most voters (Gilens 2014; Bonica 2013).

This book's findings similarly suggest that the voters who are most likely to hold state legislators accountable and legislators themselves may not be representative of American citizens. For instance, legislators with law or business backgrounds are less likely to retire than other legislators, leaving more upper-class citizens in the state house (chapter 2). Democratic women legislators are more likely to lose the general election but win their primary election, while Republican women legislators are more likely to lose their primary but win in the general election. Both these trends shape the descriptive and substantive representation in states (chapters 6 and 8). More-affluent voters with different policy views are more likely to know which party controls their state legislature (chapter 4) or have opinions about their state legislators (chapter 5), and these informed voters are more likely to hold their legislators accountable (chapter 7). These groups may back good policies, but wealthy and middle-class voters' interests do not always align (e.g., Bartels 2016). If a policy is ineffective or does not benefit most citizens, the most often proposed remedy is an election to throw bad policymakers out of office. The findings in this book demonstrate that state legislative elections do not provide such meaningful policy feedback, at least not as they are currently being used.

Studying Politics in the "Laboratories"

I do not think my current judgment about state legislatures is wrong, but I hope it is. It may seem odd that I would write a book only to end it stating to hope to be shown wrong. As a political scientist, however, I want my academic colleagues to be able to use the states as "laboratories" to learn more about the American political system, and more importantly, as a citizen of the United States and resident of Missouri, I hope the state of American democracy is not so bleak as this book suggests.

To explain from a political science perspective why I hope I am wrong, allow me to put on my inside-baseball hat and draw a parallel to an academic debate in American political science regarding the question: "Do parties matter?" This question, at first glance, may seem silly to some; but, again, consider the passage of the Affordable Care Act. When Democrats had unified control of the federal government in the first decade of the 2000s, they passed the Affordable Care Act. Not until Republicans took control of the presidency and acquired unified control of the federal government after the 2016 elections could this party repeal the individual mandate (for Americans to have health insurance) discussed at the beginning of this chapter. Such different behavior by the two major political parties followed conventional political science wisdom of the 1980s and 1990s of the "remarkable resurgence" of Congressional political parties influencing policymaking (Rhode 1991). Scholarship during this time investigated how and when parties exerted influence (e.g., when they were polarized and homogenous). Such arguments were largely accepted, as how could one question whether parties mattered in Congress?

The smart V. O. Key student David Mayhew, however, did question this wisdom. In another appropriately titled book, *Divided We Govern*, Mayhew showed that despite anecdotes like the passage of the Affordable Care Act under unified government, the number of "important laws" passed during unified and divided governments was similar (Mayhew 2005). Mayhew's finding undercut the argument that party control of Congress mattered for passing important bills. In another appropriately titled piece,

"Where's the Party?," Keith Krehbiel posed a more specific challenge to party scholars. To show that parties mattered, Krehbiel argued that one must provide evidence that "individual legislators vote with fellow party members *in spite of their disagreement* about the policy in question" (Krehbiel 1993, 238). Given that party membership and preferences highly correlate, this is a difficult task. Krehbiel went on to show there was little relationship between party membership and legislators' decisions, such as making committee assignments (see also Krehbiel 1995; 1999; 2000; and 2003, to reference a few).

Together, Mayhew and Krehbiel provided little meaningful evidence of party influence in policymaking and bucked conventional wisdom. An additional contribution of Mayhew's and Krehbiel's work is that it spurred better scholarship. Responses to Mayhew more carefully considered both the number of important laws passed and the number of important issues Americans hoped for Congress to address, leading to different conclusions about divided government's significance for lawmaking (e.g., Binder 1999). Scholars also took Krehbiel's challenge seriously. For example, Stephen Ansolabehere and coauthors (2001) estimated members' of Congress ideologies independent of their roll-call votes to create an independent measure of preferences to show on which roll-call votes parties had the most influence. In studying broader questions of legislative organization, Gary Cox and Mathew McCubbins explicitly stated their revised theory of party politics from *Legislative Leviathan* (1993) in *Setting the Agenda* (2005), which more fully considered "critiques that focus on the debility of party influence on floor votes (such as Krehbiel's)" (Cox and McCubbins 2005, 4). In this later work, Cox and McCubbins more specifically argued that party members sacrifice agenda power to the party leadership. In return, the party leadership acts like a cartel to use agenda-setting power to prevent bills unpopular with most of the party from coming to the floor, thereby protecting the party's "brand name" in elections.

The "do parties matter?" debate is a tired, academic dispute to some, but this old dog exemplifies how "null" results are results in themselves and can push scholarship in fruitful directions. I hope this book's depressing and often null results accomplish a similar task. As Mayhew and Krehbiel find little meaningful evidence that parties matter—forcing scholars to more carefully consider how parties are influential—I find little meaningful evidence of accountability in state legislatures, a finding that has implications for how scholars of politics utilize the "laboratories of democracy."

Political scientists, for example, already use state legislatures to study competing theories of legislative organization, and the "do parties matter?" debate has even reached into the states (e.g., Aldrich and Battista 2002; Anzia and Jackman 2013; Cox, Kousser, and McCubbins 2010). Cox and McCubbins with Thad Kousser test "cartel theory" in Colorado and find fewer majority party rolls—an instance where a majority of the majority party unsuccessfully opposes the passage of a bill—when the majority party has agenda-setting power. Such evidence supports cartel theory's argument that "endowing majority leaders with greater agenda-setting powers (or removing those powers) does affect their ability to influence legislative outcomes" (Cox, Kousser, and McCubbins 2010, 809).

Cox, McCubbins, and Kousser follow a tradition "of using state legislatures as laboratories to test more general theories of legislative process and behavior, usually developed in the congressional context" (Cox, Kousser, and McCubbins 2010, 809). Their evidence supports cartel theory's predictions, but Cox and his coauthors provide less evidence for the assumptions that underlie this theory. In 2016, most Coloradans knew Republicans controlled the US House, but fewer than half knew Democrats controlled the Colorado state house. Such findings concerning voters' knowledge of the state legislature bring into question whether cartel theory can explain Cox, McCubbins, and Kousser's findings. Cartel theory is predicated on the importance of a party's brand name, but why should state legislative parties care about their brand when voters do not know which brand is in charge? This is a fact many legislators recognize. Recall that 49 percent of state legislators told the National Candidate Study they do not believe voters know which party held the majority of seats in their state senate.

More broadly, political scientists often reference Mayhew's famous "electoral connection" in studies of local, state, and federal politics. It is even referenced on the first page of this book. Nevertheless, more evidence is needed to transport Mayhew's argument to lower levels of government. Central to Mayhew's argument is that members of Congress "credit claim"—or "generate a belief in a relevant political actor that one is personally responsible for causing the government . . . to do something that the actor considers desirable" in order to win reelection (Mayhew 1974, 52). But recall from chapter 5 that—when given the opportunity to answer the open-ended question, "Do you happen to remember anything special that your representative in the [lower chamber name] has done for this district or people in this district while he or she has been in the state legislature? If so, what has this legislator done?"—almost 80 percent of voters explicitly answered this question with some version of "no" or "don't know." Taken together with the proportion of Americans who could not recall their state legislator's name (chapter 4), three-fourths of Americans are unaware of both who their state legislator is and what that legislator has done for their district. These figures do not imply that state legislators do not credit claim, but they lead to a new question: should state legislators expend effort to credit claim if such actions do not resonate with voters?

The "laboratories of democracy" are useful for learning about American politics—especially considering that more governing happens in the states than in Congress. There is fantastic variation in institutional rules for political scientists to leverage. Nevertheless, political scientists need to take care before "extend[ing] theories originally developed to explain the US House to (some) state legislatures" (Cox, Kousser, and McCubbins 2010, 809). Assumptions underlying a theory need an evidentiary foundation before a theory developed at the federal level can simply be plugged into the state level. Voters' lack of awareness of brand names or credit claiming suggests that the canonical electoral connection may work differently in states, and in turn, that how state legislators achieve their electoral goals differs from their federal counterparts. When studying American legislatures, political scientists then may need to consider that "American exceptionalism" perhaps applies to studying the federal government (Lipset 1997).

I do not "prove" that accountability in state legislatures does not exist, as Mayhew and Krehbiel do not prove that parties do not matter. Meaningful accountability in state legislatures or party influence in Congress may very well exist, and we may simply be looking in the wrong places. As characterized by one of Krehbiel's well-intentioned critics: "[Krehbiel] asked 'Where's the party?', looked in only one House and answered 'Not in the attic'" (Krehbiel 1993, 259). Regarding my own study, there are many ways to hold a legislator accountable, and I searched the kitchen, den, and many other rooms of the house (and senate). Nevertheless, my search largely failed to produce meaningful evidence of electoral accountability. It concerns me that there seems to be little accountability in the rooms where we would most expect to find it, but I will continue to search along with my colleagues in hopes of finding that foyer full of electoral accountability. There could be an unexplored nook of the state house where electoral accountability exists that will help ensure better policymaking.

While previous chapters do not paint a sunny perspective on electoral accountability in state legislatures, they offer insights into how we can remodel state houses to provide at least a little more accountability. Returning to Powell's requirements for accountability one last time, for voters to have a fair opportunity to hold their legislators accountable, a legislator must want to run for reelection, and someone must want to run against him. In other words, perhaps more accountability can be achieved by making serving in the state legislature a more attractive job. Raising state legislators' salaries will likely keep incumbents running for reelection (chapter 2), and publicly financed campaigns will lead to more challengers (chapter 3). Incumbents also run more often in states without term limits, allowing them to benefit from the legislative experience they've gained in the state capitol. Such evidence provides another reason to abolish this institution in state legislatures (Masket 2020). Challengers also do not want to run if there is no chance of winning, as is often the case in partisan districts, providing another reason to curb the amount of gerrymandering in the United States.

To increase the number of voters who "know who is responsible for making policy," making state politics easier to follow is an attractive approach but one that may be challenging to achieve. For example, if more reporters cover state government or existing media pay more attention to state legislatures, then state legislatures will have a greater presence in voters' daily lives. However, achieving this goal will require a large reversal in the trend toward nationalized media and the continuing decline in statehouse reporters. Voters must still pay *some* attention to state politics. But it is important to remember that voters are not blind to state politics, particularly not when information is clear. For instance, voters have become more informed about which party controls their state legislature as more state governments have become unified instead of divided (chapter 4). A *dramatic* step toward simplification is increasing the number of unicameral legislatures, which only require voters to know the party of the governor and the unicameral legislature instead of the parties of both the state house and the state senate. With such information, voters will be better equipped to hold their state legislative parties accountable (chapter 7).

Raising legislators' pay is obviously more feasible than abolishing a state senate, and such changes to legislatures will undoubtedly affect policymaking in other ways (e.g., Cutrone and McCarty 2008). However, as put by Justice Brandeis, we have laboratories where we can experiment. For instance, in 2004, Washington adopted a top-two primary system, and California followed suit in 2010. And there is some evidence, at least from Congress, that such reforms lead to the election of more-moderate legislators

(Grose 2020; McGhee and Shor 2017). Progress may be incremental, and reforms may lead to some unhappy incidents. However, we will likely find some ways to repair the cracks in statehouse democracy. While I remain doubtful we can feasibly achieve normatively desirable amounts of accountability in state legislatures on a regular basis, state legislative elections likely *can* provide more accountability than they currently do.

Statehouse Democracy's Shaky Foundation

This book does little to add optimism to whether American democracy lives up to familiar normative expectations (Lippmann 1993; Converse 1964; Achen and Bartels 2016). It is too strong to say that relationships between legislators' behavior and election outcomes fail to exist in state legislatures or that voters *cannot* hold their state legislators accountable. And it is certainly an overstatement to say that state legislative elections are meaningless. This book's core argument is that legislators' actions have little impact on their own elections, not that elections have no impact on legislators' actions via the "threat" of electoral sanction. However, reliance on a mere threat of accountability can create a false sense of security and be dangerous both in everyday life and representative government. A town may have speed limits, and the threat of speeding tickets may create a belief that driving is then safer in this town. However, if local authorities do not enforce speed limits, drivers will learn they can speed without sanction, putting other drivers and pedestrians at risk. Similarly, the threat of electoral sanction alone may be enough for liberal states to produce liberal policies and conservative states to produce conservative policies. An *empty* threat, however, is a shaky foundation for any democracy.

Again, I hope my doubts are wrong, as state lawmakers will continue their long history of considerable authority over American lives. When discontented with the outcome of the War between the States, state governments asserted their own authority and instituted poll taxes to limit who could vote. Only when the Supreme Court overruled legislatures did these taxes end in the 1960s, and in the 1970s, the high court again famously stepped in to strike down a Texas statute in *Roe v. Wade*. During this time and by 1983, forty-nine states enacted mandatory minimums in the lead-up to the War on Drugs in the 1980s (Murdoch 2001), a development partly responsible for the subsequent incarceration in state prisons of more than half of the entire US prison population (Sawyer and Wagner 2020). After the federal government strengthened gun control laws with the Brady Bill in 1993, twenty legislatures revoked it and created "conceal and carry" laws within their state's borders (Grossman and Lee 2008). In this decade, most state legislatures also defined marriage as a relationship between a man and a woman, but in the first two decades of the 2000s, over a dozen states created laws recognizing same-sex marriages or civil unions (National Conference of State Legislatures 2015). And in the 2020s, states reclaimed the ability to determine whether a woman could have an abortion, even to save her life.

This brief tour of American lawmaking only reflects a small smattering of the important policy areas that states address. State legislatures matter. State lawmakers legislate on civil rights, education, and even immigration, and something needs to hold them in check. Elections are the primary instrument by which citizens can respond to and exert control over those who govern them. Voters are not fools but are asked to do too much in a democracy where federal politics are king. In turn, there is a lack of meaningful electoral control in state legislatures. This troubling characterization of American democracy is not lost on Americans. Eighty-three percent of Americans agreed it was very important for "elected officials to face serious consequences for misconduct," but only 31 percent thought this scenario described the American political system very well (Pew Research Center 2018). Voters are actually the optimistic ones, as only 15 percent of legislators agree with the statement that "voters know who in government to blame for policies they do not like." On the whole, it seems that neither voters nor legislators are wrong in their take on electoral accountability in the American states. But I hope that they are.

Notes

Preface

1. Proceeds from this book will be donated to the Missouri Youth and Government program.

2. Shortly after I decided to attend Princeton, a frustrated John Sides shook his finger at me and said "Larry Bartels will straighten you out" during an office hours disagreement about rational choice theory.

3. At SPPC the following year, Bob Erikson offered extensive comments on a poster that would become chapter 6 in this book. It was clear from this constructive conversation that Erikson disagreed with Rogers, which Erikson and Rogers laughed about as they closed down a bar years later at another SPPC.

Chapter One

1. See Grumbach (2022, ch. 3) for an excellent review of how states' policymaking has increased since the 1970s.

2. This example presumes that building schools instead of a sports stadium is in voters' best interest, which may not be the case. Such concerns relate to classic conflicts between delegate and trustee representation (Burke 1774). To address these different types of representation, chapters 6 and 7 assess both objective measures of legislators' representation and performance (e.g., whether the state economy was actually strong) and subjective measures of legislators' representation and performance (e.g., whether citizens thought the state economy was strong).

3. For a more thorough discussion of Key and Downs' works, I encourage readers to seek out chapter 1 of *Retrospective Voting in American National Elections* (Fiorina 1981). For a review of non-electoral ways government officials can be held accountable, see Stephanopoulos (2018).

4. This example assumes that all voters cast their ballots based on the given bill, and the median voter's opposition of a candidate reflects that a majority of voters will also oppose the candidate.

5. Federal employee figures exclude postal workers as reported by the Bureau of Labor Statistics. Federal tax figures account for individual and corporate income, payroll, excise, estate, and gift taxes, as reported by the Congressional Budget Office.

6. Studying the relationship between state-level partisan identification and Republican control of state government, 1935–2020, Caughey and Warshaw (2022, 87) similarly find that "when it comes to short-term changes in party control, party identification is the most consistent and powerful predictor" and "mass partisanship swamps all measures of mass ideology, confirming its dominance as a driver of election outcomes."

7. Benedictis-Kessner and Warshaw (2020) examine the impact of county-level wage growth on county-level vote share for state legislative candidates. To account for incumbency, they "use an indicator for the county legislative majority" (Benedictis-Kessner and Warshaw 2020, 665). In related work, James Campbell (1986) examines midterm loss for the president's party in state legislative elections, and Berry, Berkman, and Schneiderman (2000) show that the impact of the national economy on state legislative elections is less in more professionalized legislatures.

8. As explained by Banks and Sundaram (1993, 297), the voter "retain[s] the current incumbent as long as the reward remains above a certain level. Faced with this reelection rule, incumbents adopt time-invariant actions as a function of their true type, where lower cost types take higher actions, and are consequently reelected more often. Thus, as an incumbent's tenure increases, the voter is more confident she has selected a (relatively) hard-working type."

9. Retrospection is important for either the moral hazard or adverse-selection view of elections. In the moral hazard perspective, retrospection can lead to punishment to change incumbents' behavior. In the adverse selection perspective, retrospection helps inform voters of the incumbent's type to determine if the candidate will be selected again. While this book focuses on accountability, many findings of this book bring into question whether state legislative elections are effective selection mechanisms. For instance, it would be difficult to identify a legislator's type when over 75 percent of voters cannot name anything the legislator has done for their district (chapter 5).

10. Ideology or representativeness is a common—but not the only—way that one can define a legislator's type (e.g., Groseclose 2001). A voter could assess a legislator's type also for their ability to pass legislation or stimulate the economy, subjects more thoroughly addressed in chapters 5, 6, and 7.

11. Legislator ideology measures are "ideal points" estimated by Shor and McCarty using legislators' responses to surveys and roll-call records. Political

scientists frequently use ideal point estimates to quantify ideology on a numerical scale (e.g., from -1 to 1, with lower numbers reflecting liberal ideology; see Poole and Rosenthal, 2000). In figure 1.2, reported ideological measures on the x and y axes use different scales, and if a legislator's ideology is -1 and his district's ideology is -1, it does not mean this legislator perfectly represents their district.

12. To field another example of ideologically dissimilar legislators representing similar districts, consider Mike Gerber of Pennsylvania and Hunter Greene of Louisiana. Gerber and Greene both represented districts in 2010 whose ideal points were approximately 0.26 according to Tausanovitch and Warshaw, but Shor and McCarty's estimate of Greene's ideal point is a relatively conservative 0.9, and Gerber's ideal point turns out to be a much more liberal -0.7.

13. The phenomenon of midterm loss helps illustrate the balancing argument. Consider a voter who wants moderate policies and believes these policies are most likely achieved during a divided government. When voting in a presidential election, this voter casts ballots for presidential and Congressional candidates at the same time. Given these coinciding elections, this voter is uncertain which party will control the presidency after the election when they have to decide how to vote in the Congressional election (and vice versa). It is, therefore, difficult for the voter to know how to split their ticket to use their vote to create a divided government during a presidential election. This task is easier in the midterm election when the voter is almost certain who will control the presidency after the election. The voter can then vote against the president's party in the Congressional midterm election in an effort to give the power of Congress to the other party.

14. Elsewhere, Caughey and Warshaw (2022, 92) state, "Anticipatory balancing does not require that voters hold incumbents accountable for actual policy outcomes."

15. This quote was found thanks to Hirano and Snyder (2014).

Chapter Two

1. Blair and Henry (1981) found that approximately half of retiring Arkansas legislators cited family as part of the reason for their departure from the legislature in the 1970s, and in a study of Indiana and Missouri from the early 1980s, 19 percent of voluntarily departing legislators attributed their departure to family reasons (Francis and Baker 1986). Smith and Miller (1977) found that 10 percent of Texas legislators from 1970 to 1974 left the legislature for "need of family time." Thirty-eight percent of retiring state legislators from Minnesota, Mississippi, Wisconsin, and Wyoming told Zach Baumann their decision to retire was due to family reasons (Baumann 2012, table 2).

2. Response rates for this survey were well-balanced on several important observable characteristics, such as party of the candidate, whether the candidate won

the election, candidate's vote margin, and candidate's region; see Broockman and Skovron (2013).

3. In a survey of legislators from four states, Freeman and Lyons (1992) found that 58 percent of men legislators agreed with the statement that "to be really active in politics, men have to neglect their wives and children." A rich literature helps explain why so few women run for the state house (see Carroll and Fox 2013 for a review), to which this single chapter cannot do justice. Explanations for the paucity of women legislative candidates include differing levels of political ambition (e.g., Fox and Lawless 2005), the supply of candidates (e.g., Darcy, Clark, and Welch 1994), recruitment (e.g., Crowder-Meyer 2013), and personal circumstances (e.g., Carroll and Sanbonmatsu 2013).

4. This quote and example were found thanks to Squire (2012, 316).

5. Most legislative candidates come from families with incomes that exceed $75,000, but legislators' annual pay in most states was less than $25,000 in 2016 (Broockman et al. 2021).

6. Respondents could give multiple answers to this question. For instance, 4.4 percent of respondents stated that they would both retire and return to their previous career.

7. As a political *scientist*, I employ the metric system and measure distances in kilometers instead of miles.

8. These differences in means are each statistically distinguishable from zero but do not imply that women legislators provide more liberal representation, all else equal. For example, liberal districts may be more likely to elect women legislators, who would provide the same representation as a man legislator would if he represented the same liberal district.

9. The following analyses account for whether an election took place under a new redistricting regime. If a legislator sought reelection, I could identify legislators' new districts to assign district-level covariates with confidence. If a legislator did not seek reelection, I often had to assume the legislator's new district number would have been the same as the legislator's previous district number. A weakness of this assumption is that under the new district lines, a legislator may no longer live or be eligible to run in their old district. Table A.2.4 provides statistical analyses comparable to those in the main text but excludes all districts that were redistricted. Most results are similar, but the main text highlights where they most notably differ.

10. This book at times presents these differences in predicted probabilities followed by a "t-statistic of difference" in parentheticals. In a statistics refresher, if a t-statistic exceeds 1.96, the difference in probability is generally considered to be statistically distinguishable from zero or "statistically significant." If a difference in probability is reported without a t-statistic, the reader may assume that the difference in probability is statistically distinguishable from zero.

11. Nonwhite legislators are less likely to retire, all else equal, but this relationship is largely driven by legislators who represent more partisan districts.

12. In the following chapter, I more generally show that challengers less often run if their district is farther from the state capital.

13. I thank Andrew Hall for helping me develop my thoughts on these points.

14. Fowler and McClure (1990) also find evidence that higher state legislative salaries keep legislators from seeking higher office (e.g., in the US House).

15. Consistent with prior findings that show that salaries in state legislatures have little relationship with the number of legislators who come from "working class" backgrounds (Carnes and Hansen 2016), I do not find these profession relationships to vary across state legislatures with differing salaries.

16. Legislators' next jobs can also be other elected offices. I encourage readers to read work by Danielle Thomsen (2014; 2017) and Andrew Hall (2019) to learn more about legislators' ambitions and how their decisions relate to congressional polarization. In supplementary analyses that follow Thomsen's work, I identify which state legislative and US House districts overlap. I then estimate the likelihood that a legislator will leave state government when an overlapping US House seat is open and vacated by a member of the state legislator's party. If legislators strategically pursue higher office, I expect the relationships between these variables and retirement to be positive. Results are in the expected direction but do not meet conventional levels of statistical significance.

17. In 2011, the percentages of former state legislators who were lobbyists in states with and without cooling-off periods, respectively, are 6.4 percent and 5.9 percent. It is likely surprising that percentages are lower in states without cooling-off periods. However, New Hampshire, which has more than twice the number of former state legislators than any other state, influences this percentage. When excluding the Granite State, 7.3 percent of former legislators are lobbyists in states without cooling-off periods.

18. State Representative Kevin Corlew actually waited until a day before Missouri's new cooling-off regulations took place to resign.

19. Moore and Hibbing nicely note that "all voluntary departures are strategic in that the rewards of continued service are obviously perceived by the member involved to be insufficient to counteract the costs, given the way the costs and benefits appear to that member at the time" (Moore and Hibbing 1998, 1105).

20. The correlation between estimated district ideal points and district-level presidential vote is 0.80.

21. Carson and coauthors (2010) use an instrumental-variable approach to study party loyalty's impact on vote share, where the first stage regression includes "Extremism," as measured by the absolute value of a US House Member's DW-NOMINATE score. Such an approach is not currently possible in a cross-state analysis of state legislators, as one cannot bridge state-specific session ideal points. I, therefore, use a legislator's actual instead of instrumented party-loyalty score. Main findings are not sensitive to excluding this measure of a legislator's party loyalty.

22. Results are less discouraging if unrepresentative legislators who run for re-election would have been otherwise replaced by even less representative legislators (Bafumi and Herron 2010).

23. Unlike findings concerning challengers (chapter 3), the strength of the relationship between economic growth and retirement is not conditional on whether the legislator is a member of the governor's or legislative majority party.

24. When excluding districts that have been recently redistricted, statistical analyses suggest that members of the president's party are more likely to retire in the 2011 to 2020 elections.

Chapter Three

1. While any challenger is likely better than no challenger, a challenger could be detrimental to accountability if a weak challenger runs and does poorly in the election, deterring more viable challengers from running in the future.

2. For the full 2001 to 2020 time period, data on challengers' gender is unfortunately unavailable. In surveys, Moncrief, Squire, and Jewell (2001) find that 22 percent of state legislative candidates are women. More recently, Bernard Fraga, Eric Juenke, and Paru Shah (2021) identified the gender of all 2018 state legislative candidates and found that 30 percent of state legislative candidates were women and 35 percent of state legislative challengers to incumbents were women. To learn more about gender differences in who runs for the state legislature, I encourage readers to consider the work of Susan Carroll and Kira Sanbonmatsu (2013).

3. In unpublished work, Hoffman and Lyons find that a "100 percent increase in the salary is associated with a 2.5 percentage point increase in the chance an election is contested" (2014, 11). When using an index measure of professionalism that includes both length of session and salary along with legislative staff, Hogan (2004) finds more competition in more professional legislatures.

4. For clarity in presentation, I focus on decisions that may be more relevant to a potential challenger. For example, I do not examine some of the personal variables considered in the previous chapter, such as legislators' marital status, as there is less theoretical reason to expect a challenger to be more or less likely to challenge someone who is married. Analyses including these variables are available in the online appendix.

5. More specifically, my dependent variable is whether a major-party challenger ran in a district where an incumbent also sought reelection. This definition then includes incumbents who lost their primary election and did not appear in the general election. I use this definition because a major-party challenger would not know, at the time they decided to enter the race, whether an incumbent was going to lose their primary election.

6. When setting legislative salary, staff, session length, and public financing to their maximum or minimum values and incumbent-party presidential vote to

42 percent, the predicted probability of a challenger is .85 with a 95 percent confidence interval of [0.779, 0.935].

7. Berry, Berkman, and Schneiderman (2000) argue that national conditions' impact on incumbent reelection is weaker in professionalized legislatures. I similarly find that professionalism's mediating influence on national conditions occurs at the candidate-entry stage. The strength of the relationship between the state economy and challenges to gubernatorial-party state legislative incumbents is stronger in professionalized legislatures. For further detail, see Rogers (2015).

Chapter Four

1. Don't worry. In the following chapters, I won't ask you how your state legislator voted on a particular bill.

2. The Eagleton Institute asked voters to identify their state senator multiple times in the early 1970s but does not report if the survey respondent was correct. A 2006 poll found 67 percent of Utah voters acknowledged they did not know or were uncertain of their state representative or senator's names (Bernick 2006).

3. Eleven percent is an overestimate of the percentage of correct responses due to generous coding. The most specific geographic identifiers were a respondent's zip code and congressional district. I identified what state legislative district fell into a "Zip-CD" region, but multiple state legislative districts at times fell into the same "Zip-CD" region. In coding, a voter was identified as providing a "correct" answer if they provided the name of a representative who represented one of these districts. For multi-member districts, I coded a voter's response as correct if a voter accurately identified at least one of their representatives. Responses also did not need to be the full name of their representative to be marked as correct (e.g., Gibson and Caldeira 2009).

4. Voters were better able to identify their legislator's name if that legislator spent more on their most recent campaign and if the seat had been previously contested (table A.3.1). Analyses also suggest voters who live in more-partisan districts were more likely to identify their state representative's party and their state legislator's name (t-statistic of difference 1.81). Similarly, voters in the Republican state of Tennessee are more likely to identify their legislator's party if the legislator is Republican.

5. Exact search terms or topics were "president of the United States," "governor", and—for "state legislature"—"state legislature," "general assembly," "general court," "state assembly," "state house of representatives," and "state senate." Readers should note that trends in figure 5.4 do not include searches for individual governors or legislators (e.g., Governor Arnold Schwarzenegger or State Senator Barack Obama), which likely underestimates search volume for governor and state legislatures.

6. For a more extensive review of research on media coverage of state politics, see work done by Christopher Cooper and Martin Johnson (Cooper 2002; Cooper and Johnson 2006; 2007; 2009; Johnson 2013).

7. Part-time reporters made up 42 percent of newspaper reporters, 55 percent of television reporters, and 49 percent of radio reporters in 2022. For these percentages, I follow Pew's definition of "full-time" to include session-only reporters. I exclude reporters Pew designates as "students/interns" or "other."

8. In 2002, Kaplan, Goldstein, and Hale examined "122 randomly selected local television stations in the top 50 media markets in the United States" (2003, 4), and in 2004, examined forty-four local news affiliates across the New York, Los Angeles, Philadelphia, Dallas, Seattle, Miami, Denver, Orlando, Tampa, Dayton, and Des Moines media markets (2005). Given that most media markets studied are in more populous areas, readers should consider that news stations with audiences across multiple political constituencies (e.g., legislative districts) may be more likely to cover races pertinent to their full audience (e.g., a presidential or statewide contest) than to a subset of their audience (e.g., a congressional or state legislative race). There is evidence that residing in a fragmented media market correlates with lower levels of voter information (J. E. Campbell, Alford, and Henry 1984; Snyder and Stromberg 2010).

9. In interviews with news staff in Louisiana, Alvarez (2010) also finds that the governor receives more extensive coverage than the legislature. When asked about the declining number of statehouse reporters by the *American Journalism Review* (*AJR*), former *Detroit Free Press* reporter and current associate professor of communication Eric Freedman similarly characterized coverage as "pretty skimpy beyond gubernatorial coverage" (Lisheron 2010). See also Wolfson (1985, 139).

10. These figures do not reflect all the newspapers examined by the *AJR* or Pew, as some newspapers closed or started during this time period. For example, in their 2014 study, Pew examined 220 of the same newspapers as *AJR* and found that there were 467 full-time reporters in 2003, which dropped to 343 in 2009 and then to 303 in 2014, representing an overall decline of 35 percent. In their 2022 study, the Pew Research Center also notes, "It is likely that full-time statehouse reporting staff among this group of newspapers has declined by more than 44% since 2003 because the Center's 2022 data employs a broader definition of full-time statehouse reporting than the AJR data by combining full-time, year-round reporters with those who work only during the legislative session."

11. Digital and nontraditional media have also replaced some of the print media's presence in state capitols. For example, in New Jersey from 2003 to 2009, the number of full-time newspaper reporters fell from thirty-five to fifteen, the largest single-state decline in reporters during this time period (Lisheron 2010; see also Walton 2000), but as of 2013, commercial, digital reporters made up 13 percent of all full-time reporters in New Jersey. In 2013, the Pew Research Center, however, identified no full-time digital reporters in over half of states. In states where such outlets exist, audiences generally are those already particularly interested in state political news (Enda, Matsa, and Boyles 2014; Gurwitt 2008).

12. Main findings concerning the media are similar when excluding these state-level variables (see online appendix).

13. The t-statistic of the difference for 2010 is 0.014.

14. Evidence is mixed that state legislative professionalism relates to voters' knowledge of the legislature. Squire posited that shorter legislative sessions would lead to more voters focusing on the legislature. My findings from the 2010 state house and 2014 state senate support this proposition, but findings from the 2012 state house suggest the opposite relationship (table 4.1). Analyses of knowledge of the state senate indicated increased staff but lower state legislative salaries increase the likelihood that voters can correctly identify majority parties. Meanwhile, findings concerning staff and salary are more mixed when studying state house elections.

15. Analyses in the appendix investigate how characteristics of Tennessee voters relate to their knowledge of their state legislators. Unlike findings from Congress (Dolan 2011; Jones 2014), I do not find that women voters are more likely to recall or identify women state representatives. Similar to Bobo and Gilliam's (1990) study of the US House, I find that nonwhite voters are more likely to be able to identify nonwhite state legislators' names or parties, but less likely to recall nonwhite legislators' names.

16. This specification follows Hayes and Lawless and treats voters who are incorrect both in 2010 and 2014 the same as voters who are correct both in 2010 and 2014. Theoretically, one would expect that an increase in reporters would lead to fewer voters staying incorrect and more voters staying correct. When dividing voters into four instead of three categories, ordered probit estimates match this theoretical expectation but differences in predicted probabilities associated with a standard-deviation change in the reporters variable do not reach conventional levels of statistical significance.

17. Analyses in the appendix, for example, show that Tennessee voters are more likely to know their state legislator's party when that legislator spent more on their previous political campaign.

18. Analyses exclude minor mentions (e.g., when a legislator's name is only a part of a list of three or more names within an article without any real substantive content). Main findings do not change when including minor mentions.

Chapter Five

1. In a separate question, 8 percent of respondents indicated they contacted their state legislator. By comparison, 18 contacted their US senator, 15 percent contacted their US House representative, 7 percent contacted their city-council member, and 6 percent contacted their governor.

2. Some voters gave multiple issues a "100" rating. Figure 5.2 weights issues such that no one voter has a greater impact. For instance, if one voter rates education at 100 on the importance scale, education receives a value of 1, but if a voter

rates both gun control and abortion at 100, gun control and abortion each receive weights of 0.5.

3. The lack of measures of candidate ideology for all state legislative candidates prevents determination of whether all voters were correct in their candidate-level assessments, as there are likely some Democratic candidates who were more conservative than their Republican opponents.

4. Similar to Bishop's (2018) study of the 2012 CES, I find Republican voters were more likely to rate the state parties as more conservative. Republican voters rated the Republican and Democratic state legislative parties as a 76 and 33. Meanwhile, Democrats rated these parties as a 71 and 29. Republican voters were also 10 percent more likely to correctly identify whether their state legislative Democratic party was more liberal than the Congressional Democratic party and 3 percent more likely to correctly identify whether their state legislative Republican party was more conservative than the Congressional Republican party.

5. These probabilities differ by over 20 percentage points largely because of the states considered and survey weights. 42 percent of state legislative Republican parties were more conservative than the Congressional Republican party. Meanwhile, only 16 percent of state legislative Democratic parties were more liberal than Congressional Democrats.

6. Related to Mayhew's argument, when surveying Tennessee voters, I find that a legislator's increased position taking—as indicated by the number of bills they sponsor—has little relationship with voters' ability to recall or identify who their state legislators are (table A.4.1).

7. For example, Bob Erikson's (2016) "Congressional Elections in Presidential Years: Presidential Coattails and Strategic Voting" is an excellent piece that studies balancing in presidential election years, highlighting the importance of "uncertainty" for balancing.

8. When there was a gubernatorial election, 9 percent of voters in the full CES sample reported that they split their gubernatorial-legislative tickets. When there was not a gubernatorial election, 34 percent of voters voted against the governor's party in their state legislative election.

Chapter Six

1. I focus on ideological distance as this empirical setup most closely matches the spatial framework of the median voter theorem. Tausanovitch and Warshaw (2018, 227) note that this approach can be "problematic because the preferences of the voter and the position of the candidate can contribute to vote choice irrespective of the distance between them." The online appendix provides analyses similar to those in table 6.1 that include separate measures of a voter's, candidate's, and state party's ideological positions, and main results are similar. The online appendix

also provides analyses similar to tables A.6.1 and A.6.2 that include a legislator's ideal point separate from Tausanovitch and Warshaw's (2013) measure of district ideology. When controlling for these other ideological measures, I continue to find a negative relationship between ideological distance and vote share. However, I do not find a relationship between ideological distance and incumbent reelection.

2. As described in chapter 7, I adjust these approval variables such that higher values indicate approval of a Democratic state house, governor, or president. Lower values indicate approval of a Republican state house, governor, or president, and range from -2 to 2. Voters who are "not sure" if they approve or disapprove are coded as 0.

3. Unlike Adams et al. (2017), I do not find that the strength of the relationship differs between moderate versus more ideological voters.

4. To create these measures, I identify members of Congress who once served in their state legislature to bridge federal and state legislators in a similar manner to how Shor and McCarty project state legislator ideal points into a common NPAT space.

5. Within this joint analysis of Congressional and state legislative elections, I use the same mean and standard deviation of the ideological distance variable: 0.720 and 0.372.

6. When separately examining elections from 2001 to 2010 or 2011 to 2020, comparable estimates concerning the impact of governor's-party membership are not statistically distinguishable from zero.

7. This 1.2 percent change in vote share associated with a standard-deviation decrease in ideological distance from the mean is larger than the 0.8 percent change associated with a standard-deviation increase above the mean, due to the nonlinear relationship between representation and vote share.

8. These averages are lower than those found in US House elections, where reelection-seeking incumbents received average vote shares of 65 percent when facing a challenger and won 96 percent of the time.

9. Similar to findings from the vote share analyses, I do not find meaningful differences in this relationship over time.

10. Hopkins (2018, fig. 3.2) also finds an increasing correlation between county-level presidential and governor votes, but the strength of the correlation varies by whether the gubernatorial election was on- or off-cycle.

11. Despite these high correlations, split ticketing certainly occurs in state legislative elections. I encourage readers interested in state-level ticket-splitting to read Shiro Kuriwaki's dissertation (2021). Kuriwaki, for example, uses ballot images to show that up to 10 percent of South Carolina voters split their ticket between the governor and state senate or house candidates.

12. A standard-deviation change in presidential vote in the 2001 to 2010 or 2011 to 2020 elections respectively associates with 0.020 or 0.019 changes in the probabilities of incumbent reelection in all races, and 0.032 or 0.024 changes in races with a challenger.

13. When dividing districts into marginal and safe districts, where the incumbent's party received less or more than 60 percent of the presidential vote, a standard-deviation increase in ideological distance respectively associates with 0.77 and 0.49 percent losses in vote share in marginal and safe districts. See online appendix for estimates.

14. When studying elections from 2001 to 2010, Rogers (2017) finds that legislators with increased staff additionally face less punishment for poor representation. When using the same set of controls to study only the 2011 to 2020 elections, conditional staff estimates do not meet conventional levels of statistical significance. However, I do not find a similar conditional relationship when introducing the expanded set of control variables used in this manuscript.

15. In a later, colorful exchange about listening to constituency opinion concerning Maine's budget, Governor Paul LePage said Jackson "claims to be for the people but he's the first one to give it to the people without providing Vaseline" (Cousins 2013).

16. Results are similar when including the full set of state controls. I do not find evidence that the relationship between voters' opinions about individual roll-call votes and vote share is conditional on media coverage or legislative professionalism. Readers should note, however, that analyses only compare thirteen different states, limiting the amount of considered cross-state variation.

17. To illustrate this limitation, consider legislators A, B, and C who have effectiveness scores of 1, 0.75, and 0.25. The difference in ranking of each legislator is only 1, but the difference between the scores of A and B is half that of B and C.

18. Elections in 2002 also exclusively had single-member districts, but I exclude such races to avoid complications introduced by redistricting and transitioning from a multi-member to single-member system.

19. Miquel and Snyder (2006, 354) define these committees as Appropriations, Finance, Judiciary I, Rules, and Education. Miquel and Snyder's original analyses also account for a legislator's age. I was unable to identify the age of sixty-seven legislators who served from 2004–2016. Main results are similar when accounting for age where data is available.

20. Sadly, the NC Center for Public Policy Research ceased operations in 2021.

21. I thank John Sides for bringing my attention to this important point.

Chapter Seven

1. The author's father, for example, was not a fan of shortcuts, particularly when it involved riding one's bike across a nicely mowed backyard to get to a friend's house.

2. I focus on the 2006 election because this is the only time the CES asked this question to the full sample of respondents. In the 2018 CES, I asked voters what

the unemployment rate was in their state. 84 percent of Americans overestimated the unemployment rate and where the correlation between beliefs and the true rate was .21, with an average error of approximately 2.7 percent.

3. This relationship is similar to findings that voters' evaluations of the economic conditions in their city are worse in cities with higher unemployment rates (Holbrook and Weinschenk 2019).

4. To explain nationalization, Hopkins also highlights the importance of voters' identities (Hopkins 2018, chapter 7) and sources of news (Hopkins 2018, chapter 8).

5. Arceneaux (2006) finds little evidence that voters who believe the governor is functionally responsible for unemployment, education, and traffic blame or reward the governor for their perceived performance on these issues. There is, however, stronger evidence of this type of accountability for unemployment when the issue of unemployment is more accessible to voters, as indicated by their response time to survey questions.

6. One reason for "why not" is that there may be little difference between how Democrats and Republicans perform. Adam Dynes and John Holbein find that "Democrats and Republicans appear to be equal in terms of their ability to produce a wide range of policy outcomes associated with the overall well-being or social prosperity" (Dynes and Holbein 2020, 25). If the Democratic and Republican parties produce similar outcomes, it is sensible for voters to care little about policy performance. The next logical alternative here, however, is that voters would instead care about state parties' ideologies. Findings in table 6.1, however, show that voters are no more likely to vote for the state party they believe to be ideologically closer to them.

7. In addition to the education measures provided by the Correlates of State Policy Database. I also evaluate how changes in a state's average SAT score relate to state legislative election outcomes, and following findings that governors are more likely to be elected after state taxes decrease (Besley and Case 1995; Kone and Winters 1993; Niemi, Stanley, and Vogel 1995), I examine whether the party in control of the state legislature receives a similar reward for reducing taxes, as measured by the change in the maximum tax rate alone or changes in effective tax liabilities for $50,000 joint filers. Results are not sensitive to type of tax filing or level income. Substantive results are also similar when using change in a state's maximum tax rate or total state income, sales, corporate taxes collected per capita, or a dummy variable to indicate tax increases.

8. The congressional vote control is not available for state legislative elections that occur in the "off-year." New Jersey, Virginia, Mississippi, Louisiana, and sometimes Kentucky are, therefore, excluded from the main analysis. Substantive results do not change when omitting this variable and including these states. For regressions that include an indicator for the governor's party, I omit elections where the sitting governor was an independent. Results additionally are not sensitive to excluding the exposure-control variable, a particular state or year, or state fixed effects.

9. I thank Steve Smith for bringing my attention to the importance of this point.

10. See table A.4.2 for summary statistics. Approval ratings are on a five-point scale ranging from "Strongly disapprove" to "Strongly approve," which I code from -2 to 2. To maintain consistency with the dependent variable, Democratic state house vote choice, I adjust the approval variables such that positive values denote approving of the state house, governor, or president if Democrats controlled these offices. For example, strongly approving of President Bush's performance receives a value of -2, but strongly approving of President Obama's performance receives a value of 2. Substantive findings are similar when either using dummy variables for approval instead of a cardinal measure or substituting voters' assessments of the economy for their approval ratings of the political actors.

11. I examine all responses from the 2008–2020 Cooperative Election Studies but only include measures that apply to both Congress and state legislatures (e.g., a respondent's education but not state legislative professionalism measures). See table A.7.4 for probit estimates.

12. When considering individual elections, the relationship between approval ratings and vote choice was stronger in state legislatures than Congress in the 2010 and 2018 elections, but the differences between these differences in probabilities are statistically indistinguishable from zero.

13. The relationship between a voter's overall approval rating and vote choice within the subsample of CES respondents is weaker than in the full CES sample. Strongly approving instead of strongly disapproving of the state legislature increases the predicted probability that a voter in the subsample supports the state house majority party by 0.001 (t-statistic 0.003) as compared to 0.021 in the full sample. Similar to the full sample, presidential approval has a stronger impact on vote choice than overall or issue-level state legislative approval. A respondent from the subsample who strongly approved rather than strongly disapproved of President Trump was 0.391 more likely to support a Republican state legislative candidate.

14. Despite findings of differences between informed and uninformed voters, I do not find evidence that the strength of the relationship between state legislative vote choice and approval is conditional on the number of reporters devoted to state government, as found in chapter 6.

15. Arceneaux and Stein (2006, 50) similarly find that following Tropical Storm Allison, Houstonians "who are knowledgeable about local government are more likely to attribute responsibility to the county for flood preparation." This difference between high- and low-knowledge voters, however, was not found for attribution of responsibility to city governments. Gomez and Wilson (2008; but see Maestas et al. 2008) similarly find that more knowledgeable or sophisticated Louisianans are more likely to blame the state government for the poor response to Hurricane Katrina.

16. When pooling elections, strongly approving instead of strongly disapproving of the president increases the predicted probability of voting for the president's

state legislative co-partisan by 0.360. When studying US House elections, the comparable difference in probability is 0.402 (table A.7.4).

Chapter Eight

1. Alesi was helpful in this campaign, donating almost $17,000 to Grisaniti's campaign.

2. For richer theoretical predictions regarding intraparty competition in primaries, I recommend readers consider Aranson and Ordeshook (1972), Coleman (1971), and Owen and Grofman (2006).

3. Results are the same without this party assumption if we move Voter 6 to the ideological position of 6+ε where ε < 1.

4. I hold the Democratic candidate's ideological position fixed at 4 in all examples for simplicity. This tactic does not satisfy conditions for a Nash equilibrium in Scenario C. If the Republican incumbent is at 6, the Democratic candidate has the incentive to position herself at 5 to win the general election.

5. In research on primary competition that does not consider state legislators' representation, Hogan (2003) examines the 1994 and 1996 elections in twenty-five states and finds that races with an incumbent, in professionalized legislatures, are less often competitive. Studying fifteen states' elections from the 1970s, Grau (1981) finds there is greater primary competition in states with multimember districts or in the south. Focusing on 1976 and 1978 elections, Grau finds that approximately 30 percent of incumbents face primary challengers but only 3 percent do not secure their nomination. Other previous research predominantly focuses on southern elections (Jewell 1959; Jewell and Breaux 1991; Key 1949), top-two primaries (Beck and Henrickson 2013), or single states such as Indiana (Standing and Robinson 1958) or Illinois (Wiggins and Petty 1979).

6. For the below analyses, I remove observations where the primary election was a top-two primary, as in Washington and California.

7. Primary challengers run less often in states with higher state legislative salaries, and Republican primary challengers run less often in states with a publicly financed campaign option. Meanwhile, major-party challengers ran more often under both of these circumstances. Major-party challengers also run less often when a district is far from the capital, but Democratic primary challengers run more often when the district is far from the capital. I additionally find little relationship between the length of the legislative session and primary competition for incumbent state legislators.

8. In districts without a primary challenger, these percentages for Democrats and Republicans are 63.7 and 59.6 percent.

9. These relationships between incumbent renomination and representation for either Democrats or Republicans do not appear to meaningfully vary by district partisanship (table A.8.3).

10. This "deflating" statement is unrelated to the author's bitterness about Superbowl XXXVI.

11. Upset with the election's outcome, future state representative Matthew Monforton filed a lawsuit to close Montana's primaries to registered party members (Associated Press 2014). When speaking about the lawsuit, Monforton said that "the argument that someone magically becomes a Republican by spending 60 seconds in a voting booth in a primary does not create a committed political relationship between that voter and a party. That's not even a one-night stand" (Volz 2015). Earlier, Monforton told Mediatracker.org that "I don't think that Republicans should be crossing over and mucking up Democrat elections any more than they should be doing that to us" (Catlett 2014). Former Montana state senator Jim Elliot called the effort to close the primary system "a quest for ideological uniformity in the Republican Party" taken up by a "group of pious zealots" (Elliott 2015). Monforton's lawsuits were unsuccessful, and Montana's open-primary system likely contributed to Monforton's decision to exit from the legislature. On the same day Republican Walt Sales announced his candidacy for Monforton's seat, Monforton announced his retirement, angrily telling the *Bozeman Daily Chronicle*, "The Montana Republican Party will always be a charade until we stop Democrat activists from infiltrating our primaries and electing phony 'Republicans' like Ryan Zinke and Walt Sales" (Carter 2015). Sales went onto win the primary and general election and become one of the more moderate members of the Montana Republican caucus.

12. Main findings are similar in analyses that exclude a legislator's ideal point. The Pearson's R correlations for party loyalty and challenger entry are -0.12 and -0.10 for Democratic and Republican incumbents.

13. Main findings are similar if I substitute a legislator's ideal point for the ideological-distance measure.

14. These relationships are slightly stronger for Democrats than Republicans. A standard-deviation shift in ideological distance associates with a 0.007 increase, 0.018 decrease, and 0.011 increase in the probability that a Democrat will return to office in all districts, marginal districts and safe districts. The comparable figures for Republicans are -0.001, -0.018, and +0.004 in these types of districts. However, the difference in probability for Republicans in all districts is not statistically distinguishable from zero.

Chapter Nine

1. The ANES asked a similar question in 2016 and 2020 but changed the question wording to: "How often do politics and government seem so complicated that you can't really understand what is going on?" In 2016 and 2020 respectively, 5 percent and 6 percent said "always," 23 percent and 20 percent said "most of the

time," 29 percent and 25 percent said "about half the time," 35 percent and 38 percent said "some of the time," and 8 percent and 11 percent said "never."

2. Gallup asked voters in 1950, "Which political contest in this state are you,
yourself, most interested in?" Only 2 percent of respondents responded with "state
representative."

3. The penultimate paragraph of *Statehouse Democracy* walks this claim back
and states: "We do not assert that policy making in the states is determined by state
opinion exclusively or with unerring fidelity. Only the most naïve version of democratic theory would argue for such a simple equation between citizen preferences
and government action" (Erikson, Wright, and McIver 1993, 252). Caughey and
Warshaw (2018, 251, 253, 264, footnote 1) also make clear that their 2018 claims are
founded on studying responsiveness, not congruence or the extent to which states
with liberal policy opinions have more liberal policies, as in the research provided
by *Statehouse Democracy*.

4. When considering elections as a selection mechanism instead of as an accountability mechanism (chapter 1), the nationalization of state politics could lead
to a desirable clear link between voter preferences and partisan selection. However, for this result to have positive implications for representation in state legislatures, those who are elected must necessarily adhere to common party positions
across the states, which is not yet the case (Shor and McCarty 2011).

References

Achen, Christopher, and Larry Bartels. 2016. *Democracy for Realists: Why Elections Do Not Produce Responsive Government*. Princeton, NJ: Princeton University Press.

Adams, James, Erik Engstrom, Danielle Joeston, Walt Stone, Jon Rogowski, and Boris Shor. 2017. "Do Moderate Voters Weigh Candidates' Ideologies? Voters' Decision Rules in the 2010 Congressional Elections." *Political Behavior* 39, no. 1: 205–27. https://doi.org/10.1007/s11109-016-9355-7.

Aldrich, John H., and James S. Coleman Battista. 2002. "Conditional Party Government in the States." *American Journal of Political Science* 46, no. 1: 164–72. https://doi.org/10.2307/3088420.

Aldrich, John H., and Richard D. McKelvey. 1977. "A Method of Scaling with Applications to the 1968 and 1972 Presidential Elections." *American Political Science Review* 71, no. 1: 111–30.

Alesina, Alberto, and Howard Rosenthal. 1989. "Partisan Cycles in Congressional Elections and the Macroeconomy." *American Political Science Review* 83, no. 2: 373–98. https://doi.org/10.2307/1962396.

Alvarez, German. 2010. "In Search of State Government: The Lack of State Legislative Coverage in Local Television News." Master's thesis, Louisiana State University. https://digitalcommons.lsu.edu/cgi/viewcontent.cgi?article=3263& context=gradschool_theses.

American Political Science Association (APSA). 1950. "Toward a More Responsible Two-Party System." *American Political Science Review* 44, no. 3 (September): part 2, supplement. https://www.jstor.org/stable/i333592.

Anderson, Christopher J, and Daniel S Ward. 1996. "Barometer Elections in Comparative Perspective." *Electoral Studies* 15, no. 4: 447–60. https://doi.org/10 .1016/0261-3794(95)00056-9.

Anderson, Sarah E., Daniel M. Butler, and Laurel Harbridge-Yong. 2020. *Rejecting Compromise: Legislators' Fear of Primary Voters*. Cambridge: Cambridge University Press.

Andrews, Evelyn. 2018. "Buckhead Democrat Seeks to Challenge Beskin for House Seat." *Reporter Newspapers* (blog), February 5. https://www.reporternewspapers.net/2018/02/05/buckhead-democrat-seeks-challenge-beskin-house-seat/.

Ansolabehere, Stephen, James M. Snyder Jr., and Charles Stewart. 2001. "Candidate Positioning in U.S. House Elections." *American Journal of Political Science* 45, no. 1: 136–59. https://doi.org/10.2307/2669364.

Ansolabehere, Stephen, James M. Snyder Jr., and Charles Stewart III. 2000. "Old Voters, New Voters, and the Personal Vote: Using Redistricting to Measure the Incumbency Advantage." *American Journal of Political Science* 44, no. 1: 17–34. https://doi.org/10.2307/2669290.

Anzia, Sarah F., and Molly C. Jackman. 2013. "Legislative Organization and the Second Face of Power: Evidence from U.S. State Legislatures." *Journal of Politics* 75, no. 1: 210–24. https://doi.org/10.1017/S0022381612000977.

Anzia, Sarah F., and Rachel Bernhard. 2022. "Gender Stereotyping and the Electoral Success of Women Candidates: New Evidence from Local Elections in the United States." *British Journal of Political Science*, January 19: 1–20. https://doi.org/10.1017/S0007123421000570.

Aranson, Peter H., and Peter Ordeshook. 1972. "Spatial Strategies for Sequential Elections." In *Probability Models of Collected Decision Making*, edited by Richard G. Niemi and Herbert F. Weisberg, 298–331. Columbus, OH: Merrill.

Arceneaux, Kevin. 2005. "Does Federalism Weaken Democratic Representation in the United States?" *Publius* 35, no. 2: 297–311.

———. 2006. "The Federal Face of Voting: Are Elected Officials Held Accountable for the Functions Relevant to Their Office?" *Political Psychology* 27, no. 5: 731–54.

Arceneaux, Kevin, and Robert M. Stein. 2006. "Who Is Held Responsible When Disaster Strikes? The Attribution of Responsibility for a Natural Disaster in an Urban Election." *Journal of Urban Affairs* 28, no. 1: 43–53. https://doi.org/10.1111/j.0735-2166.2006.00258.x.

Arnold, R. Douglas. 1992. *The Logic of Congressional Action.* New Haven, CT: Yale University Press.

———. 2006. *Congress, the Press, and Political Accountability.* New York: Princeton University Press.

Arnold, R. Douglas, and Nicholas Carnes. 2012. "Holding Mayors Accountable: New York's Executives from Koch to Bloomberg." *American Journal of Political Science* 56, no. 4: 949–63. https://doi.org/10.1111/j.1540-5907.2012.00603.x.

Ashworth, Scott. 2012. "Electoral Accountability: Recent Theoretical and Empirical Work." *Annual Review of Political Science* 15, no. 1: 183–201. https://doi.org/10.1146/annurev-polisci-031710-103823.

Associated Press. 2011. "Illinois Lawmaker Calls it Quits One Year Early." *CBS St. Louis,* December 29. https://web.archive.org/web/20150913080547/http://stlouis.cbslocal.com/2011/12/29/illinois-lawmaker-calls-it-quits-one-year-early/.

Associated Press. 2014. "GOP Committee Sues to Close Montana Primaries." *Billings Gazette*, September 8. http://billingsgazette.com/news/government-and-politics /gop-committee-sues-to-close-montana-primaries/article_22e4899d-072d-5b34 -8b8e-155449c948f7.html.

Bafumi, Joseph, and Michael C. Herron. 2010. "Leapfrog Representation and Extremism: A Study of American Voters and Their Members in Congress." *American Political Science Review* 104, no. 3: 519–42. https://doi.org/10.1017/S000 3055410000316.

Bailey, Michael A., and Elliott B. Fullmer. 2011. "Balancing in the U.S. States, 1978–2009." *State Politics and Policy Quarterly* 11, no. 2: 148–66. https://doi.org /10.1177/1532440011406230.

Banda, Kevin K., and Justin H. Kirkland. 2018. "Legislative Party Polarization and Trust in State Legislatures." *American Politics Research* 46, no. 4: 596–628. https://doi.org/10.1177/1532673X17727317.

Banks, Jeffrey S., and Rangaram Sundaram. 1993. "Adverse Selection and Moral Hazard in a Repeated Elections Model." In *Political Economy: International Symposia in Economic Theory and Econometrics*, edited by William A. Barnett, Norman Schofield, and Melvin Hinich, 295–311. New York: Cambridge University Press.

Barber, Michael. 2022. "Comparing Campaign Finance and Vote-Based Measures of Ideology." *Journal of Politics* 84, no. 1: 613–19. https://doi.org/10 .1086/715247.

Barber, Michael J. 2016. "Ideological Donors, Contribution Limits, and the Polarization of American Legislatures." *Journal of Politics* 78, no. 1: 296–310. https:// doi.org/10.1086/683453.

Barlow, Rich. 2015. "The Impact of the Supreme Court Same-Sex Marriage Decision." *BU Today*, June 30. http://www.bu.edu/articles/2015/supreme-court-gay -marriage-decision-2015/.

Barnett, Jeffery. 2011. *State and Local Government Finances Summary: 2009*. US Census Bureau. Governments Division brief no. G09-ALFIN, October. http:// www2.census.gov/govs/estimate/09_summary_report.pdf.

Bartels, Larry M. 2016. *Unequal Democracy: The Political Economy of the New Gilded Age*. 2nd ed. New York: Princeton University Press.

Battaglini, Marco, Valerio Leone Sciabolazza, and Eleonora Patacchini. 2020. "Effectiveness of Connected Legislators." *American Journal of Political Science* 64, no. 4: 739–56. https://doi.org/10.1111/ajps.12518.

Baumann, Zach. 2012. "Just Passing Through? Explaining the Career Lengths of State Legislators." Paper presented at the State Politics and Policy Annual Conference, Houston, TX, February 16–18.

Beck, John H., and Kevin E. Henrickson. 2013. "The Effect of the Top Two Primary on the Number of Primary Candidates." *Social Science Quarterly* 94, no. 3: 777– 94. https://doi.org/10.1111/j.1540-6237.2012.00876.x.

Benedictis-Kessner, Justin de, and Christopher Warshaw. 2020. "Accountability for the Local Economy at All Levels of Government in United States Elections." *American Political Science Review* 114, no. 3: 660–76. https://doi.org/10.1017/S00 03055420000027.

Bernick, Bob. 2006. "Utahns Fail Quiz on Own Legislators." *DeseretNews.com*, March 20. https://www.deseret.com/2006/3/20/19944128/utahns-fail-quiz-on-own -legislators

Berry, Christopher R., and William G. Howell. 2007. "Accountability and Local Elections: Rethinking Retrospective Voting." *Journal of Politics* 69, no. 3: 844– 58. https://doi.org/10.1111/j.1468-2508.2007.00579.x.

Berry, William D., Michael B. Berkman, and Stuart Schneiderman. 2000. "Legislative Professionalism and Incumbent Reelection: The Development of Institutional Boundaries." *American Political Science Review* 94, no. 4: 859–74. https:// doi.org/10.2307/2586212.

Besley, Timothy, and Anne Case. 1995. "Incumbent Behavior: Vote-Seeking, Tax-Setting, and Yardstick Competition." *American Economic Review* 85, no. 1: 25–45.

Bibby, John F. 2003. *Politics, Parties, and Elections in America*. Belmont, CA: Wadsworth/Thomson Learning.

Binder, Sarah. 1999. "The Dynamics of Legislative Gridlock, 1947–96." *American Political Science Review* 93, no. 3: 519–33. https://doi.org/10.2307/2585572.

———. 2015. "The Dysfunctional Congress." *Annual Review of Political Science* 18, no. 1: 85–101. https://doi.org/10.1146/annurev-polisci-110813-032156.

Birkhead, Nathaniel A. 2015. "The Role of Ideology in State Legislative Elections." *Legislative Studies Quarterly* 40, no. 1: 55–82.

———. 2016. "State Budgetary Delays in an Era of Party Polarization." *State and Local Government Review* 48, no. 4: 259–69. https://doi.org/10.1177/0160 323X16687813.

Bishop, Bradford H. 2018. "Federal Complexity and Perception of State Party Ideology in the United States." *Publius* 48, no. 4: 559–85. https://doi.org/10.1093 /publius/pjy011.

Black, Duncan. 1958. *The Theory of Committees and Elections*. Cambridge: Cambridge University Press.

Black, Gordon S. 1972. "A Theory of Political Ambition: Career Choices and the Role of Structural Incentives." *American Political Science Review* 66, no. 1: 144– 59. https://doi.org/10.2307/1959283.

Blain, Glenn, and Kenneth Lovett. 2011. "Gay Marriage Passes New York State Senate." *New York Daily News*, June 26. http://www.nydailynews.com/news /politics/gay-marriage-legal-new-york-state-senate-passes-historic-bill-33-29 -article-1.126938.

Blair, Diane Kincaid, and Ann R. Henry. 1981. "The Family Factor in State Legislative Turnover." *Legislative Studies Quarterly* 6, no. 1: 55–68. https://www.jstor .org/stable/439713.

Boatright, Robert G. 2014. *Getting Primaried: The Changing Politics of Congressional Primary Challenges*. Ann Arbor: University of Michigan Press.

———, ed. 2018. *Routledge Handbook of Primary Elections*. New York: Routledge.

Bobo, Lawrence, and Franklin D. Gilliam. 1990. "Race, Sociopolitical Participation, and Black Empowerment." *American Political Science Review* 84, no. 2: 377–93. https://doi.org/10.2307/1963525.

Bonica, Adam. 2013. "Ideology and Interests in the Political Marketplace." *American Journal of Political Science* 57, no. 2: 294–311. https://doi.org/10.1111/ajps.12014.

Bonica, Adam, and Gary W. Cox. 2018. "Ideological Extremists in the U.S. Congress: Out of Step but Still in Office." *Quarterly Journal of Political Science* 13, no. 2: 207–36. https://doi.org/10.1561/100.00016073.

Bos, A. L., M. C. Schneider, and B. L. Utz. 2018. "Navigating the Political Labyrinth: Gender Stereotypes and Prejudice in U.S. Elections." In *APA Handbook of the Psychology of Women*, edited by C. B. Travis, J. W. White, A. Rutherford, W. S. Williams, S. L. Cook, and K. F. Wyche, 367–84. Washington, DC: American Psychological Association.

Boucher, Dave. 2015. "TN GOP Rejects Closed Primaries." *Tennessean*, February 7. http://www.tennessean.com/story/news/politics/2015/02/07/tennessee-gop-rejects-closing-primaries/23045457/.

Bowen, Daniel C., and Zachary Greene. 2014. "Should We Measure Professionalism with an Index? A Note on Theory and Practice in State Legislative Professionalism Research." *State Politics and Policy Quarterly* 14, no. 3: 277–96. https://doi.org/10.1177/1532440014536407.

Brady, David W., Hahrie Han, and Jeremy C. Pope. 2007. "Primary Elections and Candidate Ideology: Out of Step with the Primary Electorate?" *Legislative Studies Quarterly* 32, no. 1: 79–105. https://doi.org/10.3162/036298007X201994.

Broockman, David, and Christopher Skovron. 2018. "Bias in Perceptions of Public Opinion among Political Elites." *American Political Science Review* 112, no. 3: 542–63. https://doi.org/10.1017/S0003055418000011.

Broockman, David, Nicholas Carnes, Melody Crowder-Meyer, and Christopher Skovron. 2012. *2012 National Candidate Study*. Data file.

Broockman, David E., Nicholas Carnes, Melody Crowder-Meyer, and Christopher Skovron. 2014. "Who's a Good Candidate? How Party Gatekeepers Evaluate Potential Nominees." Unpublished working paper, August 20.

———. 2021. "Why Local Party Leaders Don't Support Nominating Centrists." *British Journal of Political Science* 51, no. 2: 724–49. https://doi.org/10.1017/S0007123419000309.

Brookings Institute. 2021. "Vital Statistics on Congress." *Brookings* (blog), February 8. https://www.brookings.edu/multi-chapter-report/vital-statistics-on-congress/.

Brown, Jacob R., and Ryan D. Enos. 2021. "The Measurement of Partisan Sorting for 180 Million Voters." *Nature Human Behaviour* (March): 1–11. https://doi.org/10.1038/s41562-021-01066-z.

Bucchianeri, Peter, Craig Volden, and Alan E. Wiseman. 2020. "Legislative Effectiveness in the American States." Paper presented at the American Political Science Association Conference, San Francisco, CA, September 10–13. https:// thelawmakers.org/wp-content/uploads/2020/09/Working-Paper-Legislative -Effectiveness-in-American-States.pdf.

Bullock, Will, and Joshua D. Clinton. 2011. "More a Molehill than a Mountain: The Effects of the Blanket Primary on Elected Officials' Behavior from California." *Journal of Politics* 73, no. 3: 915–30. https://doi.org/10.1017/S0022381611000557.

Burden, Barry C. 2001. "The Polarizing Effects of Congressional Primaries." In *Congressional Primaries and the Politics of Representation*, edited by Peter F. Galderisi, Marni Ezra, and Michael Lyons, 95–115. Lanham, MD: Rowman and Littlefield Publishers.

Burden, Barry C., and Rochelle Snyder. 2020. "Explaining Uncontested Seats in Congress and State Legislatures" *American Politics Research* (October). http:// journals.sagepub.com/doi/suppl/10.1177/1532673X20960565.

Bureau, Mike Dennison and Tum Lutey. 2014. "Hard-Line Conservatives Face 'Solution-Oriented' Pragmatists in Primaries." *Helena Independent Record*, May 25. http://helenair.com/news/local/hard-line-conservatives-face-solution-oriented -pragmatists-in-primaries/article_a7b6a7b0-e3d0-11e3-940f-0019bb2963f4.html.

Burke, Edmund. 1854 (1774). "Speech to the Electors of Bristol." In *The Works of the Right Honourable Edmund Burke*, 6 vols. London: Henry G. Bohn. https:// press-pubs.uchicago.edu/founders/documents/v1ch13s7.html.

Burnett, Craig M. 2016. "Exploring the Difference in Participants' Factual Knowledge between Online and In-Person Survey Modes." *Research & Politics* 3, no. 2 (April). https://doi.org/10.1177/2053168016654326.

Burnett, Craig M., and Vladimir Kogan. 2017. "The Politics of Potholes: Service Quality and Retrospective Voting in Local Elections." *Journal of Politics* 79, no. 1: 302–14. https://doi.org/10.1086/688736.

Bussing, Austin, Will Patton, Jason M. Roberts, and Sarah A. Treul. 2020. "The Electoral Consequences of Roll Call Voting: Health Care and the 2018 Election." *Political Behavior* (May). https://doi.org/10.1007/s11109-020-09615-4.

Butcher, Jordan. 2022. "Be Careful What You Count: Updating Legislative Turnover in the 50 States." *American Politics Research* (March). https://doi.org/10 .1177/1532673X221082319.

Butler, Daniel M., and David Nickerson. 2011. "Can Learning Constituency Opinion Affect How Legislators Vote? Results from a Field Experiment." *Quarterly Journal of Political Science* 6: 55–83.

Butler, Daniel M., and David R. Miller. 2021. "Does Lobbying Affect Bill Advancement? Evidence from Three State Legislatures." *Political Research Quarterly*, May 20. https://doi.org/10.1177/10659129211012481.

Cadigan, John, and Eckhard Janeba. 2002. "A Citizen-Candidate Model with Sequential Elections." *Journal of Theoretical Politics* 14, no. 4: 387–407. https://doi .org/10.1177/095162902774006804.

Campbell, Angus. 1960. "Surge and Decline: A Study of Electoral Change." *Public Opinion Quarterly* 24, no. 3: 397–418. https://doi.org/10.1086/266960.

Campbell, Angus, Philip E. Converse, Donald E. Stokes, and Warren E. Miller. 1960. *The American Voter*. Chicago: University of Chicago Press.

Campbell, James E. 1986. "Presidential Coattails and Midterm Losses in State Legislative Elections." *American Political Science Review* 80, no. 1: 45–63. https://doi.org/10.2307/1957083.

Campbell, James E., John R. Alford, and Keith Henry. 1984. "Television Markets and Congressional Elections." *Legislative Studies Quarterly* 19, no. 4: 665–78.

Canes-Wrone, Brandice, and Michael Kistner. 2020. "Out of Step and Still in Congress? The Electoral Consequences of Incumbent and Challenger Positioning Across Time." *Quarterly Journal of Political Science* 17, no. 3 (July): 389–420.

Canes-Wrone, Brandice, David W. Brady, and John F. Cogan. 2002. "Out of Step, Out of Office: Electoral Accountability and House Members' Voting." *American Political Science Review* 96, no. 1: 127–40. https://doi.org/10.1017/S0003055402004276.

Canon, David T. 1993. "Sacrificial Lambs or Strategic Politicians? Political Amateurs in U.S. House Elections." *American Journal of Political Science* 37, no. 4: 1119–41. https://doi.org/10.2307/2111546.

Canon, David T., and David J. Sousa. 1992. "Party System Change and Political Career Structures in the U. S. Congress." *Legislative Studies Quarterly* 17, no. 3: 347–63. https://www.jstor.org/stable/439734.

Carey, John M., Richard G. Niemi, Lynda W. Powell, and Gary Moncrief. 2008. "2002 State Legislative Survey." Inter-University Consortium for Political and Social Research, March 25. https://doi.org/10.3886/ICPSR20960.v1.

Carnes, Nicholas. 2013. *White-Collar Government: The Hidden Role of Class in Economic Policy Making*. Chicago Studies in American Politics. Chicago: University of Chicago Press.

Carnes, Nicholas, and Eric R. Hansen. 2016. "Does Paying Politicians More Promote Economic Diversity in Legislatures?" *American Political Science Review* 110, no. 4: 699–716. https://doi.org/10.1017/S000305541600054X.

Carroll, Susan J., and Kira Sanbonmatsu. 2013. *More Women Can Run: Gender and Pathways to the State Legislatures*. New York: Oxford University Press.

Carroll, Susan J., and Richard L. Fox. 2013. *Gender and Elections: Shaping the Future of American Politics*. New York: Cambridge University Press.

Carsey, Thomas M., and Gerald C. Wright. 1998. "State and National Factors in Gubernatorial and Senatorial Elections." *American Journal of Political Science* 42, no. 3: 994–1002. https://doi.org/10.2307/2991738.

Carson, Jamie L., Gregory Koger, Matthew J. Lebo, and Everett Young. 2010. "The Electoral Costs of Party Loyalty in Congress." *American Journal of Political Science* 54, no. 3: 598–616. https://doi.org/10.1111/j.1540-5907.2010.00449.x.

Carter, Troy. 2015. "Monforton Not Seeking Re-Election to State House." *Bozeman Daily Chronicle*, October 8.

Cass, Michael. 2012. "GOP Expects to Increase Majorities in TN House, Senate." *Tennessean*, April 22.

Catlett, Ron. 2014. "MT Legislative Candidate Hopes to End Crossover Voting." *Media Trackers*, June 18.

Catts, Everett. 2018. "Holland Challenging Beskin for District 54 House Seat." MDJOnline.com, October 5. https://www.mdjonline.com/neighbor_newspapers /northside_sandy_springs/news/holland-challenging-beskin-for-district-54 -house-seat/article_91e396b8-c8b0-11e8-8c64-c30ec25f7b9e.html.

Caughey, Devin, and Christopher Warshaw. 2018. "Policy Preferences and Policy Change: Dynamic Responsiveness in the American States, 1936–2014." *American Political Science Review* 112, no. 2: 249–66. https://doi.org/10.1017/S000305 5417000533.

———. 2022. *Dynamic Democracy: Citizens, Politicians, and Policymaking in the American States*. Chicago: University of Chicago Press.

Caughey, Devin, Christopher Warshaw, and Yiqing Xu. 2017. "Incremental Democracy: The Policy Effects of Partisan Control of State Government." *Journal of Politics* 79, no. 4: 1342–58. https://doi.org/10.1086/692669.

Center for American Women and Politics (CAWP). 2022. *CAWP Women Elected Officials Database*. New Brunswick, NJ: Eagleton Institute of Politics, Rutgers University-New Brunswick. https://cawpdata.rutgers.edu/.

Chubb, John E. 1988. "Institutions, The Economy, and the Dynamics of State Elections." *American Political Science Review* 82, no. 1: 133–54. https://doi .org/10.2307/1958062.

Clarke, Andrew J. 2020. "Congressional Capacity and the Abolition of Legislative Service Organizations." *Journal of Public Policy* 40, no. 2: 214–35. https://doi .org/10.1017/S0143814X1800034X.

Clines, Francis X. 2015. "Montana Republican Leaders Shocked to Find Moderates in Their Ranks." *Taking Note* (blog), *New York Times,* September 17. https://archive.nytimes.com/takingnote.blogs.nytimes.com/2015/09/17/montana -republican-leaders-shocked-to-find-moderates-in-their-ranks/.

Cohen, Jeffrey E. 2020. "Relative Unemployment, Political Information, and the Job Approval Ratings of State Governors and Legislatures." *State Politics and Policy Quarterly* 20, no. 4: 437–61. https://doi.org/10.1177/1532440020905800.

Cohen, Martin, Hans Noel, and John Zaller. 2011. "Without a Watchdog: The Effect of Local News on Political Polarization in Congress." Working paper.

Cohen, Marty, David Karol, Hans Noel, and John Zaller. 2008. *The Party Decides: Presidential Nominations Before and After Reform*. Chicago Studies in American Politics. Chicago: University of Chicago Press.

Coleman, James. 1971. "Internal Processes Governing Party Positions in Elections." *Public Choice* 11, no. 1: 35–60.

Conover, Pamela Johnston, and Stanley Feldman. 1982. "Projection and the Perception of Candidates' Issue Positions." *Western Political Quarterly* 35, no. 2: 228–44. https://doi.org/10.2307/448017.

Converse, Philip E. 1964. "The Nature of Belief Systems in Mass Publics." *Critical Review* 18, no. 1–3 (2006): 1–74. https://doi.org/10.1080/08913810608443650.

Cooper, Christopher A. 2002. "Media Tactics in the State Legislature." *State Politics and Policy Quarterly* 2, no. 4: 353–71.

Cooper, Christopher A., and Martin Johnson. 2006. "Politics and the Press Corps: Reporters, State Legislative Institutions, and Context." Paper presented at the State Politics and Policy Conference, Texas Tech University, Lubbock, Texas, May 19–20.

———. 2007. "News Media and the State Policy Process: Perspectives from Legislators and Political Professionals." Paper presented at the State Politics and Policy Conference, University of Texas, Austin, Texas, February 22–24.

———. 2009. "Representative Reporters? Examining Journalists' Ideology in Context." *Social Science Quarterly* 90, no. 2: 387–406.

Cousins, Christopher. 2013. "Democratic Senator Lets LePage 'Vaseline' Jab Slide off His Back." *Bangor Daily News*, June 20. https://bangordailynews.com/2013/06/20/politics/report-lepage-slips-vaseline-jab-toward-democratic-senator/.

Cox, Gary W., and Mathew D. McCubbins. 1993. *Legislative Leviathan: Party Government in the House*. Berkeley: University of California Press.

———. 2005. *Setting the Agenda: Responsible Party Government in the U.S. House of Representatives*. New York: Cambridge University Press.

Cox, Gary W., Thad Kousser, and Mathew D. McCubbins. 2010. "Party Power or Preferences? Quasi-Experimental Evidence from American State Legislatures." *Journal of Politics* 72, no. 3: 799–811. https://doi.org/10.1017/S0022381610000174.

Crowder-Meyer, Melody. 2013. "Gendered Recruitment without Trying: How Local Party Recruiters Affect Women's Representation." *Politics and Gender* 9, no. 4: 390–413. https://doi.org/10.1017/S1743923X13000391.

Cullen, Morgan. 2011. "Pay Problem." National Conference of State Legislatures. http://www.ncsl.org/research/about-state-legislatures/pay-problem.aspx.

Cutrone, Michael, and Nolan McCarty. 2008. "Does Bicameralism Matter?" *Oxford Handbook of Political Economy*, June 19. https://doi.org/10.1093/oxfordhb/9780199548477.003.0010.

Dancey, Logan, and Geoffrey Sheagley. 2013. "Heuristics Behaving Badly: Party Cues and Voter Knowledge." *American Journal of Political Science* 57, no. 2: 312–25. https://doi.org/10.1111/j.1540-5907.2012.00621.x.

Darcy, R., Janet Clark, and Susan Welch. 1994. *Women, Elections, and Representation*. Rev. ed. Lincoln: University of Nebraska Press.

Darr, Joshua P., Matthew P. Hitt, and Johanna L. Dunaway. 2018. "Newspaper Closures Polarize Voting Behavior." *Journal of Communication* 68, no. 6: 1007–28. https://doi.org/10.1093/joc/jqy051.

De Boef, Suzanna, and Paul M. Kellstedt. 2004. "The Political (and Economic) Origins of Consumer Confidence." *American Journal of Political Science* 48, no. 4: 633–49. https://doi.org/10.1111/j.0092-5853.2004.00092.x.

Delli Carpini, Michael, and Scott Keeter. 1997. *What Americans Know about Politics and Why It Matters*. New Haven, CT: Yale University Press.

Delli Carpini, Michael, Scott Keeter, and J. Kennamer. 1994. "Effects of the News Media Environment on Citizen Knowledge of State Politics and Government." *Journalism Quarterly* 71, no. 2 (July): 443–56. http://repository.upenn.edu/asc_papers/20.

Dicker, Fredric U. 2011. "GOPer's Visit Raises Gay-Marriage Hopes." *New York Post*, May 23.

Doherty, Carroll, Jocelyn Kiley, and Bridget Johnson. 2018. *The Public, the Political System, and American Democracy*. Washington, DC: Pew Research Center. http://assets.pewresearch.org/wp-content/uploads/sites/5/2018/04/26140617/4-26-2018-Democracy-release.pdf.

Dolan, Kathleen. 2011. "Do Women and Men Know Different Things? Measuring Gender Differences in Political Knowledge." *Journal of Politics* 73, no. 1: 97–107. https://doi.org/10.1017/s0022381610000897.

Dorroh, Jennifer. 2009. "Statehouse Exodus." *American Journalism Review* (April/May). http://ajrarchive.org/Article.asp?id=4721.

Downs, Anthony. 1957. *An Economic Theory of Democracy*. New York: Harper and Row.

Dynes, Adam M., and John B. Holbein. 2020. "Noisy Retrospection: The Effect of Party Control on Policy Outcomes." *American Political Science Review* 114, no. 1: 237–57. https://doi.org/10.1017/S0003055419000649.

Egerod, Benjamin C. K. 2021. "The Lure of the Private Sector: Career Prospects Affect Selection out of Congress." *Political Science Research and Methods*: 1–17. https://doi.org/10.1017/psrm.2021.10.

Eligon, John. 2012. "State Senator Loses Support of Local GOP." *New York Times*, March 21. http://www.nytimes.com/2012/03/22/nyregion/state-senator-james-alesi-loses-support-of-local-gop.html.

Elliott, Jim. 2015. "Closed Minds, Closed Primaries." *Missoulian.com*, September 23. http://missoulian.com/news/opinion/columnists/closed-minds-closed-primaries/article_e23c2d29-7625-5e62-8a2e-70240168b7bd.html.

Elliot, Rebecca. 2016. "In District 134, Incumbent Sarah Davis Touts Clout While Challenger Ben Rose Sells Change." *Houston Chronicle*, October 16. https://www.houstonchronicle.com/news/politics/texas/article/Challenger-hoping-presidential-turnout-will-help-9973955.php.

Enda, Jodi, Katerina Eva Matsa, and Jan Lauren Boyles. 2014. "America's Shifting Statehouse Press." *Pew Research Center's Journalism Project* (blog), July 10. http://www.journalism.org/2014/07/10/americas-shifting-statehouse-press/.

Energy Times. 2011. "ComEd: Energy Policy Debate First Step to Building Illinois' 21st Century Grid." February 7. https://www.exeloncorp.com/newsroom/Pages/pr_20110208_comed_modernizationact.aspx.

Erickson, Kurt. 2012. "The Revolving Door: Moves from the Statehouse Floor to the Hallways of the Capitol Spark Questions." *Illinois Issues* (April). https://

www.nprillinois.org/statehouse/2012-04-01/the-revolving-door-moves-from-the
-statehouse-floor-to-the-hallways-of-the-capitol-spark-questions.

Erikson, Robert S. 2016. "Congressional Elections in Presidential Years: Presidential Coattails and Strategic Voting." *Legislative Studies Quarterly* 41, no. 3: 551–
74. https://doi.org/10.1111/lsq.12127.

Erikson, Robert S., and Mikhail G. Filippov. 2001. "Electoral Balancing in Federal and Sub-National Elections: The Case of Canada." *Constitutional Political
Economy* 12, no. 4: 313–31. https://doi.org/10.1023/A:1012529023870.

Erikson, Robert S., Gerald C. Wright, and John P. McIver. 1993. *Statehouse Democracy: Public Opinion and Policy in the American States*. New York: Cambridge
University Press.

Erikson, Robert S., Olle Folke, and James M. Snyder. 2015. "A Gubernatorial Helping Hand? How Governors Affect Presidential Elections." *Journal of Politics*
77, no. 2: 491–504. https://doi.org/10.1086/680186.

Fearon, James. 1999. "Electoral Accountability and the Control of Politicians: Selecting Good Types versus Sanctioning Poor Performance." In *Democracy, Accountability, and Representation*, edited by Adam Przeworski, Susan C. Stokes,
and Bernard Manin, 55–97. New York: Cambridge University Press.

Fenno, Richard F. 1978. *Home Style: House Members in Their Districts*. New York:
Little, Brown.

Fiddler, Carolyn. 2016. "Kentucky Democrats Triumphant in House Special Elections." Democratic Legislative Campaign Committee, March 8. https://www.dlcc
.org/press/kentucky-democrats-triumphant-house-special-elections.

Fiorina, Morris P. 1981. *Retrospective Voting in American National Elections*. New
Haven, CT: Yale University Press.

———. 1995. *Divided Government*. New York: Longman Publishing Group.

Fitzsimon, Chris. 2022. "Journalists, Research Experts, and Industry Leaders Ex-
plore the Realities on America's State Capitols." Virtual panel hosted by Pew
Research Center, Lenfest Institute for Journalism, and Report for America,
April 29. https://lenfestinstitute-org.zoom.us/rec/play/gd8V6TIyGV0bFa8K5u
T7C828YvUTJiJpiG0zMyhNl759EXKUZeR5uJAGu9pCKaD666ahtXjA1g
KH5lM.Q8ia-mMLOOq5sS5Y?continueMode=true&_x_zm_rtaid=sjO14SE
XTA6bQuWruOKB7w.1655492938032.7144eab691527da0e8ac843d3528f70f
&_x_zm_rhtaid=148.

Folke, Olle, and James M. Snyder Jr. 2012. "Gubernatorial Midterm Slumps."
American Journal of Political Science 56, no. 4: 931–48. https://doi.org/10.1111
/j.1540-5907.2012.00599.x.

Fortunato, David, and Randolph T. Stevenson. 2021. "Party Government and Political Information." *Legislative Studies Quarterly* 46, no. 2 (May): 251–95. https://
doi.org/10.1111/lsq.12285.

Fouirnaies, Alexander, and Andrew B. Hall. 2022. "How Do Electoral Incentives Affect Legislator Behavior? Evidence from U.S. State Legislatures."

American Political Science Review 116, no. 2: 662–76. https://doi.org/10.1017
/S0003055421001064.

Fowler, Erika Franklin. 2018. "All Politics Is Local? Assessing the Role of Local
Television News in a Polarized Era." In *New Directions in Media and Politics*,
2nd ed., edited by Travis Ridout, 80–98. New York: Taylor and Francis.

Fowler, Erika Franklin, Kenneth M. Goldstein, Matthew Hale, and Martin Kaplan.
2007. "Does Local News Measure Up?" *Stanford Law and Policy Review* 18,
no. 2: 410–31.

Fowler, Linda L., and Robert D. McClure. 1990. *Political Ambition: Who Decides to
Run for Congress*. 1st ed. New Haven, CT: Yale University Press.

Fox, Richard L., and Jennifer L. Lawless. 2005. "To Run or Not to Run for Office:
Explaining Nascent Political Ambition." *American Journal of Political Science*
49, no. 3: 642–59. https://doi.org/10.1111/j.1540-5907.2005.00147.x.

Fraga, Bernard L., Eric Gonzalez Juenke, and Paru Shah. 2021. "Candidate Characteristics Cooperative (C3) 2018 Data." Harvard Dataverse, V2. https://doi
.org/10.7910/DVN/VHAPHV.

Francis, Wayne L. 1985. "Costs and Benefits of Legislative Service in the American States." *American Journal of Political Science* 29, no. 3: 626–42. https://doi
.org/10.2307/2111146.

Francis, Wayne L., and John R. Baker. 1986. "Why Do U. S. State Legislators Vacate
Their Seats?" *Legislative Studies Quarterly* 11, no. 1: 119–26.

Freedman, Eric. 2013. "Corruption Lingers 20 Years after Legislative Scandal Erupts."
Capital News Service, January 18. http://news.jrn.msu.edu/capitalnewsservice
/2013/01/18/corruption-lingers-20-years-after-legislative-scandal-erupts/.

Freeman, Patricia, and William Lyons. 1992. "Female Legislators: Is There a New
Type of Woman in Office?" In *Changing Patterns in State Legislative Careers*,
edited by Gary F. Moncrief and Joel A. Thompson, 59–70. Ann Arbor: University of Michigan Press.

Gabaix, Xavier, and David Laibson. 2005. "Bounded Rationality and Directed
Cognition." Working paper, May 1, New York University. http://pages.stern
.nyu.edu/~xgabaix/papers/boundedRationality.pdf.

Galais, Carolina, André Blais, and Shaun Bowler. 2014. "Is Political Interest Absolute or Relative?" Paper presented at the American Political Science Association annual meeting, Washington, DC, September 28–31. https://papers.ssrn
.com/abstract=2455573.

Geer, John G. 1988. "Assessing the Representativeness of Electorates in Presidential Primaries." *American Journal of Political Science* 32, no. 4: 929–45. https://
doi.org/10.2307/2111195.

Geiger, Kim. 2015. "State Lawmaker Who Crossed Madigan to Help Rauner Says
Democrats 'Vindictive.'" *Chicago Tribune*, November 11. http://www.chicago
tribune.com/news/local/politics/ct-state-lawmaker-who-crossed-madigan-to
-help-rauner-says-democrats-vindictive-20151111-story.html.

Gentzkow, Matthew, Jesse M. Shapiro, and Michael Sinkinson. 2011. "The Effect of Newspaper Entry and Exit on Electoral Politics." *American Economic Review* 101, no. 7: 2980–3018. https://doi.org/10.1257/aer.101.7.2980.

Gerber, Elisabeth R. 1996. "Legislative Response to the Threat of Popular Initiatives." *American Journal of Political Science* 40, no. 1: 99–128. https://doi.org/10.2307/2111696.

———. 2002. "Strategic Voting and Candidate Policy Positions." In *Voting at the Political Fault Line: California's Experiment with the Blanket Primary*, edited by Elisabeth R. Gerber and Bruce E. Cain, 192–213. Oakland: University of California Press.

Gibson, James L., and Gregory A. Caldeira. 2009. "Knowing the Supreme Court? A Reconsideration of Public Ignorance of the High Court." *Journal of Politics* 71, no. 2: 429–41. https://doi.org/10.1017/s0022381609090379.

Giger, Nathalie, Heike Kluver, and Christopher Witko. 2019. "Electoral Vulnerability, Party Affiliation, and Dyadic Constituency Responsiveness in U.S. Legislatures." *American Politics Research* (December). https://doi.org/10.1177/1532673X19891990.

Gilens, Martin. 2014. *Affluence and Influence: Economic Inequality and Political Power in America*. Reprint ed. Princeton, NJ: Princeton University Press.

Gomez, Brad T., and J. Matthew Wilson. 2008. "Political Sophistication and Attributions of Blame in the Wake of Hurricane Katrina." *Publius* 38, no. 4: 633–50. https://doi.org/10.1093/publius/pjn016.

Granberg, Donald, and Edward Brent. 1980. "Perceptions of Issue Positions of Presidential Candidates: Candidates Are Often Perceived by Their Supporters as Holding Positions on the Issues That Are Closer to the Supporters' Views than They Really Are." *American Scientist* 68, no. 6: 617–25.

Granberg, Donald, and Soren Holmberg. 1986. "Political Perception among Voters in Sweden and the U.S.: Analyses of Issues with Explicit Alternatives." *Western Political Quarterly* 39, no. 1: 7–28.

Grau, Craig H. 1981. "Competition in State Legislative Primaries." *Legislative Studies Quarterly* 6, no. 1: 35–54.

Greenblatt, Alan. 2016. "With Independents on the Rise, Colorado Changes Its Election Rules." *Governing Magazine*, November 9. http://www.governing.com/topics/elections/gov-ballot-measure-colorado-presidential-primaries.html.

Gregg, Katharine, Scott Mayerowitz, and Elizabeth Gudrais. 2006. "A Full-Time Legislature for R.I.?" *Providence Journal*, January 5.

Grose, Christian R. 2020. "Reducing Legislative Polarization: Top-Two and Open Primaries Are Associated with More Moderate Legislators." *Journal of Political Institutions and Political Economy* 1, no. 2: 267–87. https://doi.org/10.1561/113.00000012.

Grose, Christian R., Pamela Lopez, Sara Sadhwani, and Antoine Yoshinaka. 2022. "Social Lobbying." *Journal of Politics* 84, no. 1: 367–82. https://doi.org/10.1086/714923.

Groseclose, Tim. 2001. "A Model of Candidate Location When One Candidate Has a Valence Advantage." *American Journal of Political Science* 45, no. 4: 862–86. https://doi.org/10.2307/2669329.

Grossman, Richard S., and Stephen A. Lee. 2008. "May Issue Versus Shall Issue: Explaining the Pattern of Concealed-Carry Handgun Laws, 1960—2001." *Contemporary Economic Policy* 26, no. 2: 198–206.

Grossmann, Matt. 2019. *Red State Blues: How the Conservative Revolution Stalled in the States.* Cambridge: Cambridge University Press.

Grossman, Matt, and David A. Hopkins. 2016. *Asymmetric Politics: Ideological Republicans and Group Interest Democrats.* New York: Oxford University Press. https://doi.org/10.1093/acprof:oso/9780190626594.001.0001.

Grossmann, Matt, Marty P. Jordan, and Joshua McCrain. 2021. "The Correlates of State Policy and the Structure of State Panel Data." *State Politics and Policy Quarterly* 21, no. 4: 430–50. https://doi.org/10.1017/spq.2021.17.

Grumbach, Jacob M. 2018. "From Backwaters to Major Policymakers: Policy Polarization in the States, 1970–2014." *Perspectives on Politics* 16, no. 2: 416–35. https://doi.org/10.1017/S153759271700425X.

———. 2022. *Laboratories against Democracy.* Princeton, NJ: Princeton University Press.

Guerrero, Rafael, and Julie Wernau. 2013. "Illinois Senate Overrides Quinn Veto of Smart Grid Rate Hike." *Chicago Tribune,* May 21. http://articles.chicago tribune.com/2013-05-21/business/chi-comed-smart-grid-revenue-20130521 _1_smart-grid-bill-comed-quinn-veto.

Gurwitt, Rob. 2008. "Death and Life in the Pressroom." *Governing Magazine,* December 31. http://www.governing.com/topics/mgmt/Death-and-Life-in.html.

Hall, Andrew B. 2019. *Who Wants to Run?: How the Devaluing of Political Office Drives Polarization.* Chicago: University of Chicago Press.

Hall, Andrew B., and James M. Snyder Jr. 2015. "Candidate Ideology and Electoral Success." Working paper, September 29. http://www.andrewbenjaminhall.com /Hall_Snyder_Ideology.pdf.

Hamm, Keith E, and Robert E Hogan. 2008. "Campaign Finance Laws and Candidacy Decisions in State Legislative Elections." *Political Research Quarterly* 61, no. 3: 458–67. https://doi.org/10.1177/1065912908314646.

Hamman, John A. 2006. "Public Opinion in the State: Determinants of Legislative Job Performance." In *Public Opinion in State Politics,* edited by Jeffrey E. Cohen, 79–101. Stanford, CA: Stanford University Press.

Hanania, Ray. 2011. "Kevin McCarthy Stepping Down: Who Will Take His Place?" *OrlandParker* (blog), December 28. http://orlandparker.blogspot.com/2011/12 /kevin-mccarthy-stepping-down-who-will.html.

Handan-Nader, Cassandra, Andrew Myers, and Andrew Hall. 2022. "Polarization and State Legislative Elections." Working paper 22-05, Stanford University for Economic Policy Research, February 5. https://siepr.stanford.edu/publications /politics-and-media/polarization-and-state-legislative-elections.

Hassell, Hans J. G. 2017. *The Party's Primary: Control of Congressional Nominations*. Cambridge: Cambridge University Press.

Hayes, Danny, and Jennifer L. Lawless. 2016. *Women on the Run: Gender, Media, and Political Campaigns in a Polarized Era*. Reprint ed. New York: Cambridge University Press.

———. 2017. "The Decline of Local News and Its Effects: New Evidence from Longitudinal Data." *Journal of Politics* 80, no. 1: 332–36. https://doi.org/10.1086 /694105.

———. 2021. *News Hole: The Demise of Local Journalism and Political Engagement*. Cambridge: Cambridge University Press.

HeadCount. 2011. "NY Republican Says 'F-k It', Supports Gay Marriage Bill." June 16. https://www.headcount.org/ny-republican-says-fuck-it-supports-gay-marriage -bill/.

Hill, Seth J. 2015. "Institution of Nomination and the Policy Ideology of Primary Electorates." *Quarterly Journal of Political Science* 10, no. 4: 461–87. https://doi .org/10.1561/100.00015023.

Hillygus, D. Sunshine, and Steven Snell. 2018. "Longitudinal Surveys: Issues and Opportunities." In *The Oxford Handbook of Polling and Survey Methods*, edited by Lonna Rae Atkeson and R. Michael Alvarez, 28–52. New York: Oxford University Press.

Hinckley, Barbara, Richard Hofstetter, and John Kessel. 1974. "Information and the Vote: A Comparative Election Study." *American Politics Quarterly* 2, no. 2: 131–58. https://doi.org/10.1177/1532673X7400200201.

Hirano, Shigeo, and James M. Snyder Jr. 2014. "Primary Elections and the Quality of Elected Officials." Working paper. https://scholar.harvard.edu/files/jsnyder /files/primaries_quality_postwar_qjps2.pdf.

Hochschild, Jennifer. 2010. "If Democracies Need Informed Voters, How Can They Thrive While Expanding Enfranchisement?" *Election Law Journal: Rules, Politics, and Policy* 9, no. 2: 111–23.

Hoffman, Kim U. 2006. "Legislative Fiscal Analysts: Influence in State Budget Development." *State and Local Government Review* 38, no. 1: 41–51.

Hoffman, Mitchell, and Elizabeth Lyons. 2014. "Do Higher Salaries Lead to Higher Performance? Evidence from State Politicians." Working paper, July 2. https:// gps.ucsd.edu/_files/faculty/lyons/lyons_research_07022014.pdf.

Hogan, Robert E. 2003. "Sources of Competition in State Legislative Primary Elections." *Legislative Studies Quarterly* 28, no. 1: 103–26.

———. 2004. "Challenger Emergence, Incumbent Success, and Electoral Accountability in State Legislative Elections." *Journal of Politics* 66, no. 4: 1283–303.

———. 2005. "Gubernatorial Coattail Effects in State Legislative Elections." *Political Research Quarterly* 58, no. 4: 587–97. https://doi.org/10.1177/10659 1290505800406.

———. 2008. "Policy Responsiveness and Incumbent Reelection in State Legislatures." *American Journal of Political Science* 52, no. 4: 858–73.

Holbrook, Thomas M., and Aaron C. Weinschenk. 2019. "Are Perceptions of Local Conditions Rooted in Reality? Evidence From Two Large-Scale Local Surveys." *American Politics Research* (November). https://doi.org/10.1177/1532673 X19885863.

Hollander, Barry A. 2014. "The Role of Media Use in the Recall versus Recognition of Political Knowledge." *Journal of Broadcasting and Electronic Media* 58, no. 1: 97–113. https://doi.org/10.1080/08838151.2013.875019.

Holman, Craig. 2005. "Revolving Door Restrictions by State." Public Citizen, February. https://www.citizen.org/sites/default/files/revolving_in_states.pdf.

Holman, Craig, and Caralyn Esser. 2019. "Revolving Door Restrictions by State, 2019." Public Citizen, July 23. https://www.citizen.org/wp-content/uploads/Revolving-Door-Restrictions-by-State-2019.pdf.

Holman, Craig, and Prateek Reddy. 2011. "Revolving Door Restrictions by State, 2011." Public Citizen, June. https://www.citizen.org/wp-content/uploads/migration/state-revolving-door-restrictions-2011.pdf.

Hopkins, Daniel J. 2018. *The Increasingly United States: How and Why American Political Behavior Nationalized*. Chicago: University of Chicago Press.

Housman, Dylan. 2020. "Republicans Hold Majority State Legislatures, Potentially Giving Them An Advantage In Redistricting Process." *Daily Caller*, November 12. https://dailycaller.com/2020/11/12/redistricting-republicans-state-legislatures-2010-red-wave-2020-nancy-pelosi-house-of-representatives-election/.

Hulse, Carl. 2016. "Seeking to End Gerrymandering's Enduring Legacy." *New York Times*, January 25. http://www.nytimes.com/2016/01/26/us/politics/seeking-to-end-gerrymanderings-enduring-legacy.html.

Iyengar, Shanto, Yphtach Lelkes, Matthew Levendusky, Neil Malhotra, and Sean J. Westwood. 2019. "The Origins and Consequences of Affective Polarization in the United States." *Annual Review of Political Science* 22, no. 1: 129–46. https://doi.org/10.1146/annurev-polisci-051117–073034.

Jacobsmeier, Matthew L. 2015. "From Black and White to Left and Right: Race, Perceptions of Candidates' Ideologies, and Voting Behavior in U.S. House Elections." *Political Behavior* 37, no. 3: 595–621.

Jacobson, Gary C. 1989. "Strategic Politicians and the Dynamics of U.S. House Elections, 1946–86." *American Political Science Review* 83, no. 3: 773–93. https://doi.org/10.2307/1962060.

———. 1993. "Deficit-Cutting Politics and Congressional Elections." *Political Science Quarterly* 108, no. 3: 375–402. https://doi.org/10.2307/2151696.

———. 2012. "The Electoral Origins of Polarized Politics: Evidence from the 2010 Cooperative Congressional Election Study." *American Behavioral Scientist* 56, no. 12: 1612–30. https://doi.org/10.1177/0002764212463352.

———. 2013. *The Politics of Congressional Elections*. 8th ed. Pearson Classics in Political Science. Boston, MA: Pearson.

———. 2015. "It's Nothing Personal: The Decline of the Incumbency Advantage in US House Elections." *Journal of Politics* 77, no. 3: 861–73. https://doi.org/10.1086/681670.

———. 2021. "Driven to Extremes: Donald Trump's Extraordinary Impact on the 2020 Elections." *Presidential Studies Quarterly* 51, no. 3: 492–521. https://doi.org/10.1111/psq.12724.

Jacobson, Gary C., and Samuel Kernell. 1983. *Strategy and Choice in Congressional Elections.* New Haven, CT: Yale University Press.

Jaeger, William P., Jeffrey Lyons, and Jennifer Wolak. 2017. "Political Knowledge and Policy Representation in the States." *American Politics Research* 45, no. 6: 907–38. https://doi.org/10.1177/1532673X16657806.

Jennings, M. Kent, and Richard G. Niemi. 1966. "Party Identification at Multiple Levels of Government." *American Journal of Sociology* 72, no. 1: 86–101.

Jewell, Malcolm E. 1959. "Party and Primary Competition in Kentucky State Legislative Races." *Kentucky Law Journal* 48, no. 4: 517–35.

———. 1982. *Representation in State Legislatures.* Lexington: University Press of Kentucky.

Jewell, Malcolm E., and David Breaux. 1991. "Southern Primary and Electoral Competition and Incumbent Success." *Legislative Studies Quarterly* 16, no. 1: 129–43.

Johns, Robert. 2010. "Measuring Issue Salience in British Elections: Competing Interpretations of 'Most Important Issue.'" *Political Research Quarterly* 63, no. 1: 143–58.

Johnson, Martin. 2013. "Media Politics in the States." In *Guide to State Politics and Policy,* edited by Richard Niemi and Joshua J. Dyck, 151–60. Los Angeles: CQ Press.

Jones, Philip Edward. 2014. "Does the Descriptive Representation of Gender Influence Accountability for Substantive Representation?" *Politics and Gender* 10, no. 2: 175–99. https://doi.org/10.1017/S1743923X14000038.

Jurkowitz, Mark, and Amy Mitchell. 2013. "How Americans Get TV News at Home." *Pew Research Center's Journalism Project* (blog), October 11. http://www.journalism.org/2013/10/11/how-americans-get-tv-news-at-home/.

Justice, Glen. 2015. "States Six Times More Productive Than Congress." *State-Trackers,* January 27.

Kahneman, Daniel, and Shane Frederick. 2002. "Representativeness Revisited: Attribute Substitution in Intuitive Judgment." In *Heuristics and Biases: The Psychology of Intuitive Judgment,* edited by Thomas Gilovich, Dale Griffin, and Daniel Kahneman, 49–81. New York: Cambridge University Press.

Kaplan, Martin, Kenneth M. Goldstein, and Matthew Hale. 2003. *Local TV News Coverage of the 2002 General Election.* Lear Center Local News Archive, USC Annenberg School and University of Wisconsin. http://learcenter.org/pdf/LCLNAReport.pdf.

———. 2005. *Local News Coverage of the 2004 Campaigns*. Lear Center Local News Archive, USC Annenberg School and University of Wisconsin.

Kass, Arielle. 2018. "Three Fulton County House Races Could Be Competitive." *Atlanta Journal-Constitution*, October 16. https://www.ajc.com/news/local-govt --politics/three-fulton-county-house-races-could-competitive/Uvrfdw1HoJ PdorwsOrynIN/.

Kay, Fiona, and Elizabeth Gorman. 2008. "Women in the Legal Profession." *Annual Review of Law and Social Science* 4, no. 1: 299–332. https://doi.org/10.1146 /annurev.lawsocsci.4.110707.172309.

Kearney, Melissa, Benjamin Harris, Elisa Jacome, and Lucie Parker. 2014. "Ten Economic Facts about Crime and Incarceration in the United States." Hamilton Project policy memo, Brookings Institute, Washington, DC. https://www .brookings.edu/wp-content/uploads/2016/06/v8_thp_10crimefacts.pdf.

Kedar, Orit. 2006. "How Voters Work around Institutions: Policy Balancing in Staggered Elections." *Electoral Studies* 25, no. 3 (September): 509–27. https:// doi.org/10.1016/j.electstud.2005.06.011.

Kelleher, Christine A., and Jennifer Wolak. 2007. "Explaining Public Confidence in the Branches of State Government." *Political Research Quarterly* 60, no. 4: 707–21. https://doi.org/10.1177/1065912907304496.

Key, V. O. 1949. *Southern Politics in State and Nation*. New York: Vintage Books.

———. 1956. *American State Politics: An Introduction*. New York: Alfred A. Knopf.

———. 1964. *Politics, Parties, and Pressure Groups*. 5th ed. New York: Thomas Y. Crowell Company.

———. 1966. *The Responsible Electorate*. Cambridge, MA: Belknap Press.

Kinder, Donald R., and Shanto Iyengar. 1989. *News That Matters: Television and American Opinion*. Reprint ed. Chicago: University of Chicago Press.

Kitchener, Caroline, Kevin Schael, N. Kirkpatrick, Daniela Santamarina, and Lauren Tierney. 2022. "Abortion Is Now Banned in These States: See Where Laws Have Changed." *Washington Post*, June 24. https://www.washingtonpost.com /politics/2022/06/24/abortion-state-laws-criminalization-roe/.

Klarner, Carl E. 2021. *State Legislative Election Returns, 1967–2020*. Harvard Dataverse.

Koch, Jeffrey W. 2000. "Do Citizens Apply Gender Stereotypes to Infer Candidates' Ideological Orientations?" *Journal of Politics* 62, no. 2: 414–29. https:// doi.org/10.1111/0022-3816.00019.

Kone, Susan L., and Richard F. Winters. 1993. "Taxes and Voting: Electoral Retribution in the American States." *Journal of Politics* 55, no. 1: 22–40. https://doi .org/10.2307/2132226.

Konisky, David M, and Michiko Ueda. 2011. "The Effects of Uncontested Elections on Legislator Performance." *Legislative Studies Quarterly* 36, no. 2: 199–229. https://doi.org/10.1111/j.1939-9162.2011.00011.x.

Kousser, Thad. 2005. *Term Limits and the Dismantling of State Legislative Professionalism*. Cambridge: Cambridge University Press.

Krehbiel, Keith. 1993. "Where's the Party?" *British Journal of Political Science* 23, no. 2: 235–66.

———. 1995. "Cosponsors and Wafflers from A to Z." *American Journal of Political Science* 39, no. 4: 906–23. https://doi.org/10.2307/2111662.

———. 1998. *Pivotal Politics: A Theory of U.S. Lawmaking.* Chicago: University of Chicago Press.

———. 1999. "The Party Effect from A to Z and Beyond." *Journal of Politics* 61, no. 3: 832–40. https://doi.org/10.2307/2647831.

———. 2000. "Party Discipline and Measures of Partisanship." *American Journal of Political Science* 44, no. 2: 212–27. https://doi.org/10.2307/2669306.

———. 2003. "The Coefficient of Party Influence." *Political Analysis* 11, no. 1: 95–103.

Krosnick, Jon A. 1990a. "Americans' Perceptions of Presidential Candidates: A Test of the Projection Hypothesis." *Journal of Social Issues* 46, no. 2: 159–82. https://doi.org/10.1111/j.1540-4560.1990.tb01928.x.

———. 1990b. "Government Policy and Citizen Passion: A Study of Issue Publics in Contemporary America." *Political Behavior* 12, no. 1: 59–92. https://doi.org/10.1007/BF00992332.

Kuffner, Charles. 2016. Interview with Ben Rose. *Off the Kuff* (blog). September 26. http://offthekuff.com/wp/?p=76579.

Kuriwaki, Shiro. 2021. "The Swing Voter Paradox: Electoral Politics in a Nationalized Era." PhD diss., Harvard University. https://dash.harvard.edu/bitstream/handle/1/37368520/kuriwaki_dissertation.pdf?sequence=4&isAllowed=y.

Langehennig, Stefani, Joseph Zamadics, and Jennifer Wolak. 2019. "State Policy Outcomes and State Legislative Approval." *Political Research Quarterly* 72, no. 4 (January): 929–43. https://doi.org/10.1177/1065912918823284.

Lawless, Jennifer L. 2015. "Female Candidates and Legislators." *Annual Review of Political Science* 18, no. 1: 349–66. https://doi.org/10.1146/annurev-polisci-020614-094613.

Lawless, Jennifer L., and Kathryn Pearson. 2008. "The Primary Reason for Women's Underrepresentation? Reevaluating the Conventional Wisdom." *Journal of Politics* 70, no. 1: 67–82. https://doi.org/10.1017/s002238160708005x.

Lawless, Jennifer L., and Richard L. Fox. 2010. *It Still Takes A Candidate: Why Women Don't Run for Office.* Expanded ed. New York: Cambridge University Press.

Lax, Jeffrey R., and Justin H. Phillips. 2011. "The Democratic Deficit in the States." *American Journal of Political Science* 56, no. 1: 148–66. https://doi.org/10.1111/j.1540-5907.2011.00537.x.

Layton, Charles, and Jennifer Dorroh. 2002. "The Sad State." *American Journalism Review* (June): 18–33.

———. 2003. "Resurrection in Dixie." *American Journalism Review* (June/July): 42–53.

Layton, Charles, and Mary Walton. 1998. "State of The American Newspaper: Missing the Story at the State House." *American Journalism Review* (July/August): 42–63.

Lazarus, Jeffrey. 2006. "Term Limits' Multiple Effects on State Legislators' Career Decisions." *State Politics and Policy Quarterly* 6, no. 4: 357–83.

Lee, Deron. 2015. "A 40-Year Statehouse Reporter's Exit Interview." *Columbia Journalism Review*, January 9. https://www.cjr.org/local_news/bob_priddy_missourinet_interview.php.

Leeper, Thomas J., and Joshua Robison. 2018. "More Important, but for What Exactly? The Insignificant Role of Subjective Issue Importance in Vote Decisions." *Political Behavior*, August 28. https://doi.org/10.1007/s11109-018-9494-0.

Leigh, Andrew, and Mark McLeish. 2009. "Are State Elections Affected by the National Economy? Evidence from Australia." *Economic Record* 85, no. 269: 210–22. https://doi.org/10.1111/j.1475-4932.2009.00549.x.

Leiserowitz, Anthony, Edward Maibach, and Connie Roser-Renoug. 2009. *Global Warmings Six Americas 2009: An Audience Segmentation Analysis*. New Haven, CT: Yale Program on Climate Change Communication.

Leon, Sandra. 2012. "How Does Decentralization Affect Electoral Competition of State-Wide Parties? Evidence from Spain." *Party Politics*, February 26. https://doi.org/10.1177/1354068811436044.

Levendusky, Matthew. 2009. *The Partisan Sort: How Liberals Became Democrats and Conservatives Became Republicans*. Chicago: University of Chicago Press.

Lieb, David A. 2018. "Missouri Lawmakers Resign Ahead of New Lobbyist Limits." *AP News*, December 4. https://apnews.com/article/26d6b65b2855496a90537b3a0bc29ce6.

Lippmann, Walter. 1993. *The Phantom Public*. Reprint ed. New Brunswick, NJ: Transaction Publishers.

Lipset, Seymour Martin. 1997. *American Exceptionalism: A Double-Edged Sword*. New York: W. W. Norton.

Lisheron, Mark. 2010. "Reloading at the Statehouse." *American Journalism Review* 32 (September): 34–45.

Liu, Mingnan, and Yichen Wang. 2014. "Data Collection Mode Effects on Political Knowledge." *Survey Methods: Insights from the Field (SMIF)* (December). https://doi.org/10.13094/SMIF-2014-00009.

Lovett, Kenneth. 2012. "State Sen. James Alesi, One of 4 GOPers Who Voted for Gay Marriage Last Year, Won't Run for Reelection—Believing That Vote Weakened Him Politically." *NY Daily News*, May 9.

Lowry, Robert C., James E. Alt, and Karen E. Ferree. 1998. "Fiscal Policy Outcomes and Electoral Accountability in American States." *American Political Science Review* 92, no. 4: 759–74. https://doi.org/10.2307/2586302.

Lupia, Arthur. 2006. "How Elitism Undermines the Study of Voter Competence." *Critical Review* 18, no. 1–3: 217–32. https://doi.org/10.1080/08913810608443658.

———. 2015. *Uninformed: Why People Seem to Know So Little about Politics and What We Can Do about It*. Oxford: Oxford University Press.

Luskin, Robert C. 1990. "Explaining Political Sophistication." *Political Behavior* 12, no. 4: 331–61.

Luskin, Robert C., and John G. Bullock. 2011. "'Don't Know' Means 'Don't Know': DK Responses and the Public's Level of Political Knowledge." *Journal of Politics* 73, no. 2: 547–57. https://doi.org/10.1017/s0022381611000132.

Lyons, Jeffrey, William P. Jaeger, and Jennifer Wolak. 2013. "The Roots of Citizens' Knowledge of State Politics." *State Politics and Policy Quarterly* 13, no. 2: 183–202. https://doi.org/10.1177/1532440012464878.

Maddox, H. W. Jerome. 2004. "Opportunity Costs and Outside Careers in U.S. State Legislatures." *Legislative Studies Quarterly* 29, no. 4: 517–44. https://doi.org/10.3162/036298004X201285.

Madison, James. 1787. *Federalist* no. 10. In "Research Guides: Federalist Papers: Primary Documents in American History: Federalist Nos. 1–10," edited by Ken Drexler. https://guides.loc.gov/federalist-papers/text-1-10.

Madison, James. 1788. *Federalist* nos. 45–46. In "Research Guides: Federalist Papers: Primary Documents in American History: Federalist Nos. 41–50," edited by Ken Drexler. https://guides.loc.gov/federalist-papers/text-41-50.

Madison, James, or Alexander Hamilton. 1788. *Federalist* no. 51. In "Research Guides: Federalist Papers: Primary Documents in American History: Federalist Nos. 51–60," edited by Ken Drexler. https://guides.loc.gov/federalist-papers/text-51-60.

Maestas, Cherie D., Lonna Rae Atkeson, Thomas Croom, and Lisa A. Bryant. 2008. "Shifting the Blame: Federalism, Media, and Public Assignment of Blame Following Hurricane Katrina." *Publius* 38, no. 4: 609–32.

Maestas, Cherie D., Sarah Fulton, L. Sandy Maisel, and Walter J. Stone. 2006. "When to Risk It? Institutions, Ambitions, and the Decision to Run for the U.S. House." *American Political Science Review* 100, no. 2: 195–208.

Maine State Legislature. 2009. "State Legislative Record: One Hundred and Twenty Fourth Legislature: State of Maine." http://lldc.mainelegislature.org/Open/LegRec/124/Senate/LegRec_2009-04-30_SD_pS0510-0537.pdf.

Malhotra, Neil. 2008. "The Impact of Public Financing on Electoral Competition: Evidence from Arizona and Maine." *State Politics and Policy Quarterly* 8, no. 3: 263–81. https://doi.org/10.1177/153244000800800303.

Malhotra, Neil, and Alexander G. Kuo. 2008. "Attributing Blame: The Public's Response to Hurricane Katrina." *Journal of Politics* 70, no. 1: 120–35. https://doi.org/10.1017/s0022381607080097.

Mancinelli, Abigail. 2022. "Does Public Financing Motivate Electoral Challengers?" *State Politics and Policy Quarterly*, first view: 1–25. https://doi.org/10.1017/spq.2022.12.

Martin, Gregory J., and Joshua McCrain. 2019. "Local News and National Politics." *American Political Science Review* 113, no. 2: 372–84. https://doi.org/10.1017/S0003055418000965.

Martins, Rodrigo, and Francisco José Veiga. 2013. "Economic Voting in Portuguese Municipal Elections." *Public Choice* 155: 317–34. https://doi.org/10.1007/s11127-011-9849-0.

Maske, Todd. 2019. "Professional Backgrounds in State Legislatures, 1993–2012." *State Politics and Policy Quarterly* 19, no. 3: 312–33.

Masket, Seth. 2019. "What Is, and Isn't, Causing Polarization in Modern State Legislatures." *PS: Political Science and Politics* 52, no. 3: 430–35. https://doi.org/10.1017/S104909651900009X.

———. 2020. "Why Political Science Doesn't Like Term Limits." *Mischiefs of Faction* (blog), January 20. https://www.mischiefsoffaction.com/post/political-science-term-limits.

Mauger, Craig, and Ted Roelofs. 2017. "From Lawmaker to Lobbyist: Should the State Slow Down the Revolving Door?" *Public Sector*, January 18. https://www.bridgemi.com/michigan-government/lawmaker-lobbyist-should-state-slow-down-revolving-door.

Mayer, Kenneth R., and John M. Wood. 1995. "The Impact of Public Financing on Electoral Competitiveness: Evidence from Wisconsin, 1964–1990." *Legislative Studies Quarterly* 20, no. 1: 69–88.

Mayhew, David R. 1974. *Congress: The Electoral Connection*. New Haven, CT: Yale University Press.

———. 2005. *Divided We Govern: Party Control, Lawmaking, and Investigations, 1946–2002*. 2nd ed. New Haven, CT: Yale University Press.

McCarty, Nolan. 2019. *Polarization: What Everyone Needs to Know*. New York: Oxford University Press.

McDermott, Monika L. 1997. "Voting Cues in Low-Information Elections: Candidate Gender as a Social Information Variable in Contemporary United States Elections." *American Journal of Political Science* 41, no. 1: 270–83. https://doi.org/10.2307/2111716.

McGhee, Eric, and Boris Shor. 2017. "Has the Top Two Primary Elected More Moderates?" *Perspectives on Politics* 15, no. 4: 1053–66. https://doi.org/10.1017/S1537592717002158.

McGhee, Eric, Seth Masket, Boris Shor, Steven Rogers, and Nolan McCarty. 2014. "A Primary Cause of Partisanship? Nomination Systems and Legislator Ideology." *American Journal of Political Science* 58, no. 2: 337–51. https://doi.org/10.1111/ajps.12070.

McGreevy, Patrick. 2013. "California Lawmaker Rubio Leaves Legislature for Chevron Job." *Los Angeles Times*, February 22. https://www.latimes.com/local/la-xpm-2013-feb-22-la-me-state-senate-20130223-story.html.

McQueary, Kristen. 2012. "Legislator Who Pushed Smart-Grid Bill Hired as ComEd Lobbyist." *Illinois Review*, February 8. http://illinoisreview.typepad.com/illinoisreview/2012/02/smart-grid-sponsor-mccarthy-becomes-comeds-newest-lobbyist.html.

Melusky, Benjamin. 2018. "Legislative Pay and Voluntary Retirement in the American States." *Journal of Legislative Studies* 24, no. 4: 526–45. https://doi.org/10.1080/13572334.2018.1547945.

Milyo, Jeffrey. 2001. "What Do Candidates Maximize (and Why Should Anyone Care)?" *Public Choice* 109, no. 1: 119–39. https://doi.org/10.1023/A:101209810 4745.

Miquel, Gerard, and James M. Snyder Jr. 2006. "Legislative Effectiveness and Legislative Careers." *Legislative Studies Quarterly* 31, no. 3: 347–81.

Mitchell, Amy, Jeffrey Gottfried, Michael Barthel, and Elisa Shearer. 2016. "1. Pathways to News." *Pew Research Center's Journalism Project* (blog), July 7. http://www.journalism.org/2016/07/07/pathways-to-news/.

Mitchell, Amy, Jesse Holcomb, and Rachel Weisel. 2015. "Today's Washington Press Corps More Digital, Specialized." *Pew Research Center's Journalism Project* (blog), December 3. http://www.journalism.org/2015/12/03/todays-washington -press-corps-more-digital-specialized/.

Moncrief, Gary, Richard Niemi, and Lynda Powell. 2004. "Time, Term Limits, and Turnover: Trends in Membership Stability in U.S. State Legislatures." *Legislative Studies Quarterly* 29, no. 3: 357–81.

Moncrief, Gary F., Peverill Squire, and Malcolm Edwin Jewell. 2001. *Who Runs for the Legislature?* Hoboken, NJ: Prentice Hall.

Mondak, Jeffery. 2000. "Reconsidering the Measurement of Political Knowledge." *Political Analysis* 8, no. 1: 57–82.

Moore, Michael K., and John R. Hibbing. 1998. "Situational Dissatisfaction in Congress: Explaining Voluntary Departures." *Journal of Politics* 60, no. 4: 1088–107. https://doi.org/10.2307/2647732.

Murdoch, Stephen. 2001. "The Debate over Mandatory Minimums." *Washington Lawyer* (November).

Nathan, Richard P., and Thomas Gais. 2001. "Is Devolution Working? Federal and State Roles in Welfare." *Brookings* (blog), June 1. https://www.brookings.edu /articles/is-devolution-working-federal-and-state-roles-in-welfare/.

National Center for Education Statistics. 2019. "Public Elementary and Secondary Revenues and Expenditures, by Locale, Source of Revenue, and Purpose of Expenditure: 2016–17." *Digest of Education Statistics*, table 235.40. https://nces .ed.gov/programs/digest/d19/tables/dt19_235.40.asp?current=yes.

National Conference of State Legislatures. 2015. "Same-Sex Marriage Laws." http://www.ncsl.org/research/human-services/same-sex-marriage-laws.aspx.

———. 2017. *State Legislative Policymaking in an Age of Political Polarization.* February 18. Washington, DC: National Conference of State Legislatures. https://www.ncsl.org/Portals/1/Documents/About_State_Legislatures/Partisan ship_030818.pdf.

———. 2021a. "Size of State Legislative Staff." https://www.ncsl.org/research/about -state-legislatures/staff-change-chart-1979-1988-1996-2003-2009.aspx.

———. 2021b. "Legislative Compensation Overview." July 21. https://www.ncsl .org/research/about-state-legislatures/the-legislative-pay-problem636360604 .aspx.

———. 2022. "State Medical Cannabis Laws." https://www.ncsl.org/research/health/state-medical-marijuana-laws.aspx.

National Institute on Money in State Politics. 2022. *FollowTheMoney.org*. https://www.followthemoney.org/.

NC Center. 2016. "Rankings of Effectiveness, Attendance and Roll Call Voting Participation for the 2015 North Carolina General Assembly." NC Center for Public Policy Research, April 21. https://nccppr.org/rankings-of-effectiveness-attendance-and-roll-call-voting-participation-for-the-north-carolina-general-assembly-released/.

Nicholson, Stephen P. 2003. "The Political Environment and Ballot Proposition Awareness." *American Journal of Political Science* 47, no. 3: 403–10. https://doi.org/10.1111/1540-5907.00029.

Niemi, Richard G., and Larry M. Bartels. 1985. "New Measures of Issue Salience: An Evaluation." *Journal of Politics* 47, no. 4: 1212–20. https://doi.org/10.2307/2130815.

Niemi, Richard G., Harold W. Stanley, and Ronald J. Vogel. 1995. "State Economies and State Taxes: Do Voters Hold Governors Accountable?" *American Journal of Political Science* 39, no. 4: 936–57. https://doi.org/10.2307/2111664.

Niemi, Richard G., and Laura R. Winsky. 1987. "Membership Turnover in U. S. State Legislatures: Trends and Effects of Districting." *Legislative Studies Quarterly* 12, no. 1: 115–23.

Nyhan, Brendan, Eric McGhee, John Sides, Seth Masket, and Steven Greene. 2012. "One Vote Out of Step? The Effects of Salient Roll Call Votes in the 2010 Election." *American Politics Research* 40, no. 5: 844–79. https://doi.org/10.1177/1532673X11433768.

Obama, Barack. 2016. "Remarks by the President in Address to the Illinois General Assembly." *Whitehouse.gov*, February 10. https://obamawhitehouse.archives.gov/the-press-office/2016/02/10/remarks-president-address-illinois-general-assembly.

———. 2020. *A Promised Land*. New York: Crown.

O'Hara, Jesse. 2015. "Vote for Conscience and Constituents, Not Party Bosses." *Great Falls Tribune*, September 16. https://www.greatfallstribune.com/story/opinion/guest-opinions/2015/09/16/vote-conscience-constituents-party-bosses/32514537/.

O'Neill, Thomas P., and William Novak. 1987. *Man of the House: The Life and Political Memoirs of Speaker Tip O'Neill*. New York: Random House.

Onge, Peter St. 2008. "The Best Choices for N.C. House, Senate." *Charlotte Observer*. https://www.charlotteobserver.com/opinion/article9018536.html.

Oppenheimer, Bruce I. 2005. "Deep Red and Blue Congressional Districts: The Causes and Consequences of Declining Party Competitiveness." In *Congress Reconsidered*, 8th ed., edited by Bruce I. Oppenheimer and Lawrence Dodd, 135–58. Washington, DC: CQ Press.

Oppenheimer, Bruce I., James A. Stimson, and Richard W. Waterman. 1986. "Interpreting U. S. Congressional Elections: The Exposure Thesis." *Legislative Studies Quarterly* 11, no. 2: 227–47.

Ouellette, Nicole. 2009. "Republican Legislator Stands Alone in Support of Same-Sex Marriage Bill." *Ellsworth American*, March 17, 2009. https://www.ellsworthamerican.com/maine-news/republican-legislator-stands-alone-in-support-of-same-sex-marriage-bill-2/.

Owen, Guillermo, and Bernard Grofman. 2006. "Two-Stage Electoral Competition in Two-Party Contests: Persistent Divergence of Party Positions." *Social Choice and Welfare* 26, no. 3: 547–69.

Paddock, Joel. 2005. *State and National Parties and American Democracy*. New York: Peter Lang.

Page, Benjamin I., and Robert Y. Shapiro. 1992. *The Rational Public: Fifty Years of Trends in Americans' Policy Preferences*. Chicago: University of Chicago Press.

Parry, Janine A., Andrew J. Dowdle, Abigail B. Long, and Jessica R. Kloss. 2022. "The Rule, Not the Exception: One-Party Monopolies in the American States." *State Politics and Policy Quarterly* 22, no. 2: 226–45. https://doi.org/10.1017/spq.2022.2.

Patterson, Samuel C., Randall B. Ripley, and Stephen V. Quinlan. 1992. "Citizens' Orientations toward Legislatures: Congress and the State Legislature." *Western Political Quarterly* 45, no. 2: 315–38. https://doi.org/10.2307/448714.

Payson, Julia A. 2017. "When Are Local Incumbents Held Accountable for Government Performance? Evidence from US School Districts." *Legislative Studies Quarterly* 42, no. 3: 421–48. https://doi.org/10.1111/lsq.12159.

Pearson, Rick. 2016. "Obama Backs Challenger over Dunkin in Democratic Primary for State Rep." *Chicago Tribune*, March 7. http://www.chicagotribune.com/news/local/politics/ct-obama-endorse-straton-dunkin-primary-0308-20160307-story.html.

Pelzer, Jeremy. 2016. "Ohio Sen. Tom Patton Suggests Opponent Shouldn't Run Because She's a Young Mother." *Cleveland.com*, January 28. https://www.cleveland.com/open/2016/01/ohio_sen_tom_patton_suggests_opponent_shouldnt_run_because_shes_a_young_mother.html.

Peterson, Erik. 2019. "Not Dead Yet: Political Learning from Newspapers in a Changing Media Landscape." *Political Behavior* (June). https://doi.org/10.1007/s11109-019-09556-7.

Pew Research Center. 2013. *Modern Parenthood: Roles of Moms and Dads Converge as They Balance Work and Family*. Report, *Pew Research Center's Social and Demographic Trends Project* (blog), March 14. http://www.pewsocialtrends.org/2013/03/14/modern-parenthood-roles-of-moms-and-dads-converge-as-they-balance-work-and-family/.

———. 2018. *The Public, the Political System and American Democracy*. April. Washington, DC: Pew Research Center. http://assets.pewresearch.org/wp-content/uploads/sites/5/2018/04/26140617/4-26-2018-Democracy-release.pdf.

———. 2019a. "For Local News, Americans Embrace Digital but Still Want Strong Community Connection: Nearly as Many Americans Prefer to Get Their Local News Online as Prefer the TV Set." *Pew Research Center's Journalism Project* (blog), March 26. https://www.pewresearch.org/journalism/2019/03/26/nearly-as-many-americans-prefer-to-get-their-local-news-online-as-prefer-the-tv-set/.

———. 2019b. "For Local News, Americans Embrace Digital but Still Want Strong Community Connection." *Pew Research Center's Journalism Project* (blog), March 26. https://www.journalism.org/2019/03/26/for-local-news-americans-embrace-digital-but-still-want-strong-community-connection/.

———. 2021. "Newspapers Fact Sheet." *Pew Research Center's Journalism Project* (blog), June 29. https://www.pewresearch.org/journalism/fact-sheet/newspapers/.

Phaneuf, Keith. 2020. "CT's Unpaid Legislator Wants to Champion Push for Lawmaker Pay Reform." *CT Mirror* (blog), January 17. https://ctmirror.org/2020/01/17/cts-unpaid-legislator-wants-to-champion-push-for-lawmaker-pay-reform/.

Phillips, Susan D., and Anne R. Imhoff. 1997. "Women and Career Development: A Decade of Research." *Annual Review of Psychology* 48, no. 1: 31–59. https://doi.org/10.1146/annurev.psych.48.1.31.

Poole, Keith T., and Howard Rosenthal. 2000. *Congress: A Political-Economic History of Roll Call Voting.* New York: Oxford University Press.

Powell, G. Bingham. 2000. *Elections as Instruments of Democracy: Majoritarian and Proportional Visions.* New Haven, CT: Yale University Press.

Preston, Jennifer. 2012. "GOP Senator Who Backed Gay Unions Won't Run." *New York Times*, May 9. http://www.nytimes.com/2012/05/10/nyregion/republican-senator-who-backed-gay-marriage-wont-seek-re-election.html.

Prior, Markus. 2006. "The Incumbent in the Living Room: The Rise of Television and the Incumbency Advantage in U.S. House Elections." *Journal of Politics* 68, no. 3: 657–73. https://doi.org/10.1111/j.1468-2508.2006.00452.x.

———. 2007. *Post-Broadcast Democracy: How Media Choice Increases Inequality in Political Involvement and Polarizes Elections.* New York: Cambridge University Press.

Ranney, Austin. 1954. *The Doctrine of Responsible Party Government, Its Origin and Present State.* Urbana: University of Illinois Press.

Rasmussen Reports. 2011. "Wisconsin Poll: Support for Budget Cutting, Not for Weakening Collective Bargaining Rights." March 3. http://www.rasmussenreports.com/public_content/politics/general_state_surveys/wisconsin/wisconsin_poll_support_for_budget_cutting_not_for_weakening_collective_bargaining_rights.

Reeher, Grant. 2006. *First Person Political: Legislative Life and the Meaning of Public Service.* New York: New York University Press.

Reif, Karlheinz, and Hermann Schmitt. 1980. "Nine Second-Order National Elections—A Conceptual Framework for the Analysis of European Election Results." *European Journal of Political Research* 8, no. 1: 3–44. https://doi.org/10.1111/j.1475-6765.1980.tb00737.x.

Rhode, David. 1991. *Parties and Leaders in the Postreform House*. Chicago: University of Chicago Press.

Richardson, Lilliard, and Jeffrey Milyo. 2016. "Giving the People What They Want? Legislative Polarization and Public Approval of State Legislatures." *State and Local Government Review* 48, no. 4: 270–81. https://doi.org/10.1177/0160323X17697150.

Richardson Jr., Lilliard E., David M. Konisky, and Jeffrey Milyo. 2012. "Public Approval of U.S. State Legislatures." *Legislative Studies Quarterly* 37, no. 1: 99–116. https://doi.org/10.1111/j.1939-9162.2011.00036.x.

Rodden, Jonathan, and Erik Wibbels. 2011. "Dual Accountability and the Nationalization of Party Competition: Evidence from Four Federations." *Party Politics* 17, no. 5: 629–53. https://doi.org/10.1177/1354068810376182.

Roeder, Phillip W. 1994. *Public Opinion and Policy Leadership in the American States*. Tuscaloosa: University of Alabama Press.

Rogers, Steven. 2015. "Strategic Challenger Entry in a Federal System: The Role of Economic and Political Conditions in State Legislative Competition." *Legislative Studies Quarterly* 40, no. 4: 539–70. https://doi.org/10.1111/lsq.12088.

———. 2016. "National Forces in State Legislative Elections." *Annals of the American Academy of Political and Social Science* 667, no. 1: 207–25. https://doi.org/10.1177/0002716216662454.

———. 2017. "Electoral Accountability for State Legislative Roll Calls and Ideological Representation." *American Political Science Review* 111, no. 3: 555–71. https://doi.org/10.1017/S0003055417000156.

Rosendale, Matthew. 2015. "Declaration of Matthew Rosendale." Affidavit, document 71-9, August 28, in Ravalli County Republican Central Committee et al. v. Linda McCulloch et al., case no. CV 14-0058 (U.S. District Court, Montana).

Rosenthal, Alan. 1974. "Turnover in State Legislatures." *American Journal of Political Science* 18, no. 3: 609–16. https://doi.org/10.2307/2110635.

Rothman, Noah. 2010. "DLCC Executive Director Michael Sargeant on the Challenges and Opportunities for Democrats at the State Level." Campaigns and Elections. https://www.campaignsandelections.com/campaign-insider/dlcc-executive-director-michael-sargeant-on-the-challenges-and-opportunities-for-democrats-at-the-state-level.

Rozell, Mark J. 2003. *Media Power, Media Politics*. Lanham, MD: Rowman and Littlefield.

Ruch, John. 2018. "Voters Guide: Beth Beskin." *Reporter Newspapers* (blog), October 11. https://www.reporternewspapers.net/2018/10/11/voters-guide-beth-beskin/.

Sances, Michael W. 2017. "Attribution Errors in Federalist Systems: When Voters Punish the President for Local Tax Increases." *Journal of Politics* 79, no. 4: 1286–1301. https://doi.org/10.1086/692588.

Sawyer, Wendy, and Peter Wagner. 2020. *Mass Incarceration: The Whole Pie 2020.* Policy Prison Initiative report, March 24. https://www.prisonpolicy.org/reports /pie2020.html.

Schattschneider, Elmer Eric. 1942. *Party Government.* New York: Holt, Rinehart, and Winston.

Schuba, Tom. 2016. "Rep. Ken Dunkin's Primary Opponent Receives High-Profile Democratic Endorsements." *NBC Chicago* (blog), February 8. http://www .nbcchicago.com/blogs/ward-room/Rep-Ken-Dunkins-Primary-Opponent -Receives-High-Profile-Democratic-Endorsements-367831081.html.

Schutz, Paris. 2015. "State Rep. Ken Dunkin: 'I Don't Work for Mike Madigan.'" *WTTW,* September 4. https://news.wttw.com/2015/09/04/state-rep-ken-dunkin -i-don-t-work-mike-madigan.

Scott, Kyle. 2011. *Federalism: A Normative Theory and Its Practical Relevance.* New York: Continuum.

Shearer, Elisa, Katerina Eva Matsa, Amy Mitchell, Mark Jurkowitz, Kirsten Worden, and Naomi Forman-Katz. 2022. "Appendix B: Detailed Tables." *Pew Research Center's Journalism Project* (blog), April 5. https://www.pewresearch.org /journalism/2022/04/05/statehouse-reporters-appendix-b-detailed-tables/.

Shor, Boris, and Nolan McCarty. 2011. "The Ideological Mapping of American Legislatures." *American Political Science Review* 105, no. 3: 530–51. https://doi .org/10.1017/S0003055411000153.

———. Forthcoming, 2022. "Two Decades of Polarization in American State Legislatures." *Journal of Political Institutions and Political Economy.*

Sides, John, Chris Tausanovitch, Lynn Vavreck, and Christopher Warshaw. 2018. "On the Representativeness of Primary Electorates." *British Journal of Political Science* (March): 1–9. https://doi.org/10.1017/S000712341700062X.

Silbermann, Rachel. 2015. "Gender Roles, Work-Life Balance, and Running for Office." *Quarterly Journal of Political Science* 10, no. 2: 123–53. https://doi .org/10.1561/100.00014087.

Skovron, Christopher. 2018. "What Politicians Believe About Electoral Accountability." SSRN scholarly paper ID no. 3309906, October 31. Rochester, NY: Social Science Research Network. https://doi.org/10.2139/ssrn.3309906.

Smith, Adrienne, Jason Windett, and Jonathan Winburn. 2015. "Women's Emergence and Success in U.S. State Legislative Elections." Paper presented at the American Political Science Association Conference, San Francisco, CA, September 3–6.

Smith, Brianna, Scott Clifford, and Jennifer Jerit. 2020. "*TRENDS*: How Internet Search Undermines the Validity of Political Knowledge Measures." *Political Research Quarterly* 73, no. 1: 141–55. https://doi.org/10.1177/1065912919882101.

Smith, Edward. 2009. "A Declining State House Press Corps Leaves Readers Less Informed About Lawmakers' Efforts." National Conference of State Legislatures. http://www.ncsl.org/press-room/sl-magazine-disappearing-act.aspx.

Smith, Roland, and Lawrence Miller. 1977. "Leaving the Legislature: Why Do They Go?" *Public Service* 4, no. 4: 6–8.

Snyder, James, and David Stromberg. 2010. "Press Coverage and Political Accountability." *Journal of Political Economy* 118, no. 2: 355–408. https://doi.org/10.1086/652903.

Snyder, James M. Jr. 1996. "Constituency Preferences: California Ballot Propositions, 1974–1990." *Legislative Studies Quarterly* 21, no. 4: 463–88.

Snyder, James M. Jr., and Stephen Ansolabehere. 2002. "The Incumbency Advantage in U.S. Elections: An Analysis of State and Federal Offices, 1942–2000." *Election Law Journal* 1, no. 3: 315–38.

Songer, Donald R. 1984. "Government Closest to the People: Constituent Knowledge in State & National Politics." *Polity* 17, no. 2: 387–95. https://doi.org/10.2307/3234515.

Squire, Peverill. 1988. "Career Opportunities and Membership Stability in Legislatures." *Legislative Studies Quarterly* 13, no. 1: 65–82.

———. 1993. "Professionalization and Public Opinion of State Legislatures." *Journal of Politics* 55, no. 2: 479–91. https://doi.org/10.2307/2132277.

———. 2012. *The Evolution of American Legislatures: Colonies, Territories, and States, 1619–2009.* Ann Arbor: University of Michigan Press.

———. 2017. "A Squire Index Update." *State Politics and Policy Quarterly* 17, no. 4: 361–71. https://doi.org/10.1177/1532440017713314.

Squire, Peverill, and Christina Fastnow. 1994. "Comparing Gubernatorial and Senatorial Elections." *Political Research Quarterly* 47, no. 3: 705–20. https://doi.org/10.2307/448850.

St. Cloud State University. 2009. "Fall 2009 SCSU Survey." https://www.stcloudstate.edu/scsusurvey/_files/documents/studies-fall/fall-2009-findings.pdf.

Standing, William H., and James A. Robinson. 1958. "Inter-Party Competition and Primary Contesting: The Case of Indiana." *American Political Science Review* 52, no. 4: 1066–77. https://doi.org/10.2307/1951986.

Stassen-Berger, Rachel. 2015. "Leap from Legislator to Lobbyist a Short One in Minnesota—Twin Cities." *Twin Cities Pioneer Press*, March 27. http://www.twincities.com/2015/03/27/leap-from-legislator-to-lobbyist-a-short-one-in-minnesota/.

Stein, Robert M. 1990. "Economic Voting for Governor and U. S. Senator: The Electoral Consequences of Federalism." *Journal of Politics* 52, no. 1: 29–53. https://doi.org/10.2307/2131418.

Stephanopoulos, Nicholas. 2018. "Accountability Claims in Constitutional Law." *Northwestern University Law Review* 112, no. 5: 989. https://scholarlycommons.law.northwestern.edu/nulr/vol112/iss5/2/.

Stepp, Carl. 2004. "Why Do People Read Newspapers?" *American Journalism Review* 25 (December/January): 64–69.

Strickland, James M. 2020. "The Declining Value of Revolving-Door Lobbyists: Evidence from the American States." *American Journal of Political Science* 64, no. 1: 67–81. https://doi.org/10.1111/ajps.12485.

Sullivan, Michael Quinn. 2015. "Video: Republican Urges Liberal Democrats to Vote in GOP Primary." *Texas Scorecard*, October 27. https://texasscorecard

.com/uncategorized/video-republican-urges-liberal-democrats-to-vote-in-gop
-primary/.

Swain, John, Stephen Borrelli, and Brian Reed. 1999. "Strategic Retirement in the
U.S. House of Representatives, 1897–1996: 'You Can't Fire Me, I Quit.'" *South-
eastern Political Review* 27, no. 1: 3–31.

Tarte, Jeff. 2019. "Meet Senator Tarte." *Jeff Tarte* (blog). https://web.archive.org
/web/20190302021936/http://jefftarte.com/meetsenatortarte/.

Tausanovitch, Chris, and Christopher Warshaw. 2013. "Measuring Constituent Policy Preferences in Congress, State Legislatures, and Cities." *Journal of Politics*
75, no. 2: 330–42. https://doi.org/10.1017/S0022381613000042.

———. 2018. "Does the Ideological Proximity Between Candidates and Voters
Affect Voting in U.S. House Elections?" *Political Behavior* 40, no. 1: 223–45.
https://doi.org/10.1007/s11109-017-9437-1.

Tax Policy Center. 2020. "Who Bears the Burden of a National Retail Sales
Tax?" Last updated May 2020. https://www.taxpolicycenter.org/briefing-book
/who-bears-burden-national-retail-sales-tax.

Theriault, Sean M. 1998. "Moving Up or Moving Out: Career Ceilings and Congressional Retirement." *Legislative Studies Quarterly* 23, no. 3: 419–33.

Thomas, Charles. 2015. "Dem Dunkin Talks after Missing Key Vote in Springfield."
ABC7 Chicago, September 10. http://abc7chicago.com/978095/.

Thomsen, Danielle M. 2014. "Ideological Moderates Won't Run: How Party Fit
Matters for Partisan Polarization in Congress." *Journal of Politics* 76, no. 3: 786–
97. https://doi.org/10.1017/s0022381614000243.

———. 2017. *Opting Out of Congress: Partisan Polarization and the Decline of
Moderate Candidates*. Cambridge: Cambridge University Press.

Tidmarch, Charles M., Edward Lonergan, and John Sciortino. 1986. "Interparty
Competition in the U. S. States: Legislative Elections, 1970–1978." *Legislative
Studies Quarterly* 11, no. 3: 353–74.

Tolchin, Martin, and Susan J. Tolchin. 2010. *Pinstripe Patronage: Political Favoritism
from the Clubhouse to the White House and Beyond*. Boulder, CO: Routledge.

Trussler, Marc. 2020. "Get Information or Get in Formation: The Effects of High-
Information Environments on Legislative Elections." *British Journal of Political Science* 51, no. 4: 1529–49. https://doi.org/10.1017/S0007123419000577.

Tufte, Edward R. 1975. "Determinants of the Outcomes of Midterm Congressional Elections." *American Political Science Review* 69, no. 3: 812–26. https://doi
.org/10.2307/1958391.

Tversky, Amos, and Daniel Kahneman. 1974. "Judgment under Uncertainty: Heuristics and Biases." *Science* 185, no. 4157 (September): 1124–31. https://doi
.org/10.1126/science.185.4157.1124.

Urban Institute. 2022. "Connecticut." June. https://www.urban.org/policy-centers
/cross-center-initiatives/state-and-local-finance-initiative/projects/state-fiscal-briefs
/connecticut.

US News and World Report. 2021. "Best States Rankings." https://www.usnews
.com/news/best-states/rankings.

USNewswire. 2011. "Consumers Send Clear Message to Legislators: No to Rate Hike
Bill." *PR Newswire,* October 23. https://www.prnewswire.com/news-releases
/consumers-send-clear-message-to-legislators-no-to-rate-hike-bill-132408258
.html.

Utych, Stephen M. 2020. "Man Bites Blue Dog: Are Moderates Really More
Electable than Ideologues?" *Journal of Politics* 82, no. 1: 392–96. https://doi
.org/10.1086/706054.

Visser, Penny S., Jon A. Krosnick, and Joseph P. Simmons. 2003. "Distinguishing
the Cognitive and Behavioral Consequences of Attitude Importance and Certainty: A New Approach to Testing the Common-Factor Hypothesis." *Journal
of Experimental Social Psychology* 39, no. 2: 118–41. https://doi.org/10.1016
/S0022-1031(02)00522-X.

Visser, Penny S., Jon A. Krosnick, and Paul Lavrakas. 2014. "Survey Research." In
Handbook of Research Methods in Social and Personality Psychology, 2nd ed.,
edited by Harry T. Reis and Charles M. Judd, 223–52. New York: Cambridge
University Press.

Vogel, Charity. 2012. "Gay Marriage Vote Paying off for Grisanti." *Buffalo News,*
October 13. https://buffalonews.com/news/gay-marriage-vote-paying-off-for-gri
santi-opponents-of-same-sex-weddings-pledge-cash-support/article_801cbfae
-d4b7-501f-8d10-390ec945367a.html.

Volden, Craig, Alan E. Wiseman, and Dana E. Wittmer. 2013. "When Are Women
More Effective Lawmakers Than Men?" *American Journal of Political Science*
57, no. 2: 326–41. https://doi.org/10.1111/ajps.12010.

Volden, Craig, and Alan E. Wiseman. 2014. *Legislative Effectiveness in the United
States Congress: The Lawmakers.* New York: Cambridge University Press.

Volz, Matt. 2015. "Lawsuit Challenging Montana's Open Primaries Headed to
Trial." *Great Falls Tribune,* December 15. https://www.greatfallstribune.com
/story/news/local/2015/12/15/lawsuit-challenging-montanas-open-primaries
-headed-trial/77377446/.

Walton, Mary. 2000. "The Jersey Giant." *American Journalism Review* 22, no. 8
(October): 58–65.

Ware, Alan. 2002. *The American Direct Primary: Party Institutionalization and
Transformation in the North.* Cambridge: Cambridge University Press.

Warshaw, Christopher. 2019. "Local Elections and Representation in the United
States." *Annual Review of Political Science* 22, no. 1: 461–79. https://doi
.org/10.1146/annurev-polisci-050317-071108.

Weissert, C. S., and W. G. Weissert. 2000. "State Legislative Staff Influence in Health
Policy Making." *Journal of Health Politics, Policy and Law* 25, no. 6: 1121–48.

Wernau, Julie. 2011. "Lawmakers Override Quinn Veto; Governor Thanks Citizen
Action/Illinois for Fighting for Consumers." *Chicago Tribune,* October 26. http://

articles.chicagotribune.com/2011-10-26/business/chi-senate-overrides-quinns
-veto-of-smartgrid-bill-20111026_1_smart-grid-comed-anne-pramaggiore.

Werner, Timothy, and Kenneth R. Mayer. 2007. "Public Election Funding, Competition, and Candidate Gender." *PS: Political Science and Politics* 40, no. 4: 661–67.

Wiggins, Charles W., and Janice Petty. 1979. "Cumulative Voting and Electoral Competition The Illinois House." *American Politics Quarterly* 7, no. 3: 345–65. https://doi.org/10.1177/1532673X7900700306.

Wolak, Jennifer. 2007. "Strategic Retirements: The Influence of Public Preferences on Voluntary Departures from Congress." *Legislative Studies Quarterly* 32, no. 2: 285–308. https://doi.org/10.3162/036298007780907897.

———. 2009. "The Consequences of Concurrent Campaigns for Citizen Knowledge of Congressional Candidates." *Political Behavior* 31, no. 2: 211–29. https://doi.org/10.1007/s11109-008-9069-6.

Wolfson, Lewis W. 1985. *The Untapped Power of the Press: Explaining Government to the People.* New York: Praeger.

Worden, Kristen, Katerina Eva Matsa, and Elisa Shearer. 2022. "The Number of Full-Time Statehouse Reporters at U.S. Newspapers Has Declined 34% since 2014." *Pew Research Center's Journalism Project* (blog), April 5. https://www.pewresearch.org/fact-tank/2022/04/05/the-number-of-full-time-statehouse-reporters-at-u-s-newspapers-has-declined-34-since-2014/.

Zizzo, David. 2001. "Frozen in Time: Oklahoma Family Broke Industry Ice." *Oklahoman*, July 7. https://newsok.com/article/2747407/frozen-in-time-oklahoma-family-broke-industry-ice?

Zorn, Eric. 2016. "Ken Dunkin Gets Obama's Seal of Disapproval." *Chicago Tribune*, March 8. http://www.chicagotribune.com/news/opinion/zorn/ct-dunkin-obama-stratton-rauner-zorn-perspec-0309-20160308-column.html.

Index

abortion, 2, 8, 194, 203, 256, 265
accountability: challengers as important
for, 60, 150–51, 248–49; collective, 7, 10,
47–49, 74–75, 130–33, 181, 202–8, 250;
elites' role in, 144, 151, 230, 248–49;
expectations for, 16–18, 251; and fair
opportunity, 17–18, 22–24, 30, 49–50,
57, 59, 79, 223–27; of governor, 9, 279n5;
of governor's party, 75–77, 190, 200–
201; and ideological representation,
44–47, 71–72, 142–57, 227–28, 278n14;
individual, 7, 10, 133, 136–40, 250; for
individual roll-call votes, 155–61, 170–71;
and issue-level approval ratings, relationship between, 202–4; for issue positions, 135; for legislative effectiveness,
162–70; in local elections, 9, 189; losing
reelection, 149–51; losing votes, 145–49;
and media coverage, 100–102, 153–55;
and misinformation, 205–6; obstacles for,
22–23, 84–85; and party loyalty, 21, 146,
233–36; for policy performance, 190–94;
and presidential popularity, 78–79, 206–
8; in primaries, 209, 215–18, 229, 239–40;
for state economy, 48–49, 75–77, 149,
190–97; and state legislative approval,
200–204
Adams, James, 140
adverse-selection problem, 12–15; retrospection, 268n9
Affordable Care Act (ACA), 8, 109, 139,
246–47, 256, 259
African Americans, 32
Alabama, 128

Alesi, James, 209, 215, 217–18, 221, 281n1
"all politics are local," 20, 179–80, 208
Alvarez, German, 274n9
American Association of Retired People
(AARP), 39
American democracy, 2, 140, 182, 247, 259,
264–65. *See also* democracy
American exceptionalism, 262
American Journalism Review (journal), 96,
99–101, 104, 274n10
American National Election Study (ANES),
253, 282n1
American Political Science Association
(APSA), 182
Anderson, Sarah, 218
Ansolabehere, Stephen, 260
Anzia, Sarah, 32
Arceneaux, Kevin, 279n5, 280n15
Aristotle, 85
Arizona, 70
Arkansas, 59, 269n1
Arnold, Barbara, 22
Arnold, Douglas, 59
Articles of Confederation, 4
attribution errors, 185–87, 208, 257, 280n15;
rooted in national politics, 206, 251

balancing theory, 15, 47, 74–75; anticipatory,
48, 269n14; federal-state, 16, 77, 152–53,
195; and midterm loss, 131, 269n13; in
presidential election years, 276n7; state-
level, 16, 131–32, 149, 190
Banks, Jeffrey S., 268n8
Barber, Michael, 258